The Embassy in Grosvenor Square

Also by Alison R. Holmes

'Transatlantic Diplomacy and "Global" States', in Alan Dobson and Steve Marsh (eds.), *Anglo-American Relations: Contemporary Perspectives* (London: Routledge, 2012).

The Third Way: Globalisation's Legacy (Leicester: Troubador, 2009).

Also by J. Simon Rofe

International History and International Relations, with Andrew Williams and Amelia Hadfield (Oxford: Routledge, 2012).

'Lord Lothian's Ambassadorship to Washington August 1939–December 1940', in Michael Hopkins, Saul Kelly and John Young (eds.), *British Embassy in Washington between 1939 and 1977* (New York and Basingstoke: Palgrave, 2009).

Franklin Roosevelt's Foreign Policy and the Welles Mission (New York: Palgrave, 2007).

T

The Embassy in Grosvenor Square

American Ambassadors to the United Kingdom, 1938–2008

Alison R. Holmes

International Studies Program Leader, Politics Lecturer, Humboldt State University

and

J. Simon Rofe

Senior Lecturer in Diplomatic and International Studies, Centre for International Studies and Diplomacy, SOAS, University of London

First published 2012 by
PALGRAVE MACMILLAN

Palgrave Macmillan in the UK is an imprint of Macmillan Publishers Limited,
registered in England, company number 785998, of Houndmills, Basingstoke,
Hampshire RG21 6XS.

Palgrave Macmillan in the US is a division of St Martin's Press LLC,
175 Fifth Avenue, New York, NY 10010.

Palgrave Macmillan is the global academic imprint of the above companies
and has companies and representatives throughout the world.

Palgrave® and Macmillan® are registered trademarks in the United States,
the United Kingdom, Europe and other countries.

ISBN 978–0–230–28062–5

This book is printed on paper suitable for recycling and made from fully
managed and sustained forest sources. Logging, pulping and manufacturing
processes are expected to conform to the environmental regulations of the
country of origin.

A catalogue record for this book is available from the British Library.

A catalog record for this book is available from the Library of Congress.

10   9   8   7   6   5   4   3   2   1
21 20 19 18 17 16 15 14 13 12

Printed and bound in Great Britain by
CPI Antony Rowe, Chippenham and Eastbourne

For my family who gave me a compass for the journey,
for Duncan who makes the journey an adventure – arh

My family; and the joy of having one – jsr

Contents

Preface

The volume explores the role played by the American Embassy in London, and the US Ambassador to the Court of St James's, not only in the bilateral Anglo-American relationship, but also in wider international relations over the seventy years that the Embassy has been in Grosvenor Square. The volume covers the period from 1938 through to 2008, effectively covering the lifespan of what has often been termed 'the special relationship' from its birth in the Second World War and into the aftermath of war through the challenges of the Cold War and its aftermath to the present day. The thematic issues of this period include not only debates about the 'specialness' of the relationship in the post-war context, but also the impact of the development and demise of the 'Cold War'; the ongoing impact of the European Project and EU integration, the influence of nuclear weapons and NATO, as well as wider economic, cultural, demographic and environmental forces that have shaped the transatlantic relationship. Within this broad context, the work seeks to address three overaching and interrelated questions: first, to assess the role the Embassy has played at crucial junctures in Anglo-American relations; secondly, to consider the opportunities that arise for a US Ambassador to influence events within the transatlantic relationship; and, thirdly, to establish whether any recurring features or principles can be identified which contribute to an enhanced understanding of long-standing debates over Anglo-American relations, US Foreign Policy and International Relations. In analysing each Ambassador since 1938 and the Embassy they headed, the work posits Transatlantic Diplomacy as a concept that extends beyond Anglo-American relations in explaining the evolution diplomacy in international relations into the twenty-first century.

Acknowledgements

Alison R. Holmes would like to acknowledge the support of the Rothermere American Institute, Oxford University during the initial stages of this work; the Winston Churchill Memorial Trust for the History/Travel Fellowship that provided funds to interview the six US Ambassadors to the UK since the Cold War in their homes around the United States; and the Whitney and Betty Macmillan Center for International and Area Studies and specifically the Pierre Keller Transatlantic Fellowship at Yale University for both timely financial assistance and an incomparable experience. For expertise and patience in equal measure, thanks goes to the librarians and staff at the Ronald Reagan and the George H. W. Bush Presidential Libraries, as well as two specific former employees in the London Embassy – now Ambassadors Glyn Davies and David Johnson. Finally, thanks are due to my new colleagues at Humboldt State University and all those friends and associates on both sides of the Atlantic who read drafts, listened to papers, offered advice, and even volunteered impatience – but only when it was required.

A separate and particularly heartfelt appreciation goes to Ambassadors Price, Catto (both now sadly deceased), Seitz, Lader, Farish and Tuttle for taking so much of their time to share insight and wisdom as to how they perceived their respective experiences as Ambassador. More importantly, they, and all those serving the United States as the Presidents' personal representatives to the Court of St James's are owed a debt of gratitude. Without their efforts, and those of all the diplomats covered in these pages, *The Embassy in Grosvenor Square* would truly not be possible.

J. Simon Rofe would like to take this opportunity to thank all those who have supported his efforts in producing this book; colleagues at the University of Leicester, SOAS – University of London, and elsewhere. Particular thanks should go to the Eccles Centre for American Studies at the British Library, London who kindly made me a Fellow in 2011–12 and provided an oasis of calm to further the project; to the British Academy for providing me with a Small Research Grant in 2010–12; and to the John F. Kennedy Presidential Library, and especially the Joseph P. Kennedy Papers Donor Committee who acceded to my request and granted me access to the Ambassador's papers. Also I would to thank the patient and helpful archivists at the Library of Congress, Churchill College Cambridge, the Franklin D. Roosevelt and the John F. Kennedy Presidential Libraries.

Further, thanks must be offered to Michael Hopkins, Saul Kelly and John Young, who kindly invited me to contribute to the 2009 volume, *The*

Washington Embassy: British Ambassadors to the United States 1939–1977; and in doing so provided an inspiration for this book.

Both authors offer grateful thanks to Jenny McCall and Clare Mence at Palgrave for their efficiency and attention to detail as they carried the book through to its production.

We would also like to thank the good offices of the Transatlantic Studies Association, and its Chairman, Professor Alan Dobson, for hosting a panel at its annual conference in 2010 at the University of Durham, where initial versions of a number of these papers were presented.

Finally, we would like to thank all of the contributors to the volume. Their expert knowledge and high quality research, made the job of compiling and co-editing this volume as straightforward as it was enlightening. However, it remains the friendship at the core of the endeavour that made the task enjoyable (and survive-able), for which we are both very grateful indeed.

Note to the Cover

Front Cover: This image of the unveiling of the Franklin Roosevelt Memorial from Mary Evans/National magazines, first appeared in *The Queen Magazine*, 28th April 1948. Those attending include (r to l): Queen Elizabeth (the Queen Mother), Prime Minister Clement Attlee, Mrs Franklin D. Roosevelt, Viscount Greenwood, Queen Mary, Viscountess Greenwood, the Duchess of Kent, Prince Michael, Princess Margaret and Princess Elizabeth. The statue is the work of Sir William Reid Dick.

Back Cover: This image, taken by photographer Cliff David at the unveiling of the Ronald Reagan statue on July 4 2011, is used with the kind permission of the Ronald Reagan Presidential Foundation. Those attending include (r to l): Ambassador Louis B. Susman, The Rt Hon William Hague MP, The Honorable Condoleezza Rice, Frederick Ryan, Jr, Ronald Reagan Presidential Foundation, Ambassador Robert H. Tuttle, Congressman Kevin McCarthy and The Venerable Stephen Robbins CB QHC. The statue is the work of Chas Fagan.

Notes on Contributors

Andrew Boxer graduated in history from Selwyn College, Cambridge in 1972 before becoming Head of History and Director of Studies at Eastbourne College, East Sussex. Since 2007 he has been a postgraduate student at Pembroke College, Oxford, taking a Master's degree (2008) on the subject of Winthrop Aldrich's ambassadorship, and currently working towards a doctorate on the US response to decolonisation in Rhodesia/Zimbabwe. He is the author of *The Conservative Governments 1951–64* in the Longman *Seminar Studies in History* series as well as several school textbooks.

James Cameron is a PhD student in History at the University of Cambridge. Supervised by Professor David Reynolds, his thesis addresses the development of American ballistic missile defence policy between 1961 and 1972. He holds a BA in History from Cambridge and an MPhil in Russian and East European Studies from Oxford University. He was a Fox International Fellow at Yale University during the academic year 2010–11.

Jonathan Colman is a lecturer in History at the University of Central Lancashire, England. He is the author of *A 'Special Relationship'? Harold Wilson, Lyndon B. Johnson and Anglo-American Relations at the Summit, 1964–68* (Manchester University Press, 2004), and *The Foreign Policy of Lyndon B. Johnson: The United States and the World, 1963–69* (Edinburgh University Press, 2010). He has also published numerous journal and book articles about British and American foreign policies, and the relationship between the two countries.

Nicholas J. Cull is Professor of Public Diplomacy at the University of Southern California in Los Angeles where he directs the Master's program in Public Diplomacy. He is a historian of the communications media and its role in international relations. He is the author of pioneering studies in this field including *The Cold War and the United States Information Agency: American Propaganda and Public Diplomacy, 1945–1989* (Cambridge University Press, 2008) and *The Decline and Fall of the United States Information Agency: American Public Diplomacy, 1989–2001* (Palgrave, 2012). He is president of the International Association for Media and History.

John Dumbrell is Professor of Government at Durham University. He is a graduate of Cambridge and Keele Universities, and a former chair of the

American Politics Group of the Political Studies Association. He is the author of *President Lyndon Johnson and Soviet Communism* (Manchester University Press, 2004: awarded the Richard E. Neustadt book prize, 2005); *A Special Relationship: Anglo-American Relations from the Cold War to Iraq* (Palgrave Macmillan, 2006); and *Clinton's Foreign Policy: Between the Bushes, 1992–2000* (Routledge, 2009). His latest book is *Rethinking the Vietnam War* (Palgrave, 2012).

Martin H. Folly is senior lecturer in international history in the Isambard Centre for Historical Research in the School of Social Sciences at Brunel University, London. He is the author of *Churchill, Whitehall and the Soviet Union, 1940–45* (Palgrave, 2000), *The United States in World War II* (Edinburgh University Press, 2002), *The Palgrave Concise Historical Atlas of the Second World War* (Palgrave, 2005) and the *Historical Dictionary of United States Diplomacy from World War I through World War II* (Scarecrow, 2010). He has published articles on the negotiation of the North Atlantic Treaty and Grand Alliance relations during the Second World War.

Alison R. Holmes is Program Leader of the International Studies Program at Humboldt State University in northern California. She spent 20 years in the UK, including running two general election campaigns for the Liberal Democrats, devising communications strategy at the BBC, managing the largest British-American business organisation and as speechwriter to the US Ambassador. She was awarded her PhD in International Relations from the London School of Economics in 2005 and returned to the US in 2008 as the Pierre Keller Fellow of Transatlantic Studies at Yale University. Her current research is in the areas of diplomacy and international relations. Publications include: 'Transatlantic Diplomacy in "Global" States' in Alan Dobson and Steve Marsh (eds.), *Anglo-American Relations: Contemporary Perspectives* (Routledge, 2012); 'Ronald Reagan: Conviction Politics and Transatlantic Relations', *Transatlantic Studies Association Journal*, Winter 2010; *The Third Way: Globalisation's Legacy* (Troubador, 2009); '100 Years On: Who Are the Inheritors of the "New Liberal" Mantle', *Political Quarterly*, Winter 2006; 'The Shifting Subtleties of "Special": Differences in U.S. and UK Approaches to Public Diplomacy that Impact Global Business', *Journal of Business Strategy*, Summer 2006.

David Mayers is Professor at Boston University, where he holds a joint appointment in the History and Political Science departments. His books include *George Kennan and the Dilemmas of US Foreign Policy* (Oxford University Press, 1988), *The Ambassadors and America's Soviet Policy* (Oxford University Press, 1995), *Wars and Peace: The Future Americans Envisioned, 1861–1991* (St Martin's Press, 1998), *Dissenting Voices in America's Rise to*

Power (Cambridge University Press, 2007). His new research, currently well underway, deals with Franklin D. Roosevelt's wartime diplomacy.

Thomas C. Mills is a Lecturer in Diplomacy and Foreign Policy at Lancaster University. His research lies in the field of international relations in the twentieth century, with a particular interest in US foreign policy. His publications include 'Anglo-American Economic Diplomacy during the Second World War and the Electrification of the Central Brazilian Railway', *Diplomacy and Statecraft* (March 2009); 'The "Hemisphere Isolationists" and Anglo-American Economic Diplomacy during the Second World War', *Journal of Transatlantic Studies* (March 2011), and *Post-War Planning on the Periphery: Anglo-American Economic Diplomacy in South America, 1939–1945* (Edinburgh University Press, 2012).

J. Simon Rofe is Senior Lecturer in Diplomatic and International Studies in the Centre for International Studies and Diplomacy at SOAS, University of London, United Kingdom. His research interests lie in the field of US diplomacy and foreign relations in the twentieth century with a specific focus on the era of Franklin Roosevelt, and presidential peacemaking and post-war planning. Publications include: *International History and International Relations,* with Andrew Williams and Amelia Hadfield (Routledge, 2012); 'Pre-war Post-war Planning: The Phoney War, the Roosevelt Administration, and the Case of the Advisory Committee on Problems of Foreign Relations', *Diplomacy and Statecraft* (2012); 'Lord Lothian's Ambassadorship to Washington August 1939–December 1940', in Michael Hopkins, Saul Kelly and John Young (eds.), *The British Embassy in Washington between 1939 and 1977* (Palgrave, 2009); and *Franklin Roosevelt's Foreign Policy and the Welles Mission* (Palgrave, 2007).

Alex Spelling completed his BA in Modern History at the University of East Anglia in 2000 and received an MA in Modern History from the University of Nottingham in 2003. He was awarded his PhD in History from Nottingham in 2008 for a study of the Anglo-American relationship during the Nixon administration. He is currently a Teaching Fellow in American History at the University of Aberdeen and previously worked in a similar capacity at the University of Southampton. His other work includes 'Lord Cromer, 1971–74' in *The Washington Embassy: British Ambassadors to Washington, 1939–77* (Palgrave Macmillan, 2009), and 'Edward Heath and Anglo-American Relations 1970–74: A Reappraisal', *Diplomacy and Statecraft* (December 2009).

Paul Trickett is a PhD candidate at Coventry University. His thesis examines the public diplomacy campaign of British diplomats in the United

States during the Falkland Islands War of 1982. He teaches modern political history and American foreign policy at the University of Leicester, is a member of the University's flourishing International Relations Distance Learning programme, and also teaches Strategic Studies and Diplomacy at Coventry University. He was associate editor for the Diplomatic Studies Programme (DSP) Discussion Paper series at the University of Leicester from 1996–2002. He was also the editor of the Diplomatic Studies Programme Newsletter. He is the author of 'UK Rep and the Falkland Islands Conflict: Driving the Machine' (Diplomatic Studies Programme Discussion Papers, June 1999, No. 54).

John W. Young is Professor of International History at the University of Nottingham. His most recent books include *Twentieth Century Diplomacy: A Case Study in British Practice, 1963–76* (Cambridge University Press, 2008) and, co-edited with Michael Hopkins and Saul Kelly, *The Washington Embassy: British Ambassadors to the United States, 1939–77* (Palgrave Macmillan, 2009). He has recently published a detailed study of the ambassadorship of David Bruce in 1960s London.

Introduction

Alison R. Holmes and J. Simon Rofe

The Importance of Place: Grosvenor Square in Transatlantic Diplomacy

Sometimes known as 'Little America' or even 'Eisenhower-platz', Grosvenor Square[1] in London has served as a hub between the United Kingdom and the United States since 1785 when John Adams was appointed the first American Minister Plenipotentiary to the Court of St James's.[2] Adams was not the first diplomat sent out from the new Republic as President Washington had sent ministers to France and Spain in 1779 and following Adams, ministers were sent to Portugal in 1791 and the Netherlands the following year. At this stage, they were deliberately not given higher titles because, as Secretary of State Thomas Jefferson explained to the Senate, they 'carried the "lowest grades admissible" to keep costs to a minimum'.[3] Throughout Adams' frustrating three years, he and his family made their home at Number 9, 'in the North East Angle of Grosvenor Square in the Parish of Saint George Hanover Square' at the junction of Duke and Brook Street.[4] It was described by his wife, Abigail, to her sister: 'We are agreeably enough situated here in a fine open square, in the middle of which is a circle inclosed with a neat grated fence…in the midle…is a statue of Gorge 2d. on horse back' [*sic*].[5] Their lodgings were not paid for by the government but, as with all diplomats of the day, from his own pocket. This was a cause of constant concern to Adams, and to many that would follow, but remained core to the idea of the 'citizen diplomat' for whom humble attire and a sober demeanour would be considered core to representing the new republic. By extension, this reasoning also supported the idea of political appointees as a 'check' on the aristocratic systems of Europe.

Abigail had confused the monarchs because it was King George I who rode, 'gilted' through the Square, but it was indeed 'fine'[6] as both the largest and last square set out in Mayfair.[7] From the beginning, it was 'inhabited chiefly by People of Distinction'.[8] Unusually for London, the square's location, as well as various innovations in its design, also meant the residents ranged

1

across the social scale. In the wake of the rebuilding of Buckingham Palace in the early 1800s,[9] a period of development in the area helped pave the way for residents such as Minister Adams as well the French, Belgian, Italian and Japanese Embassies that all arrived shortly thereafter.[10]

In 1893, when the Senate confirmed President Grover Cleveland's nomination of Thomas E. Bayard to become the first American to hold the rank of Ambassador, London officially became the site of the first full American Embassy in the world.[11] Since then, the United States Chancery in Great Britain (often, but not always, combined with the Legation) has not strayed far from Grosvenor Square, including addresses at Great Cumberland Place, Piccadilly and Portland Place, the longest being a period of 29 years at 123 Victoria Street, all relatively nearby. However, in 1912 the Victoria Street location was declared by Ambassador Page to be a 'dark and dingy hall . . . between two cheap stores'.[12] He moved his residence from that 'cheap hole' back to No. 6 Grosvenor Square and a section to No. 4 Grosvenor Gardens shortly thereafter. The living conditions for ambassadors improved significantly nine years later when J. Pierpont Morgan donated his London home at 13–14 Prince's Gate as a permanent residence. Diplomats generally continued to pay for their own lodgings and to work in leased space, covering at least part of the cost by collecting consular fees. Cost control also explains why early Missions tended to be kept at the level of Legation. However, the change brought about in the diplomatic service by the Rogers Act 1924 included the building of bespoke premises around Europe for both offices and residences.[13] Paris was part of the first round, but London did not begin to benefit until 1931 when the government furnished the Prince's Gate residence and began the search for a site on which to build a permanent embassy.[14] They looked initially in Trafalgar Square, but when suitable premises could not be found at the right price, they again leased property, taking several floors of a new office building on the east side of Grosvenor Square, which they occupied until 1937.[15]

By 1938 – when we take up our story – the Embassy had moved across to No. 1 Grosvenor Square. Today, the building is the Canadian High Commission, but this was where Ambassador Winant, eschewing the Prince's Gate residence as he considered it 'a considerable distance away' opted for the 'practical advantages' of a small apartment effectively over the office: 'Flat No. 30, 3 Grosvenor Square'.[16] Early in his term, Winant was granted complete authority to coordinate both civilian and military activity, effectively giving him a staff of 4,000 and making the proximity of home to office all the more important. It was also from this rooftop perch that he was able to watch the German night-time raids on the capital, when he was not walking the streets offering help to stricken Londoners.[17] General Eisenhower, arriving in 1942, also opted for convenience and set up his initial offices as Commander-in-Chief of the Allied Forces on the west side of the square, directly opposite the Embassy.[18]

After the war, the US government used the opportunity to undertake an extensive buy and/or build programme across Europe and used war debt credits to cover the cost. As Richard Arndt explains, 'the conceptual rationale for the program was cultural; to showcase the architectural synthesis achieved by and for the American Century' although he goes on to point out that 'the phrase the "International Style" was rejected by the architects themselves, who were simply developing new forms to meet new needs with newly available materials. For them, it was the American style.'[19]

Despite a prohibition on land ownership in London, the US government was not prevented from leasing land and owning the buildings built on the property. The State Department therefore proceeded to purchase Nos. 1, 3 and 20 Grosvenor Square in 1947, paying the entire $8,337,280 in credits, while at the same time signing a 99-year lease with the Duke of Westminster (a descendant of the original Thomas Grosvenor). They added No. 5 to their portfolio in 1948 with the plan to sell this at a later date and use the proceeds to buy a large enough site for a consolidated Embassy. This took place in 1950 when they bought the entire west side of the square for $2,192,003. This was again paid entirely with credits – not including the annual fee of one peppercorn.[20]

In terms of the Ambassador's residence, Winfield House in Regent's Park, formerly owned by the Woolworth's heiress Barbara Hutton, was sold to the US government for the token price of one dollar a year after the war, but it had suffered significant damage.[21] Its state of disrepair was considered so serious that it was slated for demolition, but in 1953 Nelson Kenworthy, the person in charge of the US government building programme, vetoed the plan to destroy the house and instead brought in Perry, Shaw & Hepburn for renovations.[22] Ambassador Aldrich and his wife were the first to use Winfield House and took up residence in January 1955.[23] Prince's Gate was sold the following year for the sum of $138,198.[24] Over the years, Winfield House has benefited from the generosity of numerous ambassadors willing to use their own funds to continue the process of renovation, upgrading and updating that such a house requires, and to ensure it continues to be 'America's House' in London.

With the residence well established, it was time to turn to the task of creating a permanent Embassy. According to Jane Loeffler, the period from 1954 through 1960 was the 'heyday of the American foreign building program' and created buildings that were 'historically distinct'.[25] Despite 'austerity' being the watchword in the State Department at the time, they decided to create a competition for a new London Embassy.[26] This was the first of its kind and not repeated for another 40 years with the 1995 competition for the Embassy in Berlin (and London again in 2008).[27] Eero Saarinen, a Finnish-American modernist architect, had just won the commission for the Oslo Embassy in 1955 and was put on the list to compete for London.[28] It was a requirement of the competition that the architects visit the site which may explain Saarinen's approach to the design. He believed that every building should have its 'own look' as well as be a 'good neighbor' which, according to the cover story on Saarinen by *Time* in 1956, 'brought down the wrath of modern purists, who favour glass and steel even if it clashes with every building in the area'. As the article points out, Saarinen tried to place the design in the context of the square by 'keeping the structure modern, but keying the floor levels and spacings of the front façade to the surrounding Georgian buildings'.[29]

There were other critics of the modern approach, the most relevant being the Ambassador himself. Aldrich flew to Washington to address a special meeting of the Architectural Advisory Committee in August 1955 as they deliberated on the competition. He tried to convince them that the 'new London embassy should not only respect English architectural tradition', but more specifically, that its design should be 'in the nature of the late eighteenth-century architecture as designed by Nash'.[30] He also asserted that the Grosvenor estate would not accept a modern building on the site – despite the fact they already had accepted such buildings elsewhere. The committee's answer to Aldrich is found in the fact they invited *only* modernists to participate in the competition.[31] Happily, Aldrich was later won over.[32]

Ironically, Saarinen's winning design was not actually built, largely due to the decision to provide considerably more space. He revised the plans, but continued to alter them, even after the building was underway.[33] A prime example of this evolution is the striking gilded aluminium eagle that spreads 35 feet over the entrance. Not part of the original plan, or even the revised one, Saarinen asked Theodore Roszak to sculpt the piece and managed to get the change through the committee in 1957. This was done primarily by downplaying its significance to the overall look and using his position by that stage as the chair of the committee, to move it swiftly through.[34] The Embassy opened its doors for business in 1960.

American Mementoes

The statue of King George is long gone, though the square continues to provide a home to the landmarks of transatlantic milestones. On the north side stands a statue of Franklin D. Roosevelt. Organised by the Pilgrims Society[35] after his death in April 1945, the statue was paid for through subscription by over 160,000 British people within six days of the launch of the appeal (it took the US government 60 years after his death before the Roosevelt Memorial was opened on the Mall in Washington DC).[36] In the centre of the square stands a monument unveiled in 1986, sponsored by the Hearst Foundation, to commemorate the American Eagle Squadron formed in 1940 by American pilots who volunteered to join the British Air Force. Just outside the garden itself, steps away from his wartime office, stands a statue of General Eisenhower unveiled in 1989 during the heyday of relations between Margaret Thatcher and Ronald Reagan. One of only a few that exist of the General, the statue was the gift of the people of Kansas City, Missouri – hometown to both Eisenhower and Charlie Price, the Ambassador of the day.

More recently, the Square has been a focal point for more human transatlantic interaction with protests over issues such as Vietnam, cruise missiles and the war in Iraq. It was also the place people were naturally drawn to remember those who lost their lives in the attacks on 11 September 2001. An estimated 100,000 people from all over the world filed through the Square. Two years later to the day, a permanent memorial garden commemorating the 66 British victims (to date, still the largest number of British casualties from a single terror attack) was opened on the east side of the Square, designed to face the Embassy and paid for by the British government. Finally, on 4 July 2011 a statue of Ronald Reagan was added to the square and unveiled in the presence of the current Ambassador, Louis Susman, as well as former Ambassador (and former employee of Reagan) Robert Tuttle.

In October 2008, the US State Department announced that the US Embassy would depart from the Square with construction of a new Embassy building south of the Thames at Nine Elms in Wandsworth, set to begin in 2012 and to be America's new home from 2017.[37] It will mark over two centuries since the arrival of the first American Minister and the end of the link to Grosvenor Square.

The Embassy 'Hub'

In light of this long-standing history in Anglo-American relations it should be no surprise that the ambassadorial post to the Court of St James's is considered one of the most prestigious a President can propose, or that Grosvenor Square has been considered a vital conduit in the relationship between London and Washington.

Indeed, in the early years it was not unusual for the Ambassador to the Court of St James's to come from, or go on to, the highest US jobs. Five were President, nine were Secretary of State, and four were both.[38] Other posts held by former or future Ambassadors include: Attorney General and Secretaries of the Navy, War and Treasury. One Ambassador, Louis McLane, was Secretary of State and Secretary of the Treasury, as well as Minister to the United Kingdom – twice.[39] Cabinet posts have not been the recent pattern, though government service before and after an ambassadorial posting to London is more common than usually perceived.

Given the long-standing diplomatic relationship the full range of professional experience is reflected in the post-holders and in their influence on Anglo-American relations. Specifically, over the past 70 years 23 people have served as Ambassador: 22 men, one woman and no person of colour. Individual scenarios vary, but unlike three of their nominated predecessors, none in this cohort have been rejected by the Senate – and certainly not shared the fate of Martin Van Buren who had the added embarrassment of already being in London when word of the rejection came through.[40] Similarly, none have had their passports returned by the British authorities: the ultimate expression of a host country's displeasure. Over the years, two have declined the appointment,[41] one was recalled for disobeying direct orders[42] and two more recent Ambassadors returned home under a cloud, though not for disobedience as such, but for general presidential displeasure: Joseph Kennedy in 1940 and John Louis, Jr in 1983. Two Ambassadors have had to deal with the fall-out of impeachment proceedings against their patron.[43]

Overall, from the time of John Adams, the one thing all these emissaries have in common is the fact they have all been political appointees. In the American system, in accordance with Article II Section 2 of the Constitution the President has the power to 'nominate... by and with the advice and consent of the Senate... ambassadors, other public ministers and consuls, judges of the Supreme Court, and all other officers of the United States' which includes the entire Cabinet. The Constitution does provide that 'Congress may by law vest the appointment of such inferior officers, as they think proper', but the essential point is that each Ambassador serves effectively at the President's pleasure.[44] This approach is rooted in the early days of the republic with ideas of 'public service' and desire to have the 'common man' represent the country abroad. However, it is also firmly connected to political patronage and the rewarding of loyalty of various kinds. For London, apart from one near miss in 1898 and a single exception, namely Raymond Seitz in 1991, every Ambassador to London has been non-career.[45] As the universal role of the ambassador has always been as the official and personal representative of the sovereign, there is an understandable debate as to the distinction between professional diplomats and those sent as a personal favour or purely on financial grounds as to their subsequent effectiveness. On the one hand, an ambassadorial post can be one of the 'baubles' an American President has at his disposal to reward supporters; on the other, their real world experience and detachment from the institution of the State Department often facilitates direct access to the Chief Executive.

Many of the authors in this volume start from the premise that career diplomats are 'better' than non-career or 'political appointees'. However, it is also clear that, as they explore the question of whether access to the President translates into influence or effectiveness, their political status becomes less important than whether they used their clout and credibility to good effect. As former Deputy Chief of Mission in London (now Ambassador) Glyn Davies explains:

> The best political appointees are the best ambassadors we've got – for the really big embassies – they can be the best because you've got... the ear of the president... a stature you just can't achieve if you're essentially

a bureaucrat or a career diplomat. You can do more... You can achieve a higher point... the best political appointees, historically are the best ambassadors we've had.[46]

London has long been one of, if not the largest embassy with all of the attending work that requires for both the Ambassador and their senior team. While it is true that the Ambassador is technically the head of the mission, many of those working in the Embassy do not report solely or even regularly to him, but to their own offices back in Washington. The 'silo' effect can be intense and management a challenge. To offer a level of magnitude, there are generally anywhere from 600 to 1,000 American and locally engaged staff, approximately 17 separate government agencies represented, 6,000 visas issued daily and the hosting of approximately 20,000 official visitors a year (not including the literally hundreds of thousands unofficial exchanges, groups, civic and private bodies that often request or require some form of advice or assistance from the Embassy) to be dealt with. These numbers also tend to leave out the 'unofficial' officials working for military and intelligence agencies.[47] As such, London acts as a crucial hub, not only between agencies or between the UK and the US, but also between the US and Europe and the rest of the world. As will be clear from the chapters that follow, the global aspects of UK–US relations are never far from the surface which, for the Embassy and the Ambassador, means that London is always closely involved in a much broader range of issues than the traditional idea of 'bilateral' relations might suggest.

Period Covered

A straightforward explanation for the focus of this book could be all of the sentimental reasons associated with the American presence in Grosvenor Square and its environs for well over two centuries. However, it is the period from 1938 to 2008 that the Embassy becomes a more permanent and imposing presence as the United States evolves into a strong ally and a fierce competitor to the United Kingdom. More importantly, this period also covers the lifespan of the much debated term 'the special relationship' from its 'birth' – although not its conception – in the Second World War and its aftermath, to the challenges of globalisation in the present day. The book not only highlights the ebb and flow of that *special* link, but also provides an account of the themes which underpin the special relationship and transcend individual ambassadorships.

The thematic issues of our 70-year period include not only the 'special relationship' in the post-war context given the conflicting explanations and contested nature of its evolution, but also the development and demise of the Cold War; the ongoing impact of the European Project; the military dimension including the influence of nuclear weapons; as well as wider economic, demographic and environmental factors that have shaped the transatlantic relationship over this period.

While these issues have influenced substantial change in Anglo-American relations, by way of contrast this period has been a time of relative transatlantic stability – at least in terms of leadership. These Ambassadors have presented their credentials to only two sovereigns: King George VI and, from 1953, Queen Elizabeth II. The political leadership of the period has been similarly stable with only 15 Prime Ministers and 13 Presidents since the Second World War. Leaving Franklin Roosevelt's four election victories to one side, four of the 13 Presidents served two full terms and two served nearly two.[48] Given that only 20 per cent of all American Presidents have been re-elected, it is clearly relevant that half have in recent times. In fact, the only other concentration of single-party, single-handed leadership takes us back to George Washington's appointment of John Adams when five of the first seven Presidents were two-termers. One century and two world wars later and we are back to Franklin D. Roosevelt – a three-full-term President and the man generally considered to mark out the beginning of what is often considered to be the 'modern presidency' – and the dawn of the so-called 'special relationship'.[49]

The Framework

The time frame under scrutiny has been divided into six parts delineated by significant shifts in global affairs as reflected in UK–US relations. Each part covers individual ambassadors in chronological order, though we are conscious that strict chronological narratives often become a trawl from ambassador to ambassador which tends to lead to a 'flattening' of historical perspective. To counter this, we have used the introduction to each section to provide brief thematic digests for each period, while adding structure in terms of the issues that link the ambassadorships within and between sections in order to enhance the analytical coherence of the whole. They are as follows:

- Part I: The Wartime Ambassadors, 1938–1946
- Part II: The Cold War Ambassadors, 1946–1961
- Part III: The Cold War Ambassadors, 1961–1981
- Part IV: The Cold War Closers, 1981–1991
- Part V: The Post-Cold War Ambassadors, 1991–2001
- Part VI: The Post-9/11 Ambassadors, 2001–2008

The breadth and relevance of sources used to write a volume covering such a time span are testament to the resourcefulness of the authors. Primary resources located in archives in the United Kingdom (National Archives, Kew) and the United States (National Archives, College Park MD), as well as interviews with the last six US Ambassadors to London and other leading protagonists from the wider Diplomatic Corps, alongside a broad swathe of secondary literature indicates the range of materials that have been employed. Different resources were available to authors covering the early period – for example, the official *Foreign Relations of the United States* Series only extends to the 1970s at the present time. Whatever their particular sources, the authors have each taken the opportunity provided by the volume's approach to display their individual expertise.

'Something Old, Something New': Special Relations and Transatlantic Diplomacy

Discussion of almost any aspect of Anglo-American relations in the post-Second World War era requires a doffing of one's cap to something ubiquitously known as the 'special relationship'. Popular culture abounds with imagery of 'Uncle Sam' and 'John Bull' or 'Britannia', or the American Eagle and British Lion. Richard Curtis's 2003 film, *Love Actually*, makes direct reference to British dissatisfaction about the state of the Special Relationship. The fictional British Prime Minister rebukes a fictional American President who claims that 'our special relationship is still very special'. Reflecting popular anti-American discontent of the time, the British PM retorts: 'I fear that this has become a bad relationship. A relationship based on the President taking exactly what he wants and casually ignoring all those things that really matter to, erm … Britain. We may be a small country but we're a great one, too.' Lines in a film are one thing, but when *The Spectator* comments and a YouTube site is created to draw parallels to remarks made by leader of the Liberal Democrats and now, Deputy Prime Minister Nick Clegg to Curtis's fictional PM, a more interesting phenomenon is at play.[50]

Exploring every nuance of the special relationship is a mammoth task beyond the immediate focus of this volume. Nonetheless, we hope to be able to make a contribution to a seemingly perennial debate. First of all, what language to use: 'a' special relationship or 'the' special relationship – the latter definite article used to express more intimacy, the former indefinite used in a recent volume to describe a plurality in America's special relationships.[51] Then there is the question as to whether or not to capitalise the 'S' and the 'R' as an indication of it being a proper noun; or to italicise it for exaggerated intonation. Equally, the Celtic influence on relations between the United States and the United Kingdom should not be overlooked, despite the common concentration on the 'Anglo'. The first British Prime Minister to make an official visit to the United States in 1930 was, in fact a Scot, Ramsey Macdonald, and other significant Celts have followed. One author, writing about Philip Kerr, Lord Lothian, British Ambassador to the United States at the outset of the Second World War, entitled his article 'The Inestimable Advantage of Not Being English'.[52] As such, the prefixing of the special relationship with 'Anglo-American' is clearly not without challenge and UK–US relations may be more appropriate. Dilemmas of this sort may seem trivial, and indeed on one level they are. At a deeper level, however, they reflect the difficulties in extracting substance from verbiage.

Further evidence of the special relationship's pervasive hold on transatlantic discourse is found in the different ways of talking about it by the protagonists themselves in often rather pointed political rhetoric. The most 'Europhile' Tory leader of the post-war era, Edward Heath, disliked the term and refused to use it. At the same time, he acknowledged that Anglo-American relations had a 'natural' quality.[53] The British Foreign and Commonwealth Office have, at various times since the 1980s, performed linguistic gymnastics to avoid the phrase while the Foreign Affairs Committee in March of 2010 went so far as to declare it a 'potentially misleading' phrase and to 'recommend that its use should be avoided'.[54] However, it was not so very long ago that the Foreign and Commonwealth Office's strategy bluntly asserted that relations with the US were 'the most important individual relationship'.[55] The underlying fear being that the term only resonates amongst a British audience and therefore to use it with the US government might lead to a questioning of its existence at all. Put colloquially, it is deemed far better not to mention it, lest 'it' become the focus of the conversation.

More recently, in March 2012, President Barack Obama hosted Prime Minister David Cameron and, with strikingly different positioning than that adopted for Cameron's predecessor, attached a new prefix to the term 'relationship'. The relationship was not 'special' but should now be deemed 'essential' (the *Financial Times* commenting: 'The word "special" is worn thin through over-use'.[56]) The pair published a joint article in *The Washington Post* and *The Guardian*, stressing instead the 'essential' character of transatlantic relations while President Obama hailed the relationship as one of the 'greatest alliances the world has ever known'.[57] 'Our alliance is essential', Obama stated at a press conference on the lawn of the White House with Cameron nodding in agreement, 'it is indispensable to the prosperity and security that we seek, not only for our own citizens but for people around the world'. The idea that the Anglo-Americans are guardians of prosperity and security beyond their own citizens is something we will return to.

From an earlier era there are two dominant views of UK–US relations, special or otherwise. British economist John Maynard Keynes' reputation for driving a hard bargain with his American counterparts in Washington as the war drew to an end was well deserved. Nonetheless, as his biographer, Robert Skidelsky, states of Keynes: 'qualifying all Keynes's battles with the Americans was the underlying belief that the New World had to be yoked, and kept yoked, to the Old World, if the latter were to enjoy durable peace and prosperity'. In other words, it was important for Britain to be aligned with the United States in a special relationship. Skidelsky goes on: 'It was in Britain's long-term interest to arrange for this, even if it meant having to swallow humble pie on the way.'[58] Such a view points to the asymmetry in the transatlantic relationship – a feature that becomes acute at various points in this volume.

The second perspective on the transatlantic special relationship comes from the originator of the phrase. It would be impossible to talk of the *special relationship* without considering Churchill's rose-tinted view and lashings of prose in support of the 'English-speaking peoples'. It was in his address entitled 'The Sinews of Peace' at Westminster College in March 1946 in Fulton, Missouri, perhaps best known to the world for its line about an 'iron curtain' descending across Europe, that he first refers to a transatlantic 'special relationship'. He considered the special relationship to be 'the fraternal association of the English-speaking peoples', requiring 'not only the growing friendship and mutual understanding between our two vast but kindred systems of society'.[59]

Reference to the examples above of the use of the term 'special relationship' provides brief insight into the challenge that each of our contributors has grappled with – consciously and subconsciously – as they reflect the use of the term themselves and by their protagonists, and its associated meanings in the chapters that make up this volume.

In the realm of academia, considerable ink has also been spilt. An identifiable traditional orthodoxy of the post-Second World War Anglo-American special relationship rests on three core characteristics. The first, often seen as the principal basis of the special relationship, is the military and intelligence interconnectedness of the two states with the inter-operability of military institutions and equipment often being offered as evidence of intimacy. Although the latter is at considerable financial cost to the UK, the belief and expectation that they will be operating with the United States in the future means it is a cost they are prepared to countenance. The strategic implications in the military realm are perhaps seen most clearly in relation to Britain's nuclear capability. Whatever the political debate in the UK over the value of nuclear weapons may be, the reality is that Britain's nuclear deterrent has been built and maintained by the United States since the 1960s. As a further exemplar, the three letter acronym that UK–US militaries have enjoyed since the Second World War for their bilateral parlance is 'ABC' in describing 'American–British conversations'.

The second characteristic of the traditional view is the economic connection between the United Kingdom and the United States. It is often remarked that if 'Wall Street sneezes, the City catches the cold', an observation that holds true for the vast majority of the period under consideration here. Equally, there are extremely high levels of Foreign Direct Investment (FDI) between the two countries and despite almost 40 years of membership of the European Union in its various guises, the United States remains the UK's biggest export market.

The third characteristic within traditional views of the special relationship is that of common culture. The markers of shared language, history and language contribute to a cultural affinity which means people and policy-makers alike look across the Atlantic before turning to other potential partners. Echoing the work of Professor H. C. Allen in his seminal work *Great Britain and the United States: A History of Anglo-American Relations 1783–1952*, Inderjeet Parmar considers the key attributes of the connection to be a common political-cultural heritage of liberal institutions and anti-militarism, rule of law, respect for free speech, religious and family ties, and the English language.[60] In such an assessment, strategic and economic interests are 'subordinated to the deeper rhythms and shared histories of Anglo-Saxon peoples'.[61] Greg Kennedy writes in similar terms, referring to the special relationship as the 'long-lasting circumstances that created friendship through understanding, networking, intellectual affinity, financial ties, family or blood relations, empathy and mutual fear of deception, but remained only a sentiment, not a formal or public expression of policy'.[62] Of course there is variation in emphasis within the scholarship, but recent exponents of what might be considered an orthodox viewpoint include scholars Kathleen Burk, Alan Dobson, John Dumbrell and David Reynolds.[63]

Such views, echoing Churchillian motifs, also raise a question as to the *degree* of specialness. In other words, how special is 'special'? Alex Danchev offers a critical view in proposing ten criteria for a special relationship. Without going through them all, he identifies two key criteria as 'transparency' and the ability to 'mythicise' (as he calls it). Danchev could speak for many when he concludes: 'Specialness is semaphor. It needs to be decoded and analysed.'[64]

Transatlantic Diplomacy

Beyond the puzzle of 'specialness' in terms of bilateral or specifically diplomatic relations, there is also a broader question to be contemplated for potential future scholarship. Throughout the volume it becomes clear that there is a pattern of behaviour between these two democratic, developed, serially hegemonic states. However, it is also clear that the language of 'specialness', by whatever definition, and the existential debates regarding the relationship do almost as much to obscure as to reveal the workings of the wider international system. The focus of this volume is firmly in the realms of diplomacy, history and politics. However, the authors here, collectively, even if not overtly, offer evidence that there may be deeper, structural factors involved. We would like to pose the initial idea that it may be possible to think of still another prefix, at least in terms of the diplomatic relationship, namely 'transatlantic'. Clearly the term is regularly used in this context; however, our argument is that the term should be released from its geographic bond and applied to forms of diplomatic interaction that states develop as they increasingly move towards what has been called the 'global state'.[65]

Long before discussions of the phenomenon of globalisation became commonplace, relations between the United States and the United Kingdom have blurred the traditional line between 'foreign' and 'domestic'. Every author here spends time outlining, some in great detail, the fundamentally enmeshed nature of the bureaucratic, political, economic and social relations between these two state actors with the result that UK–US relations have become 'intermestic' rather than anything we recognise as purely international or even bilateral.

The wider point therefore, to contemplate as part of our analysis of the US Embassy in London is its implications for broader understanding of international relations. The suggestion is that the processes of globalisation, as uneven as we recognise them to be, are slowly homogenising the traits that once made the US and the UK 'special' or at least exclusive to each other. There is the possibility that, rather than a brave new world of diplomatic exchange, we are returning to an older form of continuous negotiation, but rather than Richlieu's version of *négociation continuelle,* UK–US relations exist in a world that is continuous and connected, but not secret.[66] 'Transatlantic diplomacy' as a model may, ultimately be one that is followed by others, as it operates through a process by which every issue, every policy, every debate is open and transparent to the other side. Secret diplomacy is finally, truly dead. The rest of the world may have much to learn from the eagle and the lion. Nonetheless, the eagle and lion have, as will become evident in this volume, had to learn, and re-learn lessons that embrace a meaningful relationship and engender 'transatlantic diplomacy'.

There is a thought that echoes down from the first Minister, John Adams, through the timeframe of this volume and even to the sentiments recently expressed by both President Obama and Prime Minister David Cameron. The British Ambassador to Washington, Lord Lothian (1939–40), was arguing passionately with the Foreign Secretary, Lord Halifax (his successor in Washington), that the Anglo-American relationship was essential not only to the future of each nation separately, but to all of 'civilisation'. He keenly felt, like so many others in his place before and after, that theirs was not a mission of purely bilateral relations. Rather, that the relationship's success (or failure) was important on a much wider scale and to a global audience and their actions and reactions in the diplomatic realm should be measured accordingly.

> ... it has often been said that patience is the most difficult of the statesman's arts. There is certainly no field in which it is more essential to exercise it if you believe, as I do that ... the destinies of the two countries and of the Dominions are now inextricably involved and that the future of our civilisation depends upon our gradual discovering the basis upon which we can confidently cooperate for our own and the common good.[67]

The complex tale of how the United States and the United Kingdom, the eagle and the lion, have struggled and striven, fought and cooperated in an effort to determine both their 'own *and* the common good' has, in large measure, been played out through the Embassy in Grosvenor Square. It is a saga that unfolds in the pages that follow.

Notes

1. David McCullough places the Adams household at Number 8 (David McCullough, *John Adams* [New York: Simon & Schuster, 2001], p. 349), whereas British History Online and the US Embassy website list it as Number 9 (http://london.usembassy.gov/rcgrsvnr.html). Adams himself gave his address as: 'Grosvenor Square Westminster Corner House between Duke Street and Brook Street. Aug. 31. 1785' (Docno: AFC06d103. Massachusetts Historical Society, www.masshist.org/publications/apde/portia.php?id= AFC06d103).
2. According to *Debrett's Peerage and Baronetage*, 'The correct wording when describing a foreign Ambassador accredited to the United Kingdom is indeed "accredited to the Court of St James's". The apostrophe 's' should never be dropped, either in speech or in writing…"Ambassador to the United Kingdom" is an acceptable alternative if the correct wording is likely to be misunderstood.' Correspondence with A. R. Holmes, 3 February 2010.
3. Jane C. Loeffler, *The Architecture of Diplomacy: Building America's Embassies* (New York: Princeton Architectural Press, rev. 2nd edn, 2011), p. 13.
4. Perhaps the safest expression of the address is geographic and found in the language of the lease signed 9 June 1785 attached to 'List of Visits Paid and Returned in London, June–July? 1785' (Docno: DJA03d162 www.masshist.org/publications/apde/portia.php?id= DJA03d162) and F.H.W. Sheppard (gen. ed.), 'Grosvenor Square: Introduction', *Survey of London: Volume 40: The Grosvenor Estate in Mayfair, Part 2 (The Buildings)*, (1980, pp. 112–17), British History Online, www.british-history.ac.uk/report.aspx?compid= 42125.
5. Abigail Adams to Mary Smith Cranch, 15 August 1785 (Docno: AFC06d09, www.masshist.org/).
6. *Ibid.*
7. Sheppard, 'Grosvenor Square: Introduction'.
8. Roy Porter, *London: A Social History* (Cambridge, MA: Harvard University Press, 1995), pp. 108–9.
9. *Ibid.* pp. 355–6.
10. Sheppard, 'Grosvenor Square: Introduction'.
11. Loeffler, *The Architecture of Diplomacy*, p. 15.
12. Ambassador Walter H. Page (1912–18) quoted in Beckles Willson, *America's Ambassadors to England (1785–1928): A Narrative of Anglo-American Diplomatic Relations* (London: John Murray, 1928), p. 447.
13. Richard Arndt, *The First Resort of Kings: American Cultural Diplomacy in the Twentieth Century* (Dulles, VA: Potomac Books, 2005), p. 144.
14. Loeffler, *The Architecture of Diplomacy*, p. 17 and p. 22.
15. *Ibid.* p. 193.
16. John Winant, *Letter from Grosvenor Square: An Account of a Stewardship* (Boston: Houghton Mifflin, 1947), pp. 3, 2, 1.

17. *Ibid.* pp. 60–1, 73 and Philip Seib, *Broadcasts from the Blitz: How Edward R. Murrow Helped Lead America into War* (Washington, DC: Potomac Books, 2007).
18. Loeffler, *The Architecture of Diplomacy*, p. 193.
19. Arndt, *The First Resort of Kings*, pp. 145–6.
20. Loeffler, *The Architecture of Diplomacy*, p. 195.
21. Maria Tuttle and Marcus Binney, *An American House: Winfield House* (New York: Thames & Hudson, 2008).
22. Loeffler, *The Architecture of Diplomacy*, p. 120.
23. Ambassador's Residence, Winfield House, US Embassy website: http://london. usembassy.gov/rcwinfld.html
24. *Ibid.* Loeffler, *The Architecture of Diplomacy*, p. 120.
25. Loeffler, *The Architecture of Diplomacy*, p. 163.
26. *Ibid.*, p. 104.
27. *Ibid.*, p. 253.
28. *Ibid.*, p. 191.
29. 'Art: The Maturing Modern', *Time Magazine*, 2 July 1956, available at: http://www. time.com/time/magazine/article/0,9171,891296,00.html.
30. Loeffler, *The Architecture of Diplomacy*, p. 195.
31. *Ibid.*, p. 196.
32. *Ibid.*, p. 201.
33. *Ibid.*, p. 200.
34. *Ibid.*, pp. 168, 202.
35. The Pilgrims Society – founded in 1902 as a dining club and traditionally the venue for a new US Ambassador's 'maiden speech'.
36. To commemorate their donation, people were sent a souvenir book with the following paragraph on its cover. 'THIS SOUVENIR BOOK is given to you in grateful acknowledgement of your donation of five shillings to the Franklin Roosevelt Memorial Fund. It has been produced and distributed without cost to the Fund. It is hoped that as many persons as possible will contribute five shillings in order that the memorial may be thoroughly representative of the British people's wishes to commemorate Mr. Roosevelt.'
37. 'US Takes First Steps towards Embassy Relocation', Press Release US Department of State, 2 October 2008, available at: http://london.usembassy.gov/ukpapress84. html (accessed June 2011).
38. The five Ministers or Ambassadors who were also President were: John Adams (Minister 1785–88, President 1797–1801), James Monroe (Minister 1803–1807, President 1817–25), John Quincy Adams (Minister 1815–17, President 1825–29), Martin Van Buren (Minister 1831–32, President 1837–41) and James Buchanan (Minister 1853–56, President 1857–61). The nine Ministers or Ambassadors who were also Secretary of State (SS) were: James Monroe (Minister 1803–1807, SS 1811–17), John Quincy Adams (Minister 1815–17;,SS 1817–25), Richard Rush (Minister 1818–25, Acting SS 1817), Martin Van Buren (Minister 1831–32, SS 1829–31), Edward Everett (Minister 1841–45, SS 1852–53), Louis McLane (Minister 1845–46, SS 1833–34), James Buchanan (Minister 1853–56, SS 1845–49), Thomas Bayard Sr (Minister 1893–97, SS 1885–89), John Hay (Minister 1897–98, SS 1898–1905). Two notable additions: (1) John Jay who was 'Envoy Extraordinary to the Court of London' (and Secretary of State 1789–90). Jay embarked 12 May 1794 until the successful negotiation of the Jay Treaty on 19 November of the same year. Jay stayed on to await word, unaware that both copies of the Treaty had ended up on the same ship, the *Tankerville*, which sank. Hearing nothing, Jay

returned to the US where, after much furore, Congress agreed and the Treaty went into operation on 30 April 1796. (2) Robert Todd Lincoln, Abraham Lincoln's son who was Secretary of War 1881–85 and the last Minister to the UK (1889–93) before the post became a full Ambassador. The four Ministers or Ambassadors who were both President and Secretary of State were: James Monroe, John Quincy Adams, Martin Van Buren, and James Buchanan.

39. Louis McLane (1829–31 and 1845–46) was the only Minister to hold the post twice – though a small number of Foreign Service Officers have returned to the UK including Ambassador Raymond Seitz whose term as Ambassador was his third tour.

40. Three Ambassadors were rejected by the Senate: Martin Van Buren (1832), George B. McClellan (1868) and Richard H. Dana, Jr (1876).

41. Two declined the appointment: Frederick T. Frelinghuysen (1870) was commissioned and declined and Oliver T. Morton (1870) was commissioned during a recess of Senate and declined.

42. J. Lothrop Motley angered the President by defying a direct order and was brought home 18 months later.

43. Elliott Richardson, a close colleague of President Nixon's and formerly the Secretary of Health, Education, and Welfare from 1970 to 1973, Secretary of Defence from January to May 1973, and Attorney General from May to October 1973 in the Nixon administration before going to London as Ambassador, returned home when Nixon was forced to resign despite the relatively short term gap that left in the post. (Gerald Ford appointed Anne Legendre Armstrong – the only woman to serve as Ambassador to the UK – for the remaining 12 months of his term.) Philip Lader speaks of the pressure during the impeachments proceedings against President Bill Clinton (interview with author).

44. United States Constitution, US Senate, available at: http://www.senate.gov/reference/glossary_term/advice_and_consent.htm.

45. In 1898 it is believed that the outgoing Ambassador, John Hay, favoured the appointment of his First Secretary, Henry White, as his successor. White had served in London many years and knew the job, as well as being in personal correspondence with Roosevelt, Lodge, Reid, Hay and others. However, it was noted that, 'the London Embassy was too highly esteemed as a political prize for the Administration to hand it over to a mere professional diplomat'. Willson, *America's Ambassadors to England (1785–1928)*, p. 419.

46. Alison Holmes, interview with Ambassador Glyn Davies, Washington DC, 2008.

47. Alison Holmes, interviews with Ambassadors Seitz, Davies, Johnson, Tuttle, 2008.

48. The four who served two full terms were Presidents Eisenhower, Reagan, Clinton and George W. Bush. The two who served almost two full terms were Presidents Truman (who took over after Roosevelt's death four months into a presidential term and was then elected to a full term of this own) and Nixon who was re-elected and served nearly two full terms before his resignation.

49. The 'modern presidency' was identified in scholarship on American politics in the aftermath of the Second World War, and is regularly debated within the pages of the journal *Presidential Studies Quarterly*. The following works are widely regarded as classics in the field: Richard E. Neustadt, *Presidential Power* (New York: John Wiley & Sons, 1960); Arthur Schelsinger, Jr, *The Imperial Presidency* (Boston: Houghton Mifflin, 1973); and Clinton Rossitor, *The American Presidency* (Baltimore, MD: The Johns Hopkins University Press, 1987). More

recent contributions include Fred L. Greenstein, *The Presidential Difference: Leadership Style from Roosevelt to George W. Bush* (Princeton NJ: Princeton University Press, 2004); and Louis L. Gould, *The Modern American Presidency* (Lawrence, KS: University of Kansas Press, 2004).

50. James Forsyth, 'Does Clegg Go for a Love Actually Moment?' *The Spectator*, 22 April 2010. The associated YouTube entry can be found at http://www.youtube.com/watch?v=E4HZrg1cfvw.

51. John Dumbrell and Axel Schafer (eds.), *America's Special Relationships – Foreign and Domestic Aspects of the Politics of Alliance* (Oxford: Routledge, 2009).

52. Rhodri Jeffreys-Jones, 'Review Article: The Inestimable Advantage of Not Being English: Lord Lothian's American Ambassadorship, 1939–1940', *The Scottish Historical Review*, Vol. 63, No. 175 (April 1984), pp. 105–10.

53. Alex Spelling, 'Edward Heath and Anglo-American Relations 1970–1974: A Reappraisal', *Diplomacy and Statecraft*, Vol. 20, No. 4. (2009), pp. 638–58.

54. Foreign Affairs Committee (6th) Report, *Global Security: UK/UK Relations*, House of Commons Session 2009-10 (HC 114), 28 March 2010 (London: The Stationery Office), available at: http://www.parliament.uk/business/committees/committees-archive/foreign-affairs-committee/facpn280310/.

55. For example see Foreign and Commonwealth Office, *UK International Priorities: A Strategy for the FCO* (London: The Stationery Office, 2003), p. 26.

56. Gideon Rachman, 'Cameron's "Essential" Relationship with Obama', *The Financial Times*, 13 March 2012, available at: http://blogs.ft.com/the-world/2012/03/camerons-essential-relationship-with-obama/#axzz1tecE4OKc (accessed 1 April 2012).

57. Barack Obama and David Cameron, 'United States and Great Britain: An Essential Relationship', *The Guardian*, 13 March 2012, available at: www.guardian.co.uk/commentisfree/2012/mar/13/barack-obama-david-cameron-essential-relationship (accessed 1 April 2012).

58. Robert Skidelsky, *John Maynard Keynes – Fighting for Britain 1937–1946* (London: Macmillan, 2000) p.180.

59. Winston Churchill, 'The Sinews of Peace', speech, Westminster College, Fulton MO, 5 March 1946, available at: http://www.nato.int/docu/speech/1946/s460305a_e.htm (accessed 1 April 2012).

60. H. C. Allen, *Great Britain and the United Sates: A History of Anglo-American Relations 1783–1952* (London: Odhams Press, 1954).

61. Inderjeet Parmar, 'CFR-RIIA Interconnections: A Nascent Transnational Ruling Class, Liberal Atlantic Community or Anglo-American Establishment?', Chapter 8, p. 5 (draft chapter). The final version of this chapter can be found in: *Think Tanks and Power in Foreign Policy: A Comparative Study of the Role and Influence of the Council of Foreign Relations and the Royal Institute of International Affairs, 1939–1945* (New York: Palgrave Macmillan, 2004).

62. Greg Kennedy, *Anglo-American Strategic Relations and the Far East 1933–1939* (London and Portland, OR: Frank Cass, 2002), p. 2.

63. A selection of the literature on the Special Relationship: David Reynolds, The Creation of the Anglo-American Alliance 1937–41 (London: Europe Publications, 1981); David Reynolds, 'A "Special Relationship"? America, Britain and the International Order since the Second World War', International Affairs, Vol. 62, No. 1 (Winter 1985/6), pp. 1–20; David Reynolds, 'Rethinking Anglo-American Relations', International Affairs, Vol. 65, No. 1 (Winter 1988/9), pp. 89–111; Alan Dobson, Anglo-American Relations in the Twentieth Century: Of Friendship,

Conflict, and Rise and Decline of Superpowers (London and New York: Routledge, 1995); John Dumbrell, A Special Relationship (Basingstoke: Palgrave, 2001 [2nd edn, 2006]). An excellent digest of the literature is provided in the following article which contemplates the Special Relationship's longevity: Jerome Elie, 'Many Times Doomed but Still Alive: An Attempt to Understand the Continuity of the Special Relationship', Journal of Transatlantic Studies, Vol. 3 (2005), pp. 63–83; Steve Smith, 'The Special Relationship', Political Studies, Vol. 38 (2006), pp. 126–36; Kathleen Burk, Old World, New World: The Story of Britain and America (London: Little, Brown, 2007).

64. Alex Danchev, *On Specialness: Essays in Anglo-American Relations* (Basingstoke: Palgrave Macmillan, 1998), p. ix. An earlier version of Danchev's essay was published in the Royal Institute of International Affairs Journal as 'On Specialness', *International Affairs,* Vol. 72, No. 4, The Americas: European Security (October 1996), pp. 737–50.

65. Martin Shaw, *Theory of the Global State* (Cambridge: Cambridge University Press, 2000), p. 8.

66. Cardinal Richelieu, *The Political Testament of Cardinal Richelieu: The Significant Chapters and Supporting Selections* (trans. H. B. Hill; Madison, WI: University of Wisconsin Press, 1965).

67. US Public Opinion, Secret, Despatch No. 119 from Lord Lothian to Lord Halifax, 1 February 1940, FO 800 324 National Archives, Kew.

Part I

The Wartime Ambassadors, 1938–1946

Introduction

J. Simon Rofe

As tensions in Europe began to rise in late 1937 President Franklin D. Roosevelt remarked to his Secretary of the Treasury, Henry Morgenthau, 'England is a most important post'.[1] The outbreak of war in Europe in September 1939 thrust the United Kingdom of Great Britain, and the constituent parts of its Empire, into a conflict that would last almost six years and profoundly alter London's relations with other states, large and small. The United Kingdom emerged victorious, but was, in many senses, broken by the experience. Within that context, one of the most notable outcomes of the war, and one proselytised by wartime Prime Minister Winston S. Churchill, was of a kinship between the 'English-speaking peoples' and borne out in the personal relationship between Prime Minister and President. After receiving greetings on his 60th birthday from the Prime Minister, Roosevelt, with an affection rarely seen in his written word, cabled Churchill 'It is fun to be in the same decade with you.'[2] More at home with a pen in his hand, the Prime Minister later wrote, 'I felt I was in contact with a very great man who was also a warm-hearted friend and the foremost champion of the high causes which we served.'[3] The shared wartime experience of Presidents, of servicemen and of their families, is popularly seen as a foundation to the Anglo-American 'Special Relationship'.

Alongside the overarching questions of the volume, this section is guided by the question of how far the Ambassadors and the Embassy in London played a role in the formation and early years of transatlantic 'special relations'. A senior Foreign Office official noted in January 1940 that 'the view of any US Ambassador in London on our war chances are a matter of considerable importance'.[4] While the subject of the official's concerns at the time were Joseph Kennedy's bleak remarks on British chances in the conflict, they speak to the potential influence that Kennedy and his successors would have as the United Kingdom fought for its very survival. Equally, the contributions of Joseph P. Kennedy, John G. Winant and, in the immediate post-war period, W. Averell Harriman establish important precedents – though not always helpful ones – for the Ambassadors explored in subsequent chapters.

What became known as the Second World War had already begun in the Far East when Joseph P. Kennedy arrived as Ambassador, but it was the impending European crisis that would dominate the Bostonian's time in London. Initially welcomed into London society, Kennedy came to be on remarkably close terms with British Prime Minister, Neville Chamberlain. However, as Chamberlain's appeasement policy was replaced by confrontation with Hitler, Kennedy became increasingly pessimistic in his outlook. This had significant implications for his standing in London as well as his perceived usefulness to the President in Washington. Kennedy was convinced that the war would end in the utter devastation of Europe, and surmised that Communism would rise from Europe's ashes. After war was declared in the autumn, Kennedy's views were increasingly out of step with British opinion as the country geared itself for war, and a President who was coming to accept that US interests were at stake in the conflict. Kennedy returned to the United States prior to Roosevelt's re-election for a third time in November 1940 in order to press his views on the President. Roosevelt barely provided Kennedy the opportunity to air his point. Following his re-election, Kennedy's resignation was summarily requested and to the considerable embitterment of the Bostonian he was simply ignored by the administration throughout the rest of the war.

John G. Winant was Kennedy's replacement and proved to be a more low profile appointment. Indeed, Winant served over five years in London as an accomplished diplomat and skilled administrator at a time when Great Britain and the United States were allies and prime ministerial–presidential relations were in the ascendency. He was with British Prime Minister, Winston S. Churchill, when they received the news of the Japanese attack on Pearl Harbour, the event that really sparked the Prime Minister's transatlantic connection with President Roosevelt. Despite playing an important role in coordinating a number of wartime conferences, being part of the commission which decided the zones of Allied occupation, and being resident in London for the United Nations opening meetings which took place there, Winant was not considered a prominent figure in wartime diplomacy. The same could not be said of Winant's successor. Averell Harriman arrived in London for a short stay as Ambassador (just eight months) after two and a half years as Ambassador to Moscow where he had been a crucial messenger in relations between President Roosevelt and Russian Premier, Josef Stalin.

The connection between these ambassadors is Franklin Delano Roosevelt.[5] Although the President, who was elected four times, died in April 1945, Roosevelt's influence could be felt in the appointment of Harriman the following year. The President's propensity for 'personal diplomacy', seen in Harriman's appointment to Moscow, was also apparent in Roosevelt's two appointments to London (Harriman was nominated by President Harry

S. Truman). In Roosevelt's estimation, personal diplomacy allowed him, as President, the opportunity to exert influence as and when he saw fit. Historian Michaela Hoenicke-Moore in her seminal work on American views of Nazi Germany notes how the President wanted additional information from his ambassadors. 'Roosevelt sought to complement regular State Department intelligence...by asking a number of ambassadors – both those who he trusted, like William Bullitt, Josephus Daniels and William Dodd, and others with differing political outlooks, like Joseph P. Kennedy – to report to him directly.'[6] Hoenicke-Moore's assessment that Roosevelt did not completely trust Kennedy is borne out in the following chapter, but the significance here is an illustration of Roosevelt's inclination to use individuals to further his, and US, diplomacy. The implications of this approach were wider ranging, with one historian arguing that under the stewardship of Secretary of State Cordell Hull, the State Department suffered 'almost total marginalization during the Second World War'.[7] Indeed, the value and stature of the State Department to the President in Washington would wax and wane throughout the period under consideration with the President regularly challenging procedure to advance his own policies. The knock-on effect for the standing of the London Embassy and the Ambassador would play out beyond the termination of the conflict.

For Kennedy and Winant in London, Roosevelt's personal diplomacy meant the President increasingly usurped official channels by despatching his own envoys. The Ambassador met these individuals with good grace, the former even recognising that he was not the prime channel of information from London. Indeed, by the end of Kennedy's ambassadorship the axis between leaders would be the main focus of diplomatic transatlantic relations. Harriman had, in fact, been one of the envoys Roosevelt despatched to London in 1941 deliberately to circumvent the State Department, when he was appointed as a presidential advisor with responsibility for Lend-Lease and with the title of Special Representative to the Prime Minister. Thus, the arrival of presidential envoys, with varying degrees of official endorsement from the White House, would be a feature of transatlantic relations for all of the subsequent ambassadors examined in this volume.

All of the men examined here brought distinct qualities to the role of Ambassador to London between 1938 and 1946. Kennedy became extremely close to the Prime Minister, but as Chamberlain was overtaken by events in Europe, the Ambassador continued to refuse to face the unpalatable reality of conflict. Winant, by contrast, was confronted with the realities of war from the outset of his posting. Through his night-time forays into London during the Blitz, he shared in the experience of many Londoners, becoming only the second American after Eisenhower to receive the Order of Merit in 1947. His administrative competence allowed the Embassy to effectively grow and meet the challenges posed by multiple wartime linkages between London and Washington. During Harriman's relatively brief tenure, he endeavoured to bring his experience of dealing with Stalin in Moscow to bear in London; to be a mediator of sometimes unpleasant information – seen most obviously in respect of the post-war loan. Each gentleman, to varying degrees, played a role in the UK–US relationship during the period that is regularly reminisced about as the birth of the 'special relationship'.

Notes

1. The Morgenthau Diaries, 8 December 1937, Book 101, Franklin D. Roosevelt Presidential Library.
2. *Winston Churchill, The Second World War, Vol. IV: The Hinge of Fate (Boston:* Houghton Mifflin, 1950), *p.* 62.
3. *Winston Churchill, The Second World War, Vol. II: Their Finest Hour (Boston:* Houghton Mifflin, 1949), p. 22.
4. Perowne Minute, 29 January 1940, FO 371 24248/A825, National Archives, London.
5. For sources on President Roosevelt see note 79 below.
6. Michaela Hoenicke-Moore, *'Know Your Enemy: The American Debate on Nazism 1933–1945'* (Cambridge: Cambridge University Press, 2010), p. 82.
7. Douglas T. Stuart, *Creating the National Security State: A History of the Law that Transformed America* (Princeton, NJ and Oxford: Princeton University Press, 2008), p. 35.

1
Joseph P. Kennedy, 1938–40

J. Simon Rofe

' "I have made arrangements to have Joe Kennedy watched hourly – and the first time he opens his mouth and criticises me, I will fire him".'[1] These remarks from President Franklin D. Roosevelt in conversation with Treasury Secretary Henry Morgenthau in December 1937 are not the ringing endorsement that might be expected for a man the President was about to send to London as United States Ambassador. Indeed, Morgenthau added 'he was going to send him to England as Ambassador with the distinct understanding that the appointment was only good for six months…'. Against such a background it is perhaps a surprise that Joseph P. Kennedy remained Ambassador until the end of 1940 and was able to establish close relations from his desk in Grosvenor Square with elements of the British elite as they made the transition from peace to war. Then again, we should not be surprised by Kennedy. The forthright millionaire, known for a quick Irish wit, association with Hollywood and Wall Street, and as father of nine was ambitious and politically astute in many respects. As Ambassador he sought to contribute to making policy and was not afraid to take a bold line. Within a month of the outbreak of war, he argued that the United States should intervene 'in order to be a determining factor in any peace settlement,' because '*If this war goes on* it will ultimately bring chaos to us beyond our dreams' (emphasis in original).[2] Kennedy was, and remains, a controversial character.[3]

Dual Advances in Transatlantic Diplomacy

The chapter addresses the ambassadorship of Joseph P. Kennedy and the US Embassy in London from the announcement of his appointment in December 1937 until the end of 1940.[4] Two features make Kennedy's ambassadorship unique: the first is the level of intimacy he achieved with the British government (making his fall from grace all the more stark); and second, that he achieved this closeness within just six months of his arrival. Kennedy was an immediate success in London and swiftly on intimate terms with the normally ascetic Prime Minister, Neville Chamberlain. He then acted as the critical channel of Anglo-American relations at the time of Munich in September 1938; marking the high point of his posting. Kennedy's downfall began almost immediately thereafter, and accelerated towards the outbreak of war in Europe as his views were increasingly out of line with Roosevelt in Washington. Further dislocation followed both with Washington and with the government in London as the latter geared the United Kingdom for war, leaving Kennedy in an unhappy limbo until his final return to the US on the eve of Roosevelt's victory in the 1940 presidential election.

The overarching question here is: To what extent was Kennedy effective as Ambassador and head of the American Embassy in London? The answer requires investigation of a number of second-order questions:

- How proficient was Kennedy at his job as a diplomat?
- What role did the Embassy play in London during the transition from peace to war?
- How were US interests secured during the period of his ambassadorship?

The chapter provides answers in three sections. The first provides a background to his appointment, examining Roosevelt's motivation for sending Kennedy to London at the end of 1937. The second section moves on to consider Kennedy's initial reception in London up to what can be considered the high-water mark of his ambassadorship at the time of Munich. The final section considers Kennedy's fall from grace in both London and Washington through the build up to the outbreak of the Second World War in September 1939 and his role as Ambassador to a nation at war before his return to the United States in the autumn of 1940.

The conclusion drawn is that Kennedy's ambassadorship marks a subtle but important transition in transatlantic diplomacy in two inter-related and hitherto overlooked areas. The first, and most important for its framing influence on the second, is as a foundation to at least one aspect of the Anglo-American 'special relationship'; the primacy of presidential–prime ministerial relations. The special relationship is a much debated concept with antecedents that predate Kennedy's ambassadorship. Nevertheless, in the post-Second World War manifestation of the special relationship, 'personal' presidential–prime ministerial relations are a recurrent feature. Notable to the extent that their absence is worthy of explanation when the two leaders fail to establish a personal bond. Kennedy, unwittingly, in his reaction to the onset of war ensured that the Ambassador would be a subservient channel of Anglo-American relations during the course of the war and the subsequent special relationship that developed. The shift Kennedy oversaw was from an era when the Ambassador (and Embassy) was the prime intermediary, to one in which Prime Ministers and Presidents met in person. After Kennedy's ambassadorship this would be the norm.

The second facet of Kennedy's contribution as Ambassador to relations between London and Washington are two, seemingly contrary, elements. On the one hand, Kennedy's ambassadorship illustrates how the London Embassy was bypassed on certain substantive issues in Anglo-American relations. During Kennedy's time, this meant the Embassy became peripheral to diplomatic transactions concerning the first visit of the Royal Family to the United States in June 1939, and to the destroyers-bases deal of August 1940. On the other hand, Kennedy's term illustrates the opportunity that an ambassador has to be a vital conduit for broader diplomatic activity in the Anglo-American relationship. For Kennedy this meant providing first-hand accounts to Washington of events such as the 1938 Munich crisis as well as the final moments of peace in August 1939. Kennedy's reporting serves to demonstrate the prominence, on occasion, of the individual ambassador in Anglo-American relations.

Background to the Appointment

President Roosevelt's appointment of Kennedy in January 1938 to replace Robert Worth Bingham who left London in November 1937 (and died before the year was out), raises questions in a number of areas as to the nature of the Anglo-American relationship and the importance of the ambassadorship. As was typical of Roosevelt, he left no direct account explaining his decision to appoint an Irish Catholic Bostonian to the Court of St James's. Nevertheless, a number of factors emerge in the President's thinking.[5] The motivating factors that came together for Roosevelt in late 1937 for what he envisaged being a short-term posting would be overtaken by events once Kennedy arrived in London and the European crisis escalated. Not least amongst them the success Kennedy enjoyed upon his arrival in 1938, described by Kennedy to one correspondent as 'a "hole-in-one" impression'.[6]

Roosevelt's primary aim in appointing Kennedy was to remove the Bostonian from the domestic political scene to a limited role as Ambassador in London. Kennedy was known for voicing his forthright opinions and was not afraid to voice criticism of the administration on occasion. Roosevelt was conscious that Kennedy could become a voice for conservative business interests already critical of the New Deal. Assistant Secretary of State, Adolf Berle, put it bluntly: 'Joseph Kennedy goes. A good idea; it will get him out of the country'.[7] Berle was not alone in this view; others both in the diplomatic establishment of the State Department and the administration were equally pleased to see him go. Treasury Secretary Morgenthau also recognised Roosevelt's desire to remove Kennedy from US soil: 'I certainly will be glad to have him out of Washington', Morgenthau confessed, 'and I take it that is the way the President feels'.[8]

Despatching Kennedy was not without its perils for the President. Characterising Roosevelt's assessment of Kennedy as a 'very dangerous man',

Morgenthau asked the President whether he was 'taking considerable risks by sending Kennedy who has talked so freely and so critically against your Administration'.[9] Roosevelt's riposte to Morgenthau was to point to the planned short time frame of the appointment. Kennedy shared the view that the appointment would be brief and kept an eye on the American domestic scene. Within a matter of weeks after his arrival in London, he wrote to James Landis, the New Deal 'wonderkid' and recently appointed Dean of Harvard Law School, revealing that he saw the post with a view to its utility in the American political sphere. 'I don't know what good we are going to be able to do over here', Kennedy wrote, 'but, when I get back, I am going to be able to give a better opinion on foreign affairs than I have been able to read so far in America.'[10]

Political pragmatism was also a factor for Roosevelt in two respects. First, the President recognised Kennedy's contributions to his own, and his party's victories in 1932 and 1936. Kennedy had made significant financial contributions to the Democratic Party and, during the 1936 campaign, had also authored a book entitled 'I'm for Roosevelt' to support the President's re-election.[11] For the President, the appointment to London would 'settle the ledger' between himself and Kennedy. Morgenthau recorded Roosevelt felt that 'by giving him this appointment any obligation that he had to Kennedy was paid for'.[12] The second respect in which politics was to play its part is Roosevelt's awareness of Kennedy's own political ambitions. The President knew Kennedy sought high office, possibly even the White House. With his wealth and the absence of an obvious successor to Roosevelt, Kennedy was a realistic, if prospective, candidate amongst a broad field for the 1940 election. Kennedy certainly saw the ambassadorship, initially at least, as a stepping stone to greater things. Arthur Krock, *The New York Times* Washington correspondent and long-standing critic of the Roosevelt administration, stated Kennedy 'made his desires known emphatically to the President, and by the summer of 1937... was lobbying fiercely for the appointment through every available avenue'.[13] The President would play to Kennedy's ambition, not for the last time, by acquiescing. Once he had decided to send Kennedy to London, Roosevelt continued to charm him with the prospect of a cabinet post, and endorsements for the future campaign of Kennedy's eldest son, Joe Kennedy, Jr for the 1942 Massachusetts governorship.

Further, Roosevelt recognised a number of qualities in the Bostonian. Kennedy had proven himself useful by successfully heading two New Deal institutions, the Securities and Exchange Commission in 1934, and the Maritime Commission in March 1937. Despite these successes, Kennedy was no 'Brains Truster' as historian Ralph de Bedts notes, stating he 'could not properly be considered part of the New Deal reform core'.[14] Kennedy's standing as an 'outsider' in the administration and in Washington also appealed to Roosevelt, along with an appreciation of Kennedy's capacity for 'outspoken bluntness in delivering sound advice'.[15] Nonetheless, the relationship between Roosevelt and Kennedy never reached the levels of intimacy that Roosevelt enjoyed with other Ambassadors and envoys. In fact, the President's despatch of other envoys to London in 1940, such as Undersecretary of State, Summer Welles, in March and 'Wild Bill' Donovan in July, would strain relations between Roosevelt and Kennedy to breaking point. That was all for the future at the beginning of 1938, as Kennedy prepared to depart for his post in London filled with self-confidence and an appetite to take on the role of Ambassador.

'Into the Lion's Den', January–August 1938

'…I couldn't have done anything better to make a hit in England if I had had twenty-five years to discover the best answer.'[16] Kennedy's own assessment of his first few weeks as Ambassador to the Court of St James's illustrates the impression he made and a number of factors explain the success of the first months of his ambassadorship. Of paramount importance was the relative intimacy of Kennedy's relationship with Prime Minister Neville Chamberlain. Reflecting this closeness in early 1939, in a letter to Kennedy the Prime Minister added the following note in his own hand: 'You are a most helpful friend and never more valued than now.'[17] Alongside his hard work and desire to make an impact with the government in what he believed would be a short time frame, Kennedy's initial success would also be based on the respect of the business community in the City of London engendered by his track record on Wall Street, and the positive impact he and his family made in London through what might today be described as public diplomacy. These elements all helped place Kennedy in a position to be the prime relay across the Atlantic at the time of Munich.

The paramount reason for Kennedy's initial favour was the relationship struck up with Chamberlain. Kennedy met the Prime Minister just two days after arriving in the UK. 'I dropped everything and went to Downing Street', Kennedy wrote in his diary. Kennedy's initial assessment of Chamberlain was complimentary: 'I found him a strong, decisive man, evidently in full charge of the situation here'. Kennedy added, 'I talked to him quite plainly and he seemed to take it well.'[18] The forthright tone Kennedy employed would become typical in his association with the Prime Minister.

Not known for his candour, Chamberlain nevertheless reciprocated Kennedy's open approach. Writing a month before his death in November 1940, Chamberlain wrote to Kennedy, 'As you know, I always talked to you with the most utmost frankness about the events that were happening and gave you my opinions as to our policy with complete freedom.' The 'freedom' Kennedy enjoyed was certainly in evidence in September 1938 when the Ambassador was briefed more regularly than the House of Commons. As Chamberlain recalled to Kennedy in a letter from the vantage point of October 1940, 'I found in you an understanding of what I was trying to do and an integrity of character which particularly appealed to me.'[19] The basis for their amity was a shared 'dread of war and communism' while their concern for economic security led both men to support the policy of 'appeasement as a step toward solving economic problems that . . . threatened the core of European security'.[20] Indeed, the Prime Minister 'held guarded, but fervent hopes that Kennedy would persuade his government to support an appeasement policy towards Germany'.[21] Chamberlain's hopes would be unfounded as Kennedy was never able to convince Roosevelt of the policy's merits. Nonetheless, a shared business background added another level to the relationship between Chamberlain, reflecting a unique meeting of minds between Prime Minister and Ambassador at the outset of Kennedy's posting.

Kennedy sought to be proactive as Ambassador, and did so with success in a number of areas. Historian Richard J. Whalen writes that Kennedy 'intended to be a working diplomat', in contrast to those who were content to indulge in the ceremonial aspects of an ambassadorial post.[22] The Ambassador's eagerness to be involved can be seen in his enthusiasm for his first formal speaking engagement. It is custom for the American Ambassador to make his or her first speech to the Pilgrims Society, a London society founded at the turn of the twentieth century concerned with promoting transatlantic relations. Kennedy began work on his speech as soon as he arrived and expressed a desire that 'I want to make it a good speech, saying something and thereby breaking a precedent of many years' standing'.[23] It was with some disappointment that he received word from the State Department four days later suggesting 'minor changes of language, tending to temper it down in spots where Jimmy Dunn, Sumner Welles and Pierrepont Moffatt apparently thought we had gone too strongly'.[24] These key figures on European affairs in the State Department were concerned that Kennedy's first draft was too blunt, stating that the United States would stand aloof from European affairs. Such thinking in Washington was not a prelude to action but, as Phillip Seib notes, 'Roosevelt did not want the United States to be perceived as tilting in any particular direction'.[25] The speech itself received a largely positive reception. 'Much of it was applauded', Kennedy noted. 'However, I got the feeling that parts of it fell flat'. He continued, 'I had to tell my British hosts a few homely truths, and they could not be expected to cheer their heads off.' Alluding to the possibility in Kennedy's mind that his post might be transient and the need to keep a domestic constituency in mind, he confessed: '[t]he speech was intended primarily for home consumption, as I am very anxious that my friends there should not think I have gone over to the British'.

The American political scene was to the fore in Kennedy's thinking just a month into his post. He asked Secretary of State Cordell Hull to let him be more involved saying 'if anything occurs to you, outside of the ordinary instructions, where I can be of any real assistance, please let me know'.[26]

Kennedy's eagerness to contribute to policy-making betrayed a fundamental misunderstanding of the role Roosevelt foresaw in his London Ambassador. In the same letter to Hull he wrote: 'From what I have seen of the job here and assuming nothing happens of world import, I can deliver your messages, but I probably can do nothing very constructive.' Kennedy continued: 'as matters stand today, the only possible help I can give you is to express my opinion as to events in Europe'.[27] That the role of the Ambassador was to convey communiqués from Washington and report his views on events in London without having a determinant input into the policy that resulted would seem to have passed Kennedy by. Indeed his pushing at the traditional boundaries of the role ultimately served to injure the effectiveness of Kennedy's ambassadorship, giving rise to conflict with Roosevelt.

Kennedy's success in furthering Anglo-American relations can be seen in his relations with the press, the positive impact of his family in London, and his contribution to the Anglo-American Trade Agreement. With the Press, Kennedy typically sought to be direct. In his first meeting with the American Correspondents' Association he revealed his approach. 'I told the men quite frankly', within the first week of arriving 'that I was by no means sure that an American ambassador could accomplish anything here just now: that I would go home very shortly if I found that to be the case; that I had no political aspirations whatever and any reports they had seen to the contrary were unfounded'.[28] These words were disingenuous at least in part, but indicate a frankness that would keep them engaged during Kennedy's term.[29]

Kennedy was aided in establishing a positive aura to his ambassadorship by his family and their contribution to London's social scene. Will Swift's *The Kennedys amidst the Gathering Storm* charts the impact of the family in wowing London as American 'royalty'.[30] High society welcomed Kennedy and his family to a number of events in the summer calendar including the opening day of Royal Ascot (14 June) which Kennedy described as 'A lawn party with horse racing on the side'.[31] Kennedy, as he reflected on these events, was in two minds. On the one hand, he complained to Washington about the rituals of being Ambassador, telling Hull of 'this dammed social life' in July 1938 while, at the same time, he and his family clearly enjoyed themselves.[32] 'Smiling out of the pages of London newspapers and magazines back home', Whalen writes, 'the Kennedys seemed a uniquely handsome, happy family, to whom only good things happen.'[33] A different fate would befall many of the Kennedys, but in 1938 it can safely be said that the Kennedy family enjoyed London; and London enjoyed having them.

Kennedy did provide a meaningful contribution to Anglo-American trade discussions during the early part of his ambassadorship on the basis of his experience on Wall Street, and particularly his knowledge of the movie industry. Kennedy suggested in March that he probably could 'do a good deal of missionary work on the trade pact with the newspaper owners and members of the Cabinet and leaders of the Parties'.[34] More specifically

Kennedy counselled Washington with respect to the American film industry, having been 'sounded out' by the Board of Trade in London.[35] The
discussions, which continued throughout the summer, culminated in the
Anglo-American Trade Agreement in November 1938.[36] While it would be
wrong to say that Kennedy played a particularly determinant role in the
course of the negotiations or its conclusion, it would be equally incorrect to
suggest he played no part. In fact, his facilitating role in the negotiations provided the basis for the Ambassador's proposal for an Anglo-American Barter
Deal over cotton and rubber which was concluded in June 1939 after a mere
eight weeks of negotiation.

Within the Embassy itself, Kennedy's strong start was soon felt. Shortly
after arriving, Kennedy told the Embassy's Counsellor Herschel Johnson,
'that the State Department is not viewed very seriously in the Congress or
in the country'.[37] To Kennedy's credit, within a matter of months he had
enacted a number of changes to the organisation of the Embassy, including putting the case for Johnson's promotion and all aimed at providing
the 'business-like instrumentalities which will meet the urgent requirements of the times concerning policy and the needs of the Department
regarding coordination'.[38] These changes were well received in Washington
with Welles writing to Kennedy requesting 'a personal letter suggesting
any further changes that you feel desirable in your Embassy set-up'. The
Undersecretary added 'you can be sure that everything that can be done
here will be done to meet your wishes'.[39] The impact of Kennedy's procedural changes were significant in making the Embassy an efficient outpost.
This was seen once the war had begun in the speedy and incident-free
repatriation of American citizens from the belligerent capital.

Kennedy's Munich Experience September 1938

The positive air surrounding Kennedy's ambassadorship was cemented by
the role he played during September 1938 as the world teetered on the brink
of war as a result of German designs on Czechoslovakian territory. Kennedy's
updates of the situation from London, drawn from direct discussions with
the Prime Minister, Foreign Secretary and other members of the British Cabinet, were critical in enlightening Roosevelt in Washington and explains why
it is the high water mark of Kennedy's ambassadorship.

Kennedy's proactive approach and intimacy with the British government
during these events maybe are to the fore. The tale of Chamberlain's bold
and novel flights to Munich to meet with Adolf Hitler is adequately covered elsewhere and beyond the scope of this chapter.[40] Kennedy met almost
daily with various members of the British Cabinet, including Chamberlain.
For example, Kennedy met the Prime Minister on 12 September to discuss the 'alarming developments in Czechoslovakia', while the next day
it was the Home Secretary, Sir Samuel Hoare's turn to give 'me my daily
fill-in on the Central European situation...'.[41] The sharing of information

with the Ambassador was a definite strategy on the part of Chamberlain. Historian Edward Henson argues that Chamberlain fulfilled the task of informing Kennedy with 'remarkable conscientiousness' because the Prime Minister felt US 'sympathy...particularly precious'.[42] By 21 September the situation was sufficiently serious for Sir Alexander Cadogan, the Permanent Undersecretary for Foreign Affairs, to ring Kennedy after midnight to say 'that the whole thing was very disturbing and...he feared for the whole situation'.[43] Despite the late hour, the Ambassador's reaction was to call Washington and relay to Hull what he had learned.

Kennedy's intimacy with the deliberations of the Cabinet meant he had advance knowledge over many key players in the United Kingdom. In a call on Saturday 24 September Kennedy informed Hull that he would soon learn Hitler's demands from Chamberlain when the Prime Minister returned from Bad Godesburg. 'I don't think anyone has any better information than I have', he boasted to the Secretary. Hull's response served to emphasise to Kennedy the value of his London interlocutors: 'I appreciate the benefit of this and we all do here in the department – the President will too.'[44] Significantly, Kennedy was relaying information to Washington before any public statement in the United Kingdom and even before Parliament had been informed.[45]

Two days later, Kennedy reported that he was party to a 'very secret' matter following Anglo-French talks in London. He had learnt of Chamberlain's assurance to Édouard Daladier, the French Prime Minister, that if the French went to war to defend Czechoslovakia then the British 'will definitely go [with them]'.[46] Kennedy added to Hull, Chamberlain 'gave me this assurance definitely this morning'. Given the pressure the British and French were exerting on the Czechoslovaks to acquiesce to Hitler's demands, it seems the value of such a pledge may just have been in assuring Kennedy of his supposed importance. Anglo-French capability to influence events on the ground in central Europe was ultimately limited. Nonetheless, the Chamberlain government continued to keep Kennedy in their confidence. The Ambassador was present in Parliament on 28 September when Halifax famously passed Chamberlain a note stating Italian Premier Benito Mussolini had offered to act as mediator in the crisis. The next day, Chamberlain was in Munich with Daladier, Mussolini and Hitler to sign (in the small hours of 30 September) the 'Munich Agreement' ceding the Sudetenland to Germany. The immediate danger of war receded as Hitler was apparently sated.

The sense of relief in London, and elsewhere, was palpable. There was a note of optimism in Kennedy's diary entry on the evening of 28 September. 'Tonight a feeling is spreading all over London that this [Chamberlain's imminent return to Germany] means that war will be averted. If it is it is quite likely that, with these four men around a table, and with President Roosevelt always willing to negotiation, [*sic*] it may be the beginning of a new world policy which may mean peace and prosperity once again.'[47]

Kennedy's assessment overstates Roosevelt's willingness, and opportunity, to act. The President's contribution was limited: addressing telegrams to Hitler and Mussolini on 27 September urging 'continued negotiations'.[48]

Relief aside, the passing of the crisis also allowed Kennedy a moment for reflection on a job well done. He had the Embassy geared up 'working until three or four in the morning' to keep Washington informed, and had contingency plans for evacuating Americans in the event of conflict. Further, while somewhat immodest in tone, Kennedy was quick to recognise the privileged position he had recently enjoyed. With events still fresh, he wrote to his long-standing friend, Judge John Burns, in early October:

> I have just gone through the most exciting month of my life. Between trying to keep up my contacts so we would know what really was going on before it actually happened so that we would not be caught unprepared and contemplating the possibility of the bombing of London with eight children as prospective victims, well, it is just a great page in my life's history.[49]

While Kennedy excelled in providing first-hand information on events drawn from his access to Chamberlain and Halifax, his success was not without qualification. Most importantly, the United States was not a significant influence on the outcome of the Munich crisis. Roosevelt's actions, shaped by domestic isolationist opinion, were limited to broad appeals to Berlin and Rome and, once the immediate danger had passed, sharing the relief. The President's contribution has been described as 'inherently sterile' as 'European leaders were kept guessing as to what America's reaction might be toward either the appeasement or resistance to his demands'.[50] In this sense, the volume and detail of communiqués emanating from the Embassy did little to influence US foreign policy. Nonetheless, simply because Roosevelt did not make any sort of dramatic intervention does not mean Kennedy's efforts at relaying news was superfluous. Barbara Farnham's account of Roosevelt's decision-making in respect of the Munich crisis suggests that Munich was pivotal to the President in readying the United States to influence the outcome of any conflict in favour of the democracies. Farnham argues that Munich provided 'conclusive evidence that Hitler lacked all respect for the processes of political accommodation'.[51] By relaying to Roosevelt Chamberlain's account of the German Chancellor, Kennedy influenced the future direction of US policy, the irony being that the direction of the policy was at odds with Kennedy's own view.

Kennedy's Fall from Grace October 1938–October 1940

'It is a terrible thing to contemplate but the war will prove to the world what a great service Chamberlain did to the world and especially for England at Munich.'[52] Kennedy's diary entry as war broke out in September 1939 reflected his reading of events a year previously. By then, his views were wildly out of step with Roosevelt in Washington who was prepared to aid the allies to prevent fascist domination of Europe. While the Ambassador continued to act in his capacity as transatlantic messenger, Kennedy's ability to fulfil the range of his ambassadorial function was undermined by his own views.

Though the relationship between Kennedy and Roosevelt had long had grounds for disagreement, it began a terminal decline just weeks after the Munich crisis. Three weeks later, Kennedy gave a speech to mark Trafalgar Day (21 October). His words caused significant irritation both in London, by appearing to belittle differences with Nazi Germany, and in Washington, by suggesting the US had no concerns with the fate of Europe. Kennedy stated, 'instead of hammering away at what are regarded as irreconcilables, they [the democracies and dictatorships] could advantageously bend their energies toward solving their common problems by an attempt to re-establish good relations on a world basis'. These words troubled Hull. 'The Secretary is very upset over the effect of Kennedy's recent speech', Jay Pierrepont Moffat noted (the State Department's Chief of the Division of European Affairs). Moffat continued, '[Hull] thinks we should have definitely called Kennedy off in advance, despite his claim that he was advancing a "pet theory of his own".'[53] Kennedy's explanation failed to quell a passionate reaction from the press. In conversation with journalist Arthur Krock, Moffat discussed fellow journalist Walter Lippman's reaction to Kennedy's speech. The outcome served to reawaken State Department concerns over Kennedy's suitability to be Ambassador. 'Walter Lippman says that however unsatisfactory career Ambassadors may be in certain lines, they are perhaps less of an evil than political Ambassadors who try and play individual roles instead of merely as members of the team.'[54] The Trafalgar Day speech was an important indicator of the disconnect between Ambassador and President: Kennedy's remarks 'deeply contradicted Franklin's Roosevelt's view'.[55] The risks associated with having Kennedy in London, which Roosevelt had known about from the outset, were clear.

Kennedy knew of the fissure that was developing with the President. At the end of 1938 he even contemplated resigning. He shared his concern with Lord Halifax, the Foreign Secretary. Halifax 'urged me strongly not to resign', making reference to the Ambassador's difference in opinion with Roosevelt; Halifax continued that he 'understood my arguments quite completely'.[56] Into 1939 Kennedy's disaffection continued. He had returned to the United States at the end of 1938 and was enjoying a vacation in Florida in January when Roosevelt asked him to return to London two weeks earlier than planned. Kennedy was irked by the change in plans and the conversation with the President gave him the chance to raise the prospect of him leaving London: 'I told [the] President I didn't want to go to London unless I had his confidence'. By this stage Kennedy did not have the President's confidence. Duplicity is evident in both men. Kennedy stated that he had 'never made a public statement against him [Roosevelt] or his policies and what I said privately wasn't as bad as I had said to him personally'. Roosevelt's response was 'not to worry – people just liked to make trouble'.[57] Neither was being entirely honest about their increasingly acrimonious personal relationship. In Washington in the spring of 1939 Roosevelt gave Assistant Secretary Berle orders to prevent Kennedy making a further speech because it was a 'more than usually foolish speech'.[58] Beschloss comments on the Ambassador's duplicity: during the summer 'Kennedy professed allegiance while denouncing Roosevelt in the drawing rooms of London'.[59]

Despite the growing split, Kennedy did perform the role of ambassador well in a number of areas which are routinely overlooked. The Anglo-American barter deal, trading American cotton for rubber from the British Empire of June 1938, was swiftly concluded as was mentioned above. Kennedy 'played a large role' in hastening the conclusion of the deal.[60] Earlier, in March 1939, and much to the satisfaction of his wife, Kennedy was selected to officially attend the coronation of Pope Pius XII at the Vatican. Encouraged by Welles, he took the opportunity to assess the diplomatic landscape in Rome. Reporting back to Welles, he hoped to 'keep my contacts close to the Vatican...with the hope that there might possibly be a spot for the President to do the big job – peace for the world'.[61] Such a prospect was as unrealistic in the spring of 1939 as it was when war arrived in September.

By the summer of 1939, Kennedy returned to the question of whether he should continue in London. He wrote directly to Roosevelt about his 'position in England', lamenting 'whether my experience and knowledge were not being completely wasted'. Kennedy continued: 'I do get a bit discouraged for, although I have worked harder and longer hours in this job than on any job I ever held, it seems that three quarters of my efforts are wasted because of the terrific number of things to be done which seem to have no close connection with the real job at hand.'[62] The effect of such open questioning of his worth as an ambassador had an effect on Roosevelt. Once the crisis in Europe erupted into war, Roosevelt looked increasingly to other channels of transatlantic diplomacy in the form of Lord Lothian, British Ambassador to Washington, and Winston Churchill returning to the British Cabinet as First Lord of Admiralty.

Kennedy's capacity for self-delusion was in evidence on the eve of war in August 1939. In his diary, Kennedy claims to have prompted Roosevelt to send a message to Hitler on 24 August calling for a peaceful resolution, but such appeals had a long-standing history in Roosevelt's State Department, with Munich and those to Hitler and Mussolini in the spring of 1939 being notable examples. Kennedy recorded the impact of Roosevelt's message: 'it wasn't a smash'.[63] In late August 1939 Breckinridge Long, the State

Department's Assistant Secretary, remarked 'Kennedy has been condemning everybody and criticising everything and has antagonised most of the people in the Administration'.[64] By the outbreak of war, Kennedy was marginal to the fulcrum of decision-making in the Roosevelt administration.

One reflection of this distancing of the Ambassador from his President was the fact that Kennedy played virtually no part in the visit of the British King and Queen to the United States in June 1939. With the logistical arrangements of the visit handled by the British Embassy in Washington led by Sir Ronald Lindsay (the British Ambassador who remained in post until after the visit at the request of Roosevelt), Buckingham Palace and the White House, Kennedy was peripheral.[65] Beschloss regards the royal visit as a 'monument of Kennedy's circumvention'.[66] Kennedy's diary account of the summer of 1939 glosses over implications of the first visit of a British monarch to the United States and instead stresses his personal intimacy with the royal couple. As an example, after dining with the Queen in April, Kennedy recorded that 'She wanted still very much to go to USA no matter how dangerous it was, because not to go would give satisfaction to the enemies. What a woman!'[67]

Nonetheless, the access Kennedy maintained during the late summer of that year was remarkable. He continued to file numerous reports and accounts of his conversations in London to Washington. As the British government prepared for war, Kennedy was invited by Chamberlain to attend and contribute to a Cabinet meeting on 24 August. At the meeting, Kennedy made a remarkably naive proposal for 'international economic settlement'. Kennedy's naivety lay in his estimation that such a settlement 'would be more important to Germany than what she could possibly get out of … Poland'. Kennedy was 'freelancing' this idea and there is no evidence of any direct consultation on Kennedy's behalf with Washington on such a prospect. Though Kennedy may have believed he was picking up on strands of the State Department's commitment to economic diplomacy, it seems his self-importance got the better of his judgement. Apparently oblivious to how far he was stepping out from Washington, Kennedy recorded in his diary: 'Here I was an American Ambassador, called into discussion with the PM and Foreign Secretary over probably the most important event in the history of the British Empire. I had been called in before the Cabinet and had been trusted, not only for my discretion, but for my intelligence. It was a moving experience.'[68] Though his intimacy with Chamberlain continued, based largely on personal understanding, Kennedy's charms had worn thin elsewhere in London as the war began. Eight days after Chamberlain's declaration of war, Cadogan made disparaging comments about Kennedy in his diary. Cadogan noted, after visiting King George VII, that the monarch was 'rather depressed – and a little defaitiste – result, I think, of a talk with Joe Kennedy who sees everything from the angle of his own investments'.[69] For Cadogan, whom Kennedy regarded as a close associate, to hold such a view indicates the degree to which the Ambassador was becoming superfluous to meaningful political discussion in London.

A Drawn Out End: September 1939–October 1940

Kennedy's ambassadorship to the Court of St James's had a drawn out conclusion from the outbreak of war in Europe through to his departure from London on 22 October 1940. Displaying wilful disbelief to the professed causes of the war, Kennedy's views were a mounting liability to the Roosevelt administration.

Within two days of the war beginning in September 1939 Kennedy despatched his family back to the United States. Once they had departed Kennedy's reaction to the outbreak of war was governed by his fear of the economic consequences of the war, most notably the spectre of communism extending over Europe. He wrote to Roosevelt's private secretary, Marguerite 'Missy' LeHand, after a month of war, 'I do not get carried away with this war for idealism. I cannot see any use in everybody in Europe going busted and having communism run riot.'[70] Kennedy's misreading of the German situation was stark. 'My own view is that the economics of Germany would have taken care of Hitler long before this if he didn't have a chance to wave the flag once in a while. But, of course, one isn't supposed to say this out loud.' Kennedy then confessed an equally ill-informed, but more damming indictment of his own comprehension of events. Stating the British, 'are going about this war hating it', he went on: 'I still don't know what they are fighting for that is possible of accomplishment.' Kennedy's disillusionment was not restricted to his private correspondence as he wrote to Hull a week into the war on 11 September 1939 imploring Roosevelt to intervene for the cause of peace. As German troops were conquering Poland Kennedy, in a wilful mis-reading of the facts wrote: 'it seems to me that this situation may crystallize to a point where the President can be the saviour of the world'; he went on: 'I believe that it is entirely conceivable that the President can get himself in a spot where he can save the world ...'.[71] Kennedy's belief was misguided in the extreme, and his plea fell on deaf ears.

Indicating his dissatisfaction, Roosevelt responded to Kennedy's increasingly morose communiqués from London by circumventing him. Although Kennedy maintained access to Prime Minister Chamberlain and the Embassy maintained its well-regarded correspondence with Washington, the President developed alternate channels of transatlantic communication. The most famous, and one that would become the 'partnership that saved the west' according to historian Joseph P. Lash, was between Roosevelt and then First Lord of the Admiralty, Winston Churchill.[72] The relationship between the President and the future Prime Minister has been expertly covered by Professor Warren F. Kimball and further exploration is not required here except to say that, during the winter of 1939–40 correspondence between the two men was one-sided with Churchill writing more often and at greater length than Roosevelt, who kept his responses short and convivial.[73] The implications for Kennedy by the end of 1939 was clear. He complained to his diary in early October that Roosevelt 'calls Churchill up and never contacts me', and that it was a 'rotten way to win men's loyalty'.[74] Kennedy never shared Roosevelt's faith in Churchill's galvanising ability. He opined 'Maybe I do him [Churchill] an injustice but I just don't trust him.' The Ambassador disparagingly noted that Churchill 'always impressed me that he'd blow up the American Embassy and say it was the Germans if it would get the US in'.[75] While such a prospect was an anathema to Kennedy, the candid realpolitik calculation that underpinned it would become a key facet of the wartime relationship between Churchill and Roosevelt.

In the spring of 1940, the Tyler Kent affair further illustrates the downfall of Kennedy and the marginalisation of the Embassy. The affair centred on MI5's arrest of Tyler Kent, a cipher clerk at the Embassy, on 20 May 1940 and the seizure of almost 2,000 diplomatic documents at his residence in Baker Street. Included in the documents were copies of the correspondence between Roosevelt and Churchill. Later, Churchill tacitly acknowledged the difficulties Kent posed. In a tone that suggests he was trying to convince himself as much as Kennedy, Churchill recommended that the Kent case would only be heard after the November presidential election, 'not because any information would come out...that would be embarrassing' to either himself or Roosevelt, but because he acknowledged that 'the telegrams showed too close a connection between the Prime Minister and the President'.[76] At the time of the incident, the breach of security and diplomatic protocol reflected badly on Kennedy and questioned the place of the Embassy in Anglo-American relations. The Ambassador authorised the removal of Kent's diplomatic immunity with the result that Kent was tried, convicted and spent the rest of the war in prison. Speculation has subsequently surrounded the content of the correspondence Kent had horded, particularly amongst those who argue that there was some arrangement between the President and the new Prime Minister over American involvement in the war.[77] For Kennedy the Tyler Kent affair meant, with Churchill's arrival in Downing Street in May 1940, that Anglo-American relations would be conducted through channels other than Grosvenor Square.

Beyond the Roosevelt-Churchill correspondence, Kennedy's ambassadorship was also usurped as Roosevelt resorted to utilising personal emissaries to gather information and further American foreign policy aims. The presidential envoy to arrive was Sumner Welles on a multi-faceted mission to Europe in March 1940. The details of the Welles' mission and the diplomacy that surrounded it have been discussed elsewhere, but for Kennedy it 'clearly indicated an undercutting of ambassadorial function'.[78] Although Welles invited Kennedy to accompany him to the majority of his meetings on the London leg of his mission, Kennedy's contribution was negligible and he was notably absent on 13 March when Welles met the Treasury's Permanent Secretary, Sir Horace Wilson, to discuss 'unofficial Anglo-United States cooperation to consider post-war economic problems'.[79] Welles – known as 'Sumner the Silent' by the press who followed his mission – was taciturn throughout his career. Hence his own views are notoriously difficult to identify so while he would continue to praise Kennedy for the clarity of his Embassy's reports to Washington and there are hints at a cordial relationship, there is no evidence the Undersecretary shared with Kennedy his intimate instructions from the President.[80]

Kennedy's declining influence as Ambassador to London was compounded by further visits from presidential envoys in the summer of 1940. In quick succession, Colonel 'Wild Bill' Donovan (July), and Admiral Robert Ghormley (August), met with the Churchill government to discuss intelligence and the destroyers-bases deal, respectively. The former 'was a slap at [Kennedy's] Ambassadorial integrity and was seen as such', historian Ralph De Bedts writes, as 'Donovan was clearly sent to go around him'.[81] Ghormley's visit was further proof that in the most intimate of diplomatic transactions – the transfer of British sovereign territory to the United States in exchange for US destroyers – Kennedy was being circumvented. According to Beschloss, 'The Ambassador was kept out of the destroyers bargaining by the president' who instead chose 'to conduct negotiations through the British Embassy in Washington' and the Ambassador there, Lord Lothian.[82] Kennedy was again exasperated: 'I don't understand Roosevelt'. He confided to his diary, 'I feel all the time he wants to get us into war and yet take what he says to Admiral Ghormley – [the] "Old destroyers are bad ships" [and therefore can be given to the British] – I just can't follow him'.[83] Such a view reflects Kennedy's fundamental lack of shared understanding with the President over transatlantic relations and the fate of the war in Europe.

Kennedy's final weeks in London leading up to his departure in mid-October were strained. The Ambassador increasingly focused on his own predicament even when he was party to conversations which exposed him to substantial policy issues in Anglo-American relation. So, while Lord Halifax told Kennedy that 'the great value of the bases-destroyers trade to him was in the tie-up with the United States', the Ambassador was complaining to Washington as to how he had been treated.[84] Kennedy wrote to his long-time friend Edward E. Moore at the beginning of August that he had been 'complaining bitterly to the Department about them sending people over here without giving me any notice', and also for the fact that 'arrangements for matters that properly should come through this Embassy [go] through the British Embassy in Washington'.[85] As the autumn approached, Kennedy contemplated resignation once more. In conversation with Welles in early October, Kennedy stated he was 'rather surprised the Department had not sent for me to come home, considering how well they knew my time was being wasted here'. His discontent was clear as he made plain his plan to leave: 'If the Department wanted to call me home for consultation, well and good; if however they did not want to call me home, then I would extend my resignation, to take effect here at once; that I was dammed sick and disgusted with sitting here and doing nothing.'[86] For Kennedy's frustration to reach such a level is testament to Roosevelt's canny ability to placate and postpone taking difficult decisions.

Roosevelt's management of Kennedy reflected both the President's skills in handling awkward characters, and the stark fact that the London ambassadorship was not a high priority amongst the other issues he was facing such as the destroyers-bases deal and the impending election. During the summer, while indulging other channels of communication, the President played to Kennedy's loyalty and the faint hope of a further post in government with occasional letters and phone calls to Grosvenor Square. For example, at the beginning of August 1940, the same month Roosevelt orchestrated the destroyers-bases deal, he rang Kennedy feigning intimacy by suggesting his purpose for the call was 'so that you would get the dope straight from me and not from somebody else'. Despite the Ambassador declaring to the President that he was 'not at all satisfied with what I am doing', Roosevelt soothingly replied: 'I get constant reports of how valuable you are to them over there and that it helps the morale of the British to have you there and they would feel they were being let down if you were to leave.'[87] Roosevelt, as ever, had multiple objectives. He had little inclination to consider appointing a new ambassador at such a sensitive time for Anglo-American relations, especially as domestic political matters were also in play. Having accepted his party's nomination for a third term and with Wendell Wilkie's challenge mounting, keeping Kennedy out of the country reflected Roosevelt's shrewd political acumen. Further, that Kennedy was so unceremoniously dropped by the administration after Roosevelt's re-election, suggests that any hint to a future post was purely to keep Kennedy from speaking out.

The President's capacity to keep Kennedy in line was evident in the denouement of the ambassadorship. Kennedy departed London on 22 October for New York via Lisbon. Before departing Lisbon for the transatlantic voyage, Kennedy received a note from Roosevelt 'specifically requesting me to come to the White House and make no statements to the newspaper men', upon arrival in New York a further message called him straight to Washington. Kennedy remained taciturn with the assembled press in New York and headed to Washington. If the tone of the messages Kennedy had received suggested an intimate meeting with the President, he was to be disappointed given his wife, as well as Senator James Byrnes and his wife had also been invited. Thus, as Roosevelt orchestrated, there was no opportunity for a discreet conversation between the pair. Nevertheless, despite the company, and though Kennedy's ire with Roosevelt had waned on his voyage, Kennedy accused Roosevelt of having given him a 'bad deal' on four counts: 'First, because Donovan was sent to London without consulting me: Secondly, your sending a general there and Britain's knowing about it before I did; Thirdly, carrying on negotiations on destroyers and bases through Lothian and not through me: And fourthly, the State Department's never telling me about what was going on.' Kennedy recorded, 'Roosevelt promptly denied everything.' According to Beschloss, Roosevelt turned on the State Department as having been the agents of Kennedy's frustration. Kennedy was sceptical: 'Somebody is lying very seriously, and I suspect the President.'[88] Nonetheless, and in a remarkable episode illustrating Roosevelt's charm, the Ambassador's demarche was a precursor to an invitation by the President for Kennedy to deliver a speech endorsing Roosevelt for re-election. Kennedy, with his point made, agreed, and arrangements were quickly made to provide national airtime. Kennedy's broadcast was supportive of Roosevelt in challenging the notion that he was engaging the United States in the conflict. 'Such a charge is false', Kennedy succinctly declared a week before Roosevelt defeated Wendell Willkie to become President for the third time.

Before Roosevelt's third inauguration on 20 January 1941, Kennedy's fate was sealed in perfunctory fashion. Kennedy received a letter from Hull (28 November 1940) requesting his resignation. Justified 'in the interest of efficiency of the Foreign Service...at the outset of the new Administration', the Secretary wrote '[t]he President has asked me to communicate to you and all other chiefs of our diplomatic missions', his desire to see 'their formal resignations'.[89] The brief letter carried the qualification that the resignations should be directed to Hull rather than the President. Kennedy ignored the directive. Having already offered his resignation directly to the President the day after the election (6 November 1940), he rang Roosevelt on 1 December wanting 'to get fixed up on my resignation'. By then, with Kennedy failing to remain silent on his view of the fate of the European conflict, the President was ready to accept his request. And so the relationship between President and Ambassador that had facilitated a new closeness in Anglo-American relations ceased; trumped by even more intimate transatlantic relations.

Joseph P. Kennedy's Ambassadorship: Assessment and Conclusion

> 'I should imagine there can have been few cases in our history in which the two men occupying our respective positions were so closely in touch with one another as you and I.'[90]

Neville Chamberlain's remarks to Kennedy a month before he passed away in November 1940 illustrate the intimate relationship that the Bostonian enjoyed with the Prime Minister. As United States Ambassador to the Court of St James's Kennedy had remarkable access to the highest echelons of the British government at times of acute crisis in the lead up to the Second World War. Relations between Prime Minister and Ambassador were *special* in many regards. However, the same cannot be said about the Bostonian's relationship with President Franklin D. Roosevelt. Underpinned by mutual scepticism of each other's motives, the pair's relations were often strained. Roosevelt had chosen Kennedy for the post on the basis of if being a short-term posting and one where the trappings of the ambassadorial office would limit Kennedy's capacity to meddle in the administration's policy-making. Kennedy's opening success, paving the way for a longer term than either he or the President envisaged, was therefore a surprise. Less of a surprise; the relationship deteriorated after Munich to the point Kennedy was excommunicated from the administration by the end of 1940. Given his experience, and the number of posts that arose during the plethora of wartime agencies established in Washington the fact the President did not call upon Kennedy again can only have been a deliberate act.

In London, there were contrasting views of Kennedy by the time he left. In the popular press, the departure was mourned. The *Evening News* declared gratefully: 'It is Mr. Kennedy single-handed who has strengthened Anglo-American friendship in London.' *The Times* paid him the frankest tribute: 'he has earned the respect due to a great American ambassador who never for a moment mistook the country to which he was accredited for the country of his birth'. However, those who had heard Kennedy's views directly in London had a very different view. The Chief Diplomatic Advisor at the Foreign Office noted in a memorandum that the Foreign Secretary Lord Halifax initialled: 'Mr Kennedy is a very foul specimen of double crosser and defeatist. He thinks of nothing but his own pocket. I hope that this war will at least see the elimination of this type.'[91]

With such conflicting views afoot, Kennedy's value as an ambassador is rightly questioned. Of chief significance were the Ambassador's wholly divergent views from his head of state. Throughout his time in London, Kennedy was adamant that his country should stay out of the conflict and his views blinded him to the interests the United States had in the outcome of the war. Franklin Roosevelt's foresight in assessing these threats marked him out from the vast majority of his countrymen, and Kennedy in particular.

If the measure of a US Ambassador's effectiveness is his relationship with his President, then Kennedy's ambassadorship can be seriously questioned. In retrospect, the terminal decline in presidential-ambassadorial relations seems preordained with both Kennedy and Roosevelt considering the ambassadorship a short-term appointment. From the outset, the President was managing the relationship with Kennedy on an individual level, and sought to direct his own foreign policy not through the State Department, but from the White House. In this undertaking, the President was able to practise a brand of personal diplomacy that reflected his personality. Historian James Leutze notes that Roosevelt 'seemed to enjoy the opportunities it provided for intrigue and secretiveness', and this helps explain the President's tolerance, almost humouring, of Kennedy's unconventional approach.[92] Kennedy failed to recognise Roosevelt was indulging him and became increasingly frustrated and angry. In the early days of the Churchill–Roosevelt correspondence, Kennedy noted in his diary the messages going directly from the President to the 'naval person' (the 'former' was added to the transparent codename after Churchill became Prime Minister) as 'Another instance of Roosevelt's conniving mind which never indicates he knows how to handle any organization', Kennedy complained. 'It's a rotten way to treat his Ambassador and I think shows him up to the other people. I am disgusted'.[93] Such outbursts are a regular feature of his diary. Nonetheless, Kennedy's ire toward the President was always stronger when relayed to a third party and not directly to the President. At the beginning of August 1940 having learnt of the proposed destroyers-bases deal, Kennedy told his friend Moore that he 'was dammed fresh' on the phone with the President, which does not tally up with his own diary entry on the call as being at least cordial if fractious.[94]

Kennedy's initial success and his access at the time of Munich prolonged Roosevelt's tolerance of Kennedy's dissenting views. However, as the United Kingdom became more imperilled, the dynamics changed in London, with Winston Churchill coming in from the cold and arriving in Downing Street in May 1940. From a position of intimacy with Chamberlain, Kennedy was now forced to look in on an even more 'special' relationship between Prime Minister and President.

Nonetheless, the ambassadorship of Joseph Kennedy is notable for a number of subtle but significant transitions in transatlantic diplomacy that took place during his term. Kennedy's ambassadorship illustrates his vital role as facilitator of transatlantic communications with the highest echelons of the British government, his influence on establishing the Embassy as an efficient outpost, during a shift from the pre-eminence of the Embassy as channel of communication with the White House to direct prime ministerial–presidential relations.

Kennedy's own words provide apt conclusion. Writing to Hull as he first arrived to take up his post, he said 'I hope you get some good out of my services: I am sure I will have a fine time.' While Kennedy may well have had a fine time to start with, and on occasion his services were notable in the service of transatlantic diplomacy, the ambassadorship is tainted by a failed relationship with the President and growing distance from the government he was supposed to be observing at the time of its 'finest hour'.

Notes

1. The Morgenthau Diaries, 8 December 1937, Book 101, Franklin D. Roosevelt Presidential Library, Hyde Park New York (hereafter FDRL).
2. Diary entry 17 September and 27 September 1939, Series 8. US Ambassador to Great Britain, 1931–1951, 8.1 Appointments and Diary 1938–1951, Box 100. Joseph P. Kennedy Papers, John F. Kennedy Presidential Library, Boston, MA. The chapter draws extensively upon the recently released Joseph P. Kennedy Papers, currently available only by invitation at the John F. Kennedy Presidential Library (hereafter JPK Papers, JFKL).
3. As a contemporary example of the allure of the Kennedy story, the production and broadcast of a television mini-series entitled *The Kennedys*, with British actor Tom Wilkinson playing Joseph P. Kennedy, Sr, in 2010–11 has caused considerable controversy with the History Channel in the United States declining to broadcast the series. See http://en.wikipedia.org/wiki/The_Kennedys_(TV_miniseries) (accessed 7 June 2011).
4. The announcement that Kennedy would replace Ambassador Bingham was made on 10 December 1937. According to the US Embassy in London the precise dates of his appointment are as follows: Appointment 17 January 1938; presented credentials 8 March 1938; left post 22 October 1940 (http://london.usembassy.gov/rcambex.html)
5. Elliot Roosevelt, *As He Saw It* (New York: Duell, Sloan and Pearce, 1946); Robert A. Divine, *The Reluctant Belligerent: American Entry into World War II* (New York: John Wiley, 1965); Warren F. Kimball, *Franklin D. Roosevelt and the World Crisis, 1937–1945* (Lexington, MA, and London: D. C. Heath & Co., 1973); Robert Dallek, *Franklin D. Roosevelt and American Foreign Policy, 1932–1945* (New York: Oxford University Press, 1979); Frederick Marks III, *Wind over Sand: The Diplomacy of Franklin Roosevelt* (Athens, GA: University of Georgia Press, 1988); Warren F. Kimball, *The Juggler: Franklin Roosevelt as Wartime Statesman* (Princeton, NJ: Princeton University Press, 1991); Kenneth S. Davis, *FDR: Into the Storm, 1937–1940: A History* (New York: Random House, **1993).** In more recent times, Kenneth S. Davis, *FDR: The War President, 1940–1943* (New York: Random House, 2000); Conrad Black, *Franklin Delano Roosevelt: Champion of Freedom* (New York: PublicAffairs, 2003); David F. Schmitz, *The Triumph of Internationalism: Franklin D. Roosevelt and a World in Crisis 1933–1941* (Washington DC: Potomac Books, 2007), and David B. Woolner, Warren F. Kimball and David Reynolds (eds.), *FDR's World: War, Peace and Legacies* (New York: Palgrave Macmillan, 2008).
6. Letter from Joseph Kennedy (London) to James Landis (Harvard) 22 March 1938, Papers of James M. James Landis, Box 24, Library of Congress, Washington DC (hereafter JLP LOC). Kennedy actually did score a hole in one in the first round of golf he enjoyed in the UK just days after arriving. His good fortune was compounded by the presence of newspapermen who relayed the story to their readers. 'A stroke of luck gave Kennedy's popularity a boost with the sports-loving British.' Richard J. Whalen, *The Founding Father: The Story of Joseph P. Kennedy* (Washington, DC: Regnery Gateway, 1993), p. 210.
7. 10 December 1937, Memorandum, Box 210, Adolf Berle Papers (hereafter ABP), FDRL. Berle was not an admirer of Kennedy. He continued: 'This is not because the so-called liberals want him out. It is because he has been double-dealing – anything but creditable – in some of his own matters, notably the Stock Exchange.'

8. The Morgenthau Diaries, 8 December 1937, Book 101, FDRL.
9. *Ibid.*
10. Letter from Joseph Kennedy (London) to James Landis (Harvard) 22 March 1938, JLP LOC.
11. Joseph P. Kennedy, *I'm for Roosevelt* (New York: Reynal & Hitchcock, 1936).
12. The Morgenthau Diaries, 8 December 1937, Book 101, FDRL.
13. Arthur Krock, interview recorded by Charles Bartlett, 10 May 1964, Oral History Program, JFKL.
14. Ralph F. De Bedts, *Ambassador Joseph Kennedy 1939–1940: An Anatomy of Appeasement* (New York: Peter Lang, 1985), p. 9.
15. *Ibid.*, p. 10.
16. Letter from Joseph Kennedy (London) to James Landis (Harvard) 22 March 1938, JLP LOC.
17. Neville Chamberlain to Joseph Kennedy, 19 March 1939, Box 104, Series 8, US Ambassador to Great Britain, 1931–1951, 8.2.1 Correspondence File Neville Chamberlain, JPK Papers, JFKL.
18. Diary entry 4 March 1938, JPK Papers, JFKL.
19. Neville Chamberlain to Joseph Kennedy, 19 October 1940, Box 104, Series 8, US Ambassador to Great Britain, 1931–1951, 8.2.1 Correspondence File Neville Chamberlain, JPK Papers, JFKL.
20. Michael R. Beschloss, *Kennedy and Roosevelt: The Uneasy Alliance* (New York and London: W. W. Norton & Co., 1980), p. 163.
21. Beschloss, *Kennedy and Roosevelt*, p. 159.
22. Whalen, *The Founding Father*, p. 214.
23. Diary entry 8 March 1938, JPK Papers, JFKL.
24. Diary entry 12 March 1938, JPK Papers, JFKL.
25. Philip Seib, *Broadcasts from the Blitz: How Edward R. Murrow Helped Lead America into War* (Washington, DC: Potomac Books, 2006), p. 30.
26. Joseph Kennedy to Cordell Hull, 22 March 1938, Box 109, Series 8, US Ambassador to Great Britain, 1931–1951, 8.2.1 Correspondence File Cordell Hull, JPK Papers, JFKL.
27. *Ibid.*
28. Diary entry 12 March 1938, JPK Papers, JFKL.
29. Kennedy's approach would not always effectively serve his own, or transatlantic relations. As an example in September 1938, Kennedy recorded 'The off-the-record press conference I held with American newspaper men yesterday backfired, apparently, in the case of Joe Driscoll of the *Herald Tribune*. He printed a conjecture, which was inaccurate but evidently based on a remark which we had all specifically agreed would not be referred to.' Diary entry 1September 1938, JPK Papers, JFKL.
30. Will Swift, *The Kennedy's Amidst the Gathering Storm* (New York: Harper Collins, 2008).
31. In May and June 1938 his diary was akin to a sports broadcasting scheduling; in quick succession he attended an ice hockey match (10 May), the Derby 'in Lord Derby's special train' (1 June), gave a lunch for the Walker Cup amateur golfers (7 June), attended the Wightman Cup at Wimbledon (10 June), before Royal Ascot. Diary entries May–June 1938, JPK Papers, JFKL. To complete his sporting summer, after attending a luncheon of the British Sportsmen's club in April where he was much impressed with Donald Bradman's after dinner speech, he vowed to 'attend at least one of the test matches between England and

Australia'. Kennedy recorded that Bradman 'made the best after dinner speech I ever heard in my life. They told me he is a better batsman than a speaker, but I shall have to see him before the wicket to believe it.' 25 April 1938, JPK Papers, JFKL.

32. Joseph Kennedy to Cordell Hull, 22 July 1938, Box 109, Series 8, US Ambassador to Great Britain, 1931–1951, 8.2.1 Correspondence File Cordell Hull, JPK Papers, JFKL.
33. Whalen, *The Founding Father*, p. 210.
34. Joseph Kennedy to Cordell Hull, 22 March 1938, Box 109, Series 8, US Ambassador to Great Britain, 1931–1951, 8.2.1 Correspondence File Cordell Hull, JFK Papers, JFKL.
35. 'We should be glad to have your views regarding the specific proposals...for this important American industry', Welles wrote. Telegram from Welles to Kennedy, 25 April 1938, 611.4131/1405, *Foreign Relations of the United States 1938* (Washington: Government Printing Office, series), Vol. II, p. 26 (hereafter *FRUS*).
36. Arthur W. Schatz, 'The Anglo-American Trade Agreement and Cordell Hull's Search for Peace 1936–38', *Journal of American History*, Vol. 57 (1970–71), pp. 85–103. In providing an excellent background to the importance of economic relations please see Patricia Clavin, *The Failure of Economic Diplomacy: Britain, Germany, France and the United States, 1931–36* (London: Macmillan, 1996).
37. Diary entry 13 March 1938, JPK Papers, JFKL.
38. Joseph Kennedy to Cordell Hull, 27 May 1938, Box 109, Series 8, US Ambassador to Great Britain, 1931–1951, 8.2.1 Correspondence File Cordell Hull, JPK Papers, JFKL. During July 1939, Kennedy made particular efforts to ensure the promotion of Johnson to Class I Counsellor suggesting to Hull that 'this recommendation will not be considered as beyond my scope of authority, but because I do not hesitate to say when I think a man does not do good work, I think I should not hesitate to recommend someone when he does do good work' (Joseph Kennedy to Cordell Hull, 20 July 1939, Box 109, Series 8, US Ambassador to Great Britain, 1931–1951, 8.2.1 Correspondence File Cordell Hull, JPK Papers, JFKL). In a recent article looking at the relationship between the Foreign Service and military intelligence officials during the Kennedy Ambassadorship, Martin S. Alexander argues that the cooperation was characterised by 'poor levels of preparedness' and 'ill-coordinated apparatus' as well as a 'spectacular clash of personalities' between Kennedy and Lieutenant Colonel Chyworth, the military attaché. Martin S. Alexander, ' "[...] the best security for London is the nine Kennedy children": Perceptions by US Officials in Washington DC and London of Britain's Readiness for War in 1939', *Contemporary British History*, Vol. 25, No. 1 (2011), pp. 103–4 and 110.
39. Sumner Welles to Joseph Kennedy, 1 May 1939, Box 117, Series 8, US Ambassador to Great Britain, 1931–1951, 8.2.1 Correspondence File Sumner Welles, JPK Papers, JFKL.
40. See John W. Wheeler-Bennett, *Munich: Prologue to Tragedy* (New York: Duell, Sloan and Pearce, 1948); Martin Gilbert and Richard Gott, *The Appeasers* (London: Weidenfeld & Nicholson, 1967); Donald C. Watt, *How War Came: The Immediate Origins of the Second World War, 1938–1939* (London: Heinemann, 1989); R. A. C. Parker, *Chamberlain and Appeasement* (London: Palgrave Macmillan, 1994); and Erik Goldstein and Igor Lukes (eds.), *The Munich Crisis 1938: Prelude to World War II* (London: Frank Cass, 1999).
41. Diary entries 12 and 13 September 1938, JPK Papers, JFKL.

42. Edward L. Henson, Jr, 'Britain, America, and the Month of Munich', *International Relations*, Vol. 2 (1962), pp. 291–301.
43. Diary entry 21 September 1938, JPK Papers, JFKL.
44. Telephone conversation between Joseph Kennedy and Cordell Hull, 24 September 1938, Box 109, Joseph P. Kennedy Papers, Series 8, US Ambassador to Great Britain, 1931–1951, 8.2.1 Correspondence File Cordell Hull, JPK Papers, JFKL.
45. *Ibid.*
46. Telephone conversation between Joseph Kennedy and Cordell Hull, 26 September 1938, Box 109, Joseph P. Kennedy Papers, Series 8, US Ambassador to Great Britain, 1931–1951, 8.2.1 Correspondence File Cordell Hull, JPK Papers, JFKL.
47. Diary entry 28 September 1938, JPK Papers, JFKL.
48. US Department of State Publication 1983, *Peace and War: United States Foreign Policy, 1931–1941*, (Washington, DC: US Government Printing Office, 1943), pp. 427–8, available at: http://www.mtholyoke.edu/acad/intrel/interwar/fdr14.htm
49. Letter Joseph Kennedy to John J. Burns, 10 October 1938, Box 103, Series 8, US Ambassador to Great Britain, 1931–1951, 8.2.1 Correspondence File, London 1939–1940, JPK Papers, JFKL.
50. Henson, Jr, 'Britain, America, and the Month of Munich'.
51. Barbara Farnham, *Roosevelt and the Munich Crisis: A Study in Political Decision-making* (Princeton, NJ: Princeton University Press, 1997), p. 171.
52. Diary entry 3 September 1939, JPK Papers, JFKL.
53. 21 October 1938, in Nancy Harvison Hooker (ed.), *The Moffat Papers: Selections from the Diplomatic Journals of Jay Pierrepont Moffat 1919–1943* (Cambridge, MA: Harvard University Press, 1956), p. 221.
54. 22–23 October 1938, in Hooker, *The Moffat Papers*, p. 221.
55. Beschloss, *Kennedy and Roosevelt*, p. 178.
56. Diary entry 7 December 1938, JPK Papers, JFKL.
57. Diary entry 9 February 1939, JPK Papers, JFKL.
58. 26 April 1939, Memorandum, Box 210, ADP, FDRL.
59. Beschloss, *Kennedy and Roosevelt*, p. 188.
60. Tony McCulloch, *Anglo-American Economic Diplomacy and the European Crisis, 1933–1939*, September 1978, DPhil Oxford, p. 348.
61. Letter Joseph Kennedy to Sumner Welles, 5 April 1939, Box 117, Series 8, US Ambassador to Great Britain, 1931–1951, 8.2.1 Correspondence File, London 1939–1940, JPK Papers, JFKL.
62. Letter Joseph Kennedy to Franklin Roosevelt, 9 August 1939, President's Secretary File (PSF), FDRL.
63. President Roosevelt to the Chancellor of Germany (Hitler) [Telegram], 24 August 1939, US Department of State Publication 1983, *Peace and War*, pp. 476–7; Diary entry 24 August 1939, JPK Papers, JFKL.
64. Fred L. Israel (ed.), *The War Diary of Breckinridge Long* (Lincoln, NE: University of Nebraska Press, 1966), p. 10.
65. The royal visit, and its political implications, are discussed in Benjamin Rhodes, 'The British Royal Visit of 1939 and the "Psychological Approach" to the United States', *Diplomatic History*, Vol. 2 (1978), pp. 197–211; David Reynolds, 'FDR's Foreign Policy and the British Royal Visit to the USA, 1939', *Historian*, Vol. 45 (1983), pp. 461–72; and Peter Bell, "The Foreign Office and the 1939 Royal Visit

to America: Courting the USA in an Era of Isolationism", *Journal of Contemporary History*, Vol. 37, No. 4 (October 2002), pp. 599–616.

66. Beschloss, *Kennedy and Roosevelt*, p. 187.
67. Diary entry 14 April 1939, JPK Papers, JFKL.
68. Diary entry 24 August 1939, JPK Papers, JFKL.
69. 9 September 1939, David Dilks (ed.), *The Diaries of Sir Alexander Cadogan O.M. 1938–45* (London: Cassel, 1971).
70. Joseph Kennedy to Marguerite Missy LeHand, 3 October 1939. Marguerite Missy LeHand Papers, Box 10, FDRL. Perhaps explaining in part the President's perseverance with someone at odds with his own views was a level of amity between LeHand and Kennedy. The letter of 3 October 1939 was one example and another can be found in Kennedy's diary. He recorded that he had spoken with LeHand after hearing Chamberlain's declaration of war on 3 September 1939: 'It was sad and she told me how she was thinking of me and really was terribly sweet. Asked me to call the President as he wanted to talk to me. She said how proud she was of the way I was doing this job over here and the President was too. Thanked her and said I hoped I'd see her soon. She was crying.' Diary entry 3 September 1939, JPK Papers, JFKL.
71. Joseph Kennedy to the Secretary of State 11 September 1939, 740.00111 European War, 1939/258: Telegram, *FRUS*, pp. 421–4.
72. Joseph P. Lash, *Roosevelt and Churchill 1939–41: The Partnership that Saved the West* (London: Hodder & Stoughton, 1977).
73. Warren F. Kimball (ed.), *Churchill and Roosevelt: The Complete Correspondence*. I. *Alliance Emerging October 1933–November 1942* (Princeton, NJ: Princeton University Press, 1984).
74. Diary entry 6 October 1939, JPK Papers, JFKL.
75. Diary entry 5 October 1939, JPK Papers, JFKL.
76. Diary entry 15 August 1940, JPK Papers, JFKL.
77. James Leutze remarks that 'for revisionist historians like Charles C. Tansil and Charles A Beard, and for other suspicious of Roosevelt's policies, the story [of Tyler Kent] fits their theories very neatly' ('The Secret of the Churchill-Roosevelt Correspondence: September 1939–May 1940', *Journal of Contemporary History*, Vol. 10 [1975], p. 467). For further information see Warren F. Kimball and Bruce Bartlett, 'Roosevelt and Prewar Commitments to Churchill: The Tyler Kent Affair', *Diplomatic History*, Vol. 5, No. 4 (Fall 1981), pp. 291–312; and Ray Bearse and Anthony Read, *Conspirator: The Untold Story of Tyler Kent* (New York: Doubleday, 1991).
78. De Bedts, *Ambassador Joseph Kennedy 1939–1940*, p. 188.
79. Telegram No. 224 from Lord Lothian to Foreign Office, 16 February 1940 A1236/431/45 FO 371 24248 National Archives, Kew.
80. An undated and unnamed note in Kennedy's diary files relating to Welles' time in London suggests the Undersecretary thought highly of Kennedy: 'it has been a God-given gift to the United States that Joseph P. Kennedy is our Ambassador today as the Court of St James'. And in June 1940 Kennedy recorded, 'Welles said "God help the US if it weren't for the London Embassy".' Diary entry 15 June 1940, JPK Papers, JFKL.
81. De Bedts, *Ambassador Joseph Kennedy 1939–1940*, p. 188.
82. Beschloss, *Kennedy and Roosevelt*, p. 211. By the end of 1939, and though only in office for a matter of months Lothian was being preferred as a channel of transatlantic correspondence to Kennedy. Moffat noted '[i]f Kennedy says something is black and Lothian says it is white, we believe Lord Lothian' (Hooker, *The Moffat*

Papers, p. 5). Lord Lothian's ambassadorship is discussed by J. Simon Rofe, 'Lord Lothian in Washington', in Priscilla Roberts (ed.), *Lothian and Anglo-American Relations 1900–1940* (Dordrecht: Republic of Letters, 2010). Other sources include: David P. Billington, Jr, *Lothian: Philip Kerr and the Quest for World Order* (Westport, CT: Praeger, 2006), and David Reynolds, *Lord Lothian and Anglo-American Relations, 1939–1940* (Philadelphia: Transactions of the American Philosophical Society, 1983).

83. Diary Entry 16 August 1940, JPK Papers, JFKL.
84. Diary Entry 29 August 1940, JPK Papers, JFKL.
85. Letter from Kennedy to Edward E. Moore 2 August 1940, JPK Papers, JFKL.
86. Diary Entry 11 October 1940, JPK Papers, JFKL.
87. Memorandum of telephone conversation between President and Ambassador at 3.00 p.m., 1 August 1940, JPK Papers, JFKL.
88. Diary Entry addendum 23 October 1940, JPK Papers, JFKL.
89. Cordell Hull to Joseph Kennedy, 28 November 1940, Box 109, Series 8, US Ambassador to Great Britain, 1931–1951, 8.2.1 Correspondence File Cordell Hull, JPK Papers, JFKL.
90. Neville Chamberlain to Joseph Kennedy, 19 October 1940.
91. Initialled by Sir Robert Vansittart, Permanent Undersecretary at the Foreign Office (1930–39) on Halifax Memorandum 25 January 1940, FO371/24251 1807 163 A605.
92. By way of example Moffat reveals the extent of Roosevelt's capacity for personal diplomacy, and Kennedy benefitting from it at the height of his influence in the autumn of 1938. Moffat noted that the President was prepared to usurp official channels: 'The truth of the matter is that the Secretary dislikes calling down Kennedy and Bullit as they have a way of appealing to the White House over his head' (Friday 21 October 1938; Hooker, *The Moffat Papers*, p. 221).
93. Diary entry addendum 4 October 1939, JPK Papers, JFKL.
94. Letter from Kennedy to Edward E. Moore, 2 August 1940, JPK Papers, JFKL.

2
John Gilbert Winant, 1941–46

David Mayers

President Franklin D. Roosevelt (FDR) appointed John 'Gil' Winant as Ambassador to Great Britain in early 1941.[1] From then to the end of the Second World War, he helped to steady the Anglo-US relationship and repaired damages inflicted by Joseph Kennedy. Winant drew the sting from many of those irritations that plague even the sturdiest of alliances. To countless Britons, high and low, he also symbolised American commitment to their safety. Labour party's Ernest Bevin, a wartime minister in Churchill's coalition cabinet, explained in 1946: 'It's a vivid recollection to us to see [Winant] walking round the streets during an air raid witnessing how London took it ... he shared our sorrows ... he gave one a feeling of optimism.'[2]

Alliance

Kennedy was an easy act to follow. Nearly anyone would have been preferable to him, who had, in his final British months lingered sullenly. Roosevelt, facing a grimmer world than when he lightheartedly set Kennedy upon London, was not about to burden Anglo-US ties with another dubious appointee.

Winant was a Republican. As such he belonged to FDR's effort to promote wartime bipartisanship, exemplified by enrolling two prominent Grand Old Party (GOP) figures in the Cabinet: Henry Stimson for the War Department, Frank Knox for the Navy. Apart from rival party affiliations, the differences between Kennedy and Winant were striking. The former, a conservative businessman, was recruited by the New Deal to help assuage the doubts of corporate America. Winant, by contrast, was an unapologetic progressive. Roosevelt once referred to him as 'Utopian John'.[3]

Whereas Kennedy had scrambled to escape his Irish-Boston roots, obsessively acquiring wealth plus the trappings of acceptance, Winant's pre-London life had been unexceptional. Bashful son (b. 1889) of a successful New York businessman (real estate), Winant prepped at St Paul's School in Concord, New Hampshire. After flunking as an undergraduate at Princeton

University, he returned to St Paul's to teach history. He eventually assumed the duties of assistant rector. A shambling and introverted man, he did not excel as instructor. His halting speech and fidgetiness aggravated matters. Only obvious devotion to his students – and flair for lessons on Abraham Lincoln – prevented his young charges from overt mutiny. He joined the army during the World War, paying his own way to France. He subsequently served as a pilot (rising to the rank of captain) with reconnaissance air squadrons.[4] He drifted back to St Paul's in 1919, then into a joyless marriage to a socially striving wife, Constance Rivington Russell. She liked light recreations and keenly resented her husband's growing interest in public affairs.[5]

Despite his atrocious speechifying – mumbling, inaudibility, syntactical mangling – Winant first won election in 1916 to the New Hampshire State Legislature while still on the St Paul's faculty. He returned to the legislature (Senate and House) following his wartime service. He was thrice elected governor of New Hampshire, serving two-year terms (1925–26, 1931–32, 1933–34). While in office he pushed a series of programmes, appropriately dubbed by observers as the Little New Deal, to alleviate the hardship of unemployed labourers and destitute farmers. With much in common with Roosevelt's New Deal he supported a minimum wage, advocated a reduction of the work week (to 48 hours) for women and children, promoted regulatory reform of banks, championed civil rights for African-Americans, and favoured the abolition of capital punishment. He surfaced as a possible presidential candidate in 1936, briefly winning attention by GOP kingpins, but disappointed them by backing FDR's re-election. Winant's commitment to social-political reforms had meanwhile won Roosevelt's attention, then high-level appointments: first to chairmanship of the Social Security Board, finally to the directorship in 1939 of the International Labour Organization (ILO) in Geneva. In this second job, Winant, though a disorganised and temperamental manager, established good relations with trade unionists from around the world, including Bevin, and was acknowledged as one whose feelings gravitated toward the 'common man'.[6]

Winant's 1941 assignment to London made sense in that Roosevelt did not want to identify his administration closely with the domestic programmes or electoral fortunes of Britain's Tories. Winant would, naturally, conduct himself properly with the Conservative leadership, led by Churchill and Foreign Minister Anthony Eden, but could also be counted upon to maintain cordial relations with the government's Labour ministers. A more equitable post-war Britain, implicitly promised even before the 1942 Beveridge Report, argued for support from New Deal America, a purpose abetted by Winant.[7] True to this spirit, he pleased Labour constituencies in his expressions of hope for a future expunged of class-economic injustices:

> There was something fundamentally wrong in the prewar days when, on one side, workers were standing idle, and on the other side, people

were under-fed, badly housed, short of clothes, and children were stinted on education and deprived of their heritage of good health and happiness... When war is done, the drive for tanks must become a drive for houses. The drive for food to prevent the enemy from starving us must become a drive for food to satisfy the needs of all people in all countries. The drive for physical fitness in the forces must become a drive for bringing death and sickness rates in the whole population down to the lowest possible level. The drive for manpower in war must become a drive for employment to make freedom from want a living reality.[8]

Article Five of the Atlantic Charter (14 August 1941), pledging Anglo-US cooperation to improve international labor standards and social security, gratified Winant. His later monitoring of public opinion meant that he was less surprised than most outsiders when voters turned the Conservatives out of office in July 1945. Upon his departure from the Court of St. James's in 1946, the British Trades Union Congress bestowed its Gold Badge upon him, a decoration never before conferred upon an ambassador.[9]

Britons responded warmly to Winant, an unequivocal anti-Nazi who for years had excoriated Hitler's despotism.[10] Upon his arriving in Britain, 1 March 1941, and in a dramatic break with tradition, King George VI greeted him at the Windsor train station. His first public utterance was quickly transmitted throughout the anxious kingdom: 'I am very glad to be here. There is no place I would rather be at this time than in England.'[11] Thereafter popular feeling rushed to contrast him with Kennedy's inveterate scepticism. By many accounts, women particularly liked him for his shaggy good looks and attentiveness.[12] Harold Nicolson, himself a former diplomat, was won by the 'superb character' of Winant: 'one of the most charming men that I have ever met'.[13] Intellectuals sought his company while forgiving his forensic clumsiness, notably the socialist Harold Laski, but also the historian R. H. Tawney, the economist John Maynard Keynes, the reformer Sir William Beveridge, and the writer H. G. Wells. Winant was also celebrated for his courage, demonstrable in his darting through rubble-strewn London streets with Embassy officers to succor blitz victims or douse fires caused by incendiary bombs.[14]

Only the Foreign Office harboured reservations. T. North Whitehead observed that Winant struggled hard to find the right words. Lacking the art of repose, he was 'not a restful companion'. Undersecretary R. A. Butler, originally acquainted with him in Geneva, considered his a 'mystifying' personality and predicted that, as an untrained diplomat, he would not provide Washington with 'scientific appreciations'.[15] Eden approved of Winant from the outset, however, and respected his 'instinct' for disentangling intricate questions. The two men worked closely together. They dispensed with formality and eschewed – to the regret of later historians – memoranda in preference for private conversation. They also became companionable, to the point of sharing garden chores at Eden's home in Sussex. The torment of fathers with military sons in peril proved a profound bond. (Eden's son, Simon, was killed in Burma. Winant's son, John, pilot of a B-17 Flying Fortress downed over Germany, was taken prisoner.) Churchill too felt unfeigned warmth for Winant and he became a frequent visitor to Downing Street and Chequers, even present at the latter when the BBC flashed its Pearl Harbor bulletin.[16]

London-based Americans were drawn to Winant, reinforced by relief at being rid of the mortifying Kennedy. Redoubtable newsman Edward R. Murrow befriended the new Ambassador. Colonel Raymond Lee, the Embassy's military attaché, thought him an able, if high-strung, person who deserved his subordinates' loyalty. The Embassy's Foreign Service staff respected him too.[17] He drove his people hard. Yet he was even more relentless on himself. He once confessed in a low moment: 'I have no life.'[18] His indifference to his own safety during German air raids – often avoiding even rudimentary shelter – struck acquaintances as bizarre, almost a death-wish. He never thought, in any case, to leave London for the countryside (as Kennedy famously had) but maintained a spare apartment near the Embassy office that sustained damages.[19]

Winant's 'finest hour' corresponded with his days in Britain before the United States declared war against Germany. His main contribution resided less in the realm of tangible business than in the psychological effect of his presence. He intended to reassure Britons – across a broad spectrum of caste, party, region – of US solidarity with them, that Washington would do everything, short of illegality and to the limit of what churning public opinion could abide, to ensure British security. He toured (often with Churchill) Bristol, Cardiff, Coventry, Swansea and other cities to inspect the wreckage left by Luftwaffe bombs. He offered condolences. He listened at length to homeless people in makeshift hostels. He visited hospitals. He walked through smashed factories and smoldering docksides. He promised aid, confirmed by climbing levels of Lend-Lease comfort.[20] He spoke passionately of a future free of Nazi terror. He also established sufficiently close relations by mid-1942 with Deputy Prime Minister Clement Attlee to be of use as he sought to quell restive coal miners whose work stoppages threatened to disrupt industry. Winant told a delegation of strikers in northern England:

> You, who suffered so deeply in the long depression years, know that we must move on a great social offensive if we are to win the war completely. Anti-Fascism is not a short-term military job. It was bred in poverty and unemployment. To crush Fascism at its roots, we must crush depression democracy. We must solemnly resolve that in our future order we will not tolerate the economic evils which breed poverty and war.[21]

The miners responded with praise for Winant. They returned to work, subsequently receiving boosts in salary and London's gratitude. He also took time to participate in varied good-will activities. He chaired the 'science and human needs' section of the British Association for the Advancement of Science, which met in London in September 1941. He earnestly encouraged the development of American studies in British curricula, from elementary schools to universities.[22]

The Ambassador's reports to Roosevelt in 1941 stressed several themes. On the affirmative side, the British were resolute. They were competent in waging island defence. They conducted effective, albeit limited, offensive operations. All of these factors argued for the continuance of US aid and naval-military consultation at high levels. Winant commended the skill of British soldiers, sailors, airmen, labourers, plus London's emergency services. He also extolled the virtues of British women, as imbued with endurance – as ready to sacrifice – as their men folk, both on the home front and in foreign billets. Furthermore, he made certain that reports on the British experience – from the treatment of phosphorous wounds to radar advances to warplane design – were sent to relevant US agencies, resulting in tangible benefit to national preparedness and combat efficiencies.[23]

Yet in the absence of US intervention, Winant felt that Britain would be bled, then obliged to cease hostilities on unfavourable terms. German chances, in other words, kept rising for however long America dawdled, even after the distraction of Berlin's declaring war against the USSR (June 1941). On these subjects an animated Churchill frequently discussed with him, becoming visibly impatient after the Placentia Bay conference failed to result in a US war declaration in late August 1941. The Ambassador required no persuasion, however. He repeatedly stated to compatriots: 'It will be a tragedy if we do not get into the war.'[24] Earlier he had pressed Roosevelt, with Churchill's blessing, to expand the US defence line in the Atlantic to 26 degrees west (April) and dispatch US soldiers to Iceland (July), thereby allowing the redeployments of thinly stretched British naval-military units.[25]

Ironically, given the eagerness of Winant for American intervention, his role in Anglo-US relations became less central after December 1941. Even earlier, his importance had been overshadowed: first, by the arrival in London of W. Averell Harriman (mid-March) as Lend-Lease 'expediter' with rank of Minister (and would be briefly Ambassador himself in 1946), then by Harry Hopkins (July) as Roosevelt's special emissary to Churchill to review the supplies situation. Hopkins, in charge of all Lend-Lease beneficence, stayed only briefly in Britain before leaving for Moscow to confer with Stalin about Soviet materiel requirements. The harm done to Winant's prestige was correspondingly minor. Hopkins was in any case solicitous of the Ambassador and spoke considerably of him to British officialdom. Harriman also had not intended to compromise Winant's standing, despite privately scoffing at what he viewed as the Ambassador's overwrought idealism. Nonetheless, by the nature of his urgent mission, not to mention his aplomb and ingratiating ways, Harriman became a favourite of Churchill's. He was also rightly seen by cabinet ministers as one who, like Hopkins, enjoyed FDR's particular confidence. Not deliberately, but certainly unavoidably, Harriman came to dwarf Winant in Whitehall's corridors during 1941 to 1943. Strain correspondingly developed, notwithstanding efforts by both men (more pronounced on Winant's side) to contain it. Their staffs were affected by uncertainty over lines of jurisdiction and wound up fighting a gratuitous battle for publicity and reputation.[26]

Winant felt by summer 1943 that his position had been usurped. He complained to Hopkins that, according to a persistent whispering campaign, either he or Harriman would be assigned to head the Embassy. Winant declared in pique: 'An ambassador cannot be an effective representative in London unless he is better informed and given more support than I am receiving.' As for the Foreign Office's senior figures, they sympathised with the 'perturbed' Ambassador. They were not about to question or interfere with US arrangements, however.[27] Winant's frustration was deepened by Churchill's and Roosevelt's wont to dispose directly of the main items on the Anglo-US agenda, doing so with scant ambassadorial or other consultation. Churchill later explained: 'My relationship with President Roosevelt superseded both the Foreign Office of my nation and the American Embassy.'[28]

Still Winant soldiered on. Albeit outside Churchill–Roosevelt exclusiveness, and hounded by a morbid sense of inadequacy, he did contribute usefully to Allied cooperation. He managed to find the right tone and appropriate words to buck up Churchill in 1942 as setbacks accumulated. Britain's garrison at Singapore surrendered to a numerically inferior Japanese force (February). Burma fell (May). The Afrika Korps captured Torbruk plus 30,000 British soldiers (June). The House of Commons threatened to censure the prime minister (July). Churchill told FDR amidst this bleakness: 'Everybody is inspired by [Winant].'[29]

Winant's widespread regard produced dividends for the United States. The Ambassador obtained Parliament's approval (not without grousing from members) to giving American military authorities jurisdiction over GIs charged with committing criminal acts anywhere in the United Kingdom. Winant's personal capital helped to mollify Churchill's uneasy ministers about the deployment of African-American servicemen in Britain: roughly 100,000. His prestige worked to US advantage when he defended Washington in November 1942 over the Darlan deal – an acceptable expedient, he argued, to reduce Allied casualties assaulting Vichy-controlled North Africa. His good relations with senior British officers (specifically Field Marshal Bernard Montgomery) fostered mutuality between them and American commanders, notably General Dwight Eisenhower and Admiral Harold Stark, both of whom regularly conferred with Winant. He was likewise able to lessen Anglo-US tension centred on General Charles de Gaulle's Free French movement in London, a body that excited FDR's distrust and irritability. Winant was instrumental in summer 1944 in getting British concurrence, grudgingly granted, in the rescue of thousands of Hungarian Jews from German clutches and transfer to safety via neutral and Allied territories. He meantime led a bustling embassy that conducted business with 22 different British ministries. It functioned as the nucleus of an ever-proliferating number of US agencies of varying status with their personnel sometimes seconded to the Ambassador's staff. These were concentrated on diverse projects, including such critical ones as Lend-Lease, refugee reloca-tion, scientific/atomic researches, intelligence gathering, sprawling Office of Strategic Service (OSS) operations, Operation Overlord planning.[30]

Winant's links to the American home front were comparably impressive. He informed newspaper-magazine-radio audiences that Britons were wag-ing their war with fortitude. 'The most moving thing in England today', he wrote for readers of the *Atlantic* in May 1942, 'is its unity of purpose'.[31] His interactions with ordinary US servicemen stationed in Britain were good. He encouraged them to adopt a respectful attitude toward their counter-parts. Their lower pay, shabbier uniforms and poorer rations, he taught, should not be objects of contempt but taken as a measure of sacrifices bravely borne.[32] He also intervened, when possible, to mend injured feel-ings or resolve misunderstanding when such occurred between Britons and Americans, typically involving lapses in etiquette or correct demeanor as interpreted by one side or the other. He brooded, 'It is only the caring peo-ple who get hurt.'[33] On a brighter note, he hosted congressional delegations and American celebrities in London, most notably Eleanor Roosevelt. She thought his a luminescent personality. When time came, he led the US delegation at the memorial service (17 April 1945) for Roosevelt held at St Paul's Cathedral. There he read from scriptures. He escorted and comforted a distraught Churchill.[34]

European Advisory Commission

Winant offered little advice to Washington or London on the military side of life, leaving that to the competence of the Combined Chiefs. He did, though, endorse the wisdom of daylight bombing of German targets: 'the greatest American contribution to air warfare'.[35] Otherwise, he looked forward to the prosecution of Nazis leaders responsible for atrocities and stuck closely to matters related to the Grand Alliance and Germany's future.

Winant was involved in helping British negotiators as they finalised their May 1942 treaty of alliance with the USSR, in effect getting the Soviets to back off, at least for a while, from claims to the Baltic republics and eastern Poland.[36] Respecting overall Anglo-US relations with Stalin, Winant argued for intensive cooperation and hoped, like Roosevelt, that the part-nership would continue into the post-war era. To this end, he urged prompt establishment of a second front in Western Europe to relieve the heavily engaged Red Army. He advised that the 1943 Italian surrender not be solely an Anglo-US affair but the Kremlin should be informed and, to whatever degree practicable, a party to the event; this consideration ought to produce reciprocal benefit for London/Washington in Eastern Europe when the Red Army accepted German surrenders and assumed local authority. He made a special point of staying on friendly terms with the Soviet envoys in London: first, the sophisticated Ivan Maisky, then wooden Feodor Gousev. The idea of sending Hopkins to visit Moscow in 1941, incidentally, originated with Winant and Maisky.[37]

The Ambassador attended only one of the conferences featuring the Big Three: Tehran, 27 November–1 December 1943. There, Winant met with the young shah, Mohammad Reza Pahlavi. On the eve of the conference, Winant also briefed General George Marshall and Admiral Ernest King on British thoughts concerning a range of questions: the possibility of Turkey joining the Allies, the bombing campaign against German cities, Overlord's timing, prospects for softening Germany and stretching its resources thin before commencing the final kill.[38] Winant was not, however, involved in the main Tehran conversations around the pending invasion of Western Europe, or Soviet pledges to join against Japan after Germany's defeat, or Polish matters. He later conferred with FDR in Egypt after the Yalta conference (February 1945) and expressed concern that the Grand Alliance might fracture over problems related to post-hostilities Germany, a topic then under review by the European Advisory Commission (EAC).[39]

The commission's main charge, mandated by the 1943 foreign ministers conference in Moscow, was to anticipate the Third Reich's surrender and devise methods and machinery to effect it. The EAC met in London's Lancaster House from mid-January 1944 to August 1945. The adroit Sir William Strang headed the British delegation, Gousev the Soviet. Winant led the American group. It numbered George Kennan (until detailed to Moscow in spring 1944), Brigadier Generals Cornelius Wickersham and Vincent Meyer, and Professor Philip Mosely. A French delegation, headed by the capable René Massigli, joined the EAC deliberations in November 1944.

The commission recommended the separation of Austria from Germany, plus the partition of each country into three zones of occupation, each governed by one of the conquering powers (amended by agreement at Yalta to provide for French control zones). Berlin and Vienna were likewise to be split and administered. An Allied Control Council was also proposed for Germany – similar ones for Austria and Italy – that should act consensually (originally applied to the UK, USSR and USA but then revised to include France). The EAC sought also to refine guidelines for Germany's 'unconditional surrender'.

Post-war criticisms of the commission focused on its vagueness about the duration and nature of occupation in Germany. This imprecision fostered varying Allied policies (e.g., on reparations, denazification) and two antagonistic Germanies, each with rival Cold War patrons. Divided Berlin also congealed into two entities to become a Cold War flashpoint.[40] Unlike Strang, Winant did not live long enough after the war to have to defend the EAC, but he suffered monumentally at the time from his role in the work.[41] Neither FDR, Hull nor their successors (Harry Truman, Edward Stettinius, James Brynes) provided guidance or evinced strong interest in the EAC negotiations, a third-tier operation according to Roosevelt.[42]

Winant came to fear that future Anglo-Soviet-US relations would be wholly undermined by FDR's indifference to the commission's enterprise. Making matters worse, the War Department, especially in the person of Assistant Secretary John McCloy, was unobliging. It had ideas of its own on the proper organisation of new Germany that ran against long-term EAC coordination.[43] They aimed at the retention of flexibility, prerogative, and initiative by military officers in the US zone.[44] Uncertainty about whether the punitive 'Morgenthau plan' was taken seriously by FDR contributed to the US delegation's hesitancy of manner. Winant, for one, thought this proposal both grotesque and unworkable. Meantime, the Soviets proved alternately obstinate or simply unresponsive.

The American delegation was hardly a model of unity or finesse. Winant's administrative ineptitude came crashing to the fore. He was periodically overwhelmed or ill-prepared, a sorry contrast with the efficient British. Kennan, whom he judged 'invaluable', was lost to the US Embassy in Moscow. Mosely held some views uncomfortably close to the War Department's; he was dismayed by Winant's unwillingness to secure guaranteed Anglo-US access routes to Berlin. The American group floundered. Execution of Winant's last important wartime task, in short, was botched from start to finish.[45]

Evaluation

Three discrete stages marked Anglo-US relations in 1938–1945. The first coincided with the close of what W. H. Auden aptly labelled 'this low dishonest decade'. Roosevelt, while tilting toward the Allies, adopted a policy of neutrality from the 1938 Munich meeting to France's capitulation. The United States was technically not a belligerent in the second stage, June 1940 to December 1941. Yet the administration pursued a policy toward Britain of benevolent neutrality, underscored by Lend-Lease and an undeclared naval war against Germany. The third stage, from Pearl Harbor onward, was one of full-blown alliance. Difficulty dogged Anglo-US relations throughout these periods, as shown by the vicissitudes of ambassadorial careers in London. Kennedy had momentary success before proving an irritant, then a liability. Winant's tenure was also marked by friction, notwithstanding extensive Anglo-US 'teamwork'. The crux of the matter lay with the waning of British power and prerogative and surging American might, realities that fit awkwardly in Churchill's consoling mythology rooted in a 'special relationship'.[46]

Like FDR, who needled Churchill on British rule in India, Winant never hesitated to take aim against imperialism. He enjoyed pronouncing solemnly on the imminent demise of colonialism everywhere. He insisted to British interlocutors that the maintenance of their far-flung empire troubled Americans (who, nevertheless, without compunction, and insensible to their own unreflecting hegemonial purpose, took over Caribbean bits of the receding empire in compensation for 50 old destroyers). He lectured an agitated gathering at the Royal Empire Society in July 1942, just as Gandhi was preparing to launch his *Quit India* campaign: 'We [Americans] have [little] in common with your colonial empire. A careful survey of public opinion in the United States showed there was a greater divergence of viewpoint on British colonial policy than on any other subject that divided us.'[47] In line with aroused Irish-American feeling, from Boston to San Francisco, Winant pressed FDR's preference upon Churchill regarding Northern Ireland: the six provinces should be exempt from conscription.

In another demonstration of cracks in the special relationship, an embarrassed Winant delivered to Churchill in November 1944 a proposal on arranging future international civil aviation routes that baldly advantaged the United States over Britain. Bundled with it were intimations that London's rejection would trigger reductions of Lend-Lease aid. Churchill's private secretary, John Colville, called the idea 'pure blackmail'.[48] Still, it was not allowed to disrupt cordiality with Winant. Like his jabs against empire or his Northern Ireland meddling or his defence of the Eisenhower-Darlan accord, the civil aviation proposal did not count against him. His unusual standing insulated him from the resentment and barbs that rained upon his predecessor.[49]

Whereas the war embittered Kennedy and led to his recommending in the 1950s that Americans should renounce global activism, the London experience of Winant fortified his confidence in internationalism. He had not only looked hopefully toward post-war Anglo-US collaboration with the Soviet Union, but he had also urged that modalities be devised to harness atomic science to benefit all nations. He was, consequently, upset by Churchill's 1946 'iron curtain' gloominess, the Grand Alliance's disintegration, and rising Moscow-Washington acrimony. Never without ambition, he hoped to win appointment as Secretary General of the United Nations, from which perch he might foster the peace cause. Such an appointment, though, was never realistically in the offing. Roosevelt had toyed with the idea of making Winant his vice-presidential running mate in 1944 and briefly considered him for a cabinet post, perhaps to head the State Department (after Cordell Hull) or the Labor Department (if vacated by Frances Perkins).[50] Bypassed by FDR, Winant stood no chance of favour from Truman. He preferred tougher diplomats than 'Utopian John', whose intellectual reflexes seemed suspiciously like those of Henry Wallace.[51] Hence Truman's April 1946 appointment of Harriman, who had no illusions about the developing East–West dispute, to the Court of St James's.

Winant had been enervated by his London duties and rattled by blackening premonitions. Nervous fatigue swept him. Outbursts of uncontrollable rage shook him, directed, most uncharacteristically, at his subordinates. All of this misfortune was compounded by bursitis, drinking problems, continuing unhappiness in marriage (aggravated by extramarital tugs), and financial distress with indebtedness around $750,000 by 1947.[52] He spoke with confidants about the purported wisdom of suicide.

Winant nevertheless tried to find constructive release as US representative to the United Nations Economic and Social Council, an assignment from which he resigned in despondency as Cold War quarrels swamped the agency's usefulness. He served as chair of the Fourteenth Annual Brotherhood Week in 1947, then wrote his wartime memoirs, finishing one of two-projected volumes.[53] He played a small part in trying to foster Jewish–Christian reconciliation.

Ultimately nothing calmed him. His personality unravelled in cascading self-recriminations and despair. He ended his life with a pistol shot to the right temple on 3 November 1947 in his New Hampshire home. He was essentially, as a few observers noted at the time, a casualty of the war and of the dismal peace that followed.[54]

Winant had received numerous British tributes plus honorary degrees from universities, among them Oxford and Cambridge in autumn 1945. King George awarded him the Order of Merit in 1947 in a ceremony at Buckingham Palace.[55] His most handsome recognition, he might have judged, was given posthumously and meant to perpetuate his memory. Winant House was opened in London on 5 July 1951. British and American benefactors established this safe haven (a dozen apartments of varying size) for impecunious elders and young couples. The housing stock in London at the time was woefully inadequate, not recovered from the destruction wreaked by Luftwaffe bombers or V-1 and V-2 rockets. Families in need of accommodation on the waiting list of the London County Council numbered 207,000, of which more than 60,000 constituted emergency cases.[56]

Ten years before the doors of Winant House were officially opened, nearly to the day, the Ambassador had visited a shelter (Abingdon House) for homeless men in the desolate area of London's bombed dockland. He had conversed with the residents. He had taken tea with them. He had inspected their quarters and played games. The shyness of these men, their inarticulateness and elusiveness, Winant's own traits, did not inhibit them from cheering when time came for leave-taking.[57] The impression made at Abingdon and places like it stamped him. He had never faltered in his 'faith', as he phrased it to FDR, 'in the common people of England'.[58]

Notes

1. Winant was appointed ambassador on 11 February 1941. He presented his credentials on 1 March 1941. His appointment terminated on 10 April 1946.
2. Farewell Dinner to Mr J. G. Winant at Lancaster House, 23 April 1946, p. 2, Box 196, John Winant Papers, FDRL.
3. Bernard Bellush, *He Walked Alone: A Biography of John Gilbert Winant* (The Hague: Mouton, 1968), p. 118.
4. *Ibid.*, pp. 41–50.
5. Lynne Olson, *Citizens of London: The Americans Who Stood with Britain in its Darkest, Finest Hour* (New York: Random House, 2010), pp. 13–14. Constance Winant raised show dogs. She enjoyed horse races, shopping expeditions, and luxury spas. Her husband was censorious on the subject of her gambling.
6. Leon Anderson, untitled 'sketch' of John Gilbert Winant, 15 January 1970, John Winant Papers, New Hampshire Historical Society (NHHS). For an unflattering view of Winant in Geneva, see Geoffrey Partington, 'John Gilbert Winant at Geneva: The Testimony of Sir Walter Crocker', *National Observer*, Spring 2003.
7. Entry of 15 February 1941, Fred Israel (ed.), *The War Diary of Breckinridge Long: Selections from the Years 1939–1944* (Lincoln, NE: University of Nebraska Press, 1966), p. 181; Mr R. Butler, Minute, 23 January 1941, FO371/26224 (File 409), Foreign Office Records, National Archives, London (NAL); W. Averell Harriman and Elie Abel, *Special Envoy to Churchill and Stalin 1941–1946* (New York: Random House, 1975), p. 5; David Reynolds, *From World War to Cold War: Churchill, Roosevelt, and the International History of the 1940s*, (Oxford: Oxford University Press, 2007), pp. 150–62.
8. John Winant, *Our Greatest Harvest: Selected Speeches* (London: Hodder & Stoughton, 1950), p. 58.
9. Robert Sherwood, *Roosevelt and Hopkins: An Intimate History* (New York: Harper & Brothers, 1948), pp. 839–40; Farewell dinner to Mr J. G. Winant at Lancaster House, p. 4, 23 April 1946, Box 196, John Winant Papers, FDRL.
10. Charles Rumford Walker, 'Winant of New Hampshire', *The Atlantic*, May 1941, p. 553.
11. Winant, *Our Greatest Harvest*, p. 4.
12. Bert Whittemore, 'A Quiet Triumph: The Mission of John Gilbert Winant to London, 1941', *Historical New Hampshire*, Spring 1975, p. 7.
13. Nigel Nicolson (ed.), *Harold Nicolson: Diaries and Letters 1939–1945* (London: Collins, 1967), pp. 186, 263.
14. John Colville, *The Fringes of Power: 10 Downing Street Diaries 1939–1955* (New York: W. W. Norton & Co., 1985), pp. 372, 773; Bellush, *He Walked Alone*, pp. 168, 180; John Winant, *Letter from Grosvenor Square: An Account of a Stewardship* (Boston: Houghton Mifflin, 1947), pp. 61–62; Ethel Johnson, 'The Mr. Winant I Knew', *South Atlantic Quarterly*, January 1949, p. 37; Farewell dinner to Mr J. G. Winant at Lancaster House, p. 2, 23 April 1946, Box 196, John Winant Papers, FDRL.
15. Mr T. North Whitehead, Minute, 22 January 1941 and Mr R. Butler, Minute, 23 January 1941, FO371/26224 (File 409), Foreign Office Records, NAL.
16. Interview of Winston Churchill, p. 2, 4 July 1951, Box 1, interview of Virginia Crawley, p. 4, 3 July 1951, interview of Anthony Eden, pp. 15–17, 7 and 8 July 1951, Box 2, Bernard Bellush Papers, FDRL; Johnson, 'The Mr. Winant I Knew', p. 38; Winant, *Letter from Grosvenor Square*, pp. 92, 96–7; Bellush, *He Walked Alone*, p. 178; David Reynolds, *In Command of History: Churchill Fighting and Writing the*

Second World War (New York: Random House, 2005), pp. 263–4. Winant's son John survived German prison and the war. A younger son, Rivington, survived tours with the Marine Corps in Pacific combat.

17. Edward R. Murrow to Winant, 10 November 1941, Box 209, John Winant Papers, FDRL; A. M. Sperber, *Murrow: His Life and Times* (New York: Freudlich Books, 1986), p. 189; entries of 14 April and 3 August 1941, James Leutze (ed.), *The London Journal of General Raymond E. Lee 1940–1941* (Boston: Little, Brown & Co., 1971), pp. 241, 361; Bellush, *He Walked Alone*, p. 166.

18. Notes made from the diary of Maurine Mulliner, p. 3, Box 7, Bernard Bellush Papers, FDRL. Also Winant to Howard Braucher, 12 November 1941, Box 186, John Winant Papers, FDRL.

19. Robert St. John to NBC, 15 January 1943, John Winant Papers, NHHS.

20. Lend-Lease, enacted by Congress in March 1941, did ultimately provide tangible aid, valued between $21 and $25 billion, to the British Empire. See Reynolds, *From World War to Cold War*, p. 109; I. C. B. Dear and M. R. D. Foots (eds.), *The Oxford Companion to World War II* (Oxford: Oxford University Press, 1995), p. 680.

21. Winant, *Our Greatest Harvest*, pp. 56–7.

22. *Ibid.*, pp. 26–7, 102–3; Ivan Maisky, *Memoirs of a Soviet Ambassador* (New York: Charles Scribner's Sons, 1968), p. 214; Reynolds, *From World War to Cold War*, pp. 187–8.

23. Winant, *Our Greatest Harvest*, p. 198; Bellush, *He Walked Alone*, p. 163.

24. Colville, *The Fringes of Power*, pp. 434–43; entry of 29 August 1941, Leutze, *The London Journal of General Raymond E. Lee*, p. 382.

25. Bellush, *He Walked Alone*, p. 173.

26. Olson, *Citizens of London*, pp. 169–70; Sherwood, *Roosevelt and Hopkins*, pp. 269, 311, 919; Rudy Abramson, *Spanning the Century: The Life of W. Averell Harriman, 1891–1986* (New York: William Morrow & Co., 1992), pp. 302–4; Harriman and Abel, *Special Envoy*, p. 26; Entries of 14 and 27 April, 15 and 25 and 30 July, 29 August 1941 in Leutze, *The London Journal of General Raymond E. Lee*, pp. 241, 259, 340, 353, 359, 382; Bellush, *He Walked Alone*, p. 175; interview of Virginia Crawley, 3 July 1951, pp. 7–8, Box 2, Bernard Bellush Papers, FDRL.

27. Winant to Hopkins, 16 October 1943, Box 257, Harry Hopkins Papers, FDRL; memorandum, 9 August 1943, Secretary of State, Northern Department, FO371/34121, Foreign Office Records, NAL; Sherwood, *Roosevelt and Hopkins*, pp. 754–6.

28. Interview of Winston Churchill, p. 1, 4 July 1951, Box 1, Bernard Bellush Papers, FDRL.

29. Churchill to FDR, 1 April 1942, Warren Kimball, *Churchill and Roosevelt: The Complete Correspondence* (Princeton, NJ: Princeton University Press, 1984), Vol. I, p. 439.

30. William Phillips to FDR, 13 August 1942, Box 38, PSF, Franklin Roosevelt Papers, FDRL; General George Marshall to FDR, 9 September 1942 and FDR to John Winant, 10 September 1941, Box 38, PSF, Franklin Roosevelt Papers, FDRL; Paul Kellogg to Winant, 16 May 1944, Box 211, John Winant Papers, FDRL; Henry Morgenthau to Winant, 19 August 1944, Box 209, John Winant Papers, FDRL; interview of General Dwight Eisenhower, 8 August 1951, p. 2, Box 2, Bernard Bellush Papers, FDRL; Leutze, *The London Journal of General Raymond E. Lee*, p. 338; Olson; *Citizens of London*, pp. 288–9; Bellush, *He Walked Alone*, p. 215.

31. John Winant, 'How Britain Controls Its Manpower', *The Atlantic*, May 1942, p. 63.

32. Article for American Red Cross Booklet to be Given to American Soldiers and Sailors in the British Isles, 6 June 1942, Box 181, John Winant Papers, FDRL.
33. Frances Perkins to Winant, 8 December 1944 and Winant to Perkins, 16 January 1945, Box 214, John Winant Papers, FDRL.
34. Martin Gilbert, *Churchill and America* (New York: Free Press, 2005), p. 345; Eleanor Roosevelt, *This I Remember* (New York: Harper, 1949), p. 266.
35. Winant to Hopkins, 16 October 1943, Box 257, Harry Hopkins Papers, FDRL.
36. Churchill to FDR, 4 June 1942, Kimball, *Churchill and Roosevelt*, Vol. I, p. 505; also see pp. 393–4.
37. Winant, *Letter from Grosvenor Square*, pp. 207–9; Maisky, *Memoirs of a Soviet Ambassador*, pp. 180–1, 268; Bellush, *He Walked Alone*, pp. 189–90; Warren Kimball, *Forged in War: Roosevelt, Churchill, and the Second World War* (New York: William Morrow & Co., 1997), p. 223.
38. *Foreign Relations of the United States: The Conferences at Cairo and Tehran 1943* (Washington: Government Printing Office, series), pp. 301–3 (hereafter *FRUS*).
39. Winant to John McCloy, 24 February 1945, Box 195, John Winant Papers, FDRL.
40. Robert Murphy, *Diplomat among Warriors* (Garden City, NY: Doubleday, 1964), pp. 230–3.
41. Lord William Strang, *Home and Abroad* (London: Andre Deutsch, 1956), pp. 205, 225.
42. *FRUS 1944*, Vol. III, pp. 3–6; *FRUS: The Conferences at Cairo and Tehran 1943*, pp. 883–4; Bellush, *He Walked Alone*, pp. 192, 204.
43. Winant to Hopkins, 19 December 1944, Box 257, Harry Hopkins Papers, FDRL.
44. Winant to FDR, 28 January 1945 and Winant to John McCloy, 24 February 1945, Box 195, John Winant Papers, FDRL.
45. Winant to FDR, 21 January 1944, Box 257, Harry Hopkins Papers, FDRL; Murphy, *Diplomat among Warriors*, p. 232; George Kennan, *Memoirs: 1925–1950* (Boston: Little, Brown & Co., 1967), pp. 164–80; Bellush, *He Walked Alone*, pp. 192–210.
46. Reynolds, *From World War to Cold War*, p. 312.
47. Winant, *Our Greatest Harvest*, p. 65.
48. Colville, *The Fringes of Power*, pp. 391, 528; Gilbert, *Churchill and America*, pp. 318–19.
49. Nicolson, *Harold Nicolson*, p. 263.
50. Alonzo Hamby, *Man of the People: A Life of Harry S. Truman* (New York: Oxford University Press, 1995), p. 280; interview of Anthony Eden, 7 and 8 July 1951, p. 19, Box 2, Bernard Bellush Papers, FDRL; John Allison, *Ambassador from the Prairie or Allison Wonderland* (Boston: Houghton Mifflin, 1973), p. 102; Frances Perkins, *The Roosevelt I Knew* (New York: Viking Press, 1946), p. 392.
51. Winant and Truman met only once, briefly and informally, while FDR was still alive. Winant had hoped to meet Truman at the time of the Potsdam conference. Winant's request for such a meeting with the President either went unanswered or, more likely, was simply refused. See Roger Tubby to Alvin Knepper, 23 December 1952, Box 1359, Official File and John Winant to Truman, 13 June 1945, Box 9, Naval Aide File, Papers of Harry Truman, Harry Truman Presidential Library.
52. Winant had been in love with Churchill's married daughter Sarah. They conducted a discreet affair during the days of his ambassadorship. He later entertained notions of marrying her, but she failed to go along. See Olson, *Citizens of London*, pp. 113, 370–1, 385. Maurine Mulliner was a devoted friend of Winant and special assistant. Perhaps they too were romantically attracted to each other.

See suggestive Notes from the Diary of Mulliner, Box 7, Bernard Bellush Papers, FDRL.

53. John Winant, 'Fundamental Freedoms', *Conference: The Magazine of Human Relations*, Winter 1947, p. 5.
54. Louis Fischer, 'John G. Winant: Casualty of the Peace', *The Saturday Review*, 6 December 1947, p. 21; editorial by James Langley, *Concord Monitor* (New Hampshire), 4 November 1947; Sperber, *Murrow: His Life and Times*, p. 298.
55. Bellush, *He Walked Alone*, pp. 227–8.
56. Speech by Robert Sherwood at dedication of Winant House in London, 5 July 1951, item 2237, Robert Sherwood Papers, Houghton Library, Harvard University; Dedication and Presentation of Winant House (pamphlet), 5 July 1951, Box 7, Bernard Bellush Papers, FDRL.
57. The Anglo-American Committee for War Refugees in Great Britain to Lady Abingdon, 30 June 1941, John Winant Papers, NHHS.
58. Winant to FDR, 17 October 1942, Box 38, PSF, Franklin Roosevelt Papers, FDRL.

3
W. Averell Harriman, 1946

Martin H. Folly

Averell Harriman's term as Ambassador to London lasted barely six months. Harriman's long and prominent career in US foreign policy has been extensively discussed, but invariably little is said of his term as Ambassador in London, beyond the circumstances of his appointment and of his resignation.[1] Anglo-American relations were going through a period of change and tension, but the impression is given that Harriman, for once, was on the periphery, and that he was of no consequence in these developments. This chapter will, for the first time, explore this neglected period in Harriman's career.

The Expediter

Averell Harriman both inherited wealth – his father, E. H. Harriman was a railroad tycoon – and made millions himself as an investment banker and venture capitalist.[2] He was a fully paid up member of the 'east-coast establishment' and was comfortable with the polo-playing, Ivy League set and the wealthy upper class who were his neighbours in the Hudson Valley in New York state.[3] The instincts of his class were, by default, conservative, but the progressive tradition was not alien and neither was the tradition of combining public service with the continued pursuit of wealth in private enterprise. Harriman became a supporter of Franklin D. Roosevelt's interventionist, activist style of government, and was a national officer of the National Recovery Administration (NRA) until it was declared unconstitutional by the Supreme Court in 1935. He returned to his business career with the demise of the NRA, but served as head of the Business Council from 1937 to 1939. The Council was one of Roosevelt's major links to the business community.

Harriman was eager to participate in US mobilisation efforts in 1940 and successfully pushed himself forward, becoming Chief of the Materials Branch and Production Division in the Office of Production Management (OPM) in early 1941.[4] Harriman became concerned that a German hegemony of Europe would soon extend to South America, with disastrous effects on American commerce and national security. When, at the start of January 1941, Harry Hopkins was sent on a mission to Britain to discuss aid, Harriman begged to go too, pleading a previous acquaintance with Winston Churchill and with Britain. The Hopkins mission was deliberately kept very low-key to avoid negative public reactions and Harriman was refused. Harriman did make sure he was present to greet Hopkins when he returned, along with newly appointed Ambassador to London, John Gilbert Winant (who had more business being there).

The ploy of putting himself forward in this way worked, for he was called to see Roosevelt, who offered him the job of special liaison in London.[5] Harriman's discontent with OPM and Roosevelt's own preference for parallel bureaucratic structures meant that Harriman was to be independent of both OPM and the State Department, reporting directly to Hopkins and the White House. Within weeks of his appointment, therefore, Winant, the Ambassador, had been effectively undermined. There is no doubt that Harriman, despite Roosevelt's own vagueness about the scope of the role, saw himself as no less than the direct point of contact between Churchill and Roosevelt. Harriman could not have been closer to the heart of matters and, as he preferred, connected to power not by organisational structures but by personal connections. Roosevelt invented the title of 'defence expediter' for him and told the press when asked whether Harriman would report direct or through Winant, 'I don't know and I don't give a damn, you know.'[6]

This effectively set the pattern for Harriman's tour of duty in London. The 'expediter' acted independently of the London Embassy, though operating out of an office in 3 Grosvenor Square, adjoining the official Grosvenor Square residency. He was assiduous in developing contacts with those at the heart of power, and by making his home at the Dorchester hotel, made sure that he was physically in close contact with the British elite.[7] Of his relationship with the Ambassador, Harriman told Roosevelt 'we are working together as one team': the truth was far from that. Harriman interfered in matters unconnected with Lend-Lease, played host to American visitors and diligently cultivated Churchill.[8]

Harriman came to London with a strong belief that the United States should be more active in its support of Britain, and that it should identify Britain's cause as its own. While Harriman was not always kept well informed by Washington, Churchill took him up closely, in the belief that the expediter had a direct channel to Roosevelt. He became, as Churchill undoubtedly intended, a keen advocate of the British cause to Washington. Churchill may, though, have over-estimated Harriman's position in the administration. Roosevelt had many informal advisors, and Harriman was not of the very inner circle, despite his good relationship with Hopkins. Harriman, eager to be involved, voluntarily became part of the British hierarchy instead. He was shown everything, given maximum security clearance and treated by Churchill virtually as a member of his extended family – though he was unaware that his American friend was having an affair with his daughter-in-law, Pamela Digby Churchill.

This cherished position of Harriman's came under threat in 1943. The US Embassy in Moscow had been a problem for some time. The Ambassador, Admiral William Standley, had suffered in the same way as Winant, only more intensely. A succession of special envoys, including Harriman himself, had gained access to the Soviet leadership when it was denied to the regular ambassador, who was regarded by the Soviets as a gatherer of intelligence and therefore to be kept at arm's length. Indeed, Standley had noted in 1942 that Harriman, who had come to Moscow with Churchill, was self-important and insensitive.[9] The Lend-Lease organisation in Moscow was a thorn in the Ambassador's side as it was for the Ambassador in London. Standley finally lost his patience in a press conference and expressed his discontent at his treatment and at Soviet ingratitude for Allied aid. While many in Washington sympathised with the sentiment, he had to be relieved.[10] Secretary of State Cordell Hull at first wished to send Hopkins, but poor health ruled him out. Hull turned then to Harriman who had been approached in 1941 but had replied that he had no wish to be a simple messenger.[11] Harriman's own experience side-lining ambassadors no doubt influenced his desire to avoid the potential trap of such a post, bogged down in day-to-day minutiae, beholden to the Secretary of State and probably blind-sided by the President's preference for working through special envoys and informal channels. However, Roosevelt appealed to his ego by emphasising the importance of the posting.[12] Harriman argued that he was of more use in London than as a 'glorified communications officer' in Moscow, but he could not resist the blandishments of Hopkins and Roosevelt and he duly agreed to become Ambassador at Moscow in August 1943, taking up his post on 18 October.[13]

Harriman did insist on a reorganisation of US representation in Moscow, so that it was clear who was in charge. He also asked for an expert on the USSR to help with the business of political analysis: his first choice was Charles 'Chip' Bohlen. When Bohlen could not be released from his post as liaison to the White House, Harriman was given George Kennan instead.[14]

A 'Glorified Communications Officer'

This is not the place for a detailed account of Harriman's ambassadorship at Moscow: it has been much discussed elsewhere.[15] Harriman was at pains at the start to ensure he was not simply the mouthpiece of the State Department. He kept lines of communication open to General George Marshall, the Army Chief of Staff, and into the White House via Hopkins. Although that link declined when Hopkins' ill-health precipitated his move out of the White House in 1944, Harriman's connections (including with the British government) kept him at least on the fringes of the inner circle. He attended the major conferences attempting, as before, to act as a fixer and a link-man. Harriman regarded his business background as equipping him for this role, making him a calm, pragmatic negotiator with a readiness to deal with the realities of varied positions held by protagonists and to accept the force of self-interest, while seeing how it could be managed and satisfied.

Harriman was not a deep theoretical analyst or philosophical thinker.[16] He did formulate his own view of the motivations and direction of Soviet foreign policy and the optimum way to handle it. This view developed over time, under the influence of Kennan and of the difficulties of life for a foreign diplomat in Moscow. He was proud of the fact that he had more personal meetings with Stalin than any other American, and his belief in the efficacy of his own personal diplomacy gave his views a particular slant that kept them from being merely a recitation of those of the eloquent Kennan. Thus, when involved in negotiations, Harriman adopted flexible positions and took into account the views of the other side – as he had done with the British, so he did with the Soviets.[17]

As an ambassador, he attracted the loyalty of his subordinates, if also the frustration of the more theoretically minded, like Kennan, for his lack of interest in grappling with deep analysis of the USSR. There were few public duties and this fitted Harriman's tastes. Otherwise, like most foreign diplomats, he grew frustrated with the petty restrictions imposed by the watchful and suspicious Soviets. He continued to aspire to the role of 'fixer', as his secretary Robert Meiklejohn observed, and contrived to attend all the major summit meetings.[18] He served with the British Ambassador, Sir Archibald Clark Kerr, on the Moscow committee on the reorganisation of the Polish government following the Yalta conference, and later in the year, on a commission to Romania.[19] Both were exercises in frustration as the Soviets took positions from which they would not budge, showing no desire for the kind of compromises necessary for cooperation.

The conclusions he developed during the first year of his ambassadorship have led to his being characterised as a hard-line anti-Soviet thinker, but this is a misrepresentation. Harriman came to believe that Soviet policy could be influenced by American actions: that they respected firmness and a decisive and clear defence of US interests, but were suspicious of goodwill gestures. The USSR was a potential bully – but, like all bullies, would respond to firm treatment. While such language appealed to many in the State Department and the military, and, after Roosevelt's death on 12 April 1945, to the new President, Harry S. Truman, Harriman quickly lost influence once James F. Byrnes became Secretary of State.[20] He became determined to leave Moscow, and resigned in December 1945.

The Posting to London

Harriman was initially very reluctant to take on the ambassadorship in London. He had resigned from the Moscow Embassy at least partly because he disliked working with Byrnes, who had not shown Harriman the respect that he thought he was due during the Potsdam conference in the summer of 1945, effectively keeping the Ambassador on the sidelines.[21] Harriman was not accustomed to being in such a position. On Roosevelt's death, he had made an immediate attempt to place himself at the centre of policy-making, by flying back to Washington DC to try and persuade the new President, Harry S. Truman, of the wisdom of the policy that he had been recommending towards the USSR. Byrnes, however, made a concerted effort to run foreign policy himself, pushing aside those who had been important advisors to Roosevelt, such as Admiral William Leahy, as well as Harriman.

Harriman was not in any sense a career diplomat – or even public servant – and he left Moscow in January 1946 not so much for a rest as to return to his business activities.[22] When he got word that he was to be offered the London posting, his instinct was to refuse it for these reasons – and also because he feared it would be largely ceremonial. For him, a regular ambassadorial post implied a messenger role quite at odds with his own sense of self and the qualities he believed he possessed. Harriman wished to be an insider, but one free to act flexibly, to be a fixer and 'go-between' and deploy his talents as a reasoned intermediary. For all his ostensible desire to return to private life, Harriman remained attracted to the idea of being at the centre of power. He also felt, as a result of his years in Moscow and unmatched experience of dealing with the USSR, that he had vital insight to impart to policy-makers, and, in the uncertain state of US–Soviet relations, a mission to ensure that US policy was based on being open-eyed towards what he saw as the dangers of certain aspects of Soviet policy. He was determined, therefore, to resist the suggestion by Byrnes in March that he go to London.

Harriman's resolve was broken, however, by the fact that Truman himself pressed him to go. When they met at the White House, Truman explained that he feared that relations with the USSR were going to reach crisis point: indeed, there are some accounts that Truman said 'We may be at war with the Soviet Union over Iran.'[23] Harriman's own recollection was that Truman was anxious that it was the British, who were involved in the Iranian issue by formal treaty, who would be the ones dragged into war.[24] Truman argued that he needed a man in London who he could depend upon and who had knowledge of both the British and the Soviets. Thus, while Harriman was to be a regular ambassador, not a 'special envoy', Truman strongly implied that Harriman's mission would be limited to the duration of the crisis, and that he was being sent to act as a 'fixer' between Britain and the USSR. On that basis, Harriman felt he could not refuse.[25] There was always, of course, the mitigating factor that he would be able to renew contact with Pamela Churchill. Whether it was because of this personal factor, or the urgency of getting to London to handle the Iran crisis, Harriman left for London immediately after he was sworn in, catching Winant unprepared and leading to some confusion.[26]

As it turned out, by the time Harriman arrived in London on 21 April, the Iranian crisis was close to resolution, with Stalin backing down from confrontation when it was clear that the Iranian government was holding firm against his demands.[27] Soviet forces left the country in early May.[28] Despite Truman's informal undertaking, Harriman now found himself the regular ambassador, ensconced at Grosvenor Square and with an indefinite period of service ahead of him. He would now have to undertake the full range of public diplomacy duties that fell to an ambassador, which he had not had to perform either as Lend-Lease expediter nor as ambassador at Moscow. Such duties did not appeal to him.[29] He found it 'rather a hectic job', and complained to James Forrestal, 'This job is much more work than I thought it would be, partially because of the many Americans, both government and private, that I have to see and look after.'[30] Harriman was not equipped with the all-round skills ideally sought in an ambassador. He had earned the nickname 'the Crocodile' because of the way his habitually drowsy and plodding manner could suddenly give way to sharp action. As an ambassador, he was not a deep analyst, nor was he interested in extensive reportage: he saw his role as a facilitator and problem-solver.[31] He was certainly possessed of the social skills to make the necessary impression in public diplomacy. He was urbane and charming. He was always immaculately dressed (the contrast to Winant was noted).[32] He was, however, not a natural conversationalist, and was a wooden public speaker. However, his great asset was his reputation as a friend of Great Britain and a wartime comrade of Churchill and Roosevelt. His coming was widely welcomed. It was mis-read as an indication of the importance Truman attached to Anglo-American relations, and as a sign of generous American economic intentions towards Britain, given Harriman's association with Lend-Lease.[33]

Harriman avoided encouraging this tendency. In his early speeches he emphasised American commitment to close relations with Britain, calling up wartime memories of the Supreme Headquarters, Allied Expeditionary Force (SHAEF). He also, however, was at pains to say that the US was committed to the United Nations, and therefore that its relations with Britain were not exclusive. In this way he avoided associating himself with Churchill's recent plea in his 'iron curtain' speech at Fulton, Missouri, for the rebuilding of an Anglo-American special relationship. He stated that Americans could not be 'prosperity isolationists' but the US also needed to avoid the two extremes of being 'an international Santa Claus' or of interfering in other people's affairs. The US, he said, needed world prosperity and security in order to achieve these for itself.[34]

Anglo-American relations were going through difficult times. The closeness of the wartime relationship had quickly dissipated. The glue of closely intertwined military operations had been removed. Moreover, the US was engaged in rapid demobilisation. It was also involved in reverting to peacetime economic activities, which meant, if business was continued as usual, that Britain was now an economic rival. While the American public and Congress had embraced internationalism so far as supporting US membership in the United Nations, isolationism had not disappeared, but took the form of economic nationalism and fiscal conservatism. With Britain no longer a partner in war, visceral anti-British feelings in the US could re-emerge. There was hostility to British imperialism, and concern about the socialist intentions of Britain's new Labour government. While there were growing suspicions of the aims of the USSR, the same applied to Britain. This was reflected in the long and bitter debate in Congress on the passage of a loan to Britain. Lend-Lease aid had ceased immediately at the end of the war, throwing British reconstruction plans into disarray. Economic conditions, with this aid removed, deteriorated sharply. Rationing of food and clothing increased.[35] When a team headed by the economist Lord Keynes arrived in Washington, they found American officials drove a hard bargain, in terms of the conditions attached to a $3.75 billion loan. There was no choice but to accept. There then followed long congressional debates, where strong anti-British feelings were on show.[36] The loan was not approved until after Harriman arrived in London but left a bitter taste in the mouth. The Senate voted in favour of it 46–34 on 10 May 1946, and the House of Representatives followed suit by only 219–155 on 13 July.[37] In the House of Commons, 100 MPs rejected the deal and 169 abstained. Foreign Secretary Ernest Bevin said he hated the loan, but there was no alternative.[38] While still in Moscow, Harriman summed up Britain's state of dependency on the US, telling staff that the British government 'could ill afford an independent foreign policy in spite of Bevin's distaste for Byrnes and his high-handed measures . . . England is so weak she must follow our leadership. She will do anything that we insist upon and she won't go out on a limb alone.'[39]

The combined committees that had integrated the Anglo-American war effort were all wound down, except the Combined Chiefs of Staff, which maintained a shadow existence, meeting rarely. The short-term impact of Churchill's Fulton speech was negative, stoking the suspicions of isolationists in Congress, but it was observed by the British Embassy in Washington that anti-Soviet feelings, and the perception of Britain as a partner in standing up to the USSR, undoubtedly swayed congressional opinion in favour of the loan.[40]

In the summer of 1946, however, the process by which Britain and the United States became Cold War allies was still very much in its early stages. Byrnes had tried various strategies to make progress with the USSR, and had made little attempt to coordinate policies with the British. While Truman had famously told him he was 'tired of babying the Soviets', there was still a sense at the time of the Iran crisis that it was really a matter between Britain and the USSR, from which the US was somewhat detached, though running the risk, as Truman intimated to Harriman, of being dragged in.[41] Byrnes, however, was now hardening his stance as illustrated by his handling of the Iran situation, and then in the Council of Foreign Ministers (CFM) in Paris in May. Bevin had already been engaged in some bitter arguments with his Soviet counterpart, Vyacheslav Molotov, though, like Byrnes at this time, still clung to the hope that the USSR might still see it had an interest in reaching compromise agreements over the issues that divided them: notably the economic arrangements for occupied Germany and Austria, the future political structure of Germany and peace treaties with the other defeated Axis powers in Europe: Italy, Finland, Romania, Bulgaria and Hungary.[42]

These issues made it a lively and dynamic period of Anglo-American relations, but, as Harriman feared, the Grosvenor Square Embassy was something of a backwater in these matters of great moment. They were being decided either in Washington, with the loan negotiations, or in meetings in Paris. Harriman's self-defined specialism on the USSR was to be rarely called upon while he was in London. After the end of the Iran crisis and an initial conversation with the Foreign Office's chief official concerned with relations with the USSR, Christopher Warner, Harriman's thoughts on the Soviet Union were most commonly in demand for lectures and speeches to organisations like the Staff College at Camberley.[43] As it turned out, as we will see below, the main issue on which Harriman was called to make a contribution was Palestine, a significant and divisive element in Anglo-American relations, but one about which he had no claim to specialist knowledge and one which tested his skills as a fixer to the limit.

Harriman at Grosvenor Square

Harriman's relationship with Clement Attlee's Labour government did not reach the level of intimacy he achieved with Churchill. The wartime Prime Minister had deliberately cultivated the relationship as a direct line of connection to Roosevelt. Attlee and Bevin did not follow a similar strategy. Perceiving the importance of relations with congressmen and with the Washington bureaucracy, the emphasis was on conducting relations through their Ambassador in Washington, who was Harriman's former colleague in Moscow, Archie Clark Kerr, now Lord Inverchapel.[44] Moreover, with the CFM in May followed quickly by the Peace Conference in Paris from July to September, which settled treaties with the minor Axis states, Bevin had direct personal contact with Byrnes through much of Harriman's term of duty.

This is not to suggest that Harriman was on bad terms with the Labour government. In spite of his close personal relationship with Churchill, now Leader of the Opposition, there is no evidence that Harriman was cold-shouldered by Bevin nor Attlee. They knew him well from the war period, when both were key members of the Churchill coalition, and while Harriman's predecessor, Winant, was ideologically closer to them and had good connections with the British labour movement, Harriman's service in the New Deal tended to mitigate the effect of his being a millionaire capitalist. From his side, Harriman was happy to accept an invitation to speak at the Durham miners' gala and connect with British working people in a non-political way to balance the more usual appointments with businessmen and chambers of commerce.

Fulfilling this engagement produced a short disagreement with Churchill, reflecting perhaps a somewhat proprietorial attitude on the part of the former Prime Minister towards the Ambassador. Attlee had also spoken at the miners' gala, though on a separate platform. Attlee had sharply attacked the Conservatives, and the newspapers reported his and Harriman's speeches together. Churchill's friend Lord Beaverbrook complained to Harriman that he was meddling in internal British politics by appearing on a platform with the leader of the Labour Party at a political event. Harriman answered him sharply that the gala was non-political and that he had not seen Attlee there at all. He later noted: 'I told Beaverbrook that it would do me untold good with the government and public if Churchill complained that I was in close touch with British Labor.' Churchill let the matter drop.[45]

Harriman's speech to the Durham miners was part of a conscious effort to forge relations with British labour.[46] His labour attaché, Sam Berger, made sure that the Ambassador met leading trade unionists and Labour back-benchers at a series of cocktail parties.[47] While Harriman's tastes and lifestyle made him a natural member of the elite, complete with honorary membership to a number of London clubs, such as the Beefsteak and the Travellers, he had an easy and charming manner with working people and no tendency to put on airs. He genuinely enjoyed, and was moved by, the Durham meeting.[48] He clearly viewed the programme of the Labour government without hostility – indeed even the more radical wing of the party were described by him as like zealous New Dealers, no more.[49] With the leadership, he seems to have been on good terms, if not to the same degree of intimacy that he had enjoyed with Churchill. He did address Attlee as 'Clem', indicating an informal personal relationship.[50] He was on good social terms with Hector McNeil, Bevin's deputy at the Foreign Office.[51]

Harriman thought that there were two main preoccupations of the Attlee government in their relations with the US. There was, first, a passionate desire for military and diplomatic cooperation with the US, albeit accompanied by a fear of American economic power. Second, the British were, Harriman thought, desperately afraid of another US depression that they feared would lead to another world-wide catastrophe. Appraising the government for his friend James Forrestal, Harriman thought its main deficiency was the lack of practical knowledge in the fields of administration and management (areas of course in which Harriman regarded himself as expert). They were biting off more than they could chew in attempting to nationalise the steel industry.[52]

Like most people at the time, Harriman had initially under-rated the self-effacing Attlee, but came to see him as a 'real leader'. He sympathised with Attlee over an issue that arose soon after his arrival in London: the sharing of atomic research. In their first conversation after Harriman's arrival, Attlee expressed bitter feelings about the passage of the McMahon Act (the Atomic Energy Act 1946), which abruptly terminated the Anglo-Canadian-American cooperation that had produced the atomic bomb. Harriman knew from personal experience of the importance of the British contribution in the early stages of the project: he was aware that they had passed over all their knowledge, much of it further advanced than that of the Americans. Now they were debarred from any exchange of information. Britain was determined to be a nuclear power, and the decision by Congress forced the Attlee Cabinet to develop Britain's own bomb, at colossal expense. Harriman did try to help, by getting permission for Lord Portal, controller of production (atomic energy) at the Ministry of Supply, and British atomic scientists, to visit some atomic facilities in the US.[53]

Harriman did not really get the opportunity to forge a close working relationship with Bevin, because the Foreign Secretary was in Paris during most of Harriman's tour of duty. Moreover, most of the meetings that they did have were concerned with Palestine, an issue of considerable Anglo-American tension. There was, however, no animosity between the two, and Harriman seems to have achieved his usual goal of convincing his foreign interlocutor that he was not only sympathetic to their viewpoint, but was actually arguing their case in Washington as part of his preferred role as intermediary-fixer. This was not just an illusion, for in some early reports he did very much incline his view to sympathy with the British – for instance over British food shortages and high American commodity prices. In his opening press conference he had been asked rather aggressively about American abundance, compared to British rationing, and he had said he thought resentment justified. He subsequently reported on the food situation from a distinctly British perspective.[54]

Harriman did not make any attempt to publicly adopt an austere lifestyle himself, as Winant had done during the war. This was most clearly shown in the 4 July party that he hosted. Harriman had moved into 14 Prince's Gate, a sizeable property donated by the banker J. P. Morgan for the Ambassador's use. Winant had lived in a flat in the Embassy in Grosvenor Square and Prince's Gate had been used as a dormitory for female staff. Soon after Harriman took up residence, he resumed cocktail parties there – an important part of public diplomacy, to be sure, and having the advantage for him of allowing him to meet important people collectively rather than individually. This reduced the time he spent on glad-handing and freed him to spend his weekends in the country at Great Enton, a house in Surrey donated rent-free by Robert Sherwood, the playwright, who was a close friend of Harriman and Hopkins.[55] The hospitality at Prince's Gate occasionally attracted snide comments in the press, though the British were by and large so positive towards Harriman that they preferred to dwell on his immaculate dress and continuing good looks (it was often repeated that he was one of the ten most handsome men in the US). However, *Time* magazine could not resist poking fun, printing a gossipy report of the 4 July party, attended by 2,000 guests including Attlee and Deputy Prime Minister Herbert Morrison, and implying that American officials were considerably worse for drink. Harriman was bitter about the report, but it made little dent on his popularity with the British media or public.[56]

Palestine

Harriman continued to take a view inclined towards that of his hosts in his intervention on another Anglo-American issue: the US use of bases on British territory in the Pacific. This was an issue, however, which Bevin preferred to deal with directly with Byrnes.[57] The main Anglo-American matter in which Harriman was involved was the contentious issue of Palestine, rather than the issues of aid to Britain or relations with the USSR, which might be regarded as his areas of expertise. The issue proved too intractable to be susceptible to Harriman's 'fixer' approach of representing and mediating each side's views in his own communications, and this may be the reason why he says nothing of his role in this matter in his memoir – Palestine is not mentioned in the book at all – an omission then repeated in accounts of Harriman's career that mostly depend upon his own account.

Bevin's first meeting with Harriman was to address the Palestine issue, and throughout Harriman's brief tenure the vast majority of his meetings with the Foreign Secretary were concerned with this issue. Much of the time, Harriman was merely delivering messages – as he had always feared – but he also reported British views back to Washington in a tone that makes it seem that he was seeking to get American understanding of the British position. Thus, after his first meeting with Bevin, he wrote to Dean Acheson, acting Secretary of State at the time, 'I hope you will consider the long past history of Great Britain's responsibility for Palestine, and the problem which . . . Bevin and his associates now have to face and deal with.'[58]

The Palestine issue was to replace the loan as a major focus of tension between the US and Britain by the fall of 1946. In the US, the anti-British sentiments expressed during the loan debate were capitalised on by Zionist publicists, who skilfully presented British policy as equivalent to that of the Nazis, as the British sought to deny passage to Palestine to Jewish refugees in Europe and took military action against the Jewish Agency in Palestine. With Jewish voters perceived as a significant bloc, especially in New York, and close contests predicted in the Congressional elections in November, Truman was under domestic political pressure to distance himself from British actions. It is possible that broader strategic aspects were also influential: Britain and the US were competing for influence with the Arab states and a failure to satisfy Arab demands in Palestine could fatally undermine British dominance in the region.[59] As far as the British were concerned, the Palestine mandate, which they had taken up after World War I, had become a burden. The area was regarded by the British military and by Bevin as strategically vital – especially as Egypt was pressing for the withdrawal of British forces from its territory. Britain had made conflicting promises to the Arabs of Palestine and to Jews regarding the future of Palestine. Jewish aspirations for it to be a Jewish state had grown and had much international support after the genocidal actions of the Nazis. The neighbouring Arab states opposed such a move. Prior to the Second World War the British had steered an uneasy path between the two communities in Palestine, pleasing neither and facing increasing militancy from both. The rising significance of oil production in the Middle East, not to mention the spectre of Soviet expansionism raised acutely in the Iran crisis, made the British – and also many in the State Department – anxious not to alienate Arab opinion. Bevin, who took a close interest in the Palestine issue – though matters internal to the territory were under the direction of the Colonial Secretary, George Hall – was eager to associate the US with a Palestine settlement. He felt that US financial aid for Palestine was crucial, and US backing might well sway opinion in the two communities behind it.[60]

A first crucial step in achieving this goal appeared to have been achieved with the formation of an Anglo-American Committee (AAC) on Palestine, which produced its report just as Harriman took up his post in London.[61] One of the recommendations was a proposal that Truman had endorsed in 1945, namely the immediate admission into Palestine of 100,000 Jews from displaced persons camps in Europe.[62] Having identified himself so strongly with this, Truman felt it important to push it through, and pressed for it to be actioned in advance of consideration of the other recommendations in the report. In Washington a Cabinet committee of State, War and Treasury was to be formed to deal with Palestine questions, which would send representatives, headed by Ambassador Henry F. Grady, but Harriman was instructed to proceed immediately with discussions on the 100,000. Thus, Harriman found himself involved in heading an American delegation, assisted by two officials from Washington, to a series of committee meetings with the British, headed by Sir Norman Brook.[63]

These meetings were Harriman's main diplomatic activity through June. In them, differences immediately became clear. The British saw many practical problems with the proposal, and in particular held that the pace of immigration should be shaped by the availability of housing and employment in Palestine. They thought a maximum of 4,000 a month could be moved. The American delegation pointed out that this was less than the number moving into the camps in Germany, Italy and Austria from Eastern Europe.[64] Their initial proposal was 20,000 a month, determined not by practicalities, but by the desire to have all 100,000 moved by the end of 1946. The material supplied to Harriman from Washington mostly originated from the Jewish Agency. The Agency wished to manage the whole immigration itself, and took a much rosier view of the potential for the Palestinian economy to absorb such a large influx of refugees. They did, however, propose a figure of 10,000 a month, and Harriman's group swung behind that.[65]

The British had no desire to hand control of the process over to the Jewish Agency, which they suspected of collaborating with terrorist groups. They also pressed two points to assuage Arab opinion, which they knew would be extremely hostile. They wanted it made clear that the majority of surviving European Jews would remain in Europe, and moreover that many of those who did migrate would be taken in by other countries, thus indicating that the burden was not solely falling on Palestine. The US remained interested only in the immigration to Palestine, and offered to fund it. The British pressed that part of the package had to be a funding of economic development of the Arab areas, and they hoped also to have the Americans commit to providing security forces. These issues and differences were all aired in the meetings, and sub-committees were formed to investigate the various issues.

Harriman himself clearly found it difficult to bridge the gap between the two sides. In the end, the report of the committee was a fudge: it recommended 'between 4,000 and 10,000 a month', and simply put forward the British and Jewish Agency viewpoints without resolving the distance between them. Although Harriman's remit did not involve going much further than exploring the issue, it was not Harriman's finest hour as a 'fixer', which perhaps accounts for its absence from his memoir.[66]

Harriman actually performed better as a mediator in one-on-one meetings rather than in a committee environment. He discussed the Palestine problem with McNeil on 5 July, and agreed that the issue could have an adverse impact on the forthcoming House vote on the loan. He urged on McNeil that an affirmative statement supporting the recommendations of Harriman's Anglo-American committee would help. McNeil flew to Paris to discuss this with Bevin, to ask him to put to Attlee the idea of a statement affirming British sympathy with the Jews. Harriman told Byrnes in confidence that the British were prepared to support the migration of the 100,000 as soon as practicable: they were just more conservative with regard to how fast this could be achieved. Also they did not feel able to commit themselves until they knew how far they could count on help from the US in terms of finance and construction materials for housing. Harriman urged Byrnes to encourage Bevin to take this action. Harriman was thus actively promoting the American agenda, but also operating within the constraints of a sympathetic understanding of British views, which he was in effect defending. The immediate result was disappointing, as the Cabinet turned down a draft statement, on the grounds it would do more harm than good. Harriman did not give up: he saw Attlee on hearing of this and persuaded him to issue a short statement through the FO announcing the arrival of Grady on 12 July and hoping for constructive conclusions to be reached as soon as possible. This was not exactly what Harriman had wanted, but he hoped it would help a little with the House. Given the closeness of the vote, the effort was probably worthwhile, even if the impact of the statement was small.[67]

One of the points that the Harriman-Brook committee did agree upon was that the issue of the immigration could only be dealt with alongside the broader issues of the future of Palestine – which did not meet Truman's desire to get on with it separately, but was what Attlee had been saying all along. Grady's mission duly took over from Harriman, whose subsequent involvement was largely in delivering messages, both in London and then in Paris. Harriman had the ticklish task of reporting Truman's rejection of the Morrison-Grady plan for autonomous regions in a unitary Palestine under British control.[68] In Paris, his secretary noted they were having the Palestine question 'for breakfast, lunch and dinner'.[69] There are continuing signs in his reportage that he strove to do justice to British viewpoints, and that he may well have sympathised with their difficulties, of which he had been made fully aware in his June committee meetings. This had no impact on the conduct of policy by Truman, who showed little inclination to help the British with the dilemmas they faced in Palestine.[70]

Paris Interlude

Harriman spent most of the second half of his brief ambassadorship away from London.[71] In spite of their poor personal relations, Byrnes called on Harriman to assist at the Paris Peace talks that began at the end of July 1946.[72] The purpose of the conference was for 21 participating states to agree on the text of treaties with the minor Axis powers that had been drawn up in the CFM. This was done by individual commissions for each of the Axis countries, though their purpose was merely to report the treaties back to the CFM for final approval. Moreover, the Council members, the big four, were committed in advance to support the texts as they stood, having already been negotiated in the CFM. The other states present were not pleased, and much of the contentious discussion was provoked by states such as Australia advancing substantive changes. In addition, matters were complicated by the territorial disputes between some of the ex-enemy states, notably Hungary and Romania, and the fact that the USSR now controlled these countries. The Soviets, therefore, were to be found often arguing for more leniency towards them, for instance in the issue of reparations, than they did towards Italy, which was in the western sphere.

Harriman found Soviet behaviour unsurprising: 'Nothing much is being accomplished at Paris except that more and more people are realizing what we are up against in the way of political warfare from our gallant allies and that we have to face and deal with the discomfort and unpleasantness of this situation over a considerable number of years.'[73]

Harriman attended the meetings on Romania through August and September, and claimed in his memoirs to have expedited matters by private discussions that he arranged with the chair of the commission, Dmitri Manuilsky, who was nominally representative of Ukraine, but in reality was directed by Molotov. Harriman claims that this back-channel approach meant that the Romania treaty was settled long before those for the other ex-enemy states, Finland, Hungary and Italy.[74] The records of the conference do not give clear evidence of this.[75] The main issues raised were the Romanian-Hungarian frontier in Transylvania and economic questions such as reparations and the restoration of foreign property or compensation for its loss. Harriman was unable to make much headway against the Soviet stance – so while it could be said that the Romanian commission was less contentious than some others, which may have been down to unrecorded informal dealings between Harriman and Manuilsky, the end result was simply an endorsement of the draft Romanian treaty as it stood, and none of the changes that the Americans would have liked were made. Harriman thus made little mark on the proceedings.[76]

Harriman also suggests his work in Paris was completed by the time Byrnes gave his Stuttgart speech on 6 September, when in fact Harriman was still attending meetings in Paris up until 12 September at least, and the Romanian commission did not conclude its business until 24 September.[77]

By that time, Harriman's days in London were numbered. On 12 September Secretary of Commerce Henry Wallace made a speech in which he criticised the British and advocated a policy of goodwill towards the USSR. Truman had seen the speech in advance and Wallace believed he had Truman's approval for his remarks. Probably Truman had merely skimmed through it, and had not spotted that Byrnes would see it as a direct attack on his conduct of American foreign policy. Quite possibly Truman regarded himself as in charge of policy, and if he did not mind, it was no concern of Byrnes. The Secretary of State, however, made it an issue of confidence and effectively issued an ultimatum on 19 September that either he or Wallace go. On 20 September, Wallace was induced to resign.[78] On 21 September, Truman telephoned Harriman. The Ambassador was at Great Enton with Pamela Churchill – apparently gloomy that he was likely to be passed over for Wallace's job because he was stuck in London – but had gone over to Chartwell to lunch with Churchill. In his memoir, Harriman gives the impression he was staying with Churchill, but newspapers reported the excitement at the local exchange near Great Enton in finding the President of the United States on the line.[79] Truman, speaking from the presidential yacht *Williamsburg*, asked one question, would Harriman like to be Secretary of Commerce, and Harriman replied, 'hell, yes…'[80] According to

Harriman's account, he asked Churchill what he should do, and the former Prime Minister said he must of course take it, for 'the centre of power is in Washington'.[81] This was a fact of which Harriman had become all too aware during his brief quasi-exile in Britain, so it is unlikely that he was in any doubt at all about accepting the post. However, he delayed his definite acceptance until the Sunday because he needed to check the legal position with regard to his connections to Brown Brothers. Harriman was concerned that his capital would not be available to the firm while he was Secretary of Commerce, because of a possible clash of interests between his role as impartial manager of US commerce and his status as an executive of a business heavily involved in that commerce. Assured by his attorneys on the Sunday morning that this was not a problem, he then experienced some delay getting through to Truman to confirm his acceptance of the post.[82] There is no doubt, however, that the essence of the sentiment in his memoir is accurate – he welcomed a return to the centre of power. By 1 October he was on his way.

W. Averell Harriman: Conclusions

Harriman was a less than enthusiastic ambassador. To be sure, he enjoyed his popularity in London. He was, however, not much interested in the day-to-day business of the Embassy, and staff members found him 'reticent, aloof and not altogether engaged'.[83] With the possible exception of the over-large 4 July party, his public diplomacy was effective and successful. As far as private diplomacy was concerned, the problems and issues in Anglo-American relations, while of vital importance and considerable contention, were less susceptible to Harriman's 'insider-fixer' approach. Bringing together the British and the Truman administration on the Palestine issue was beyond him. His claim to have 'fixed' the Romania negotiations behind the scenes is unsubstantiated. All this having been said, Harriman's standing as a friend of Britain was an asset for both the US and British governments, and it is tempting to speculate that had he served out a full term as Ambassador, he might be remembered as one of the best, for he was well equipped to deal with the developments in Anglo-American relations that were to follow, and British frustrations evident during 1947 about their views and position not being understood in Washington might well have been much less had Harriman still been present at Grosvenor Square.[84] On the other hand, it should be noted that as Secretary of Commerce he had some opportunity to take British interests into account, notably in presiding over the Committee on Foreign Aid considering Marshall Aid in the fall of 1947.[85] While there was regret in London at his departure, his appointment to replace Wallace was seen as a welcome rebuttal of the strongly anti-British sentiments that Wallace had uttered in his notorious speech. Harriman was still widely seen as a friend of Great Britain.[86]

Harriman's later career was distinguished. He served in the administrations of John F. Kennedy, Lyndon B. Johnson and Jimmy Carter. He and Pamela Churchill were eventually married, and Pamela served as US Ambassador in Paris after Harriman's death in 1986.

Notes

1. See, for example, Abramson, *Spanning the Century*, pp. 409–10, Walter Isaacson and Evan Thomas, *The Wise Men: Six Men and the World They Made* (New York: Simon & Schuster, 1986), pp. 366–7.
2. Harriman's investment firm, Harriman Brothers (later Brown Brothers, Harriman), was established in 1920 and was one of the US businesses involved in investment in the USSR during the 1920s, most notably in connection with manganese concessions.
3. Harriman represented the United States at polo in 1928. In earlier days, he was Dean Acheson's rowing coach at Yale.
4. Abramson, *Spanning the Century*, p. 268.
5. Harriman meeting with Roosevelt 18 February 1941, Meiklejohn Diary Vol 1, ii, W. Averell Harriman Papers, Library of Congress, Box 211 (hereafter cited as WAHP with box and file number).
6. Harriman and Abel, *Special Envoy*, p. 5.
7. Harriman to Winant, 27 May 1941, Harry L. Hopkins Papers, FDRL, Box 124; Olson, *Citizens of London*, pp. 117–19.
8. Abramson, *Spanning the Century*, p. 303.
9. William Standley, *Admiral Ambassador to Russia* (Chicago: Henry Regnery, 1955), pp. 209–13.
10. Harriman and Abel, *Special Envoy*, p. 213.
11. *Ibid.* p. 214; Abramson, *Spanning the Century*, pp. 349–50.
12. Mary E. Glantz, *FDR and the Soviet Union: The President's Battles over Foreign Policy* (Lawrence, KS: University Press of Kansas, 2005), pp. 147–9. The Roosevelt-Harriman meetings were in June 1943, including dinner at the White House on 17 June. See Harriman and Abel, *Special Envoy*, pp. 218–19; Beatrice Bishop Berle and Travis Beal Jacobs (eds.), *Navigating the Rapids, 1918–1971: From the Papers of Adolf A. Berle* (New York: Harcourt, Brace, Jovanovich, 1973), p. 446.
13. Harriman to Roosevelt, 5 July 1943, *FRUS: Cairo and Teheran Conferences 1943*, pp. 13–15.
14. Harriman and Abel, *Special Envoy*, p. 219; Abramson, *Spanning the Century*, pp. 347–8, 350–1.
15. See David Mayers, *The Ambassadors and America's Soviet Policy* (Oxford: Oxford University Press, 1995); Frank Costigliola, 'Archibald Clark Kerr, Averell Harriman, and the Fate of the Wartime Alliance', *Journal of Transatlantic Studies*, Vol. 9 (2011), pp. 83–97.
16. Charles E. Bohlen, *Witness to History, 1929–1969* (New York: W. W. Norton & Co., 1973), pp. 127.
17. Harriman to Hull, 6 February 1944, *FRUS 1944*, Vol. IV, p. 822; Larry I. Bland, 'Averell Harriman, the Russians and the Origins of the Cold War in Europe, 1943–45', *Australian Journal of Politics and History*, Vol. 23 (1977), pp. 408–9, pp. 415-1-6; William Larsh, 'W. Averell Harriman and the Polish Question,

December 1943–August 1944', *East European Politics and Societies*, Vol. 7 (1995), pp. 534, 538–40.

18. Meiklejohn Diary, 1 December 1943, WAHP 211, Vol. 2.

19. For the Romania mission, see *FRUS 1946*, Vol. VI, pp. 555ff. In private, Clark Kerr regarded Harriman as a 'bum-sucker' (of Churchill), which was probably not a completely unfair description, and also a 'weather-vane' in terms of the fluctuations of his views, which reflected Harriman's ambiguity about relations with the USSR, Clark Kerr diary, 13 August 1942, Clark Kerr papers, British National Archives, Kew (hereafter TNA) FO800/300, Clark Kerr to Eden 16 July 1944 FO800/302; Costigliola, 'Archibald Clark Kerr, Averell Harriman', p. 91.

20. Bland, 'Averell Harriman, the Russians', pp. 415–16; Diane S. Clemens, 'Averell Harriman, John Deane, the Joint Chiefs of Staff, and the "Reversal of Cooperation" with the Soviet Union in April 1945', *International History Review,* Vol. 14 (1992), pp. 287, 305–6.

21. David McCullough, *Truman* (New York: Simon & Schuster, 1992), p. 451.

22. Truman formally accepted Harriman's resignation on 14 February; Harriman had returned via India, China, Korea and Japan (Harriman and Abel, *Special Envoy*, p. 546).

23. Herbert Feis, *From Trust to Terror* (New York: W. W. Norton, 1970), pp. 82–3. Harriman and Abel, *Special Envoy*, p. 550.

24. Under the Treaty the USSR was supposed to withdraw its troops in March 1946. They did not do so – and prevented the Iranian government from moving its own troops into Iranian Azerbaijan to deal with unrest. FO meeting, 16 April 1946, Foreign Office correspondence files, TNA FO371/52673/E3459; Terry H. Anderson, *The United States, Great Britain, and the Cold War, 1944–1947* (Columbia, MI: University of Missouri Press, 1981), pp. 122–3.

25. Harriman and Abel, *Special Envoy*, p. 550: according to Harriman, he said to Truman, 'I hope you realize that I'm not looking on this as a regular appointment. I don't want to go to London for a full term. This is, as you say, an emergency. As soon as the emergency is over, I'd like to come home.' Truman replied, 'All right, I'll remember that' but then did nothing to facilitate Harriman's early return when the Iranian crisis blew over.

26. Foreign Secretary Ernest Bevin had requested a meeting with Winant in 24 April, unaware that he was no longer Ambassador: Freeman Matthews described Winant's apparent failure to inform the FO of the date of the end of his ambassadorship as 'hard to fathom'. Harriman wrote to Byrnes that this caused some bewilderment, 'as never before has any outgoing ambassador remained after the new ambassador's arrival. I don't attach much importance to it as most people put it down to Winant's usual vague way of handling things. Some questions, however, have been asked as to why I was so precipitous in arriving without giving Winant time to take his leave. In any event I don't feel any real embarrassment as I am so well known here', thus acknowledging the fault was not all Winant's (Harriman to Byrnes, 26 April 1946, Matthews to Harriman, 7 May 1946, WAHP 223/5).

27. Robert J. Donovan, *Conflict and Crisis: The Presidency of Harry S. Truman 1945–48* (Norton: New York, 1977), p. 195.

28. Bullard to FO, 21 April 1946, TNA FO371/52674/E3668.

29. Waddell to Meiklejohn, 13 June 1946, WAHP 223/2.

30. Harriman to Major General Anderson, 14 June 1946, WAHP 212/10; Harriman to Forrestal, 29 June 1946, WAHP 212/3; Harriman to Kirk, 30 April 1946, spoke

of 'the appalling diplomatic calls' looming as 'the largest cloud at the moment', WAHP 220/3.

31. Isaacson and Thomas, *The Wise Men*, pp. 20, 347.

32. *Titbits*, 17 May 1946.

33. Harriman told the press that Bevin opened their first meeting with the words 'welcome home' (*Daily Telegraph*, 29 May 1946; *Sunday Times*, 23 June 1946); Gallman (chargé at the Embassy) to Harriman, 25 March 1946, WAHP 220/3. Harriman's salary was $17,500 plus expenses. Among the effects he brought with him were 19 cases of Old Grandad bourbon.

34. *New York Herald Tribune*, 23 April 1946; *Daily Express*, 23 April 1946; *Yorkshire Post*, 29 May 1946, *The Times*, 29 May 1946.

35. David Dimbleby and David Reynolds, *An Ocean Apart* (New York: Random House, 1988), p. 180.

36. Richard N. Gardner, *Sterling-Dollar Diplomacy: Anglo-American Collaboration in the Reconstruction of Multilateral Trade* (Oxford: Clarendon Press, 1956), pp. 237, 239, 251.

37. A number of hostile amendments were defeated more narrowly still.

38. Bevin conversation with Senator Arthur Vandenburg, 28 January 1946, Bevin papers, TNA FO800/513.

39. Harriman and Abel, *Special Envoy*, p. 531.

40. Anderson, *The United States*, pp. 124–5, Ronald Powaski, *Toward an Entangling Alliance* (New York: Greenwood, 1991), p. 186; Caroline Anstey, 'The Projection of British Socialism: Foreign Office Publicity and American Opinion, 1945–50', *Journal of Contemporary History*, Vol. 19 (1984), p. 436.

41. Donovan, *Conflict and Crisis*, pp. 156–8.

42. Harriman to Byrnes, 24 May 1946, *FRUS 1946*, Vol. II, pp. 448–9.

43. Harriman conversation with Warner, 8 May 1946, State Department papers Record Group 59 761.00/5-846; Harriman speech at Camberley, 1 July 1946, Kennan to Harriman, 3 September 1946, WAHP 213/1.

44. Martin H. Folly, 'Lord Inverchapel', in Michael Hopkins, John Young and Saul Kelly (eds.), *The Washington Embassy, 1939–77* (Basingstoke: Palgrave Macmillan, 2009), pp. 55–9.

45. Harriman and Abel, *Special Envoy*, pp. 550–1.

46. He told the miners that Britain would 'get full value for the loan' and that 'our two countries will be partners in the world of the future', speech 20 July 1946, quoted in *The New York Times*, 23 September 1946.

47. Berger memorandum, 20 May 1946, WAHP 223/5.

48. Lawson (MP) to Harriman, 22 July 1946, WAHP 213/5; Harriman to Watson, 27 September 1946, WAHP 225/1; Harriman to Morris, 2 September 1946, WAHP 883/18. This file has an interesting set of photographs of Harriman addressing the 'Big Meeting'.

49. Harriman to Lovett, 9 July 1946, WAHP 213/5. Harriman wrote, 'the British are making real progress, forcibly by keeping their belts tight and expanding their exports rapidly – no troubles with labor.... Incidentally, the doctrinaire socialists (the other half of the Labor Party) have much the same approach as the New Deal boys – enthusiasm for their theories, full confident that they know all the answers, and they are incessantly at work to put their ideas across.'

50. Though he was also in the habit of spelling his last name 'Atlee': this from a man annoyed by the way so many people spelt his own name 'Averill' (Harriman to

Byrnes, 6 July 1946, WAHP 224/1; Harriman to Cherwell, undated, September 1946, WAHP213/1).

51. See, for example, McNeil to Harriman, 5 July 1946, WAHP 224/1.
52. Walter Millis (ed.), *The Forrestal Diaries* (New York: Viking, 1951), entry for 22 July 1946.
53. Harriman and Abel, *Special Envoy*, p. 551.
54. *The New York Times*, 23 April 1946; Harriman to Acheson, 9 May 1946, WAHP 223/5.
55. Waddell to Meiklejohn, 13 June 1946, WAHP 223/2.
56. Article 'Embarrassing Binge', *Time*, 15 July 1946; Harriman to W. S. Anderson, 25 July 1946 WAHP212/10. The party cost £866 4s – see invoice in WAHP 224/1: over $3,500 by the prevailing exchange rate.
57. Memorandum of talk with Bevin, 24 April 1946, WAHP 224/1; Harriman to Acheson, 11 May 1946, WAHP 220/7; Alan Bullock, *Ernest Bevin: Foreign Secretary, 1945–51* (Oxford: Oxford University Press, 1983), pp. 200–2: Bevin minute, 7 September 1946, TNA FO800/513.
58. Harriman to Acheson, 24 April 1946, WAHP 224/1; Harriman to Byrnes, 6 June 1946, *FRUS 1946*, Vol. V, pp. 565–6; Harriman to Byrnes, 8 July 1946, WAHP 224/1.
59. Amikam Nachmani, ' "It Is a Matter of Getting the Mixture Right": Britain's Postwar Relations with America in the Middle East', *Journal of Contemporary History*, Vol. 18 (1983), p. 128.
60. Brook conversation with Bevin, 10 July 1946, TNA FO800/485.
61. For a summary of the report, see Acheson to Diplomatic Officers, 25 April 1946, *FRUS 1946*, Vol. VII, pp. 585–6.
62. Truman to Attlee, 5 June 1946, *FRUS 1946*, Vol. VII, pp. 617–18.
63. Byrnes to Harriman, 10 June 1946, *FRUS 1946*, Vol. VII, pp. 624–5.
64. 18 June 1946 meeting, WAHP 223/6.
65. US group report P-7, 17 June 1946, WAHP 223/6.
66. 21 June 1946 meeting, final report P-20, 26 June 1946, WAHP 223/6; Harriman to Byrnes, 27 June 1946, *FRUS 1946*, Vol. VII, pp. 638–9.
67. McNeil to Harriman, 5 July 1946, Harriman to Byrnes, 6 July and 8 July 1946, WAHP 224/1.
68. Harriman to Acheson, 31 July 1946; Harriman conversation with Hall, 2 August 1946,Truman to Attlee, 13 August 1946, WAHP 224/1.
69. Newton to Waddell, 21 August 1946, WAHP 213/7.
70. Harriman to Byrnes, 14 August, Harriman conversation with Bevin, 15 August, with Attlee and Hall, 15 August, Harriman to Acheson, 21 August and 30 August 1946, WAHP 224/1. Loy Henderson, of the State Department Division of Near Eastern Affairs, where there was more sympathy for the British position, thanked Harriman for his efforts, letter 6 August 1946, WAHP 213/3.
71. Harriman regularly flew back to England for long weekends, leaving on Saturday and often returning on Tuesday afternoon, only two hours before the Romania meetings at 4 p.m. However, he spent most of that time at Great Enton, not in London. His Paris schedule is in WAHP 216/5: see also the appointments diary in 220/1.
72. Harriman's secretary reported to London, '... the plan seems to be that Mr Byrnes wants to divide the work into four parts: 1/4 Byrnes, 1/4 Harriman, 1/4 Smith [Ambassador at Moscow], 1/4 Caffery [Ambassador at Paris]. This may not work out, but the plan as I gain it is exactly that', Waddell to Warburg, WAHP 216/5.

73. Harriman to Colonel Frank N. Roberts, 28 August 1946, WAHP 213/7; Powaski, *Toward an Entangling Alliance*, p. 181. Harriman wrote to Kennan towards the end of the conference, 'Paris is a gloomy business, but not surprising. Our "Gallant Allies" are running true to form. It seems to me that there has been great value in allowing the people of the Western World to see what the Russians and their satellites are up to...' (letter 20 September 1946, WAHP 213/5).

74. Harriman and Abel, *Special Envoy*, p. 551.

75. No meetings with Manuilsky are recorded in the appointments diary, 220/1, though they could have met informally before or after commission meetings.

76. Harriman at 5 September 1946 and 11 September 1946 meetings, WAHP 218/2. Baranovsky chaired the meetings from 31 August.

77. Harriman to Sherwood, 20 September 1946, WAHP 213/7.

78. James F. Byrnes, *Speaking Frankly* (New York: Harper & Brothers, 1947), pp. 239–42.

79. *London Evening Standard*, 23 September 1946; *Manchester Guardian*, 24 September 1946.

80. Robert H. Ferrell (ed.), *Truman in the White House: The Diary of Eben A. Ayers* (Columbia, MI: University of Missouri Press, 1991), entry for Sunday 22 September 1946. Ayers was Truman's assistant press secretary.

81. Harriman and Abel, *Special Envoy*, p. 553.

82. Harriman to Truman, 22 September 1946, WAHP 224/5.

83. Abramson, *Spanning the Century*, p. 409.

84. *Manchester Guardian*, 24 September 1946; Folly, 'Lord Inverchapel', p. 62.

85. Harriman oral history interview 1971, Truman library, available at: www. trumanlibrary.org/oralhist/harriman.htm, p. 24.

86. *The New York Times*, 23 September 1946. *The Star* described Harriman as 'a mighty friend of Britain', 23 September 1946.

Part II

The Cold War Ambassadors, 1947–1961

Introduction

J. Simon Rofe

As 1945 began and the Second World War drew to its conclusion, the Big Three – Franklin Roosevelt, Winston Churchill and Soviet Premier Josef Stalin – envisaged the essential fabric of their relationship, and those of the countries they led, extending into peacetime. Little did they know that, by high summer one of their number would be dead (Roosevelt, 12 April) and another ousted from the prime ministership (Churchill, 26 July), leaving Stalin as the final part of the troika who held the expectation of the wartime alliance continuing.[1] Such changes in the geopolitical landscape were to be followed by others of equal or even greater magnitude in marking out the beginning of what can retrospectively be identified, neatly, as the Cold War. Confronting this fast changing situation was President Harry S. Truman who had succeeded Roosevelt. Truman's was a baptism by fire as he faced confrontation with the Soviet Union in Europe, the Middle East and the Far East before the end of 1946. In respect to the United Kingdom, he was ultimately responsible for the decision to cease Lend-Lease and instigate negotiations for an Anglo-American loan (July 1946) – the final payment of which was made in 2006.[2] The Anglo-American relationship was changing from one of wartime allies to one where the asymmetry in economic and military wealth was clear. It was in this environment that he recalled his first appointment to the Court of St James's, Averell Harriman, to Washington to become his Secretary of Commerce (October 1946) and leaving a vacancy in London. As the wartime alliance devolved into increasingly open conflict with the Soviet Union, greater responsibilities came to rest on shoulders of the United States Ambassadors to London during this early Cold War period.

However, such thoughts were not paramount in Truman's thinking as he made the decision as to who would replace Harriman. The initial person under consideration was, in fact, not Lewis Douglas whose ambassadorship Jonathan Colman covers presently, but O. Max Gardner.[3] The former North Carolina Governor headed a powerful caucus of Southern interests within the Democratic Party, and allied himself to many early New Deal social causes while establishing a corporate law business in Washington. When Truman announced, on 6 December 1946, that Gardner stepping down from the position of Undersecretary of the Treasury was to become the next Ambassador, it bore all the hallmarks of political patronage. After the announcement, *Time* magazine commented of Gardner that he had two 'great assets' for what the magazine saw as a 'socially exacting, financially burdensome job at the Court of St. James's: he is social-minded and he is wealthy'.[4] Fate, however, intervened and Gardner died on 6 February 1947 before leaving for London. Thus providing the opportunity for Douglas to become Ambassador, and the first covered in this section of early Cold War Ambassadors.[5]

During this period the Embassy was increasingly engaged in policy-making in Anglo-American affairs. Antecedents to such a development existed from the wartime experience, and the onset of the Cold War with its attendant crises, such as the Berlin Airlift (1948–49) meant increasing Anglo-American cooperation to meet them. Interestingly, the London Embassy was also acquiring a reputation as an unofficial hub between Washington and continental Europe. One manifestation of this was Truman committing the United States to participation in the North Atlantic Treaty (4 April 1946) alongside the United Kingdom, Canada and nine other European states. The number of American personnel who passed through the Embassy during the years covered here, even if on their way to the continent, allowed for greater levels of interaction between US and UK officials fostering opportunities for further understanding.

Noticeable in Douglas, and his successors Walter Gifford, Winthrop Aldrich and John Whitney are their efforts to engage in what would now be called public diplomacy. That is to say, they increasingly undertook engage-ments beyond the metropolis, with the aim of improving the standing of the United States in the eyes of the British people. For Whitney at least, this task was a very real one after the Suez crisis of 1956 and the questioning of the then recently applied motif of the special relationship.

Institutional change also served to facilitate UK–US relations. After the Rogers Act 1924 offered fundamental reform in creating the US Foreign Ser-vice from separate consular and diplomatic services, there was little change in the formal structures of the State Department until after the Second World War.[6] The National Security Act 1947 would ultimately have profound effects on the State Department, but initially the newly founded National Security Council remained subservient to Truman. At the same time, the ramifica-tions of the war, and the escalating Cold War, meant increasing dislocation between Washington and diplomatic posts overseas. While the State Depart-ment reeled from the blows, subsequently unfounded, applied by Joseph McCarthy, it was subjected to a major review undertaken as part of the Hoover Commission led by former President Herbert Hoover, to reduce federal waste and inefficiency. The upshot for the State Department was the Wriston Report (1954) covering personnel practices undertaken at the behest of Secretary of State, John Foster Dulles led by Brown University President Henry M. Wriston. The report integrated, albeit slowly over a period of years, civil service employees with Foreign Service officers so that 'By the end of 1957, the Foreign Service had more than doubled in size to 3,436 officers.'[7] The ramifications for London were not felt immediately by Aldrich or Whitney. Nonetheless, the formalising of the concept of 'tours of duty' at home and overseas meant it was possible for officers to make a return to favoured locations on the basis of a combination of personal preference and professional expertise. London became a favourite destination, with numerous US Foreign Service officers passing through Grosvenor Square, in furthering their careers.[8]

While the Cold War crystallised during the era covered in this section and governed much of the time period covered in this volume, another, even longer-standing character in our volume enters the stage: Queen Elizabeth II. Beginning her reign in 1952, following the death of her father, and her coronation in June 1953 she is still on the throne in 2012. Her role in the life of the US Ambassador to the United Kingdom is wholly ceremonial, in receiving the Ambassador's credentials. Thus far she has received sixteen Ambassadors from the United States beginning with Aldrich.

While her reign has not been without incident, the longevity of Queen Elizabeth's reign speaks to continuity within the British body politic. From the vantage point of the Queen's Diamond Jubilee in 2012, the certainty now readily identified as a hallmark of US–UK relations was not preordained in the early Cold War period. A plethora of challenges bilaterally and in the wider world were met by varying degrees of cooperation, and a crystallisation of Churchillian rhetoric into a harmony of interests in international affairs. Albeit tested at times, and not in symmetry, nonetheless the opening years of the Cold War reveal a shared approach and no major reason to question it. Gifford's words in 1953, quoted by Colman, somewhat prophetically point to this shared understanding: 'British attitudes on basic international issues are of course identical with our own. They will stay that way.'[9]

Notes

1. Frank Costigliola, *Roosevelt's Lost Alliances* (Princeton, NJ: Princeton University Press, 2012).
2. Philip A. Grant, Jr, 'President Harry S. Truman and the British Loan Act of 1946', *Presidential Studies Quarterly,* Vol. 25, No. 3 (Summer 1995), pp. 489–96.
3. Statement by the President, 6 December 1947, Public Papers of the Presidents, Harry S. Truman, 1945–1953, available at: http://trumanlibrary.org/publicpapers/index.php?pid=1827&st=Gardner&st1 (accessed 1 April 2012).
4. 'To England', *Time*, Vol. 48 Issue 24 (9 December 1946), p. 28.

5. Statement by the President on the Death of O. Max Gardner, 6 February 1947, Public Papers of the Presidents, Harry S. Truman, 1945–1953, available at: http://trumanlibrary.org/publicpapers/index.php?pid= 2223&st= Gardner&st1 (accessed 1 April 2012).

6. Geoff Berridge, *Diplomacy: Theory and Practice* (Basingstoke: Palgrave, 2nd edn, 2002), p. 8.

7. 'By August 1959, 1,523 Foreign Service officers were assigned to positions in the Department in an effort to improve communications between Washington and the overseas missions and to fulfill the legal requirement that Foreign Service officers spend a portion of their careers in the United States.' Office of the Historian, US Department of State, A Short History of the Department, available at: http://history.state.gov/departmenthistory/short-history/containment andcoldwar (accessed 1 April 2012).

8. A function of these reforms was to provide for support to the Ambassador. Their closest advisor during this period was known as Counsellor, sometimes with specific prefixes such as 'political' or 'economic', until 1965 when the title of Deputy Chief of Mission (DCM) first appears in the Foreign Service List. Clarification received from the Office of the Historian at the Department of State, April 2012.

9. Gifford to Secretary of State, 14 March 1951, *FRUS 1951*, Vol. IV, Part I, p. 922.

4
Lewis Williams Douglas, 1947–50

Jonathan Colman

In February 1947, O. Max Gardner suffered a fatal heart attack soon before he was due to sail to Britain to take up the post of Ambassador to the Court of St James's. The position had been vacant for five months, when Averell Harriman had been called to become Secretary of Commerce. Harriman had recommended Lewis W. Douglas to take his place, although Douglas's name was not prominent among those under consideration. Now, with Gardner's death, Douglas was in with a chance once more. Undersecretary of State Dean Acheson and Harriman both proposed Douglas to Secretary of State George C. Marshall, who, in turn, put forward the proposal to President Truman.[1]

Douglas, the 17th Ambassador to Great Britain and the 46th Chief of Mission, would find himself very busy during his three years in London. This was due to the impact of intensifying Cold War tensions and the concomitant renewal of Anglo-American cooperation on a variety of economic and security matters. Issues included the coal shortage in Britain engendered by the bitter winter of 1946–47; the provision of Marshall Aid to Britain and other Western European states; and the Berlin Crisis of 1948–49. Douglas was at the centre of these events, addressing them admirably and winning the confidence of senior American and British policy-makers. Such were Douglas's contributions that he has been described as a policy-maker in his own right.[2] Events in this period also had an impact on the development of the London Embassy as an institution. While the Second World War had made the Embassy one of the United States' 'largest and most important offices' abroad, the growing volume of work in the Douglas years made the Embassy more important than had ever been the case in peacetime.[3]

Douglas was a former Congressman and advisor to Franklin D. Roosevelt, as well as a successful businessman with a background in mining and insurance. His political credentials for the London post were good. In 1940 he had supported the extension of economic aid to Britain, and in his position as Deputy War Shipping Administrator (based in London) he had argued to his superiors that it was essential to maintain intimate cooperation with Britain and the Commonwealth. Similarly, he stressed to General Hastings Ismay the 'bald necessity of our playing together, working together, and cementing our relationships by specific engagements and detailed undertakings... The two of us together can lay the foundation for world order, but there can be no world order unless we are together.'[4] During his wartime stint in London, Douglas made the acquaintance of leading figures in the British Labour Party such as Ernest Bevin and Clement Attlee. Labour had won the general election of 1945 and, despite straitened economic circumstances, pursued the creation of a welfare state. Douglas got along well with British officials and politicians. One commentator suggested in 1947 that this was because 'he manages to be thoroughly American, yet manages to be the complete antithesis of the grotesque caricature so many Britons have built up of the typical American: loud-mouthed, loud-suited and inclined to give a condescending slap on the aching British back'.[5]

However, there were concerns in some quarters in Britain about Douglas's conservative economic outlook – he had resigned in 1934 as Roosevelt's Director of the Bureau of the Budget in protest at the growth of government spending. A 1947 article in the journal *New Republic* suggested that sending Douglas to a Labour-governed Britain was 'a bit like sending a Methodist missionary as Ambassador to the Pope'.[6] Douglas did express some harsh judgements about the Attlee government's economic and financial management, once arguing to his superiors in Washington that British economic problems were partly self-inflicted because of the failure to modernise industrial machinery, the commitment to social spending, and the continued drain of dollars for sterling expenditures outside Britain.[7] Yet F. B. A. Rundall of the Foreign Office noted that Douglas had taken a generous attitude to British war debts to the United States and had consistently supported Washington's liberal international trade policies. Rundall believed that Britain had 'little to fear from Douglas's alleged conservatism and devotion to free enterprise', and that he was sensitive to the strategic implications of Britain's economic difficulties.[8]

The first major issue with which Douglas dealt was one that, with his mining background, he was well equipped to navigate: the shortage of coal in Britain which crippled transportation and led to widespread power cuts. Douglas considered that the coal problem was of profound consequences: 'every single issue here in England, of whatsoever kind, can be traced to the original sin – coal. It touches the exports... It touches Britain's exchange position and dollar position. It affects seriously and adversely her political power in the continent of Europe, and her authority in the Middle East – and indeed, everywhere throughout the world.'[9] Douglas felt that the Attlee government's failure to close marginal mines, to encourage greater productivity through a revised wage structure and tax regime, to stem absenteeism, and to recruit more miners had contributed to the problem.[10]

The coal shortage meant that the British government was keen to secure increased imports of American coal through the European Coal Organisation (ECO), but a particular obstacle was the intransigence of fellow ECO members, the French, who had their own claims on American coal.[11] Douglas spent a great deal of time working with representatives of Britain, France and other members of the ECO, and was central to the negotiation of a revised US coal allocation for Britain. He helped to devise a formula that would moderate the British demand and help the French to save face.[12] Douglas's success in this matter also helped to preserve the integrity of the ECO as an organisation. His efforts won the gratitude of Clement Attlee as well as other British politicians and officials, and demonstrated how his work in London had as much to do with multilateral European questions as well as bilateral Anglo-American ones.[13]

The bitter winter of 1946–47 exacerbated an already shaky economic situation in a country still reeling from the impact of the war. In May 1947, Douglas explained to Washington that the British situation was more difficult than was commonly appreciated, with a limited supply of dollars, imported goods costing more and more, and the impact of a faltering economic recovery in Europe and Asia.[14] Despatches such as this found a ready audience in a Washington gravely concerned, in the context of the Cold War, about the future of key Western European states, and contributed to the decision to initiate a large-scale programme of reconstruction assistance.[15] In June 1947, Secretary of State Marshall announced his famous 'Plan', known officially as the 'European Recovery Programme' (ERP). The intention was to improve the capacity of Western Europe to remain non-communist as well as to create a market for American goods. Douglas had high hopes for Britain's participation in the ERP, not least because a boost to Britain's economic status would bolster the country's 'moral position ... among other countries. She will be able to provide the direction and leadership, and she will be able to play the role only Britain can play in integrating the economic programme for Europe'.[16] Just as he had while in London during the war, Douglas attached great importance to helping Britain maintain its international strength. He now also saw the need for a strong Western political bloc to help contain communism.

There was, however, some scepticism in Congress about how far the aid programme would serve American interests, and Douglas was chosen to testify in Congressional hearings. He visited Washington several times in 1947–48 for this purpose, and during his time there he garnered a reputation on Capitol Hill for sound judgement. Douglas's performances and his administrative contributions in London (there were strict conditions attached to the aid and many aspects of the programme were highly technical) played an important role in the success of the ERP and won the particular gratitude of Foreign Secretary Ernest Bevin. Bevin told him in April 1948 that:

> I wish I could find words adequate to express the depth of my feeling and the gratitude which I feel towards you for what you have done in connection with the European Recovery Programme.... We worked closely together during the crisis last summer arising out of the non-discrimination question. You then helped us to smooth out all the difficulties which might so easily have led to division between the English-speaking peoples, and which might therefore have seriously affected the whole world situation.... I can well understand the great physical and mental strain which has been imposed upon you – not least in flying backwards and forwards between London and Washington.... Above all, I should like you to know how very much I have appreciated your advice and help.[17]

ERP negotiations in Washington nearly collapsed in June 1948, over various technical difficulties. However, when the venue for talks was changed to London, Douglas was able to play a central role in breaking the deadlock, not least because after lengthy talks with Bevin and Stafford Cripps (Chancellor of the Exchequer) he advised Washington not to press the issue of extending most-favoured-nation treatment to Japan.[18] The result was that the bilateral Anglo-American ERP agreement was signed in July 1948.

Subsequently, to ensure the continued progress of the aid programme, Douglas worked closely with the Economic Cooperation Administration (ECA),[19] the American agency responsible for administering the ERP. Late in 1948, Paul G. Hoffman, ECA's head in Washington, praised Douglas's contribution to a number of meetings with Bevin:

> Only as I reviewed mentally the details of our interviews with Mr Bevin did I realize how superbly you handled the situation. There were at least half a dozen times when if you hadn't come up with the right word and right inclination a real explosion might have taken place. You have my heartfelt thanks.[20]

An intervention of this sort is not surprising given that an ambassador bears ultimate responsibility for what goes on in the Embassy and that he was keen that the ERP and the Anglo-American relationship should run smoothly, but it does seem that his contributions to the ECA's work were of special value. Douglas's efforts came to the attention of President Truman, who wanted to appoint him to the role of Economic Coordinator Administrator for Europe. However, Douglas felt that the envoy to London could not perform two major roles, and that even if he resigned in favour of the European role he would be suspected of bias towards Britain.[21]

In the first few months of 1948, London was host to a three-power conference over the future of the western-occupied portion of Germany. Douglas was appointed to be the chief US representative. The conference dealt with matters such as German economic recovery, the international control of the Ruhr, and the creation of a new political framework for Germany. Douglas's approach to the German question was evident in his statement that while he appreciated 'dangers of potential German aggressive power' he considered it essential either to take 'all reasonable steps to consolidate Western Germany with Western Europe, or admitting this couldn't be done and letting Western Germany move eastward'.[22] Much of the work of the conference was carried on informally in small meetings and conversations between members of the various delegations,[23] creating ample opportunity for bilateral Anglo-American collaboration. There were differences of view. At one stage, Ernest Bevin feared that the United States might use the ERP to induce Britain to end reparations to the Soviet Union from western Germany. This, Bevin suggested, would 'react badly against the US'.[24] There was also some Anglo-American cooperation against France. After discussion with Douglas, Bevin instructed the British Ambassador in Paris to make the 'strongest representations' to the French, who were not enthusiastic about the prospect of a West German government.[25]

In June 1948, the Soviet Union blocked the land routes to West Berlin after the Allied efforts, agreed in London, to treat the western part of Germany as a single unit. Douglas felt that abandoning Berlin in the face of Soviet pressure would be

> a calamity of the first order. Western European confidence in us, in the light of our repeated statements that we intend to remain in Berlin, would be so shattered that we would, with reasonable expectancy, progressively lose Western Germany, if not Western Europe. Fear, uncertainty, and lack of faith in us would weaken the determination of Western Germans and the people of Western Europe, and would probably cause failure of the European Recovery Program, if it would not cause the beneficial effects, which we hope it will produce, to evaporate like water on a hot stove.[26]

He also felt though that the issue should not be pushed to the point of war because the outbreak of a further conflict would, among other things, destroy liberal attitudes in Europe.[27]

In June 1948, Secretary of State Marshall agreed that London should be one of the centres, alongside Berlin and Washington, for managing the crisis. From June to September 1948, when the crisis was especially tense, London was the primary location for coordinating Western policy. Marshall ordered that Douglas was 'furnished copies of all messages', including those of the

Department of the Army.[28] On the British side, too, there was a desire to keep London the centre of Allied policy. Douglas reported Bevin's view that 'decisions can be reached more promptly by maintaining this close association [in London] than by the circuitous method of communicating directly with the British Embassy in Washington which in turn communicates with the US'.[29] There were frequent meetings between Douglas, Bevin, William Strang of the Foreign Office, and the French Ambassador, René Massigli, plus other officials. The meetings often took place in Douglas's office at the US Embassy while he talked on the telephone to Marshall.[30] There were some minor differences of view between the British and the Americans, but Douglas helped to work out a coordinated diplomatic response to the Soviet demarche, including a simultaneous protest to the Soviet government in Moscow.[31] The success of the Allied 'airlift' to supply West Berlin with essential provisions, and the Soviet lifting of the blockade in May 1949 represented a major success for Western resolve in the Cold War, and was an own-goal for the Soviets. In 1949 the new Federal Republic of Germany became a founder member of the North Atlantic Treaty Organisation (NATO), and a few years later was permitted to rearm. This suited Douglas, who was keen to see West Germany contribute to the strength and prosperity of the West.

Another of Douglas's contributions was promoting the 'special relationship' as a mainstay of US foreign policy.[32] During 1948 and 1949 Britain had taken the lead in discussions and negotiations which had led to seminal developments such as the Brussels Pact and the Council of Europe, but there was, among the British, a general resistance to further measures of integration with the continental powers. This gave rise to frustration among some American diplomats. During the run-up to talks in Paris in 1950, State Department officials produced a paper on the nature of the Anglo-American 'special relationship' which led Ambassador David K. E. Bruce in France to argue that an avowedly close relationship with Britain would prejudice US bonds with other European states and could discourage British participation in European unity. To be sure, Douglas sympathised with the desire to see greater European integration, to the point he once urged Ernest Bevin to take a more positive attitude towards European integration.[33]

However, this was not an issue he wanted to push at the expense of the bilateral Anglo-American relationship. He wasted no time in replying with what were, by now, his long-standing views. In a lengthy, forceful analysis, he argued that tight bilateral bonds with Britain were a strategic necessity as there was no country 'whose interests are so wrapped around the world as the UK'. As the heart of a global Empire and Commonwealth, Britain was 'in more vitally strategic areas than any other nation among the community of Western nations', the centre of the sterling area, and the only power west of the Iron Curtain 'capable of wielding substantial military strength'.[34] While Dean Acheson – now Secretary of State – approved of the general conception of a 'special' Anglo-American relationship, he did agree with Bruce that US diplomats should avoid proclaiming that relationship.[35]

The tightening Anglo-American bonds in these years bolstered the importance of the London Embassy as an institution. A 1949 report reflected how the growing 'identity of interests' between the United States and Britain in the Cold War 'interplay of power' had underlined the need for coordinated policies. This meant that in addition to performing the normal functions of a diplomatic mission, namely, 'the conduct of negotiations...and reporting on domestic, political, economic and sociological developments and evaluating their significance from the standpoint of US policy', the Embassy had to 'participate in the implementation, and in many cases, the actual formulation of joint US-UK policies'. The example of Germany's political and economic future was a notable example of this process. British cooperation was vital for the recovery and integration of the continent, with the result that the US Embassy saw a 'continuing stream of special missions and international conferences' on a host of political and economic matters.[36] Embassy personnel also advised the British government on issues such as the Atlantic Pact, the Brussels Treaty and the Council of Europe.[37]

The wartime Lend-Lease programme had involved the employment of many trained economists in US Embassies, and there was further work for economists with the ECA. ECA London began with around 30 people, but soon there were over 100. In 1950, ECA London comprised 11 units, such as the Trade and Overseas Development Division, Industry Division and the Labour Division.[38] Kathleen Burk has noted that ECA country missions varied greatly in how far they intervened in the economic policies of the host country. ECA Athens, for example, was 'practically a second government', but ECA London was less intrusive in furthering American policy preferences. This led some ECA officials to believe that the UK mission had, in effect, been captured by the British. Richard M. Bissell, Assistant to the Deputy Administrator of ECA in Washington, stated that 'We were suspicious that the mission reflected the view of the British Government'.[39] Douglas remarked in 1948 that ECA representatives worked with the British 'in an atmosphere of mutual collaboration and confidence'.[40] Besides the ECA, there were many other Embassy activities designed to promote prosperity and trade (albeit on American terms), including efforts to reduce discriminatory practices or prohibitive trade barriers implemented by Britain.[41] Further Embassy activities in the politico-economic realm included administering the stockpiling of strategic materials, acquiring scrap metal from occupied Germany, and overseeing the supply of steel. The Embassy also extended help to American business interests and produced numerous research reports and special studies on the British economy.[42]

Douglas proved himself an eminently capable ambassador, but many Foreign Service officers whose formative experiences had taken place before the Second World War reflected the isolationist traditions and policies of the United States and were unused to dealing with the sort of problems stemming from a more activist foreign policy.[43] The Foreign Service expanded substantially during the war and became more democratic in its recruitment. However, the process of diplomatic evolution could not take place overnight. W. John Kenney, head of ECA London 1949–51, commented that there were still many people, 'old line Foreign Service officers, that just did not comprehend the broader role the United States was playing and would continue to play for some time'.[44]

Yet Embassy personnel were still notably successful in their relations with British officials. Waldemar J. Gallman, Deputy Chief of Mission 1947–49, remembered the willingness of Whitehall personnel to share information.[45] Thomas K. Finletter, Kenney's predecessor in charge of ECA London, noted that British officials often 'went over documents' with him 'before they presented them officially to us'.[46] Thomas Dunnigan, who was posted to the Embassy in 1950 to deal with German affairs, recalled that information 'went back and forth' readily between British and American diplomats.[47] Labour Attaché Samuel Berger was responsible for developing some particularly 'special' personal relationships while working in Britain. While on a research fellowship before the war, Berger made many contacts among Labour and trade union leaders when the Embassy was paying them relatively little heed. Berger was able to use and develop these ready-made friendships during the Second World War and especially after 1945 when the Labour Party won the general election.[48] A later Embassy official described Berger as 'the key member of the Embassy'.[49] While the post of ambassador is more senior and in most circumstances provides the readiest entry into the highest official circles, the example of Berger confirms that some – if not most – US diplomats found it very easy to secure meaningful access to British politicians and officials.[50] This was because the experience of wartime collaboration was fresh in peoples' minds, and because the emergent threat of communist expansionism made coordinated foreign policies a necessity.

London had been a large Office of Strategic Services station during the war, and became a major base for the Central Intelligence Agency (CIA) when the organisation was established in 1947.[51] The creation that year of an Embassy liaison office for the CIA and for the Federal Bureau of Investigation (FBI) strengthened Anglo-American sharing of clandestine intelligence material.[52] In 1949, official procedures for sharing diplomatic intelligence material between the US Embassy and the British Foreign Office were implemented: US State Department intelligence research reports and documents on topics of potential value to British policy-makers were screened in the Department and then either withheld or forwarded to the London Embassy. The Embassy provided further vetting of the material, but most, if not all was then passed on to the British Foreign Office by a designated intelligence liaison officer. This officer was also responsible for obtaining material from the Foreign Office.[53] Britain and the United States were generally much freer in sharing sensitive information among themselves than with other allies, as was evident in some elements of the Embassy's work.

Growing Anglo-American interdependence brought some instances of friction, mainly because of the imbalance of the relationship: by 1945 Britain had found itself displaced as the leading global actor and reliant on American largesse. Deputy Chief of Mission (DCM) Julius Holmes reflected in 1950 that the abrupt ending of Lend-Lease aid in 1945 had caused a 'violent shock' in Britain and raised doubts among British policy-makers about how far Washington could be relied upon in the future; there were divisions in August 1947 over the crisis caused by making sterling convertible with the dollar; in 1947–48 the issue of Palestine 'imposed a most serious strain' on the relationship; and in the spring and summer 1949 the foreign exchange crisis and the devaluation of sterling for Britain was 'accompanied by mutual recriminations in both countries'. It was the duty of US diplomats to resolve these issues while preserving cordiality and cooperation as far as possible, but sometimes the task was complicated, as many of the officials coming to London on Anglo-American business paid scant regard to British sensibilities. Holmes complained that there had been a 'stream of American visitors, public and private, demanding to see top leaders of government, asking impertinent or intrusive questions'. The Embassy did its best 'to handle these cases tactfully and skilfully, but we know they have caused irritation here'.[54]

For all the closeness between high-level policy-makers on the Anglo-American scene, there was some anti-Americanism to address. In 1948, DCM Waldemar Gallman noted the Labour Party's suspicion of American capitalism, while British Conservatives feared American trade competition and the threat to the favourable trading system of Imperial Preference within the British Empire. All shades of political opinion considered that US foreign policy 'may be erratic in particular instances' and that the United States might drag Britain into misplaced adventures.[55] Douglas concluded early in his ambassadorship that a 'steadily conducted, well conceived and competently organized educational programme' was needed to ensure that US foreign policy was not misunderstood or even frustrated by the British people.[56] Measures included compiling a digest of anti-American views expressed by individuals, periodicals and newspapers. The digest was then evaluated at weekly meetings of the United States Information Service (USIS) and other Embassy staff to address the problem. The decision was taken to implement 'a better organized and more considered campaign'.[57] Soon USIS provided coverage for propaganda from offices in London, Edinburgh and Manchester. The impact of US 'public diplomacy' is hard to gauge, however, in part because of the ERP's success in assuaging some hostility towards the United States. Contrary to some of Douglas's fears, anti-Americanism did not inflict significant damage on the Anglo-American relationship and most American diplomats in Britain met with friendly receptions from the public and officials alike.

Conclusion

Lewis Douglas was not without his flaws as an ambassador. For instance, some of his interlocutors considered that he often went into issues in tiresome detail,[58] and that his frequent dealings with leader of the opposition Winston Churchill caused some irritation among Labour politicians.[59] All the same, Douglas developed close and productive ties with Ernest Bevin and garnered 'immense prestige and popularity' on the Anglo-American diplomatic scene.[60] His contributions were certainly recognised in Washington. When personal reasons led Douglas to consider resigning in early 1949, Truman responded that he was 'most anxious for him to remain at his post', so that matters such as the future of Germany, Palestine, the ECA and the North Atlantic Treaty could be addressed.[61] In 1950, referring to the Atlantic as 'the great river of Anglo-American association' and to the US and British embassies as 'the two great channels through which the lively waters run', British Ambassador to Washington Oliver Franks praised the 'superb skill with which the American faucet had been managed in London [which] has greatly helped the pressures on the British tap in Washington'.[62] Franks was acknowledging the US Embassy's role in furthering the Anglo-American relationship during a critical period.

The US Embassy in Douglas's time was notable for its liaison role, that is, helping to formulate joint or complementary policies. This was, of course, closely related to the representation and negotiation functions of an embassy that have been noted by G. R. Berridge, but there are differences.[63] While negotiation, representation and liaison all involve communication and interaction, negotiation and representation can feature in adversarial or even hostile situations as well as more harmonious ones. An example of an adversarial situation in which the Embassy had a major role were the 1947–48 talks over the British imposition of a tax on imported feature films. By contrast, liaison is more constructive and occurs when the states concerned have similar outlooks and overlapping interests in relation to a common issue. The Embassy's liaison function derived predominantly from the need to coordinate British and US policies in the developing Cold War and helped to lay the foundations for the long-term 'special relationship' that Douglas helped to develop and was so keen to extol.

The stature of the US Embassy was also enhanced by its strength in coordinating policies in relation to given geographical areas.[64] Britain had diplomatic expertise and influence stemming from decades, if not centuries, of global policies, so liaison in London had an especially valuable quality from the perspective of US Foreign Service personnel. At the same time, many of the important Anglo-American issues in the late 1940s were addressed mainly in Washington, reflecting American preponderance as well as the recognition that the British Embassy in Washington was in especially capable hands under Oliver Franks. Most of the negotiations about NATO in 1949, which institutionalised the US security commitment to Western Europe, took place in Washington.[65] Yet, partly due to the stature of Douglas as an envoy, and partly due to the institutional impact of the Cold War, the Embassy in London had, by 1950, reached a level of unprecedented peacetime importance.[66]

Notes

1. Robert Paul Browder and Thomas G. Smith, *Independent: A Biography of Lewis W. Douglas* (New York: Knopf, 1986), p. 241. Douglas had long been a personal friend of Acheson. John T. McNay, *Acheson and Empire: The British Accent in American Foreign Policy* (Columbia, MI: University of Missouri Press, 2001), pp. 43–4.
2. Marc Trachtenburg, *A Constructed Peace: The Making of the European Settlement 1945–1963* (Princeton, NJ: Princeton University Press, 1999), p. 76.
3. 'Information for the Survey Group Proceeding to London', 24 February 1945, Box 22, Lot 54D224, Record Group (RG) 59, National Archives and Record Administration (NARA II), College Park, MD.
4. Quoted in Browder and Smith, *Independent*, p. 241.
5. Quoted in 'Ambassador Lewis Douglas: Diplomacy is Big Business', *Time*, 1 December 1947, p. 12.
6. Child minute, 12 March 1947, FO 371/61000, National Archives (TNA), Kew, Surrey.
7. Michael F. Hopkins, *Oliver Franks and the Truman Administration: Anglo-American Relations, 1948–1952* (London: Cass, 2003), p. 58.
8. Rundall minute, 12 March 1947, FO 371/61000, TNA.
9. Quoted in Browder and Smith, *Independent*, p. 255.
10. Douglas to Secretary of State, 28 March 1947, *FRUS 1947*, Vol. III *British Commonwealth, Europe* (Washington, DC: USGPO, 1972), pp. 497–8.
11. Douglas to Secretary of State, 17 May 1947, *FRUS 1947*, Vol. III, p. 511.
12. Douglas to Secretary of State, 18 March 1947, *FRUS 1947*, Vol. III, pp. 494–5.
13. See Douglas to Secretary of State, 22 and 23 May 1947, *FRUS 1947*, Vol. III, pp. 513–14.
14. Douglas to Secretary of State, 20 May 1947, *FRUS 1947*, Vol. III, pp. 14–15.
15. Browder and Smith, *Independent*, p. 257.
16. Douglas to Secretary of State, 25 July 1947, *FRUS 1947*, Vol. III, p. 44.
17. Quoted in Browder and Smith, *Independent*, pp. 275–6. See *FRUS 1947*, Vol. III, pp. 52 and 267, on Douglas's relationship with Bevin. On Bevin, see Bullock, *Ernest Bevin*.

18. Kathleen Burk, 'Britain and the Marshall Plan', in Chris Wrigley (ed.), *Warfare, Diplomacy and Politics: Essays in Honour of A.J.P. Taylor* (London: Hamish Hamilton, 1986), p. 219; Secretary of State to President Truman, 26 June 1948, *FRUS 1948,* Vol. III *Western Europe* (1974), p. 458.

19. Douglas to State Department, 31 August 1948, *FRUS 1948,* Vol. III, p. 1118.

20. Quoted in Browder and Smith, *Independent,* p. 277.

21. Browder and Smith, *Independent,* p. 277.

22. Douglas to Secretary of State, 21 April 1948, *FRUS 1948,* Vol. II *Germany and Austria* (1973), p. 198.

23. Editorial note, *FRUS 1948,* Vol. II, p. 191.

24. Douglas to Secretary of State, *FRUS 1948,* Vol. II, pp. 129–30.

25. Douglas to Secretary of State, 1 June 1948, *FRUS 1948,* Vol. II, pp. 308–9.

26. Douglas to Secretary of State, 17 July 1948, *FRUS 1948,* Vol. II, pp. 968–9.

27. Bullock, *Bevin,* p. 576; Lucius D. Clay, *Decision in Germany* (Melbourne, London and New York: Heinemann, 1950), p. 376.

28. Browder and Smith, *Independent,* pp. 293 and 302.

29. Douglas to Secretary of State, 26 June 1948, *FRUS 1948,* Vol. II, p. 923; Hopkins, *Oliver Franks,* p. 83.

30. Norman Moss, *Picking up the Reins: America, Britain and the Post-War World* (London: Duckworth, 2008), pp. 156–7.

31. Clay, *Decision in Germany,* p. 369; Smith (Soviet Union) to Secretary of State, 30 July 1948, *FRUS 1948,* Vol. II, pp. 995–6.

32. Surveys of Anglo-American relations include Kathleen Burk, *New World, Old World: The Story of Britain and America* (London: Little, Brown, 2007); Danchev, *On Specialness*; David Dimbleby and David Reynolds, *An Ocean Apart: The Relationship between Britain and America in the Twentieth Century* (London: BBC/Hodder & Stoughton, 1988); Alan P. Dobson, *Anglo-American Relations in the Twentieth Century: Of Friendship, Conflict and the Rise and Decline of Superpowers* (London: Routledge, 1995); John Dumbrell, *A Special Relationship: Anglo-American Relations in the Cold War and After* (Basingstoke: Macmillan, 2006); and Ritchie Ovendale, *Anglo-American Relations in the Twentieth Century* (Basingstoke: Macmillan, 1998). See the bibliographies of these works for accounts of the Anglo-American relationship in the early Cold War.

33. John W. Young, *Britain, France and the Unity of Europe, 1945–51* (Leicester: Leicester University Press, 1984), pp. 126–7.

34. John Baylis (ed.), *Anglo-American Relations since 1939: The Enduring Alliance* (Manchester: Manchester University Press, 1997), pp. 62–7. See also Richard J. Aldrich, *The Hidden Hand: Britain, America and Cold War Secret Intelligence* (London: John Murray, 2001), p. 354; Browder and Smith, *Independent,* pp. 338–9; and Dobson, *Anglo-American Relations,* pp. 98–9. 'Special Relationship' versus 'European Unity' arguments would of course be rehearsed for decades. See the views of Henry Kissinger in Baylis, *Anglo-American Relations,* pp. 162–4.

35. Baylis, *Anglo-American Relations,* pp. 74–5.

36. G. R. Berridge, *Diplomacy: Theory and Practice* (Basingstoke: Palgrave, 3rd edn, 2005), p. 122.

37. 'Supplemental Budget Request', 6 May 1949, Box 20, Lot 54D224, RG59, NARA II.

38. 'Organization Administration for Congressional Briefing: ECA Special Mission to the United Kingdom', 10 January 1950, Box 2, Mission to UK, Office of Deputy Chiefs of Mission Subject Files (Entry 1417), RG59, NARA II.

39. Burk, *New World, Old World*, p. 585; Bissell, quoted in Moss, *Picking up the Reins*, p. 134.
40. Douglas to State Department, 31 August 1948, *FRUS 1948*, Vol. III *Western Europe* (1974), p. 484; Burk, *New World, Old World*, p. 585. See also Burk, 'Britain and the Marshall Plan', pp. 210–30.
41. See, for example, Jonathan Colman, 'The US Embassy and British Film Policy, 1947–48: A "Lesser but Highly Explosive Question"', *Journal of Transatlantic Studies* (December 2009), pp. 413–30.
42. Hall to Bartlett, 12 April 1948, Box 22, Lot 54D224, RG59, NARA II.
43. *Hearings before the Subcommittee on National Security Staffing and Operations of the Committee on Government Operations United States Senate*, Eighty-Eighth Congress, First Session, 24 July and 18 September 1963, Part 3 (Washington, DC: USGPO, 1963), p. 267.
44. Oral History Interview with W. John Kenney, 29 November 1971, Harry S. Truman Presidential Library, Independence, Missouri (hereafter HSTL).
45. Michael F. Hopkins, 'The Washington Embassy: The Role of an Institution in Anglo-American Relations, 1945–1955', in Richard J. Aldrich and Michael F. Hopkins (eds.), *Intelligence Defence and Diplomacy: British Policy in the Post-War World* (London: Cass, 1994), p. 82.
46. Interview with Thomas K. Finletter, 25 February 1953, Price Papers, HSTL.
47. Author's telephone conversation with Thomas Dunnigan, 16 June 2007.
48. On the development of the post of Labour Attaché, see Andrew L. Steigman, foreword by Carol C. Laise, *The Foreign Service of the United States: First Line of Defense* (Boulder, CO and London: Westview Press, 1985), pp. 146–8.
49. Philip M. Kaiser, *Journeying Far and Wide: A Political and Diplomatic Memoir* (New York: Scribner's, 1992), p. 120; Hugh Wilford, *The CIA, the British Left and the Cold War: Calling the Tune?* (London: Cass, 2003), pp. 164–7 and 186 (fn. 20); and Hugh Wilford, 'American Labour Diplomacy and Cold War Britain', *Journal of Contemporary History*, Vol. 37, No. 1 (2002), pp. 45–65.
50. *Hearings before the Subcommittee on National Security Staffing*, p. 243.
51. Aldrich, *The Hidden Hand*, p. 83.
52. Tom Bower, *The Perfect English Spy: Sir Dick White and the Secret War 1935–1990* (London: Heinemann, 1995), p. 90. Also see Aldrich, *The Hidden Hand*, pp. 83–6, on the exchange of intelligence documents.
53. Holmes to State Department, 15 February 1950, 611.41/2-1550, Central Decimal 1950–1954, RG59, NARA II.
54. Telegrams (London), London to Secretary of State, 7 January 1950, Box 165, PSF: Subject Files 1940–53, HSTL.
55. Gallman to Acheson, 30 January 1948, *FRUS 1948*, Vol. III, pp. 1074–5.
56. Memorandum, 9 May 1947, Box 24, Lot 54D224, RG 59, NARA II.
57. Gallman to Wailes, 8 January 1947, Box 24, Lot 54D224, RG 59, NARA II. On the Embassy's wartime propaganda operations, see Charles A. H. Thomson, *Overseas Information Service of the United States Government* (Washington, DC: Brookings, 1948), pp. 64, 69–75.
58. Burrows to Wright, 29 December 1950, FO 371/81779, TNA.
59. Browder and Smith, *Independent*, pp. 336–7.
60. 'Confidential Report', author unknown, 16 August 1951, Box 154, Foreign Affairs File, PSF: Subject File 1940–1953, HSTL.
61. Conversation between Acheson and Truman, Box 65, Mem Cons File 1949-53, Sec State File 1945–1953, Acheson Papers, HSTL.

62. Quoted in Browder and Smith, *Independent*, p. 353.
63. See Berridge, *Diplomacy*, pp. 119–32.
64. Author's telephone interview with Thomas Dunnigan, 16 June 2007.
65. Hopkins, *Oliver Franks*, pp. 86–97 and p. 252.
66. Douglas commented in 1948 that 'Anglo-American unity today is more firmly established than ever before in peacetime'. Douglas to Marshall, 11 August 1948, *FRUS 1948*, Vol. III, p. 1113. See also Dimbleby and Reynolds, *An Ocean Apart*, p. 180.

5
Walter Sherman Gifford, 1950–53

Jonathan Colman

Walter Gifford took up the post of US Ambassador to London late in 1950, a troubled time for the Anglo-American relationship. This was due in large part to differences of view over the Korean War.[1] While the British contributed troops to the American-led campaign, there were concerns that US policies were rash and provocative. Additionally, Gifford dealt with issues of European security, including the response to a series of notes from the Soviet Union in 1952 proposing the neutralisation and reunification of Germany. He also dealt with British demands for support after the Iranian nationalisation of British oil assets. Gifford was not a notably proactive or interventionist ambassador, nor did he seek to shape policy directly, but – as will be seen – he did foster greater mutual understanding between Washington and London. Despite tensions, he did not find himself having to address any major crises in the Anglo-American relationship while he was in Britain; the broad international objectives of the two countries remained mutually compatible.

Gifford was not the only candidate for the ambassadorship in 1950. Lewis Douglas had wanted Thomas K. Finletter, head of the European Cooperation Administration in London 1948–49, to be his successor.[2] Finletter's experience would have stood him in good stead, but it would have been a break with precedent to have selected a professional diplomat for an important post such as London.[3] President Harry Truman is said to have considered appointing James Bruce, Ambassador in Buenos Aires and brother of David K. E. Bruce, Ambassador in Paris. While the President no doubt realised that having two brothers in the two most prestigious ambassadorships (London and Paris) would have attracted criticism, Bernard Burrows at the British Embassy in Washington suggested that the chief reason for Bruce's rejection was that he was 'too much in [Secretary of Defence] Louis Johnson's pocket'. Secretary Johnson had been vigorously 'plugging' Bruce's 'case with the President ... and it would certainly only have been over [Secretary of State] Dean Acheson's dead body that Bruce would have been appointed'.[4] Acheson's hostility may also have derived from allegations of corruption.

When it emerged that Bruce was under consideration for London, one jour-nalist wrote that 'The London Embassy will soon be sold for cash on the barrelhead.'[5]

Washington was keen to secure the early *agrément* to Walter Gifford's appointment. A Foreign Office official was worried about the reasons for Gifford's divorce in 1929 (there might have been scandal or gossip), but Buckingham Palace considered that as over twenty years had elapsed it did not matter.[6] British Ambassador in Washington Oliver Franks suggested that he campaign for the Congressional mid-term elections then 'at full blast makes things very difficult for the President if he tries to hold up publica-tion of the name of the new Ambassador'. Truman had 'gone outside all party considerations' in naming Gifford, a Republican, as the next Ambas-sador in London.[7] Burrows suggested that Gifford was 'one of the reasonable and sensible Republicans'. He had been 'a member of Dewey's Finance Com-mittee during the 1948 Presidential campaign', and was presumed to be 'a fairly heavy contributor to Republican Party funds'.[8] Gifford's wealth also meant that he could bear the substantial cost of the London position. More-over, Truman's appointment of a Republican turned out to be a wise thing to do in the light of Republican success in the Congressional elections.

The Harvard-educated, 65-year-old Gifford had spent most of his life in business. He had risen from modest origins to become president of the American Telephone and Telegraph Company in 1925, spending 25 years in that role. He had some public service experience, too. During the First World War he had been executive director of the Council of National Defense, and later he was Secretary to the American delegation of the Inter-Allies Munitions Council. In the Second World War he held the post of Chairman of the American Red Cross War Campaign, headed the Industry Advisory Committee of the Board of War Communications and was a member of the War Finance Committee of New York State.[9] Dean Acheson suggested that Gifford had 'excellent qualifications' due to his 'valuable services to the United States government in both wars'.[10] However, Gifford had no diplo-matic experience, and his acquaintance with Britain was confined solely to a motoring tour during the 1930s. Given this background, Bernard Burrows believed that he would be

> more like the American Ambassadors we used to have in London before the war...and that while he will be an admirable representative and do all the public side of things very well, he will be much less interested in the day-to-day work than Lew Douglas and will not intervene himself in nearly so many detailed problems – such for example as the level of German industry – as has his predecessor.[11]

A Foreign Office official concluded bluntly that Gifford was merely 'an effi-cient but remarkably colourless business-man'.[12] Few other officials were so negative, though, and they looked forward to the arrival of the new Ambassador.

Gifford took as axiomatic the United States' close relationship with Britain, recognising that the country still had global diplomatic entrée and was the strongest of the Western European states. However, he recognised that the British were 'overextended economically, politically and militarily...their commitments, which they have inherited from days of their greater strength, are now too great for their resources'. They were 'trying desperately to maintain their position as a first class power, seat of empire, head of Commonwealth and center of sterling area'. Operating on a thin margin made the British 'extremely sensitive to any hint that their [the UK] position is not consistent with theirs [the US], especially in areas where they have primary responsibility'.[13] Gifford was a supporter of European political and economic integration, seeing it as a way of bolstering the strength of the continent. As Britain was still reluctant to participate in this process – looking instead towards close bonds with the United States and to the Commonwealth – he did not, unlike his successors, have to consider what British participation in a unified Europe would have meant for the 'special relationship'. He was, as one would expect, a firm believer in the need to stand up to communism, through military alliances such as NATO and mechanisms of collective security such as the United Nations. The Ambassador had drawn the simple lesson of the 1930s that it was essential to resist dictators or their aggression would never cease. He noted, for example, that the 'breakdown of sanctions against Italy' had been disastrous for the League of Nations.[14]

The Cold War meant that the Anglo-American 'special relationship' was well-established by the time Gifford arrived in London in November 1950, in large part due to the work of the US Embassy. As noted in the previous chapter, there had been intensive collaboration in London over Marshall Aid and the Berlin Blockade. Meanwhile, the British Embassy in Washington had hosted talks that led to the signing of the North Atlantic Treaty. However, the development of institutional links in diplomacy, defence and economics, and the general intermingling of British and American interests, meant that the policies of one partner could antagonise the other partner all the more easily. There were particular differences of view over the Far East, especially concerning communist China.[15] The United States had supported the Chinese nationalist forces under Chiang Kai-shek in the long-running civil war, but when the communist Mao-Tse Tung triumphed in 1949 there were bitter domestic recriminations about the administration's so-called 'loss' of China. The State Department considered that Britain's diplomatic recognition of Mao's government made matters worse, as the move helped to strengthen and legitimise the regime (the British had acted out of concern for their regional commercial interests and political influence).

Gifford noted that while the London government recognised the need to keep Formosa (Taiwan) – now the outpost of the defeated, US-backed nationalist forces – in friendly hands, the British felt that this objective could be accomplished more effectively by seeking constructive relations with mainland China instead of relying on Chiang's discredited army. Furthermore, the British, unlike the Americans, wanted communist China to have a seat in the United Nations, as it was felt that this would be more constructive than leaving Beijing in isolation. Gifford concluded that the British were more inclined to accommodate the 'Asiatic viewpoint' than they were the views of their American ally.[16] However, there was some collaboration between Britain and the United States to recover lost American assets in China, so the issue of China in Anglo-American relations was not solely one of discord.

In June 1950, communist North Korea had, with Moscow's assent, invaded South Korea, a US protégé. Neither the United States nor Britain had attached particular importance to South Korea, but they agreed readily that this demonstration of communist aggression should be resisted. Britain, seeking to maintain influence with the United States as well as to stand up to communist advances, provided the second highest number of troops for the American-led, UN-sponsored, war effort. Numerous Commonwealth countries took part too. After making rapid headway, the UN forces took the war up to North Korea's border with China in November, only to be greeted by 200,000 Chinese troops. There was little complaint in Britain when things were going well, but Gifford noted that subsequent retreat reduced American standing considerably.[17] British worries about Korea focused partly on the grandiose personality of General Douglas MacArthur, who commanded the UN forces and bridled at civilian restraints imposed on the conduct of the war.[18] Gifford noted in May 1952 that most British people welcomed Truman's replacement of MacArthur by General Matthew Ridgway as helping to reduce the chance of the Korean conflict spreading. There was among the British 'much quiet satisfaction from their unjustified belief that they had played a part in securing [MacArthur's] removal', Gifford suggested.[19]

The fear in Britain that American policies could spark a wider war in Asia and beyond was of particular resonance given that in April 1950, the United States had secured four permanent air bases in Britain. These would undoubtedly be targets for a Soviet atomic attack in the event of a superpower conflict.[20] According to Oliver Franks, Ernest Bevin, the British Foreign Secretary, feared that Gifford might 'call him up some night and say, "Our planes are taking off in five minutes from your fields, do you mind?" '[21] Intimations in November 1950 that US policy-makers were considering dropping the bomb in Korea led a fearful Prime Minister Clement Attlee to cross the Atlantic for a summit conference in Washington. Gifford attended the gathering, acting as an advisor to the President. The Ambassador's face-to-face briefings of his Washington colleagues helped to convey the climate of opinion in Britain in a way that telegrams, however comprehensive and insightful, could not. The summit communiqué stated that the United States intended to keep the British government 'informed' of any developments which might change the situation concerning the use of atomic weapons. This fell short of an agreement to engage in consultation, but, as Gifford reported, Attlee's visit helped to ease British worries about the immediate use of the bomb.[22]

Yet the British continued to doubt their American allies. Early in 1951 Gifford asked the State Department to send certain high-ranking officials to London to discuss American policy in the Far East with British politicians and officials.[23] However, the State Department felt that there was already enough Anglo-American consultation, in London, in Washington and elsewhere. Instead, the London Embassy should itself initiate certain measures. These might include the use of Embassy and other speakers to talk on 'grass-roots platforms, brain trust discussions, etc'; 'frank on the record discussions with key editors, BBC commentators...to give [the] full picture of [the] immense US effort and the goodwill and faith behind our desire to work with Britain as [an] honored, experienced partner'; and 'honest indoctrination to moulders of Brit public opinion', such as newspaper editors.[24] Soon, Gifford requested additional support for the operations of the United States Information Service in London, to explain the American point of view in relation to issues such as Korea, Formosa and the UN.[25]

Gifford noted on one occasion that the United States created its own problems with British public opinion. Constant publicity about American military developments gave the impression that the Americans had adopted a 'warlike purpose' in their international stance. Examples included the official release of information about a 'hitherto secret base at Thule...under 1000 miles from the North Pole', a reported statement by US officials that 'targets in Russia were within the range of jet bombers flying from American-operated bases abroad', a remark that 'all American aircraft carriers now carry planes – or will shortly carry planes – capable of dropping the atomic bomb', and the release of information about the perfection of atomic cannon.[26] To counter negative perceptions, Gifford's Embassy built on some earlier initiatives and became notably active in the fields of propaganda and public diplomacy. By early 1953 the various information services of the US government in Britain included 93 staff operating in London with an annual budget of nearly a million dollars, having expanded considerably first under Lewis Douglas and then under Gifford.[27]

The United States initiated a substantial rearmament programme with the beginning of the Korean War, and wanted Britain to follow suit. Gifford reported in January 1951 that – partly due to Embassy promptings – Attlee and the most influential ministers in the Cabinet recognised that British rearmament had to reflect military needs rather than economic ones.[28] The London government agreed to increase defence spending from £3,600 million to £4,700 million for 1951–54. However, this fell short of the £6,000 million that American policy-makers had in mind.[29] British representatives,

Gifford noted, responded to American entreaties by stating that they had nearly 40,000 troops fighting communists in Malaya, that proportionately the size of British forces compared with that of American ones, that military service in Britain was longer and universal, that until the outbreak of war in Korea, Britain spent a higher proportion of GNP on defence than did the United States, and that since Korea that amount had been increased substantially.[30]

Defence spending was a sore subject. In spring 1951, Aneurin Bevan, Harold Wilson and John Freeman resigned from the Cabinet in protest against National Health Service prescription charges, which had been introduced to help cover the cost of rearmament. Gifford wrote that the way these politicians had dramatised the 'allegedly disastrous effects' of the defence programme on the British economy 'not only brought into [the] open some latent fears' about the 'incompatibility of large-scale rearmament with [the] welfare state concept but also capitalised on the smouldering resentment toward [the] US' occasioned by continued shortages of raw materials. Bevan *et al.*, Gifford suggested, had exploited the 'widespread belief that US had put strong pressure' on Britain to rearm.[31] Dean Acheson made a press statement rebutting the view that American stockpiling was responsible for the raw materials shortages, while the announcement of new allocations (under the Mutual Security Act 1951) helped to ease the controversy. The London Embassy noted that more and members of the British public now believed that their government was at least partly responsible for the shortages, having concentrated on building up gold and dollar reserves instead of stockpiling raw materials.[32]

By the time the Labour government left office in October 1951, Anglo-American differences over the Far East had become much less pressing, in large part because the military situation in Korea had become stabilised (an armistice was secured in 1953).[33] A side effect of the Korean War was to create the momentum for greater integration of the defences of the Western European states. In particular, the war is said to have put the 'O' into NATO, with a number of reforms designed to create an integrated command structure. However, the selection of US Admiral William Fechteler to fill the post of NATO's Supreme Allied Commander Atlantic (SACLANT) piqued British pride. Dean Acheson concluded in a despatch to the Embassy in April 1951 that Winston Churchill, leader of the Conservative Opposition, was exploiting patriotic sentiment over the appointment.[34] Churchill wanted a joint Anglo-American structure comparable to those of the Second World War. After becoming Prime Minister in October 1951, he gained only minor concessions from the United States: the British command was extended to the 100 fathom mark around the British coast, and there would be more command flexibility in the eastern Atlantic.[35]

Britain refused to participate in the European Defence Community (EDC). This was a scheme for a supranational army that would bring about the rearmament of West Germany within a controlled framework. Gifford noted how Churchill thought that the EDC was 'not the kind of European army he had in mind in his early speeches'.[36] The Ambassador took the view that the EDC was an important step in the construction of united defences, and that the British, with their decision not to participate in this and other measures towards unification, had a 'negative attitude' towards European integration.[37] Gifford had further concerns that certain of Churchill's policies might – unwittingly – disrupt the augmentation of Western defences. The Prime Minister considered that his experience with Stalin during the Second World War placed him in the best position of all the Western statesmen to deal with Moscow, and that there should be an East-West summit conference to ease the Cold War.[38] This had been all the more essential since 1949, by which time both the United States and the Soviet Union had the atomic bomb (Britain detonated its own bomb in 1952). However, American diplomats did not want to get sidetracked into the pursuit of détente and to give up the quest for a position of strength in the Cold War. Gifford was required to dissuade Churchill from making any public proposal for a summit without prior consultation with the Americans.[39] While the precise effects of any such entreaties are hard to measure, the Prime Minister did not make any unilateral moves to initiate a summit while Gifford was Ambassador (although he would do so in 1953, after Stalin died). As for the EDC, France rejected the scheme in 1953, and West Germany was soon rearmed under the auspices of NATO.

In late 1952, the London Embassy was the centre of discussions between the United States, Britain and France about how to respond to a series of Soviet notes proposing a four-power conference about West Germany's possible reunification and neutralisation.[40] While answering to Dean Acheson in Washington, Gifford dealt extensively with Foreign Secretary Anthony Eden and French Ambassador to London René Massigli. There was a consensus among the allies that, as Gifford noted, the Soviets' main purpose behind making the proposals was to 'delay and impede' plans for West German rearmament, but there were differences about how best to respond.[41] Gifford and his colleagues believed that the absolute priority was to push forward with the signature and ratification of the EDC, but the British and the French were more inclined to consider public opinion in West Germany and in their own countries, and to explore matters such as the Russian proposal for a treaty with West Germany.[42] At one stage, too, the British criticised part of an American draft reply to one of the Soviet notes as being too propagandistic.[43] Gifford provided able stewardship of the talks in London, helping to ensure that the differences between the allies did not become so exaggerated that they prevented a unified response. By September 1952 the Soviets had dropped their diplomatic initiative. Stalin was preoccupied with the forthcoming Nineteenth Party Congress, and, quite likely, was awaiting the result of the US presidential election.[44]

A further, and more prolonged, issue for Gifford was Iran's nationalisation of the British-controlled Anglo-Iranian Oil Company in 1951 by the left-leaning regime of Mohammed Mossadeq. This was a significant blow to Britain, as Anglo-Iranian represented the country's only non-dollar source of oil, and it was also a question of prestige in a region where British influence was waning. Gifford noted the 'growing Near East practice of twisting the lion's tail' at a time when Britain's diminished power kept it from taking 'preventive or retaliatory action'.[45] The preferred option for British policy-makers was to use force to regain the oil assets in Iran, but American help would be needed. However, the Americans – bogged down in Korea until 1953, fearing that military intervention would encourage direct Soviet involvement, and by no means rueing the edging out of British imperial interests in the Middle East – were not as sympathetic as was hoped, and the White House and State Department wanted a negotiated settlement.[46] Gifford noted on one occasion that the Labour Foreign Secretary, Herbert Morrison, was in a 'petulant and angry mood', feeling that US policy had presented him as much as a wrongdoer as was the Iranian leader, who had disregarded the recommendations of the International Court of Justice and had 'generally refused to cooperate in any way in reaching equitable solution'. Morrison even wondered if Washington was willing to see the downfall of the Labour government over the Iranian oil issue.[47] Nor was Foreign Secretary Anthony Eden impressed by American policy. Soon after the general election, Gifford argued that the latest American proposals for a negotiated solution were no more likely to commend themselves to Mossadeq than previous ones. Unlike Washington, the British (in the absence of the military option) were not prepared to abandon the principle that financial compensation had to be determined by an impartial international body.[48]

While not supporting armed intervention, Gifford was definitely more sympathetic to British concerns than were most of his colleagues in the United States – a stance which garnered considerable gratitude in London.[49] He felt that the Iran issue should not be permitted to damage Anglo-American bonds. On one occasion, he told Washington that the British had 'conducted themselves responsibly...and whatever their inclinations otherwise may have been, have deferred to our views at a number of crucial points'. It was 'no time for Anglo-American differences to become apparent on a question to which so much moral importance is attached here'.[50] The matter dragged on. In December 1952, Gifford expressed concern to the State Department about its consideration of a lump-sum settlement with Mossadeq without conferring with the British. As the Iranian leader was likely to reject such an approach to the issue of compensation, it was not worth the likely damage to Anglo-American relations.[51] The Ambassador's arguments created a fuller understanding in Washington about British concerns, but he did not succeed in modifying American policy. A new approach would have to wait until the Eisenhower administration – which was especially worried about Mossadeq establishing links with the Soviet Union – had entered office. Anglo-American covert action in 1953 helped to bring about the downfall of the Iranian nationalist and, subsequently, the regime of the Shah agreed to provide suitable compensation to the British. However, this led to the destruction of Britain's oil monopoly in Iran, with the United States taking a notable share.

Conclusion

Ambassador Gifford never did, as Bernard Burrows in Washington had predicted late in 1950, involve himself much in the day-to-day work of his Embassy. He barely needed to, given that he had the valuable support of Julius Holmes, Deputy Chief of Mission 1949–52. Holmes was notably adept in a role that is especially important in major embassies with non-career ambassadors. After a visit to London in 1950, the former Ambassador to London (1946) Averell Harriman commented that 'I...want to say how fortunate...we are in having as effective and objective a man' in the Embassy as Holmes.[52] Thomas Dunnigan, who dealt with German questions at the Embassy from 1950 to 1952, suggested that Holmes 'held all the reins in his hand'.[53] An unsigned report in August 1951 (possibly from Harriman, who was in London around that time) suggested that Holmes was even ahead of Gifford as 'the most knowledgeable interpreter of Anglo-US affairs' and 'the most effective worker on our behalf behind the scenes'.[54] Holmes provided close administrative support for the Ambassador, and kept the Embassy running smoothly when Gifford was in Washington for consultations or was taking his annual leave.

The observer noted above did not find the Ambassador particularly impressive. It was suggested that while he was 'very able...and [a] conscientious worker in his country's cause', he was 'inexperienced in the world of politics and diplomacy'. Gifford had himself stated privately that he was 'too old for the political-cum-social amenities which go hand-in-hand with a post such as his at the Court of St James's. It was 'a curious fact that more can be done in a private house, club or at weekends in London than in any government office or during "working" hours'. Although 'a kindly and essentially good man, doing the best he can', and with 'many friends in high places', Gifford had 'irritated others as well, due mainly...to his inexperience'. The report suggested that it would have been 'difficult to select anyone who could have competed favourably with the immense prestige and popularity of Lewis Douglas. Whoever was selected to follow must suffer in comparison.' Douglas, who was then in Britain in a private capacity, still had 'more inside information and exercises more political (as opposed to official) thinking than does the Ambassador himself'.[55]

It is axiomatic that diplomats need to maintain a wide range of contacts to produce the highest quality of reporting and to exert influence. However, the 1951 report expressed concerns that contacts between US and British officials in London could have been better. Although the US Embassy had

> a large representation in Britain...somehow the liaison does not seem as effective as it might; neither American nor British...interpret their views to one another clearly enough for tolerant understanding, and social integration and 'mixing' are more formal than need be....The desire for intimacy is there but the method of creating it is found wanting.[56]

The importance of the US Embassy in London had begun to wane with Douglas's return to Washington. This development reflected his high calibre as an envoy, the relative stability of the European situation by this stage and the new, and in many ways problematic, focus upon Asia as an arena of Cold War crisis. Douglas suggested in July 1950 that 'the responsibilities which were formerly lodged in this Embassy...have gradually and very properly diminished' – only 'the routine reporting, combined with an occasional task of some significance, remains for this Embassy to do'.[57] The forecast proved correct, which meant that Gifford did not have the chance to participate in any epochal Anglo-American initiatives, such as the response to the Berlin Blockade, as had Douglas.

There was the growing importance of the Washington Embassy to contend with, too. Dean Acheson was less inclined to delegate authority to ambassadors than was his predecessor, George C. Marshall, and when Acheson worked through London it was mainly indirectly via Oliver Franks, a reflection of his friendship with Franks.[58] The situation in Korea brought enhanced military liaison between the British Embassy and the Pentagon.[59] Like Franks, Roger Makins was a skilled ambassador to the United States (1952–56) and thereby helped to boost the stature of the British Embassy in Washington over the US Embassy in London.[60]

Gifford was little inclined to seize the initiative, perhaps because of his status as a diplomatic novice, and he did not immerse himself in matters of detail. However, his interventions on matters such as the German notes of 1952 helped to ease Anglo-American differences, and generally he was assiduous in reporting promptly to Washington events and conditions which might influence the relationship with the United States. His business background was valuable in enabling him to understand economic affairs. This was valuable, for example, in the context of American aid to Britain and for the GATT (General Agreement on Tariffs and Trade) talks that took place in Torquay in 1950–51.[61] He also helped to moderate the relationship between top-level policy-makers on at least one occasion. After a 1952 *Newsweek* article suggested that there was a 'Clash of Personalities' between Acheson and

Eden, Gifford was required to reassure the latter that the article was spurious and that Acheson held him in the highest regard.[62]

Gifford's personal role was such that he performed a number of G. R. Berridge's 'ten commandments' of an embassy: negotiating (especially in relation to the Stalin notes about West Germany in 1952), promoting friendly relations with elites, clarifying intentions, and gathering information and producing political reports.[63] He seemed to grow into his post, becoming increasingly well regarded by his British hosts. Eden suggested that the Ambassador was

> wise enough to find his way cautiously. He carefully considered every position gained and, by his third year, was proving himself an outstanding ambassador. Gifford's background, with its wide experience of men and affairs, taught him how to handle the British. He soon won our respect, and affection followed.[64]

Eden and his colleagues 'were surprised and sorry to say goodbye to the Giffords. So were all who cared for the tough reality of Anglo-American relations.'[65] After the presidential election of November 1953, Winston Churchill urged Eisenhower to break with precedent by leaving Gifford in London, instead of making a new, party-political appointment. Eisenhower agreed in principle but felt obliged to award the diplomatic prizes to those who had contributed generously to his election campaign.[66] Although the Anglo-American alliance had its tensions during Gifford's time in London, there was no major breach; the two countries maintained common cause in the Cold War. As the Ambassador noted, 'British attitudes on basic international issues are of course identical with our own. They will stay that way.'[67] By promoting mutual understanding between the United States and Britain, Gifford helped to contribute to that state of affairs.

Notes

1. Although the war had begun in June, Lewis Douglas's departure from London soon after had meant that he missed much of the furore.
2. Tydings and Acheson conversation, 13 April 1949, Box 65, Mem Cons File 1949–1953, Sec State File 1945–1953, Acheson Papers, Library of Harry S. Truman (HSTL), Independence, MI.
3. The precedent would be broken with the appointment of Raymond Seitz as ambassador, 1991–94.
4. Burrows to Wright, 29 December 1950, FO 371/81779, The National Archives, Kew (TNA).
5. Nelson K. Lankford, *The Last American Aristocrat: The Life of David K.E. Bruce* (New York: Little, Brown, 1992), pp. 213–15.
6. Lascelles (Buckingham Palace) to Strang, 23 November 1950, FO 371/81779, TNA.
7. Franks to Prime Minister, 26 September 1950, FO 371/81779, TNA.
8. Burrows to Wright, 29 December 1950, FO 371/81779, TNA.

9.   'US Ambassador to Britain', *The Times*, 28 September 1950; Gifford biography, FO 371/81779, TNA.
10. New York to Foreign Office, 26 September 1950, FO 371/81779, TNA.
11. Burrows to Wright, 29 December 1950, FO 371/81779, TNA.
12. Curle minute, 23 October 1950, FO 371/81779, TNA.
13. Gifford to Department of State, 28 December 1951, *Foreign Relations of the United States (FRUS) 1952–1954*, Vol. VI *Western Europe and Canada Part I* (Washington, DC: USGPO, 1986), p. 720.
14. Gifford to Secretary of State, 20 January 1951, *FRUS 1951*, Vol. IV *Korea and China Part I* (1983), p. 896.
15. Anglo-American differences in the Far East also included a peace treaty for Japan. See Hopkins, *Oliver Franks*, pp. 144, 198, 202, 214–18, 256.
16. Gifford to Secretary of State, 20 January 1951, *FRUS 1951*, Vol. IV Part I, p. 896.
17. Baylis, *Anglo-American Relations since 1939*, p. 69.
18. Gifford to Secretary of State, 20 January 1951, *FRUS 1951*, Vol. IV Part I, p. 896.
19. Gifford to Secretary of State, 11 May 1951, *FRUS 1951*, Vol. IV Part I, p. 941.
20. See Jonathan Colman, 'The 1950 "Ambassador's Agreement" on USAF Bases in the UK and British Fears of US Atomic Unilateralism', *Journal of Strategic Studies*, Vol. 30, No. 2 (April 2007), pp. 285–308.
21. Memorandum of Conversation, 14 January 1951, *FRUS 1951*, Vol. I, p. 803.
22. The pledge was of doubtful value. An American government document from 1952 confirmed that consultations with the British or indeed any other government were ranked a low priority if the President was ever called upon to consider using the bomb. Circumstances permitting, the order of priority for US consultation would be, first, the Joint Chiefs of Staff, the Secretary of Defence, the Secretary of State, and the Chairman of the Atomic Energy Commission; second, other departments and agencies of the government (the remaining members of the National Security Council, the Cabinet, Civil Defence, etc.); third, 'the American people'; fourth, other governments such as that of Britain, and, finally, the President could consult the United Nations if he wanted. Gleason to Truman, enclosing study of 11 June 1952, Box 175, NSC: Atomic File, NSF: Subject Files, HSTL. Gifford to Secretary of State, 20 January 1951, *FRUS 1951*, Vol. IV Part I, p. 896.
23. Gifford to Secretary of State, 20 January 1951, *FRUS 1951*, Vol. IV Part I, p. 896.
24. Secretary of State to Embassy in United Kingdom, 25 January 1951, *FRUS 1951*, Vol. IV Part I, p. 901.
25. Gifford to State, 16 March 1951, 511.41/3-1651, Decimal File, RG 59, National Archives and Record Administration, College Park, Maryland.
26. Summary of Telegrams, 10 October 1952, Box 25, SMOF: Naval Aide File, Harry S. Truman Papers, HSTL.
27. Aldrich, *The Hidden Hand*, p. 452. For a general account of US propaganda activities in Britain, including cooperation with British officials, see Aldrich, *The Hidden Hand*, pp. 447–52. See also Hugh Wilford, *The CIA, the British Left and the Cold War: Calling the Tune?* (London: Cass, 2003), pp. 164–7.
28. Gifford to Secretary of State, 4 January 1951, *FRUS 1951*, Vol. VI Part 1, pp. 890–1.
29. Hopkins, *Oliver Franks*, p. 189.
30. Gifford to Secretary of State, 20 January 1951, *FRUS 1951*, Vol. IV Part I, p. 898.
31. Gifford to Secretary of State, 11 May 1951, *FRUS 1951*, Vol. IV Part I, pp. 942–3.
32. Summary of telegrams, 27 April 1951, Box 24, State Department Briefs File, SMOF: Naval Aide File, HSTL.

33. Gifford to Secretary of State, 4 May 1951, *FRUS 1951,* Vol. VII *Korea and China* (1983), pp. 415–16.
34. Secretary of State to Embassy London, 28 April 1951, *FRUS 1951,* Vol. III *European Security and the German Question Part I* (1981), p. 517.
35. Dobson, *Anglo-American Relations in the Twentieth Century,* pp. 104–5.
36. Gifford to Secretary of State, 19 December 1951, *FRUS 1951,* Vol. III Part I, p. 971.
37. Gifford to Secretary of State, 20 January 1951, *FRUS 1951,* Vol. IV Part I, p. 896.
38. See John W. Young, *Winston Churchill's Last Campaign: Britain and the Cold War, 1951–55* (Oxford: Clarendon Press, 1996).
39. Acting Secretary of State to Embassy in the United Kingdom, 25 October 1951, *FRUS 1951,* Vol. IV Part I, pp. 978–9.
40. For the text of the Stalin notes, see *FRUS 1952–1954,* Vol. VII *Germany and Austria* (1986), pp. 169–73, 199–202, 247–52, 291–7. For the responses see *ibid.,* pp. 189–91, 242–7, 288–91, 324–6. See also Ruud Van Dijk, 'The 1952 Stalin Note Debate: Myth or Missed Opportunity for German Unification?', Woodrow Wilson International Center for Scholars, Working Paper No. 14, May 1996; Henry Kissinger, *Diplomacy* (New York: Simon and Schuster, 1994), pp. 493–9; Rolf Steininger, *The German Question: The Stalin Note of 1952 and the Problem of Reunification* (New York: Columbia University Press, 1990).
41. Gifford to Department of State, 17 April 1952, *FRUS 1952–1954,* Vol. VII, p. 209.
42. Secretary of State to Embassy in France, 17 March 1952, *FRUS 1952–1954,* Vol. VII, pp. 183–4; Gifford to Department of State, 11 May 1952, *FRUS 1952–1954,* Vol. VII, p. 239.
43. Gifford to Department of State, 2 September 1952, *FRUS 1952–1954,* Vol. VII, p. 309.
44. Kissinger, *Diplomacy,* p. 499.
45. Quoted in Mary Ann Heiss, 'The United States and Great Britain Navigate the Anglo-Iranian Oil Crisis', Council on Middle East Studies, Working Papers, available at: http://www.yale.edu/macmillan/cmes/papers.htm.
46. CIA estimate, 24 September 1951, *FRUS 1951,* Vol. I, p. 206.
47. Gifford to Department of State, 5 October 1951, *FRUS 1952–1954,* Vol. X *Iran* (1989), pp. 205–8.
48. Gifford to Department of State, 13 October 1951, *FRUS 1952–1954,* Vol. X, pp. 493–4.
49. Gifford to State Department, 26 June 1951, *FRUS 1952–1954,* Vol. X, p. 69.
50. Gifford to Department of State, 1 October 1951, *FRUS 1952–1954,* Vol. X, pp. 188–200.
51. Note 2, *FRUS 1952–1954,* Vol. X, p. 551.
52. Harriman to the President, 13 March 1950, Box 149, Foreign Affairs File, PSF: Subject File 1940–1953, HSTL.
53. Author's telephone interview with Thomas Dunnigan, 16 June 2007.
54. 'Confidential Report', author unknown, 16 August 1951, Box 154, Foreign Affairs File, PSF: Subject File 1940–1953, HSTL.
55. *Ibid.*
56. *Ibid.*
57. Quoted in Browder and Smith, *Independent,* p. 343.
58. *Ibid.,* p. 318.
59. Author's telephone interview with Thomas Dunnigan, 16 June 2007.
60. For Franks, see Hopkins, *Oliver Franks,* and *idem.,* 'Oliver Franks, 1948–52', in Michael F. Hopkins, Saul Kelly and John W. Young (eds), *The Washington*

Embassy: British Ambassadors to the United States, 1939–77 (Basingstoke: Palgrave, 2009), pp. 71–90. For Makins, see Saul Kelly, 'Roger Makins, 1952–1956', in Hopkins *et al.*, *The Washington Embassy*, pp. 91–109; and Saul Kelly, 'Transatlantic Diplomat: Sir Roger Makins, Ambassador to Washington and Joint Permanent Secretary to the Treasury', in Saul Kelly and Anthony Gorst (eds.), *Whitehall and the Suez Crisis* (London: Cass, 2000), pp. 157–77.

61. See *FRUS 1951*, Vol. I, pp. 1245–572, for US policy – including a number of despatches from Gifford – towards the Torquay round.

62. Draft letter from Acheson to Eden, 11 April 1952, Box 70, Acheson Papers, HSTL.

63. See Berridge, *Diplomacy*, pp. 119–32.

64. Anthony Eden, *Memoirs: Full Circle* (London: Cassell, 1960), p. 203.

65. *Ibid.*

66. John Colville, *Footprints in Time* (London: Collins, 1976), p. 236.

67. Gifford to Secretary of State, 14 March 1951, *FRUS 1951*, IV Part I, p. 922.

6
Winthrop Aldrich, 1953–57

Andrew Boxer

When Winthrop W. Aldrich arrived at London Airport on 10 February 1953, one bystander quipped: 'He looks like a British ambassador arriving in the United States.'[1] This was an astute observation – Eisenhower could hardly have chosen a more Anglophile figure. For Aldrich, aged 68 when he took up the post, the London Embassy promised an opportunity for glittering social success as a coda to his distinguished banking career. One US newspaper thought his lack of diplomatic experience an asset: 'Mr. Aldrich should be particularly useful in this post in a day when so many of the chief problems in the relationship between Great Britain and the United States are financial, rather than political, in nature.'[2] However, the first Eisenhower administration was to prove a period of exceptional and highly publicised political difficulty between the US and Britain, culminating in the Suez Crisis of 1956, arguably the most serious rupture in Anglo-American relations of the twentieth century. Aldrich, despite his excellent relations with most of the British elite, played only a minor role in the development and resolution of the Suez Crisis and it is hard to avoid the conclusion that his performance as ambassador was, at best, modest.

The circumstances surrounding Aldrich's appointment were inauspicious. He later told research interviewers: 'I'm not at all sure I would have taken the job if I'd known that Eisenhower was going to appoint Dulles as Secretary of State ... I had known him very well at the bar in New York and I knew the rigidity of his character and I had never been really sympathetic to him.'[3] Dulles being a dour, workaholic Presbyterian, and Aldrich a sociable Baptist with numerous compelling hobbies, prestigious club memberships and outdoor-sports interests, the two men were temperamentally at odds, to put it mildly.[4] The consequence was that Dulles never trusted Aldrich with any substantial diplomatic tasks, and Aldrich hugely resented being sidelined as Dulles took every opportunity to conduct diplomatic negotiations himself. Dulles's predilection was facilitated by the development of international jet aircraft travel; both he and Eisenhower travelled abroad much more extensively than their immediate predecessors. Truman made four overseas visits while President; Eisenhower made 17. Truman's three Secretaries of State made a combined total of 24 foreign trips (almost exclusively to Europe) whereas Dulles made 50, often visiting a range of capitals on one trip, and travelling nearly 500,000 miles all over the globe.[5]

Aldrich's treatment by Dulles rankled with him for the rest of his life. In 1964 he told an interviewer:

> If a Secretary of State uses his ambassadors simply as messenger boys, doesn't keep them fully informed about the inner workings of his own mind, if on every occasion he arrives with a great corps of people, the ambassador finds great difficulty in knowing exactly what's going on. I knew a hell of a lot more about what was going on through my conversations with his staff, all of whom were men who were trying to keep me fully informed, than I did from Dulles.[6]

The result of this personal and professional discord was that the US Embassy in London was less effective than it might have been at a time when the US administration was accused by many in Britain, especially during the Suez Crisis, of failing to explain its policies with sufficient clarity and emphasis.

Sadly, Aldrich seems inadvertently to have contributed to his fractious relationship with Dulles by spreading the news of his ambassadorial appointment among friends and colleagues at a time when it was still supposed to be confidential. Eisenhower blamed Aldrich for this indiscretion and for the minor diplomatic incident it provoked, writing in his diary on 13 February 1953:

> [The selection of Aldrich] was made on the most confidential basis, but to our consternation it was soon public knowledge in New York City – and indeed, throughout the nation. Foster Dulles considered this situation so embarrassing that he felt he would have to make a prompt public announcement of the fact that we intended to nominate Winthrop Aldrich when the new administration should take over.[7]

That Dulles made this announcement before the British government had even been informed about, much less given its consent to, the appointment was a clear breach of diplomatic protocol. A waspish protest followed from the British government, already concerned that the campaign rhetoric of the victorious Republicans signalled a weakening of both the 'special relationship' and the support that the Truman administration had given to Western Europe.[8]

Aldrich's principal advantage as Ambassador was that his wealth and social connections put him on a comfortable footing with the British political and social elite; future Prime Minister Harold Macmillan (the son-in-law of a duke) enthused in his diary: 'the Aldriches are really very charming people – the nice, simple, rich and rather old-fashioned Americans one likes so much'.[9] It was generally agreed that Aldrich was sufficiently wealthy to take the post. As Claire Boothe Luce observed: '[Ambassadorships in] Rome, London, Paris, are posts around which a dollar curtain has long been drawn. They can be assumed for any reasonable length of time only by men with private fortunes.'[10]

Born in November 1885, Winthrop Williams Aldrich enjoyed an upbringing, education, family connections and career which were typical of the east coast establishment that some historians have seen as forming almost a mid-century US aristocracy.[11] Claiming descent from one of the original Mayflower pilgrims and from General Nathaniel Greene, the Revolutionary War hero, Aldrich grew up in a wealthy, political family. His father, Nelson Wilmarth Aldrich, was a self-made millionaire with extensive business interests and investments. A Republican senator for over 30 years, Nelson Aldrich was the principal Republican power-broker in the Senate from 1892 until 1910.[12]

Winthrop Aldrich studied law at Harvard and, after service in the navy during the First World War, spent most of the 1920s handling the legal affairs of the Equitable Trust Company, which was owned by his brother-in-law, John D. Rockefeller. Aldrich became the company's president in 1929. The following year, having overseen the company's merger with the Chase Bank of New York, he became president of this new institution. Although, like his father, he was a committed and active Republican, he also possessed what historian Thomas Ferguson has called a 'highly cultivated sense of bipartisanship' and was prepared to transcend narrow party affiliations and work for Democratic administrations if he thought the national interest required it.[13] This explains why he supported some of President Franklin D. Roosevelt's early banking reforms, believing that weaknesses in the American banking system had contributed to the severity of the depression.[14] By 1936, however, he had reverted to his Republican loyalties and supported Alfred Landon's presidential bid in opposition to many of the New Deal economic policies. Nonetheless, in 1940, according to historian Jeffery M. Dorwart, Aldrich was again assisting Roosevelt by allowing a Chase Bank mission to Japan to be used as a front for US spies because the President had 'become desperate to discover ways to counteract foreign aggression, subversion and espionage without alienating the isolationists'.[15] This concern about US isolationism was another consistent feature of Aldrich's thinking.

Aldrich's strong Anglophile sentiments appear to date from the 1920s. By then he was married to Harriet Alexander, the moneyed grand-daughter of a railroad magnate, and was the father of four daughters and two sons (one of whom died as an infant). A keen yachtsman who competed in the America's Cup at Cowes in 1930, he formed a number of friendships with wealthy Britons from the sailing fraternity. Immediately war broke out in 1939 he headed two charitable organisations to raise funds for medical help for Britain and funded a secret programme for British aircraft pilots to train in the US.[16] By 1943, he was in charge of the National War Fund, an organisation which coordinated American charitable efforts for the Allies. During his wartime visits to Britain, he developed warm relationships with members of the British establishment. He toured bombed cities, was received at Buckingham Palace, and met Churchill, Eden and Mountbatten as well as other leading politicians. In August 1945, he became the first recipient of the King's Medal for Service in the Cause of Freedom in a ceremony at Buckingham Palace, and in 1947 King George VI appointed him a Knight Grand Cross of the British Empire.[17]

The issue of post-war economic reconstruction further strengthened Aldrich's identification with Britain, whose recovery he believed was essential to the strength and stability of post-war capitalism. As the first chairman of Truman's Advisory Committee for Financing Foreign Trade he was an enthusiastic supporter of the Marshall Plan. But this work for the Truman administration did not prevent him from playing a major part in raising money for Thomas Dewey's bid for the presidency in 1948 and it is possible that, in a Dewey administration, Aldrich would have been given a cabinet post as Secretary of the Treasury.[18]

By the early 1950s Aldrich had become part of a strong cabal of Republican grandees who were alarmed at the prospect of the party's nomination going to Senator Robert Taft of Ohio because they feared he would overturn the internationalist, free trade, Eurocentric emphasis of the Democratic Truman administration. Aldrich joined others in organising and financing the campaign to enlist Eisenhower (and, in June 1951, played the almost obligatory round of golf with him).[19] Nevertheless, he did not become a close personal friend of Eisenhower and it is highly probable that his indiscreet talk in November 1952 about what was then still his confidential appointment to the London Embassy soured his relationship with the administration from the outset. The episode clearly made Eisenhower doubtful of Aldrich's calibre. He wrote in his diary:

> Winthrop Aldrich should be warned to keep his mouth shut when he has knowledge of any subject which is not public knowledge. The whole difficulty arose out his impatience and his naive supposition that the people he talked to in New York would keep his confidence. If he should be guilty of that kind of thing in his present office, he would quickly lose his usefulness.[20]

By April 1953, however, Aldrich – by this time in post as Ambassador – was at the centre of another controversy, having delivered what one US journalist described as an 'April Fool's day address' to the English Speaking Union in

London. This time, his *faux pas* had the dubious honour of being debated in Congress:

> Senator Malone (R) of Nevada told the Senate last night that Winthrop Aldrich, American ambassador to Britain, has committed the United States to war in advance, without action by Congress. Malone said Aldrich made the commitment...April 1, when Aldrich apologized in a speech before the English Speaking Union for this country's 'slowness' in coming to Britain's defense in two world wars and promised that the United States won't be slow next time.[21]

This was not to be the last of Aldrich's apparently pro-British indiscretions. British Cabinet minister Harold Macmillan recorded in his diary dining with Aldrich and his wife on 12 May 1953, the day after Prime Minister Churchill had made a major foreign policy speech in the House of Commons. Churchill, hoping to end his career with a dramatic peace initiative, wanted to resurrect the summit diplomacy of the war years and called for the Western powers to respond positively to the new regime in the USSR. He proposed that 'a conference on the highest level should take place between the leading Powers without long delay'.[22] Eisenhower had already expressed his reservations about this in a message to Churchill (copied to Aldrich) six days before his speech: 'We should not rush things too much and should not permit feeling in our countries for a meeting between heads of states and governments to press us into precipitate initiatives.'[23] Far from endorsing the line taken by his President, Aldrich's views, according to Harold Macmillan, echoed those of his British hosts:

> The Ambassador (without the slightest regard to discretion) criticised – or rather attacked – the Secretary of State, Dulles. He was in 100% disagreement with him. Either he or Dulles would have to go. It was also clear that Julius Holmes (his minister) and the rest of the 'boys' in the Embassy had listened to Churchill's speech with alarm and indignation. The Ambassador thought it 'great stuff' and was in almost complete agreement.[24]

Aldrich's poor relationship with Dulles is likely to have been widened by their differing attitudes to Britain. Dulles took a negative view of British imperialism, believing that the determination of Britain and France to cling on to their colonial empires (especially in the Middle East) undermined the ability of the Western democracies to confront the USSR.[25] Aldrich, however, was much more supportive of British imperialism. His attitude can be gleaned from remarks he made to an interviewer in 1964. In the final version of the interview Aldrich's more outspoken comments – indicated, below, by the words that have been scored through – were edited out at his request.

We were hustling them [the British] out of their colonial positions all over the world ~~and I disagreed with that~~. I think we should have been much more sympathetic with the achievements of the British in bringing about the gradual evolution of their colonial possessions into new nations. ~~Of course the British in my opinion have been much too hasty about it recently and the way they've been spawning new nations in the Caribbean is simply extraordinary~~.[26]

Aldrich's exasperation with his own government surfaced early in his ambassadorship. C. L. Sulzberger, chief correspondent of *The New York Times*, recorded in his diary a conversation with Aldrich on 3 June 1953: 'Aldrich says he hasn't the vaguest idea what American policy is because every time Eisenhower sets it out in a speech, Dulles makes another speech modifying it.'[27] This frustration may have undermined Aldrich's self-confidence and his effectiveness. In April 1954, only just over a year into Aldrich's tenure, Clarence Randall, Eisenhower's special consultant on foreign economic policy, found him in a distinctly gloomy mood and made a perceptive analysis of the Ambassador's unhappy situation:

He ... is very, very tired, and wonders how long he can stay with it. His staff's morale is low. Some resign, others are transferred, and no one is ever quite sure of his future, so the Ambassador lives constantly in a state of disorganisation. My heart went out to him because he is a fine man trying hard to do a good job, and one for which, in frankness, he is not too well equipped. Winthrop is not an intellectual, and it takes great concentration on his part to deal steadily one after the other with subjects of world-wide significance for which he has not been trained. He knows this, and said to me with a frankness that drew me to him, 'I am just not mentally up to this job.'[28]

A few months later, the State Department was even wondering whether Aldrich might want to retire early. Assistant Secretary, Thruston B. Morton, reported to Dulles: 'Aldrich's performance has been adequate but in view of his age and the burdens of the post, it is felt he might be interested in retiring after completion of two years of duty.'[29] Aldrich clearly found some of his duties irksome. In a personal letter of May 1955 to thank Alfred Gruenther for the gift of a bottle of whisky, Aldrich admitted, with a certain gallows humour, 'I am afraid I am generally allergic to high power conferences and I will always need quite a lot of alcoholic support to see me through.'[30]

Those who worked in the Embassy had mixed views about both Aldrich's personality and his effectiveness. John Edgar Williams, his aide from 1955 to 1956 dismissed him as 'kind of a stuffed shirt'.[31] Robert W. Zimmermann and Walter M. McClelland, who were political officers at the Embassy, found him remote. Zimmermann recalled: 'My impression was that everybody looked to the DCM (Deputy Chief of Mission) more than to Aldrich. The DCM was really running the operation. He ran the staff meetings and everything else. Aldrich was seldom there.'[32] However, Thomas J. Dunnigan, Aldrich's staff aide from 1952 until 1954, was impressed by his boss:

> [Aldrich] was a formidable person . . . He worked on the big problems and understood them . . . When there was something to be taken up with the prime minister or the foreign minister, Winthrop Aldrich would do it. And he'd do it well. He had their confidence. And he was well connected socially in Britain. He knew every duke and duchess and many of the earls and so forth in the UK. He lived well, entertained well.[33]

Aldrich made a conscientious effort to travel around Britain, his private aeroplane (a twin-engine Dakota) facilitating visits to far-flung meetings of chambers of commerce and businessmen's clubs, while the Embassy car carried him to nearer-at-hand London-based institutions such as city livery companies and the Imperial Defence College. A US Embassy administrative order of 15 June 1956 on speaking engagements summed up his views on getting out and about as Ambassador:

> It seems obvious that if this mission is to report back to the United States what the British public – not merely the political leaders and newspaper editors – are saying, we must not bypass opportunities to meet and speak with people in their own groups, where, surrounded by friends whose opinions they know, they are likely to indicate their true thoughts.[34]

Whatever Aldrich's skills as a diplomat, his staff aide Dunnigan was certainly correct about the Ambassador's social connections. Aldrich both relished and was highly successful at the social side of his job, an impression confirmed by his son:

> He was a deeply social person, going to parties, flirting with ladies. That sort of thing was his principal activity. He had lots of royal and highly social friends, such as the Buccleuchs. He knew the Duchess of Buccleuch as Molly, adored her, and constantly visited her castle, Drumlanrig, in Scotland. A very substantial amount of my father's time was taken up with embassy parties and British social matters, and with the people he liked. He loved the ambassadorship. It fed his ego.[35]

The Embassy parties were many and they were successful, the sociable and stimulating Mrs Aldrich having a major talent for entertaining on the grand scale, and a reputation for working hard to make sure her guests enjoyed her parties as much as she did. 'My mother's view was that, if you weren't amusing, you weren't serious', says her son.[36] An internal US Embassy memo of 1956 informed the Ambassador: 'during the fiscal year 1956 you gave the following functions: 21 cocktail receptions, 17 lunches, 15 dinners, 2 dinner-dances, 3 teas. Your two dinner-dances, on November 15 and June 5, cost $2565.25 and $4433.66, respectively.'[37]

A series of long, gossipy letters written by Mrs Aldrich to their children back home in the US indicates how frequently they socialised with the British elite. Aldrich (described as 'Daddy' in these letters to his children) appears to have formed a particular bond with the Queen Mother, as these three extracts from letters from 1953 and 1956 attest:

> The Queen Mother came. She was very gracious and attractive, and as usual singled out Daddy and talked to him and everybody else seemed quite impressed by that...

> Staying the weekend at Boughton with the Buccleuchs. We were invited over to have tea with the Duke and Duchess of Gloucester, who live about 10 miles away, and with whom the Queen Mother was staying. Nobody else except Daddy and me. Their place is called Barnwell Castle. I thought Daddy and the Queen Mother would never stop walking around and discussing every kind of thing...

> Standing quite near us was the Queen with Lord Mountbatten and a few other people. Daddy said to the Rockefellers, 'Would you like to meet the Queen?' and of course they said they would, and it was very easy. We took them over and we all of us stood around and had a most genial conversation...The Rockefellers and I went home shortly after that, around 2 o'clock. Your gay father of course stayed another hour and had supper with the Queen Mother.[38]

The Aldriches also regularly socialised with leading members of the Conservative government, and Aldrich's friendship with Harold Macmillan enabled him to play a significant part in the backstairs intrigue that accompanied Macmillan's accession to the premiership in the aftermath of Suez – a task made easier by the fact that Aldrich's relationship with Anthony Eden was much cooler.[39] Aldrich also had 'great admiration and affection for Salisbury' and regularly visited him at his Hertfordshire seat, Hatfield House.[40] (The 5th Marquess of Salisbury, who boasted a political ancestry that dated back to the reign of Queen Elizabeth I, was the leading Conservative in the House of Lords and a key power-broker in the Party.) There may have been an element of snobbery in Aldrich's friendships because he did not get on well with Selwyn Lloyd – whom Macmillan patronisingly dubbed 'a middle class lawyer from Liverpool'.[41] Lloyd, promoted to the Foreign Office by Eden in December 1955, lacked the aristocratic clubbability that Aldrich found so congenial among his British friends. Lloyd for his part dismissed Aldrich in his memoirs as 'the amateur', although he did acknowledge that Aldrich was 'enthusiastic for Anglo-American co-operation publicly avowed'.[42] Historian Robert Rhodes James maintains that, at the height of the Suez Crisis in early November 1956, 'relations between Lloyd and Aldrich...were very bad indeed' although this could be explained as much by the tension of that particular time as by the personal relationship of the two men.[43]

Aldrich was the first US Ambassador to occupy Winfield House, the ambassadorial residence in Regent's Park. This palatial mansion had been built in neo-classical style in 1936 for the Woolworth heiress Barbara Hutton who donated it to the US government after the Second World War. According to *The New York Times*:

> State Department officials said that at a cost of about $190,000 Winfield House, a red brick three-story [sic] structure set in a twelve-acre estate, would be converted into a 'simple, economically operated residence.' The decision to move was made, the officials said, because the present residence at 14 Prince's Gate, which is owned by the United States Government, was found to be unsuitable. They said the building was sixty years old, was inconveniently laid out, and presented some security hazards in that it was in a row of attached houses.[44]

The *St Louis Post-Dispatch* reported that 'three American ambassadors in a row [had] declined to occupy [Winfield House] because of the personal expense involved in keeping it up and maintaining the ten [sic] acres of lawns and gardens around it' and that Aldrich was 'reported to spend some $25,000 a year of his own money maintaining [it]. The State Department does not allow ambassadors money enough to keep it going'.[45]

The Aldriches' housewarming party at Winfield House early in 1955 was a typically lavish affair, as this *Time* magazine report makes clear:

> Although Aldrich wanted everything 'informal', invitations to 330 guests called for 'evening dress and decorations', a sure tipoff that royalty would be present. With some 50 Scotland Yardmen and bobbies barring gate-crashers (including all newsmen), the regal parade was led by Queen Elizabeth II, Prince Philip and Queen Mother Elizabeth. After Aldrich whirled the Queen about the ballroom in a lively foxtrot, some of his countrymen started cutting in on the faintly startled Elizabeth. Protocol soon died an informal death. When the Queen's customary departure hour of midnight came, she stayed on, danced with all cutters-in, wound up having ham and eggs at 3 a.m. London's press next day upbraided Aldrich for his news blackout and the ballroom manners of the crude Americans (observed by an *Evening Standard* spy). But apparently the

Queen had seldom had such a ball. Said one guest: 'I've never known the royal family to be so happy.'[46]

Rather more prosaically, this move to larger premises also enabled Mrs Aldrich to expand the activities that she organised for the wives of Embassy staff members, as *The Washington Post* reported:

> These women – they number about 120 – carry out a great amount of social and welfare activities. They are active in the Red Cross, the Women's Voluntary Services, organisations for the blind, and in the Docklands Settlements. Last year $3,000 was raised at a ball they organised to aid Crosby Hall, a famous residence for foreign women – one third of them are Americans – attending universities in London.[47]

In the more serious world of international politics, there is little reason to doubt the accuracy of Aldrich's complaint (reiterated to all the interviewers who subsequently talked to him) that Dulles treated him as little more than a 'messenger boy'.[48] He was virtually a bystander in the crisis over German rearmament that prompted Dulles to threaten an 'agonising reappraisal' of the American commitment to Europe, a warning the British government took seriously.[49] Dulles directed the US diplomatic effort himself. Aldrich was in Washington in July 1953 as part of the United States delegation at a series of meetings with the foreign ministers of Britain and France but he did not contribute to the discussion.[50] He also attended the nine-power conference in London in the autumn of 1954 as part of the US delegation, but any contributions he may have made were not recorded. Aldrich's messages to Washington during the crisis were few and contained only routine information. There is little evidence that Dulles instructed him at any time during the negotiations. Aldrich played an even smaller role in the 1954 crisis over Indo-China, even though this produced a more serious rift in Anglo-American relations than the problem of German rearmament had done. He did not attend the Geneva conference and there is no evidence that Dulles solicited his opinion at any stage. The messages between the State Department and the US Embassy in London were largely about procedural matters or formal statements of one or other government's negotiating position.[51]

Dulles also dominated US diplomacy during the Suez Crisis, which began in July 1956 when the Egyptian leader, Gamal Abdul Nasser, nationalised the Suez Canal. The British and French governments, majority shareholders in the Suez Canal Company, were determined to recover control, by force if necessary, and hoped that by doing so they would bring down Nasser's government. They wanted US diplomatic support, but the US government believed (as Eisenhower told Eden in September) that 'American public opinion flatly rejects the thought of using force' against Nasser, and that 'Suez is not the issue on which to attempt...Nasser's deflation'.[52] Dulles, however, who travelled to Britain three times in August and September 1956 and led the US delegation at both the international conferences held in London, was never as unambiguously clear about this as Eisenhower, and his apparent shifts and turns during the crisis exasperated both the British and Aldrich.

Aldrich was flying to the US for a holiday when news of Nasser's action broke (and indeed he was one of a number of political diplomatic appointees criticised by the Senate Foreign Relations Committee in 1957 for taking too many days off).[53] It is perhaps an indication of how dispensable Washington considered Aldrich that he was not sent straight back to London. With Dulles away in South America, Eisenhower dispatched Robert Murphy, the Deputy Undersecretary of State, to liaise with the British. Dulles, when he returned to Washington, attended two meetings on the crisis before travelling to London. Aldrich attended neither. His biographer implies that, although he and Dulles arrived in London on the same day, they did not cross the Atlantic together.[54] Three weeks later, at a time of particularly fraught Anglo-American relations, Aldrich was permitted to resume his interrupted holiday.

Dulles did, however, request one important diplomatic initiative from Aldrich as the crisis came to a head. In late October, the US administration received intelligence reports about Israeli mobilisation and suspected (correctly, as it turned out) that the British and French were colluding with the Israelis to provide themselves with an excuse to attack Egypt and take back the Canal by force. Aldrich, instructed by Dulles to find out about possible British involvement, dined with Foreign Secretary Selwyn Lloyd on 28 October. His telegram to the State Department indicates that he found Lloyd's denial of British complicity convincing:

> [Lloyd] said with feeling, and I believe evident conviction, that major Israeli attack either on Jordan or Egypt at this time would put Britain in impossible situation...Lloyd inclined believe Israeli attack more likely to be directed against Jordan than Egypt...He unwilling believe Israelis would launch full scale attack Egypt despite temptation to do so, in present circumstances...His concern over the consequences of Israeli initiative carried sufficient conviction for me to conclude that any UK complicity in such a move is unlikely.[55]

Aldrich's willingness to accept Lloyd's denial is slightly surprising. Just six days before this dinner, he had received a sufficiently strong hint from Walter Monckton (the British Minister of Defence who had resigned on 18 October) about the possible use of force that he cabled Washington about it. Aldrich reported Monckton as saying that he had resigned 'not only because of his physical exhaustion but also because he was convinced that the use of force in Suez would be a great blunder. He said he felt that you [i.e. Dulles] were on the right track regarding this matter'.[56]

Aldrich seems to have been rather easily convinced of Selwyn Lloyd's good faith at their dinner. Lloyd disliked the collusion plan and, if the testimonies of two of the Israeli negotiating team at Sèvres (where the collusion plan was concocted by the French, British and Israelis) are to be believed, was not good at disguising the fact.[57] On the other hand, since part of the purpose of the Sèvres collusion plan was to keep the Americans in the dark, it is not surprising that Lloyd blatantly lied to Aldrich.

Eisenhower was outraged by the Anglo-French attack on Egypt in early November and used American financial muscle to force a ceasefire. He also refused to have any further contact with Eden or Lloyd. This snub to Eden (which Aldrich attributed to Dulles's influence) sealed the Ambassador's disenchantment with the behaviour of his own government. His more outspoken comment is scored through:

> I myself was surprised at the vitriolic nature of Eisenhower's reaction to what happened. I think it was un-statesmanlike; I think it was a dreadful thing, the way the United States government permitted itself to act because of pique or petulance or any of the emotions which may sway personal actions. I don't think personal feelings should enter into international affairs. ~~But you can gather that I don't think too much of Mr. Dulles.~~[58]

Aldrich was arguably at his most active as US Ambassador when, with the worst of the crisis over, Dulles became *hors de combat* following an operation for cancer in early November, just before Eisenhower's re-election, and Herbert Hoover became acting Secretary of State. Then, when Prime Minister Eden, drained and ill, left Britain on 23 November for what he hoped would be a recuperative vacation in Jamaica, Aldrich became the medium for vitally important post-crisis communications between Washington and the three men (Macmillan, Rab Butler and Salisbury) who ran the British government in Eden's absence.[59] This gave him a significant role in the backstairs intrigue that eventually led to Eden's replacement by Macmillan as British Prime Minister early in 1957. Macmillan's eagerness to repair Britain's relationship with the US, as well as to restore something of her former world reputation and financial status, made him especially keen to exploit his friendship with Aldrich, who appears to have relished being part of the cloak-and-dagger secrecy involved in this. In a telegram of 19 November 1956 Aldrich told the acting Secretary of State, Herbert Hoover:

> [Macmillan] asked me if I would be available to him at any minute, day or night. I replied that that was what I was here for and that I would deem it a great privilege if he would keep constantly in touch with me. Obviously, Macmillan asked me not to communicate all of this to anyone at this moment and I am therefore sending this message in utmost confidence.[60]

On the eve of Aldrich's departure as Ambassador, Macmillan paid him a warm tribute. Possibly no more than a standard farewell address, it nevertheless hints at Aldrich's influential role behind the scenes:

> Ambassador Aldrich...has played a remarkable and indeed historic role during these anxious weeks. We owe him a debt which we cannot easily repay; and I like to think that his countrymen will feel that they should be equally grateful for what he has done.[61]

The irony of the Suez Crisis is that, had Eisenhower and Dulles put greater trust in Aldrich, the Ambassador might have been more successful than Dulles in persuading the British that the US administration really did oppose the use of gunboat diplomacy to regain control of the Suez Canal. Aldrich enjoyed much more cordial personal relations with the British elite than did Dulles, yet he thought the British were wrong to use force. One of Harriet Aldrich's letters to her children expresses the anguish she and her husband felt in opposing a policy carried out by people they liked and admired:

> I went to the House of Commons to hear the debate. It was really a tragic afternoon. I felt so upset that I was almost in tears, hearing Gaitskell [the leader of the Labour Opposition] talking about the invasion as if this was the greatest tragedy in the world (which I agree with), as opposed to the Prime Minister who spoke, naturally, in defense of having done it. Daddy and I feel so strongly that it was a mistake that we have to be very, very careful what we say...In my mind there can be no question, really, that the government is dead wrong to use force in support of a belligerent in the Middle East.[62]

In his account of the role he played in the crisis, written a decade later, Aldrich argued that the tragedy of Suez had occurred because Eden could not be brought to understand Dulles's position: 'Eden did not see that in this language [of Dulles's] there was no *commitment* to use force and that when it came to the final and formal decision we might not be willing to use it.' He went on to assert in the same article that 'every effort was made to make our position clear', although the evidence shows that, in fact, Dulles allowed him very little scope to make that effort.[63] Given that the Secretary of State placed so little faith in the Ambassador it is perhaps not surprising that the British authorities ignored any warnings Aldrich may have given them.

Conclusion

It is hard to avoid the impression that the ends of US diplomacy were ill served during Aldrich's tenure of the London Embassy, particularly in 1956. He appears to have wanted the job because it provided him with an opportunity to resume socialising with the British elite; he cannot have expected to have to deal with a crisis of the magnitude of Suez. His wife certainly did not. Even before Nasser nationalised the Suez Canal, it is clear that she often fretted when the Aldriches' long-arranged personal plans had to be disrupted because business kept Aldrich at his Embassy desk. In a letter to her children dated 22 July 1956, four days before Nasser's nationalisation of the Suez Canal, she regretted that Aldrich would not, after all, be able to fly to the US with her that night to attend a wedding in Newport 'because of... the fact that he had to hand some kind of official letter to Selwyn Lloyd on a certain day – very sad, and yet I am glad for him that he will be able to go to the Laurence Olivier party for Marilyn Monroe'.[64] It is, perhaps, a fitting comment on Aldrich's tenure of the Embassy that partying with Hollywood stars appears to have been more important to him than fulfilling irksome diplomatic duties.

Aldrich should not be held wholly responsible for his mediocre record as Ambassador. First, Dulles must share some of the blame for their poor personal relations, and his failure to entrust Aldrich with anything significant undoubtedly led to the Ambassador feeling undervalued and ill used. Secondly, Aldrich shared with the British the conviction that it was Dulles, and not the President, who ran US foreign policy:

> [Eisenhower] just turned foreign affairs over to Dulles and he simply coasted along. A lot of people felt that way. In a way it was his great strength. He could make people work together, and so forth, but he seemed to depend entirely on Dulles in foreign affairs.[65]

This view remained historical orthodoxy until the 1980s.[66] Although Eisenhower spelt out to Eden very clearly and repeatedly his opposition to the use of force against Egypt, it is understandable that both the British government and Aldrich paid greater attention to what Dulles said – and the evidence that he was more opaque than Eisenhower seems incontrovertible.[67] Finally, it is unlikely that even a more effective ambassador could have prevented the disastrous turn of events in the autumn of 1956, given the determination of Eden's government to use force against Nasser's Suez Canal coup.[68]

Notes

1. *The Baltimore Sun*, 12 February 1953.
2. *The New York Herald Tribune*, 1 December 1952.
3. Tape recorded interview with Aldrich by David Berliner, October 1972, pp. 4–5, Columbia Oral History Project, Eisenhower Library, Abilene, Kansas; interview with Aldrich conducted by Richard D. Challener, Dark Harbor, Maine, 15 July 1964, MSS938 SG3 Series 3 SS1 Folder 31, p. 3, Rhode Island Historical Society, Providence, Rhode Island.

4. The dislike was mutual. Evelyn Shuckburgh, a British Foreign Office official, recorded in his diary written while accompanying Eden, then British Foreign Secretary, to Washington in March 1953 for a conference where they were met by Dulles at the airport. 'We dashed off to the White House. Dulles tried to prevent A.E. taking Roger Makins [the British Ambassador to the US] with him, primarily to avoid having to take Winthrop Aldrich' (Evelyn Shuckburgh, *Descent to Suez, Diaries 1951–56* [London: Weidenfeld, 1986], p. 79).

5. US Department of State website; Arlington Cemetery website.

6. Aldrich interview by Challener, 15 July 1964, *op. cit.*, p. 48; Rhode Island Historical Society, Providence, Rhode Island.

7. Louis Galambos and Duan Van Ee (eds.), *The Papers of Dwight David Eisenhower*, Vol. 14. *The Presidency: The Middle Way* (Baltimore, MD: The Johns Hopkins University Press, 1996), p. 44 (hereafter *DDE*).

8. Stephen E. Ambrose, *Eisenhower: The President*, Vol. 2. 1952–69 (London: Lee Cooper, 1984), p. 50.

9. Peter Catterall (ed.), *The Macmillan Diaries* (Basingstoke: Palgrave Macmillan, 2003), p. 256.

10. Clare Boothe Luce, 'The Ambassadorial Issue: Professionals or Amateurs?' *Foreign Affairs*, Vol. 36, No. 1 (October 1957), pp. 114–15. Luce pointed out that ambassadors in European capitals were expected to spend lavishly on entertaining in a style that could not be paid for by their salaries and allowances.

11. Aldrich's milieu and attitudes were remarkably similar to those of the six 'wise men' analysed by Walter Isaacson and Evan Thomas in their book about Acheson, Bohlen, Harriman, Kennan, Lovett and McCloy, the influential US diplomats of the Truman era who, in the authors' judgement, were the 'architects of the American century' (Isaacson and Thomas, *The Wise Men*, p. 17). Robert Dallek's biography of Kennedy indicates just how many influential 'Boston clans' there were, including the Rockefellers, to whom Aldrich was connected by marriage. Robert Dallek, *John F. Kennedy, An Unfinished Life 1917–1963* (London: Penguin Books, 2003), p. 26.

12. Allen Johnson (ed.), *Dictionary of American Biography* (New York: Scribner's, 1964), pp. 151–7.

13. Thomas Ferguson, 'History, Politics, Statistics: A Preface to Walter Dean Burnham's Electoral Archive', *The Journal of the Historical Society*, Vol. 7, No. 4 (December 2007), p. 496.

14. Thomas Ferguson, *Golden Rule: The Investment Theory of Party Competition and the Logic of Money-Driven Political Systems* (Chicago: University of Chicago Press, 1995), pp. 148–54.

15. Jeffery M. Dorwart, 'The Roosevelt-Astor Espionage Ring', *New York History*, Vol. 62, No. 3 (July 1981), pp. 314–15.

16. *Ibid.*, p. 316.

17. Arthur M. Johnson, *Winthrop W. Aldrich: Lawyer, Banker, Diplomat* (Boston: Graduate School of Business Adminstration, Harvard University, 1968), pp. 305–6.

18. Frank Kofsky, *Harry S. Truman and the War Scare of 1948* (New York: St Martin's Press, 1993), p. 44; Richard N. Smith, *Thomas E. Dewey and his Times* (New York: Simon & Schuster, 1982), pp. 489–90.

19. Letter from Aldrich to Eisenhower, 16 June 1951; DDE Papers, Pre-Presidential, 1916–52, Principal File, Box 3, Eisenhower Library, Abilene, Kansas.

20. *DDE*, Vol. 14, p. 46. Sir John Colville suggests in his autobiography that Eisenhower disliked the tradition of appointing political nominees to senior

diplomatic posts but felt 'obliged to reward those who had contributed gener-ously to his election campaign'. Colville also claims that Aldrich was Eisenhower's second choice for London after Churchill rejected Claire Boothe Luce because 'a woman, and a former actress at that, as American Ambassador to the Court of St James was, in 1953, something too ludicrous to contemplate' (Colville, *Footprints in Time*, p. 236).
21. *The Washington Times*, 15 April 1953.
22. Martin Gilbert, *Winston S. Churchill, Volume 8: Never Despair, 1945–65* (London: Heinemann, 1988), p. 831.
23. *DDE*, Vol. 14, p. 207.
24. Catterall, *Macmillan Diaries*, pp. 231–2.
25. Richard H. Immerman, *John Foster Dulles: Piety, Pragmatism, and Power in U.S. For-eign Policy* (Lanham, MD: Rowman & Littlefield, 1999), pp. 147–56. The force of Dulles's visceral dislike of British 'colonialism' is evident in his impassioned denunciation of British and French policy at a National Security Council meeting in Washington on 1 November 1956 – the day after the RAF had begun bomb-ing Egypt at the start of their military campaign to recover control of the Suez Canal. *Foreign Relations of the United States, 1955–57 (FRUS)*, Vol. XVI, Doc. 455, pp. 906–7.
26. Aldrich interview by Challener, 15 July 1964, *op. cit.*, pp. 58–9.
27. C. L. Sulzberger, *A Long Row of Candles, Memoirs and Diaries 1934–54* (New York: Macmillan, 1969), p. 737.
28. Clarence B. Randall, *Unpublished Journals, 1953–61*, Box 1, Washington after the Commission, 1954, Volume II, 14–29 April 1954, pp. 15–16, Eisenhower Library, Abilene, Kansas.
29. Dulles Papers, Personnel Series, Box 1: Evaluation of Chiefs of Mission, September 1954, File 3, Eisenhower Library, Abilene, Kansas.
30. Gruenther Papers 1941–83, General Correspondence Series, Box 21, Eisenhower Library, Abilene, Kansas.
31. John Edgar Williams, interview with Dr Anne R. Phillips, 1995, *Coun-try Reader, United Kingdom*, Association for Diplomatic Studies and Training, Washington DC.
32. Robert W. Zimmermann, interview with Charles Stuart Kennedy, 10 June 1992; Walter M. McClelland, interview with Charles Stuart Kennedy, 20 November 1995, *Country Reader, United Kingdom*, Association for Diplomatic Studies and Training, Washington DC.
33. Thomas J. Dunnigan, interview with Charles Stuart Kennedy, 1990, *Coun-try Reader, United Kingdom*, Association for Diplomatic Studies and Training, Washington DC.
34. Box 235C, Aldrich papers, Baker Library, Harvard Business School, Harvard, MA.
35. Author's interview with Alexander Aldrich, Albany, New York, 19 October 2010.
36. *Ibid.*
37. Box 200, Aldrich papers, Baker Library, Harvard Business School, Harvard, Boston, MA; Correspondence File III, American Embassy, London Expenses 1953–1956.
38. MSS938 SG3 Series 1 SS2, Folder 2, 20 March 1953; Series 1, SS2 Folder 20, 2 June 1956; Series 1, SS2 Folder 20, 26 June 1956; Rhode Island Historical Society, Prov-idence, Rhode Island. Harriet's use of the word 'gay' to describe her husband should not be misunderstood. In the 1950s the word meant 'light-hearted and carefree' rather than 'homosexual'.

39. Their mutual loathing of Dulles brought Eden and Aldrich closer together in retirement. The two men visited one another's homes from time to time and corresponded warmly. Aldrich happily responded to Eden's request for advice about investments and they both admired Herman Finer's 1964 book which was highly critical of Dulles's policy during the Suez Crisis. Avon Papers, AP23/5/5; AP23/5/B; AP23/5/7; AP23/5/7A; University of Birmingham; Herman Finer, *Dulles over Suez: The Theory and Practice of his Diplomacy* (London: Quadrangle Books, 1964).

40. Catterall, *Macmillan Diaries,* p. 256.

41. D. R. Thorpe, *Selwyn Lloyd* (London: Jonathan Cape, 1989), pp. 1, 461.

42. Selwyn Lloyd, *Suez 1956: A Personal Account* (London: Jonathan Cape, 1978), p. 61.

43. Robert Rhodes James, *Anthony Eden* (London: Weidenfeld, 1986), p. 568.

44. *The New York Times,* 2 March 1954.

45. *St Louis Post-Dispatch,* 14 November 1956.

46. *Time,* 7 March 1955.

47. *The Washington Post,* 18 November 1956.

48. Aldrich interview by David Berliner, October 1972, *op. cit.,* p. 11.

49. Kevin Ruane, 'Agonising Reappraisals: Anthony Eden, John Foster Dulles and the Crisis of European Defence, 1953–54', *Diplomacy and Statecraft,* Vol. 13, No. 4 (December 2002), pp. 151–85.

50. *FRUS 1952–54,* Vol. V, pp. 1608–708.

51. *FRUS 1952–54,* Vol. XVI, pp. 470–1, 496–7, 1066–7, 1304–5.

52. Peter G. Boyle (ed.), *The Eden-Eisenhower Correspondence 1955–57* (Chapel Hill, NC: University of North Carolina Press, 2005), p. 163.

53. 'It has been ascertained ... that in the past two years [1955 and 1956] "political" ambassadors have been absent from their posts, on other than health grounds, for more than twice as long, on average, as career diplomatists ... Prominent absentees during this period [included] Mr. Winthrop Aldrich, then ambassador to London (169 days)' (*The Times,* 10 August 1957).

54. Johnson, *Winthrop W. Aldrich,* p. 380.

55. *FRUS 1955–1957,* Vol. XVI, Doc. 405, p. 818.

56. Telegram from London Embassy to Department of State, No. 2215, 23 October 1956, Department of State Central Files, 974.7301/10.2456, College Park, Maryland.

57. Israeli Chief of Staff Moshe Dayan recalled Lloyd's behaviour at the Sèvres meeting. Lloyd was unable to disguise his reluctance at having to participate in the collusion negotiations: 'His whole demeanour expressed distaste – for the place, the company, the topic'. Moshe Dayan, *The Story of my Life* (London: Weidenfeld & Nicolson, 1976), p. 180. Another of the Israeli delegation thought that Lloyd 'gave the impression of something stinking hanging permanently under his nose'. Mordechai Bar-On, *David Ben-Gurion and the Sèvres Collusion,* in William Roger Louis and Roger Owen (eds.), *A Revolutionary Year: 1958 in the Middle East* (London: I. B. Tauris, 2002), p. 157. Interestingly, although Lloyd, in his memoirs (*Suez: A Personal Account*), discusses the Sèvres meeting at some length, he makes no mention of his dinner with Aldrich on 28 October.

58. Aldrich interview by Challener, 15 July 1964, p. 61.

59. In a 1966 interview with the author of his biography, Aldrich claimed that 'The contact between the American government and the British government was through me and this triumvirate of Salisbury, Rab Butler and Macmillan, who were acting for the British government as a triumvirate and the President

wouldn't have anything to do with Eden. Or with Selwyn Lloyd either.' Aldrich Papers, Box 242, File 12, Johnson Interview with Aldrich, 18 October 1966, pp. 41–2, Baker Library, Harvard Business School, Boston, MA.

60. *FRUS 1955–1957*, Vol. XVI, Doc. 593, p. 1163.
61. Macmillan's farewell address to Aldrich at a Pilgrims Society dinner on 31 January 1957, marking Aldrich's retirement as Ambassador, reported in *The Times*, 1 February 1957 in a feature headed 'Anglo-U.S. decisions on Suez'.
62. Harriet Aldrich's letter to her children, 2 November 1956, MSS938 SG3 Series 1, SS2, Folder 20, Rhode Island Historical Society, Providence, Rhode Island.
63. Winthrop W. Aldrich, 'The Suez Crisis, A Footnote to History', *Foreign Affairs*, Vol. 45, No. 3 (1967), p. 543.
64. MSS 938 SG3, Manuscripts Division, Series I: Correspondence, Subseries 2: Harriet A. Aldrich, Box 2, Folder 20, Rhode Island Historical Society, Providence, Rhode Island.
65. Aldrich interview by Berliner, October 1972, p. 29.
66. It was overturned by Fred I. Greenstein, *The Hidden-Hand Presidency: Eisenhower as Leader* (Baltimore, MD: The Johns Hopkins University Press, 1982).
67. Boyle, *The Eden-Eisenhower Correspondence*.
68. The minutes of the first meeting of the British Cabinet's Egypt Committee on 30 July 1956 make this clear. 'While our ultimate purpose was to place the Canal under international control, our immediate objective was to bring about the downfall of the present Egyptian Government' (quoted in David Carlton, *Britain and the Suez Crisis* [Oxford: Blackwell, 1988], p. 37).

7
John Hay Whitney, 1957–61

Thomas C. Mills

Taking up his post as American Ambassador to the Court of St James's in February 1957, John Hay Whitney entered Grosvenor Square just a few months after the Suez crisis of the previous year. As such, his principal task on behalf of the Dwight D. Eisenhower administration was to repair relations with Harold Macmillan's new Conservative government in the aftermath of the greatest crisis in the Anglo-American special relationship since the Second World War. The rapprochement that did indeed transpire between the two nations was expressed most vividly in the Anglo-American conferences at Bermuda and Washington in 1957. Notwithstanding Macmillan's hopes to establish Anglo-American interdependence, Britain's status in the special relationship was in reality that of a junior partner. Such a status was compounded by the failure of the Eisenhower administration to fully consult its transatlantic ally in matters of joint concern to the two countries. Reluctant to accept such an inferior status, Britain continued to exercise its independence, leading inevitably to tensions with the US. Relations between the two countries reached something of a nadir with the collapse of the Paris Peace summit in May 1960 – where Macmillan's hopes for an improvement in relations with the Soviet Union were dramatically dashed – and the subsequent deterioration in Anglo-American relations that followed.

So what did John Hay Whitney's role amount to in these broader developments in Anglo-American relations? To judge by the existing literature, not a great deal. Both in surveys of Anglo-American relations during the twentieth century and in similar works focused specifically on the late 1950s, Whitney barely receives a mention.[1] The argument presented here is that such an oversight is unwarranted. Whitney did in fact play a central role in repairing the special relationship in the immediate aftermath of the Suez crisis. And while unable to wholly prevent the later souring of relations that followed, he remained alert to British sensitivities to such an extent to at least prevent a further major crisis between the two countries from occurring. Furthermore, examining Whitney's role as Ambassador to London sheds light on some of the more general issues of concern to students of diplomacy. Most notably, Whitney's ambassadorship highlights the gains to be achieved by summitry and public diplomacy, as well as some of the problems likely to be experienced by high profile political appointees. Perhaps most importantly, exploring Whitney's time as Ambassador to London will further our understanding of this largely neglected period in Anglo-American relations.

Whitney's Appointment to London

In some respects Whitney's route to Grosvenor Square was fairly predictable. For one thing his appointment continued a family tradition, with Whitney's maternal grandfather, John Hay, having served in the same post in the 1890s.[2] Moreover, having raised substantial funds for both of Eisenhower's presidential campaigns, Whitney's subsequent reward of the job of Ambassador to London followed a familiar pattern of political patronage.[3] In reality, Whitney's appointment to the prized diplomatic post was not straightforward.

Following the death of his father in 1927 Whitney inherited business interests worth roughly $180 million, making him one of the richest men in America at the age of 23.[4] While Whitney used his immense wealth to forge high profile public roles in the worlds of theatre, film and sport, he showed little initial interest in politics.[5] When Whitney did express a political orientation he tended to identify with the east coast liberal wing of the Republican Party and showed little enthusiasm for the conservative leadership embodied in the likes of Robert A. Taft or even the more centrist Thomas Dewey.[6] Indeed, Whitney's only significant foray into governmental affairs prior to his ambassadorship came during Franklin D. Roosevelt's wartime presidency, when Whitney headed the Motion Picture Division of Nelson Rockefeller's Office of the Coordinator for Inter-American Affairs.[7]

It was only the emergence of Eisenhower's 'dynamic conservatism' in the 1950s that ensured Whitney would enter political life in earnest. Serving during 1952 as chief fundraiser of Citizens for Eisenhower-Nixon, Whitney had fully entered the Republican Party's fold by the time of Eisenhower's re-election bid in1956.[8] By then acting in the official capacity of chairman of the United Republican Finance Committee, Whitney had taken on a number of minor roles within the administration and forged a close friendship with the President.[9] While never quite gaining access to Eisenhower's innermost circle, Whitney did enjoy frequent correspondence with the President and occasional visits to the White House.[10] He was also able to pander to Eisenhower's fondness for bird shooting by offering the use of his extensive plantation in south-west Georgia.[11]

As Whitney's stature within Eisenhower's coterie of friends and advisors rose, rumours of a major ambassadorial posting began circulating. Indeed, there was talk of Whitney becoming Ambassador to Britain for Eisenhower's first term in 1952. But – beginning a pattern of self-denial – Whitney let it be known that he expected no such reward for his assistance in getting Eisenhower elected and the post went to Winthrop Aldrich.[12] However, Aldrich only ever expected to serve four years, and it was therefore not long before speculation that Whitney would replace him in London began. With Aldrich backing Whitney for the post, and no signs of opposition from Congress, this seemed inevitable in the event of a Republican victory in the 1956 election.[13]

The sole remaining obstacle to Whitney's appointment as Ambassador to London turned out to be his own self-doubts. Beyond a natural shyness and mild stutter that would have to be overcome in the public duties of an ambassador, Whitney's principal concern was that Anglo-American relations would be undermined if the post of US Ambassador went to someone with his lack of diplomatic experience. Writing to Eisenhower in August 1956, Whitney went so far as to argue that the post might be better offered to someone of greater public stature in order for the US to 'serve notice that we believe that the importance of our English-speaking alliance ... is far greater than the reaffirmation of our good intentions. Such an ambassador', Whitney went on, 'would be on a mission and not on a visit'. However, in keeping with many of his predecessors, Eisenhower – once he had secured re-election – opted for loyalty and personal acquaintance over experience in his choice of Ambassador to London. On receiving a formal offer, Whitney accepted his new posting, pledging to 'work at it with enthusiasm'.[14] This would certainly be a necessary attribute given the dismal state of Anglo-American relations that greeted Whitney on his arrival in London.

Reconciliation: From Bermuda to Washington

Following the British invasion of Egypt in November 1956 many in Britain were shocked when the Eisenhower administration condemned the action in the United Nations and applied financial pressure on Britain that eventually forced a humiliating withdrawal of troops.[15] Resentment against US action was acute in Britain, with many viewing it as a betrayal of the special relationship between the two countries. Indicative of the strength of feeling were the hundred-plus signatures supporting an Early Day Motion in the House of Commons censuring the Eisenhower administration for 'gravely endangering the Atlantic Alliance'.[16] Duncan Sandys, the British Minister of Defence, conveyed a similar message directly to the Eisenhower administration. In a meeting with the US Secretary of State, John Foster Dulles, Sandys pointed to the 'deep and widespread anti-American sentiment in Britain' and the sense among officials that the country had been 'badly let down' by their erstwhile ally.[17] Such resentment towards the US was still apparent during the opening months of Whitney's ambassadorship. Writing to the State Department in March 1957 Whitney was at pains to convey that anti-American sentiment was by no means confined to the most vocal critics on the right wing of the Conservative Party, but extended to all parts of the political spectrum. 'Latent anti-Americanism', Whitney warned, 'will be a factor in our relations for some time to come'.[18]

While US disapproval of the British intervention in Egypt had indeed been genuine it soon became clear that Eisenhower was keen to overcome the bitter legacy of the crisis and restore Anglo-American relations to a more cordial status.[19] Despite the differences between the two countries in the Middle East, Washington still viewed Britain as a vital ally in the Cold War struggle. The President made this point in a letter to Winston Churchill where he expressed his hope that the Suez affair could be 'washed off the slate as soon as possible' in order that the 'old time closeness' between the US and Britain could be restored.[20] During a round of golf with Whitney prior to the new Ambassador's departure for London, Eisenhower put things more succinctly, instructing him to 'stop the rot' in Anglo-American relations.[21]

The first step towards this goal had already been initiated when Whitney arrived in Grosvenor Square. In January 1957 Eisenhower invited Macmillan to an Anglo-American summit to be held on the Atlantic island of Bermuda in March of that year.[22] Whitney's principal hope for the forthcoming meeting was that it would provide an opportunity to restore faith in the Anglo-American alliance among the British government and public. During preparations for the talks with the State Department, Whitney advocated doing everything possible at Bermuda 'to create an intense feeling of mutual trust and friendliness' between the two nations. Demonstrating a keen eye for what would nowadays be termed political spin, Whitney advised that pictures of Eisenhower and Macmillan 'talking, eating, relaxing, and press reports showing [the] intimate nature of the talks, will have a powerful impact'.[23]

Whitney attended the conference in Bermuda, but played little active part in the substantive discussions that took place there.[24] And while the conference left many issues unresolved between the US and Britain – most prominently those concerning the Middle and Far East – the summit did seem to have the more general effect desired by the Ambassador.[25] By the end of the meeting Macmillan described to a Cabinet colleague how 'personal relations between myself and the President have been established on a level of confidence which is very gratifying'.[26] Similarly, an editorial in *The Times* described 'the biggest achievement of Bermuda' as having put 'relations between the two Governments on the old informal and trustful basis'.[27] In restoring a good degree of British faith in the Anglo-American alliance, the summit at Bermuda could therefore be deemed a success. Whitney acknowledged as much in a letter to Dulles shortly after returning from Bermuda. 'From the point of view of my problem', Whitney stated, the Bermuda conference 'will be worth at least a year of work in its effect on British opinion towards the United States'.[28]

On returning to London, Whitney was able to solidify relationships with the key political figures in Britain. Already acquainted with the leader of the Labour Party, Hugh Gaitskell, and the Colonial Secretary, Alan Lennox-Boyd, from a brief tenure during his youth studying at Oxford, Whitney also quickly established contacts with the Foreign Secretary, Selwyn Lloyd, and Macmillan.[29] Writing to Eisenhower in June 1957 the Prime Minister stated: 'we like our new ambassador very much and I find it a great help to talk with him on things at large'.[30] Indeed, Macmillan had set the terms of his relationship with Whitney the previous month when he informed the Ambassador that he was welcome to come and see him whenever he had anything important to discuss.[31] In the subsequent months and years that followed Whitney regularly took up this invitation and developed a close relationship with the British leader, leading Macmillan to remark in the spring of 1959 that Whitney was 'the best American ambassador here in many years'.[32]

However, Whitney's early success at winning the confidence of British leaders was threatened when it emerged that the Ambassador was being excluded from certain communications by the State Department relevant to Anglo-American relations. Whitney became aware of this immediately following the Bermuda conference when it came to light that British officials were in possession of documents relating to the talks that he had not been privy to. The absence of such documents was becoming 'increasingly embarrassing', noted Whitney, when engaging in discussions with the British.[33] Concerned by a series of leaks in European capitals, the State Department had indeed placed restrictions on the distribution of certain communications.[34] However, following a terse note to Washington in which Whitney expressed his hope that 'these important records may be received in the next few days', the State Department complied and ensured Whitney was included in all correspondence.[35]

Whitney also raised the matter privately with Eisenhower and secured the President's assurance that he would be kept informed of all relevant developments in Anglo-American relations.[36] This did not turn out to be the case completely, however, as the Foreign Office – acting on previous advice from the State Department – continued to convey messages from Macmillan to Eisenhower through its Embassy in Washington, without always involving Whitney's Embassy in London.[37] There was, in fact, a certain hypocrisy to Whitney's complaints about being excluded from diplomatic correspondence. For the Ambassador himself often wrote privately to the President, precisely to avoid the correspondence being seen by his superiors in the State Department.[38] While this practice solidified the relationship between the President and the Ambassador, it is indicative of the tension always likely to exist between the Foreign Service establishment and a high profile political appointee such as Whitney.

The Ambassador's public profile did, however, mean that he was already known to some extent by the British public on his arrival in London.[39] Seeking to capitalise on this recognition, Whitney embarked upon an ambitious round of public diplomacy during his first year as Ambassador in an attempt to improve the image of the US, and thereby further strengthen the Anglo-American alliance. Travelling a total of 5,600 miles, while visiting 22 cities, Whitney went beyond the formal dinners and receptions usually attended by ambassadors. Visiting a Yorkshire textile factory and a Welsh coalmine, Whitney was even granted the honour of switching on the Blackpool illuminations.[40] During the course of his various public engagements Whitney invariably sought to press home the message of Anglo-American unity. Speaking as guest of honour at the Pilgrims of Great Britain annual dinner, Whitney employed the words uttered by his grandfather at a similar function some 60 years earlier. 'All of us who think', Whitney informed his audience of the British elite, 'cannot but see that there is a sanction like that of religion which binds us to a sort of partnership in the beneficent work of the world'.[41] Whitney's message of Anglo-American amity was boosted when he and his wife accompanied Queen Elizabeth II and Prince Philip on a state visit to the US in October 1957.[42] Following the trip Whitney paid for 10,000 copies of a pictorial souvenir album to be distributed to schools and other institutions throughout Britain.[43]

The impact of such public diplomacy is always difficult to gauge. Certainly Whitney believed that, 'on the surface' at least, British opinion of the US had improved since the low point in the immediate aftermath of the Suez crisis. 'But the wounds of injured pride', Whitney wrote to a friend, 'are deep and don't quite ever clot and heal'.[44] The limits of any Anglo-American rapprochement were confirmed by a Gallop poll from June 1957 showing that the percentage of the British public that regarded the US as 'Britain's best friend' stood at just 43 per cent.[45] A similar message was conveyed to Whitney during a meeting with a group of right wing Conservative MPs the following month. They argued that anti-Americanism was still rife among the British public, based on the belief that recent 'Anglo-American relations have been a one-way rather than a two-way street'.[46] However, the views of this group were dismissed by the leadership of the Conservative Party, and even one of the MPs expressing the misgivings wrote to Whitney following the meeting to state his 'admiration for what you are so fairly and perseveringly doing to ameliorate the situation'.[47] Nevertheless, it was clear by the autumn of 1957 that, notwithstanding Whitney's efforts, much work was still to be done in improving relations between the US and Britain.

Attempts to reinvigorate the Anglo-American special relationship subsequently entered a new phase and were this time initiated by the British. The trigger for this was the launch on 4 October 1957 of the Soviet Union's *Sputnik* satellite. This surprise display of Soviet prowess in the field of ballistic missile technology created a clamour in the US for more effective cooperation with allies in the Cold War struggle.[48] Macmillan sought to take advantage of this atmosphere by writing to Eisenhower suggesting that, in order to better confront the Soviet threat, the US and Britain should 'go further towards pooling our efforts and decide how best to use them for the common good'.[49] This suggestion was received sympathetically in the US and the second Eisenhower-Macmillan meeting of the year was scheduled for late October in Washington.[50]

In preparation for the meeting Whitney returned to the US for talks at the State Department. During these discussions he sought to impress upon his colleagues the need to move beyond the general expressions of good-will produced at Bermuda and ensure that the Washington meeting resulted in substantive policy agreements between the US and Britain.[51] The joint statements released at the end of the Washington talks certainly seemed to facilitate the kind of institutional framework for much closer Anglo-American collaboration in confronting the common threats faced by the two countries. Reporting on the meeting to the Cabinet in November 1957, Macmillan stated that the 'Declaration of Common Purpose' signed by himself and Eisenhower amounted to 'a declaration of interdependence' between the US and Britain, which would result in the two countries 'combining their resources and sharing their tasks'.[52]

In the months that followed such Anglo-American interdependence did indeed seem to transpire. This was most notable in the exchange of nuclear weapons materials and information, and the establishment of a series of regional and topical 'working groups' designed to coordinate Anglo-American policy.[53] But beneath Macmillan's rhetoric of interdependence lay a reality of growing British subordination to the US. This left Whitney with the awkward task of trying to maintain good Anglo-American relations against the backdrop of trends that threatened to rupture the special relationship.

The Limits of Interdependence

Whitney was well aware that Britain's status as a world power in the late 1950s was declining and that any talk of an 'equal partnership' between the US and Britain was at odds with the stark realities of the differing economic and military might of the two countries. As he explained to a meeting of US diplomats in September 1957, Britain was operating from a 'weakened world position' and the government had to learn to 'cut [its] coat to fit a relatively smaller piece of cloth'.[54] Nevertheless, Whitney shared the general view of the Eisenhower administration that the country remained an important ally.[55] Moreover, Whitney believed that good relations between the two countries could be maintained so long as consultation took place on global issues of joint concern. As he wrote to the State Department, British opinion towards the US was incredibly sensitive in the aftermath of Suez, and this would not diminish until the British people were convinced that their government was being 'fully consulted' and was acting as a 'full partner in decisions'.[56] Whitney expanded upon this point publically when addressing a dinner of the English Speaking Union in June 1957. 'After the shock of Suez', he explained, 'it is more important than ever that we consult together on the major issues with which we are concerned.'[57]

The consultation that Whitney believed to be so vital to a successful Anglo-American partnership had in fact been promised in the communiqué produced at the end of the Bermuda summit.[58] Moreover, it had subsequently taken place to some extent throughout 1957 with regard to developments of concern to the US and Britain in Syria.[59] However, it increasingly became clear to Whitney that such Anglo-American consultation was in danger of being overridden by a unilateralist tendency within the US administration.

An early instance of this emerged in relation to the Middle East during the spring of 1957. For some time both Washington and London had been concerned that the king of Jordan's position was under threat from forces in the country supportive of Egypt's Gamal Abdul Nasser. In order to demonstrate its support for the king, the US sailed its Sixth Fleet into Jordanian waters. While this action seemingly had the desired effect of bolstering the King's status in Jordan, the failure even to inform the British government of the forthcoming action was a cause of great concern to Whitney. 'This business of consultation, a flowering of Bermuda, a proof of our togetherness', Whitney wrote to the State Department, 'is terribly important here. It cannot bloom alone in Washington'. The reply from the State Department that the Eisenhower administration did in fact 'want consultation to bloom in London as well as Washington' did little to reassure Whitney.[60]

A similar situation arose the following year, again in relation to the Middle East. Concerned for the fate of the pro-Western regime in Lebanon following the union of Egypt and Syria to form the United Arab Republic, US and British officials undertook detailed contingency planning for military operations in the region.[61] However, when a coup in Iraq provided the trigger for intervention in July 1958, the US invasion of Lebanon was carried out independently of British troop landings in Jordan.[62] Macmillan berated Eisenhower that 'we ought ideally to have had a proper joint long-term plan before embarking on any operations'.[63] Following the intervention Whitney sought to coordinate policy between the US and Britain in terms of the length of the Middle Eastern campaigns, but the US penchant for unilateral action had been made abundantly clear.[64]

The fact that military operations in the Middle East could instigate a dispute in Anglo-American relations is indicative of the global interests that the two countries shared. More accurately, the lack of US consultation with Britain prior to the interventions is illustrative of the divergence between the two nations' perceptions of their shared global interests. The danger of the

US not consulting Britain on matters of joint concern, believed Whitney, was that it would encourage the Macmillan government to exercise its own independent foreign policy, thus further straining the Anglo-American alliance. Notwithstanding Britain's declining world power status, Whitney was well aware of a tendency among the country's leaders to rally against subservience to the US and 'from time to time go out of their way to assert their independence'.[65]

This trait was certainly in evidence when it came to policy towards communist China. Whereas the US had refused to recognise Mao Zedong's government, Britain had done so in 1950.[66] By the end of the decade the main issue of contention between the US and Britain was the stringent economic controls operated against China by the US. Britain had long been calling for a relaxation of these and in June 1957 broke with the US policy in order to facilitate greater trade with China.[67] The issue remained a constant source of conflict during Whitney's time in London and the Ambassador attracted personal criticism in the press following a speech where he reiterated US policy towards China. In this instance senior British figures supported Whitney's right to articulate US policy.[68] But while Britain's deviation from US policy on this front could be accommodated, a more serious cleavage in the Anglo-American alliance resulted when Macmillan sought to chart an independent course towards the Soviet Union.

Motivated by domestic political pressure, Macmillan had for some time been gently promoting the idea of a great power disarmament summit with the Soviet Union, having first raised the notion with Whitney in a meeting in May 1957.[69] The Ambassador relayed the Prime Minister's thoughts to Eisenhower, noting that 'a meeting at the top level on this most dramatic of all issues would, of course, be a fine piece of personal promotion for' Macmillan.[70] The President and Dulles, however, were generally unenthusiastic about the idea, fearing the fall-out if such a summit were to take place and fail to achieve concrete results.[71] Whitney expressed such misgivings publicly in a speech in the City of London. Seeking talks with the Soviets, he warned, put the West in a position of 'skating on thin ice'.[72] Privately Whitney expressed his concern to Lloyd that Britain and the US 'were getting off our joint track' when it came to dealing with the Soviets.[73]

Initially, Macmillan accepted the Eisenhower administration's reticence, but the incentives for a summit with the Soviets were drastically increased when on 27 November 1958 the Soviet Premier, Nikita Khrushchev, set a six-month deadline for the Western powers to reach an agreement with the Soviet Union over the status of Berlin.[74] This motivated Macmillan to visit Moscow in February 1959, despite the Eisenhower administration's misgivings. The eventual result of Macmillan's diplomacy was the Paris Peace summit of May 1960. Macmillan hoped that this meeting would lead to a substantial reduction in Cold War tensions, but it was immediately disrupted by Khrushchev's dramatic revelation that an American U-2 spy plane had been conducting reconnaissance missions over the Soviet Union. Eisenhower refused to offer what would have been a humiliating apology for the invasion of Soviet air space – despite Macmillan's pleading for him to do so – and the summit subsequently collapsed in disarray.[75]

Recriminations began immediately, with many in the US placing the blame for the Soviet propaganda coup on Macmillan, as the summit's chief instigator.[76] Observing these events in Paris, Whitney noted that while many were rushing to 'blame the British for being soft', the US would be wise 'not [to] forget their best friends, difficult as they may be'.[77] Others in the US were far less forgiving, and when the *New York Herald Tribune* launched a scathing attack on Macmillan this caused a particular headache for Whitney. The Ambassador had purchased control of the newspaper in August 1958, as the latest expansion of his business empire.[78] In a front-page story a few days after the summit, the newspaper editorialised that the failure of the Paris summit had discredited Macmillan's whole strategy of attempting to ease Cold War tensions through such meetings. The result, the piece went on, was likely to be a drastic lessening of Macmillan's influence in Washington, and a subsequent 'period of some strain between London and Washington'.[79]

While Whitney may have remained an absent owner of the newspaper while in London, his association with the source of such criticism of the British premier unsurprisingly caused a backlash. The *Daily Express* decried the 'extraordinary...attack' on Macmillan and, noting Whitney's ownership of the *Herald Tribune*, demanded an explanation from the Ambassador. A brief Embassy statement followed, declaring that Whitney exercised no editorial control over the newspaper's content.[80] Similarly, Whitney conveyed a message from the State Department to Lloyd deploring the criticisms of Macmillan made in the *Herald Tribune*.[81] And while this put an end to the controversy, the incident certainly highlights one of the potential pitfalls for an Ambassador with business interests as extensive as Whitney's.

Regardless of Whitney's conflict of interest regarding the *Herald Tribune*, the substance of the editorial – that Anglo-American relations had taken a turn for the worse in the final months of the Eisenhower administration – was undoubtedly true. Indicative of the hostility between the two countries that existed by the end of Whitney's term in London is the frustration the Ambassador expressed during a farewell dinner hosted by the Pilgrims Society in January 1961. Referring to criticisms of the allegedly aggressive US policy in South-East Asia from the British press and public, Whitney declared that he simply could not 'believe that this is really what you think of us, or the President who has worked with such devotion for eight years in the cause of peace'.[82] So with Anglo-American relations finishing on such a low, how are we to judge an ambassador who was sent to London with the principal mission of improving relations between the two countries in the aftermath of the Suez crisis?

Conclusion

Given the dire state of Anglo-American relations at the beginning of his time in London, Whitney certainly deserves credit for the rapid improvement that materialised throughout 1957. Yet in the end there was only so much that summitry and positive press reports could do to disguise the tensions that characterised Anglo-American relations during this period. As British power in the world declined and the country reluctantly came to terms with its dependency on the US, rifts between Washington and London were inevitable. Affecting such underlying currents in the global balance of power is, perhaps, beyond the abilities of any ambassador, regardless of their talents. However, while unable to fundamentally alter the negative trajectory of Anglo-American relations during his ambassadorship, it is quite possible that relations could have been much worse – and minor ruptures turned into major crises – had there been an ambassador in post less astute to British sensitivities. By the early 1960s the two nations still remained allies, albeit, in Christopher Thorne's phrase, 'of a kind'.[83]

On leaving London Whitney certainly received lavish praise from both sides of the Atlantic. Writing in November 1960, Eisenhower stated: 'I am quite sure that your four years' service in your vital post has done much to strengthen the basic friendship between the Governments of Great Britain and the United States'.[84] Similarly, in a message delivered to Whitney shortly before he departed, Macmillan stated that 'during four difficult and testing years' the Ambassador had 'done so much to strengthen the friendship between our two countries'.[85] These tributes perhaps reflect more the close personal relationships that Whitney had forged with both Eisenhower and Macmillan than his true impact on Anglo-American relations. Whitney himself provided a more balanced view when asked years later what he considered to be the chief accomplishment of his ambassadorship. 'I like to think', replied Whitney, 'that we did set an aura of good feeling'.[86] This more modest appraisal of Whitney's achievements in Grosvenor Square seems a fair verdict.

Notes

1. For examples of the former, see Dobson, *Anglo-American Relations in the Twentieth Century*; and Ovendale, *Anglo-American Relations in the Twentieth Century*. For examples of the latter, see Michael Dockrill, 'Restoring the "Special Relationship": The Bermuda and Washington Conferences, 1957', in Dick Robinson and Glyn Stone (eds.), *Decisions and Diplomacy: Essays in Twentieth Century History* (London: Routledge, 1995), pp. 205–23; Matthew Jones, 'Anglo-American Relations after Suez, the Rise and Decline of the Working Group Experiment, and the French Challenge to NATO, 1957–59', *Diplomacy and Statecraft*, Vol. 14, No. 1 (2003), pp. 49–78. For a rare exception, see the brief reference to Whitney in Donald Cameron Watt, *Succeeding John Bull: America in Britain's Place, 1900–1975: A Study*

of the *Anglo-American Relationship and World Politics in the Context of British and American Foreign-Policy-making in the Twentieth Century* (Cambridge: Cambridge University Press, 1984), p. 138.

2. E. J. Kahn, Jr, *Jock: The Life and Times of John Hay Whitney* (New York: Doubleday, 1981), p. 223.

3. *Ibid.*, pp. 208 and 214.

4. 'Whitney, John Hay', in *American National Biography*, Vol. 23 (New York: Oxford University Press, 1999–2005), pp. 305–6.

5. *Ibid.*, p. 306; Kahn, *Jock*, p. 205.

6. Khan, *Jock*, pp. 205–6. In later life Whitney was an active member of and substantial donor to the Ripon Society, a think-tank representing the liberal wing of the Republican Party. See *ibid.*, p. 206.

7. Antonio Pedro Tota, *The Seduction of Brazil: The Americanization of Brazil during World War II* (Austin, TX: University of Texas Press, 2009), pp. 36–44.

8. Kahn, *Jock*, pp. 208–14.

9. *Ibid.*, pp. 212–14. See also 'National Affairs: The Gifted Amateur', *Time*, 7 January 1957, available at http://www.time.com/time/magazine/article/0,9171,808886-1, 00.html (accessed 29 June 2010).

10. For a discussion of Eisenhower's advisors, see 'Eisenhower's 'Inner Circle'', *The New York Times* (magazine), 3 February 1957, p. 9.

11. Kahn, *Jock*, pp. 210–12.

12. *Ibid.*, p. 214.

13. *Ibid.*, pp. 214–15.

14. *Ibid.*, pp. 215–16. Whitney's nomination was confirmed unanimously by the Senate on 5 February 1957. See 'Senate Group Backs Whitney', *The New York Times*, 6 February 1957, p. 17.

15. Dobson, *Anglo-American Relations in the Twentieth Century*, pp. 117–18.

16. Keith Kyle, *Suez: Britain's End of Empire in the Middle East* (London: I. B. Tauris, 2003), p. 507.

17. The National Archives (TNA), Kew, FO371/126683/AU1051/28, Washington to Foreign Office, 28 February 1957. See also Dockrill, 'Restoring the "Special Relationship"', pp. 207–8.

18. US National Archives and Records Administration (NARA), Maryland, State Department Central Decimal File, 611.41/3-757, Record Group 59, London to State Department, 7 March 1957.

19. Dobson, *Anglo-American Relations in the Twentieth Century*, p. 119.

20. Dwight D. Eisenhower, *The White House Years: Waging Peace, 1956–1961* (London: Heinemann, 1966), pp. 680–1.

21. Kahn, *Jock*, p. 220.

22. TNA, FO371/126683/AU1051/33, Kirkpatrick to Caccia, 18 January 1957; Dockrill, 'Restoring the "Special Relationship"', p. 208.

23. NARA, 611.41/3-757, RG59, London to State Department, 7 March 1957.

24. Kahn, *Jock*, p. 227.

25. Stephen Blackwell, 'Britain, the United States and the Syrian Crisis, 1957', *Diplomacy and Statecraft*, Vol. 11, No. 3 (2000), pp. 139–58, p. 144; Dockrill, 'Restoring the "Special Relationship"', pp. 215–16.

26. Quoted in Dockrill, 'Restoring the "Special Relationship"', p. 215.

27. 'Bermuda', *Times*, 25 March 1957, p. 11.

28. Quoted in Kahn, *Jock*, p. 227.

29. Kahn, *Jock*, p. 225; 'Whitney', in *American National Biography*, Vol. 23, p. 305.
30. *FRUS 1955–57*, Vol. XXVII, pp. 775–77.
31. *FRUS 1955–57*, Vol. XX, pp. 544–55.
32. Kahn, *Jock*, pp. 240–1.
33. NARA, 611.41/4-357, RG59: London to State Department, 3 April 1957.
34. Kahn, *Jock*, pp. 231–2.
35. NARA, 611.41/4-357, RG59, London to State Department, 3 April 1957; NARA, 611.41/4-857, RG59, Fisher Rowe to Whitney, 8 April 1957.
36. Kahn, *Jock*, pp. 231–2.
37. TNA, FO371/132330/AU1051/28, Hoyer-Millar to Brook, 18 August 1958 and Hoyer-Millar to Brook, 26 August 1958; TNA, FO371/132330/AU1051/29, Brook to Hoyer-Millar, 20 August 1958.
38. See, for example, *FRUS 1955–57*, Vol. XX, pp. 544–55.
39. Kahn, *Jock*, p. 224.
40. *Ibid.*, p. 232.
41. Quoted in Kahn, *Jock*, p. 228. See also 'U.S-British Tie Cited', *The New York Times*, 8 October 1957, p. 4.
42. 'Queen's Schedule in US a Full One', *The New York Times*, 1 October 1957, p. 10.
43. Kahn, *Jock*, p. 235.
44. Quoted in Kahn, *Jock*, p. 228.
45. NARA, Records of the Foreign Service Posts of the Department of State, Great Britain, London Embassy, Box 494, RG84, London to State Department, 9 July 1957.
46. *Ibid.*, 5 July 1957.
47. 'British Discount Anti-US Attitude', *The New York Times*, 11 July 1957, p. 7; NARA, 5 July 1957.
48. Nigel J. Ashton, ' "A Rear Guard Action": Harold Macmillan and the Making of British Foreign Policy, 1957–1963', in T. G. Otte (ed.), *The Makers of British Foreign Policy from Pitt to Thatcher* (Basingstoke: Palgrave Macmillan, 2002), pp. 238–60, pp. 246–47.
49. *FRUS 1955–57*, Vol. XXVII, pp. 785–6.
50. *Ibid.*, pp. 789–96.
51. *Ibid.*, pp. 791–4.
52. Quoted in Dockrill, 'Restoring the "Special Relationship" ', p. 218.
53. John Baylis, 'The 1958 Anglo-American Defence Agreement: The Search for Nuclear Independence', *Journal of Strategic Studies*, Vol. 31, No. 3 (2008), pp. 425–66; Jones, 'Anglo-American Relations after Suez', pp. 49–78.
54. *FRUS 1955–57*, Vol. IV, pp. 608–36.
55. Dobson, *Anglo-American Relations in the Twentieth Century*, pp. 119–20.
56. NARA, 611.41/3-757, RG59, London to State Department, 7 March 1957. Whitney was supported in these views by the Deputy Chief of Mission in the London Embassy, Walworth Barbour. See NARA, 611.41/12-3057, RG59, London to State Department, 30 December 1957.
57. 'US Ambassador Urged Closest Consultation', *The Times*, 5 June 1957, p. 4.
58. NARA, 611.41/3-2457, RG59, USDEL Bermuda to State Department, 24 March 1957; 'Bermuda', *The Times*, 25 March 1957, p. 11.
59. Blackwell, 'Britain, the United States and the Syrian Crisis', pp. 139–58; 'Macmillan Sees US Aide', *The New York Times*, 24 August 1957, p. 4; Jones, 'Anglo-American Relations after Suez', pp. 52–3.

60. *FRUS 1955–57*, Vol. XXVII, pp. 772–3.
61. Diane B. Kunz, 'The Emergence of the United State as a Middle Eastern Power', in William Roger Louis and Roger Owen (eds.), *A Revolutionary Year: 1958 in the Middle East* (London: I. B. Tauris, 2002), pp. 77–100, 86; Ashton, " 'A Rear Guard Action' ", p. 249.
62. Ashton, " 'A Rear Guard Action' ", p. 249.
63. Quoted in Blackwell, 'Britain, the United States and the Syrian Crisis', p. 154.
64. *FRUS 1958–60*, Vol. XI, pp. 451–53.
65. *FRUS 1955–57*, Vol. IV, pp. 608–36. See also 'British Discount Anti-US Attitude', *The New York Times*, 11 July 1957, p. 7.
66. Ritchie Ovendale, 'Britain, the United States, and the Recognition of Communist China', *The Historical Journal*, Vol. 26, No. 1 (1983), pp. 139–58.
67. Dobson, *Anglo-American Relations in the Twentieth Century*, p. 121.
68. Kahn, *Jock*, p. 237.
69. NARA, 611.41/2-2458, RG59, London to State Department, 24 February 1958.
70. *FRUS 1955–57*, Vol. XX, pp. 544–55.
71. *Ibid.*, pp. 616–17.
72. 'Soviet Termed Wary', *The New York Times*, 25 April 1958, p. 3.
73. *FRUS 1958–60*, Vol. VIII, pp. 86–8.
74. NARA, 641/12-459, RG59, London to State Department, 4 December 1959.
75. Ashton, ' "A Rear Guard Action" ', pp. 249–50.
76. 'Macmillan's Summit Role', *The New York Times*, 24 May 1960, p. 16.
77. Kahn, *Jock*, p. 245.
78. 'Whitney Obtains Control of Herald Tribune', *The New York Times*, 29 August 1958, p. 1 and p. 16; Kahn, *Jock*, pp. 237–8.
79. 'Summit Casualty – Macmillan', *New York Herald Tribune*, 23 May 1960, p. 1 and p. 11.
80. 'Macmillan Story Assailed by Beaverbrook's Papers', *New York Herald Tribune*, 26 May 1960, p. 13.
81. *FRUS 1958–60*, Vol. VII, pp. 868–9.
82. 'Whitney Honored by British Group', *The New York Times*, 12 January 1961, p. 2. See also Watt, *Succeeding John Bull*, p. 138.
83. Christopher Thorne, *Allies of a Kind: The United States, Britain, and the War against Japan, 1941–1945* (London: Hamish Hamilton, 1978).
84. Kahn, *Jock*, p. 247.
85. 'Ambassador Wants More Candid Anglo-US Explanations', *The New York Times*, 12 January 1961, p. 6.
86. Quoted in Kahn, *Jock*, p. 251.

Part III

The Cold War Ambassadors, 1961–1981

Introduction

Alison R. Holmes

Much of the special relationship narrative relies on the cornerstone of belief in an alliance born of conflict and based on a quality of trust that could only have been produced by the tempering effects of war. There is little to explain how the relationship 'should' work during peace or indeed in wars in which the enemies were not shared or through times in which the asymmetry of different types of power becomes acute. There is even less in this traditional approach to guide our understanding of the ongoing resilience of such a relationship, except perhaps the persistence of their shared global perspective on the changes going on in the world around them.

All of the parts of this volume reflect, yet struggle with the war versus peace dichotomy framework of UK–US relations. The preponderance of qualifiers for the term 'Cold War' in the titles of each part is an indication that, while security and intelligence – the basic links of conflict and war – remain key, these issues cannot stand alone. Nowhere is this struggle more apparent than in the next time frame, which encompasses simultaneous economic and social change in both countries. This period of peaceful 'revolution' was seeded in wartime, but came to fruition as the next generation questioned almost every aspect of authority and power that the Anglo-American relationship had, to that point, promoted and protected.

The 20-year period from 1961 to 1981 carries our story of the Embassy through the weight of Vietnam, the building of the Berlin Wall, the Cultural Revolution as well as the opening of China, the Soviets in Afghanistan, one Middle East crisis after another – including oil with the attendant 'discovery' of rampant stagflation – and closes with the Iranian revolution and the taking of hostages at the American Embassy in Tehran. Domestically, Americans travelled from Camelot, Martin Luther King and the Civil Rights trail through the beginning of environmental awareness, Woodstock and Watergate to the door of the Reagan Revolution. And, as Ambassador Brewster found, political parties can make a difference to 'specialness', at least in terms of specific issues such as South Africa.

For the British, economic crises were relentless, as was the realisation that the Empire was finally dead along with the ability to extend national power – though not necessarily influence – to other parts of the world. At home, the crumbling of the aristocracy combined with demands for civil rights, particularly in Northern Ireland (including the beginning of issues regarding US visas for nationalist sympathisers as Ambassador Richardson found, or the best way to achieve one's aims as again Ambassador Brewster found on the issue of US guns arming British police in Northern Ireland) were all part of the fundamental reordering of British society. The left and the right of politics on both sides of the Atlantic were forced to reinvent themselves in the face of growing demands at home and abroad for a fundamentally different order within the international system. As always, these two, sometimes passive, sometimes active, but constantly engaged global actors were affected by, and had an effect on, all these new realities.

The five Ambassadors of the post-Cold War period in Part III have relatively little in common. They represent a range in terms of length of tenure with Ambassador Bruce being one of the longest serving across this time frame, while Richardson and Armstrong had barely enough time to unpack before it was time to head back to the US. As usual, they are all political appointees, but with a wide range of actual political experience. Bruce was arguably 'to the embassy born' and, crucially, brought a wide and deep system of contacts in Washington, with whom he stayed in constant contact over his long term and used to powerful effect. On the other hand, and despite their short tenure, Richardson and Armstrong both had strong government experience to back them up. They did not have traditional diplomatic pedigrees, but they did have potentially useful experience in terms of the economic issues facing the UK at the time. Perhaps indicative of the wider social change, this period also includes both the first Jewish Ambassador in Walter Annenberg and the first woman, Anne Legendre Armstrong. Annenberg is particularly interesting for a number of reasons; a wealthy businessman and not the first man to come to the post without giving much financial support directly to the President he served, he became known for his often lavish contributions both to the post through massive renovations to Winfield House and as a benefactor of a number of British institutions. Annenberg, like Richardson after him, was good on business issues but both men were cut out of 'high politics' often through no 'fault' of their own, but due to political brinkmanship on the part of their own colleagues. Unlike other Ambassadors, in retirement Annenberg became a 'fixer' for a number of future Ambassadors to the UK by way of his initial and early support for Ronald Reagan, though later a supporter of Nixon. Armstrong, a Texan, represents the beginning of the strong line of connections to Texas over the coming decades.

The relatively rapid turnover at the end of this period, the result of elections and scandal, did offer the staff, particularly the Deputy Chiefs of

Mission, more opportunity. Their ability and initiative are surely reflected in the fact so many of them went on to become ambassadors themselves – although this is not an unusual aspect for London 'alumni'. A constant theme that continues throughout this period is the tendency for London to as act as a 'hub' on global issues as Bruce found over the issue of Cyprus and London as a go-between for Greece and Turkey. As such, London has always been and remains a premier training ground for professional development and offers unparalleled networking opportunities for career staff (even if it is at the cost of providing logistical support for a relentless number of US delegations to the UK).

In terms of relations between Presidents and Prime Ministers the second 'high water mark' of relations between President Kennedy and Prime Minister Harold Macmillan seemed to be draining away over this period, with changing parties, changing electorates and changing faces at the top taking a toll on the intimacy of the past. As we shall see, it is an interesting question if this was more about the ambassadors and their qualifications, or a personality issue. Full *dis*credit should also be attributed here to Henry Kissinger and the group that came to be known as 'Eagleburger men' whose style and ego belied a view of cooperation as weakness – even with their own team. On the other hand, it also points to an ongoing reality that, throughout this entire timeframe, information was more freely shared by the British than the Americans; and that all US Ambassadors, regardless of party or time frame, came to use, if not rely on, their British contacts for the most up to date information rather than their own 'official chain'. This had interesting consequences for the British as they tried to keep track of who was sharing information with whom on the American side so as not to annoy the 'higher' links of command.

In terms of the practical issues for the authors here, it is also at this point that we begin to have more *realité* from those involved in the events being discussed. Archive material for this period becomes more difficult to come by, and therefore interviews are used more to support their work. This does, however, also introduce the issue of memory and position and should be balanced accordingly as new material will inevitably come to light on all the issues covered here.

The urge to define periods of time by issues of peace versus conflict is strong. We could have simply put the Cold War into a single category and left it at that. However, it seemed clear to us that 1960 – at least as far as the British and American public were concerned – represented a step change not only in their domestic politics, but in their view of the world. More importantly, and as we see over and over again in these chapters, despite, or perhaps because of, the upheaval at home and around the world, they continued to move in the same direction. From Vietnam to the hostage crisis in Iran, the five Ambassadors covered here had their work cut out for them.

8
David K. E. Bruce, 1961–69

John W. Young

According to his diary, David Bruce virtually selected the London Embassy for himself: before his inauguration as President, John F. Kennedy told the veteran diplomat and Democratic Party supporter that he could have any post he wanted and Bruce had no hesitation in opting for London.[1] The appointment was entirely without controversy. Indeed, while Bruce was a political appointee rather than a career diplomat, it is difficult to imagine anyone better suited to the post. He was a long-standing member of the American foreign policy hierarchy during the first decades of the Cold War, with a particular expertise in relations with Western Europe, serving under both Democratic and Republican administrations. Not only did he have experience as a soldier, journalist, lawyer, investment banker and, in 1923–25 Democratic member of the Maryland House of Delegates, but also in 1926–27 he had, albeit briefly, served as a professional diplomat in Rome. Before his appointment to London, he had taken a leading role in administering the Marshall Plan (as Chief of the European Cooperation Administration in Paris, 1948–49) and acted as Ambassador to both France (1949–53) and West Germany (1957–60). He was also well acquainted with key policy-makers of the 1960s like George Ball, Dean Rusk and Dean Acheson. Acheson had even urged Kennedy to make Bruce his Secretary of State before Rusk was selected.[2]

Before taking up the post, the new Ambassador already had close links with the United Kingdom. Indeed, his career, friendships and marriage reflected the fact that Britain and America are bound together culturally and socially, at least at the level of the upper classes. He had served in London during the Second World War in the Office of Strategic Services, and had numerous acquaintances there – including the James Bond novelist Ian Fleming, with whom he had worked on intelligence matters. At the personal level, Bruce's second wife, Evangeline Bell, whom he married at the end of the war, was half-English, the grand-daughter of a Conservative MP. Evangeline was an excellent asset in London. With her family connections, cosmopolitan outlook and enthusiasm for entertaining she made the

Ambassador's residence at Winfield House a focus of high society dinners. Bruce was already in his sixties when he arrived in London, having been born into a wealthy Virginia family back in 1898. He was also a smoker, a wine lover and a gourmet. Yet, despite the first signs in December 1966 of the heart trouble that would eventually kill him, his health was good and he had no trouble coping with the demands of an ambassador's life, which often involved late nights, transatlantic flights and the stresses of crisis management. Unsurprisingly, his time in London has already attracted some academic discussion.[3] Its appeal as a subject has, no doubt, been boosted by his personal diary, typed up at length, on an almost daily basis, which gives a remarkable insight into his life as ambassador. In its detail, it may be unique as a record of the routine of a modern envoy.

Bruce's Contacts with Washington

Bruce's ambassadorship coincided with an accelerating threat to the very institution of the Embassy. One of his colleagues, George Ball, Undersecretary of State in 1961–66, came to believe that 'jet planes and telephones...largely restricted ambassadors to ritual and public relations'.[4] Swifter communications, summit meetings, the growth of international organisations and the 'instant' reports from a global media all undermined the significance of ambassadors as the twentieth century progressed, but the expansion of jet transport in the 1960s was probably the most significant factor. Heads of government and foreign ministers could meet at short notice. In those European countries who were members of both NATO and the European Economic Community (EEC), foreign ministers met several times a year, pushing ambassadors into the background. Yet, the role of the Embassy was far from extinguished. In 1961, the year Bruce arrived in London, the Vienna Convention on Diplomatic Relations set out the functions of embassies as follows: to represent one state in another state; 'protecting in the receiving State the interests of the sending State and of its nationals'; negotiating agreements; reporting on 'conditions and developments' in the receiving State; and 'promoting friendly relations'. The resident embassy was a flexible institution, with multiple roles that evolved over time.[5] Certainly, a study of Bruce shows that an experienced and energetic ambassador could meet the challenges of the time and preserve an essential position in bilateral relations.

It helped, of course, that Bruce had such good connections to the levers of power in Washington. He had easy access to the State Department throughout his time in London. In February–March 1963, he even spent several weeks working in the Department, after Kennedy asked him to prepare a paper on the future of US–European relations. Aside from this unusually long stay, Bruce returned to the US for consultations several times a year and was, almost always, present to brief the President ahead of summit meetings with the British Prime Minister. During Bruce's first nine months in London, he visited Washington three times and these may serve as an indication of his good connections to the policy machine. His first trip back was only 18 days after he had arrived in the UK to deliver his credentials. Its main purpose was to attend a meeting between Kennedy and Macmillan, and to brief the President on Anglo-American relations before this summit began. However, the Ambassador also took part in separate meetings between the two foreign ministers, Rusk and Lord Home. He talked to British officials about the chances of a British application to the EEC and had a one-to-one discussion about the same subject with the National Security Advisor, McGeorge Bundy.[6] Bruce's next visit, in September–October, was more focused on the State Department, the key issues being the future of Berlin (following the building by the Soviets of a wall between the Eastern and Western sectors) and British Guiana (a British colony where the Americans feared a left-leaning government might come to power after independence). He also had personal meetings with such leading figures as Rusk, Bundy, Ball and CIA Director Allen Dulles.[7] Bruce's third visit, in December, which he combined with a Christmas stay at his family home in Virginia, meant he could accompany Kennedy to the summit meeting with Macmillan on Bermuda[8] as well as staying into the New Year to attend a meeting in the State Department with a British delegation about trade and labour questions.[9]

In addition to visiting Washington and receiving instructions from the State Department, Bruce also kept in touch with US policy through American officials who made personal visits to London. Again, just looking at the first year of his ambassadorship, there were visits from such figures as Mennen Williams, the Assistant Secretary of State for African Affairs (July 1961), Robert McNamara, the Defence Secretary (also July 1961), Ambassador-at-Large Averell Harriman (September 1961), Kennedy's military representative General Maxwell Taylor (March 1962) and Undersecretary of State George Ball (April 1962). These visits demonstrated the regular high-level contacts between Britain and America on such political-security issues as decolonisation, the Cold War, the future of South-East Asia, NATO and European integration. Bruce's diary is rather less forthcoming about intelligence links, although they are sometimes noted in a cursory way, as in August 1961, when a special courier arrived from Washington with a message about a new CIA Director being appointed, which required 'consultation with officials in the security departments of the British Government'.[10] The tone of one diary entry, saying that 'The volume of US officials, correspondents, and telegrams from the Department and foreign posts never diminishes', reveals that the regular contacts with Washington, while they kept the Ambassador closely informed about US thinking, could also seem relentless.[11] Bruce was never one to act independently, even when he doubted the wisdom of instructions from Washington. During the Cuban Missile Crisis he accepted State Department instructions to carry a pistol with him when he went to meet Acheson off an airplane, despite both men being bemused by this. Bruce then acted as 'armed escort' to the (equally bemused) Central Intelligence Agency officer, Chester Cooper, who had been sent by Kennedy to explain the discovery of Soviet missiles on Cuba to Macmillan.[12]

Presidents and Prime Ministers

The Ambassador had regular access to both the President and the Prime Minister. Bundy once noted that Bruce was one of the very few ambassadors who 'wrote with a sense of style' that ensured the President was happy to read his telegrams.[13] Whilst he was never a personal friend of Kennedy or Johnson, Bruce expressed fulsome praise for both in his diary and was felt by his staff to 'have the ear of the White House and he knew when to use it. He was sought out by the White House rather than the other way around'.[14] Bruce's biographer, Nelson Lankford, has argued that Kennedy relied on the unorthodox British Ambassador to Washington, David Ormsby-Gore, to smooth transatlantic relations. The latter was of Kennedy's own generation and they developed a warm friendship. Only when Lyndon B. Johnson (LBJ) became President in November 1963, argues Lankford, 'did Bruce come into his own as Ambassador to Britain'.[15] This was partly because LBJ was far less close than Kennedy had been to Ormsby-Gore, or to the latter's successor (1965–69), Patrick Dean.[16] It is also a fact that Johnson never visited London, whereas Kennedy passed through in May 1961 (en route to the Vienna summit with Nikita Khrushchev) and met Macmillan for a summit meeting in late June 1963, seeing Bruce on both occasions. It is interesting, however, that in 1969 the Political Counsellor of the Embassy, William Galloway, told a British official that he 'did not believe that the US Embassy here could ever take the place of Washington for the day-to-day business of Anglo-American relations'.[17] From a professional viewpoint, even under Johnson, it seems the British Embassy in Washington retained its eminence over Grosvenor Square in bilateral dealings. Bruce himself complained to the State Department in 1964 that part of his job involved 'carrying out instructions to make representations to the Foreign Office, all too often duplicatory of conversations already held with the efficient British Embassy in Washington...'[18] Nonetheless, Bruce did have the advantage of being able to talk to British Prime Ministers at key points. For example, his access to Downing Street was such that he met Macmillan in January 1963 just after the French President, Charles de Gaulle, had vetoed Britain's first application to join the EEC. Bruce had 'thought that perhaps he would be bristling with indignation over the General's utterances. On the contrary, he was cool as a cucumber.'[19]

There can be little doubt that the relationship between LBJ and Macmillan's successors was lukewarm and that this helped Bruce become more important in smoothing transatlantic differences. Bruce himself felt that, under Kennedy, the high level 'team work' between Britain and the US was 'exceptionally satisfactory'. This was not only because of Ormsby-Gore's friendship with the President, but also because of the 'mutual esteem and trust' between Kennedy and Macmillan, reinforced by relations at foreign ministers' level between Rusk and Home.[20] Under Johnson, any mutual esteem was far less apparent. The President only met Alec Douglas-Home – Prime Minister for a year after October 1963 – once at summit level and that was overshadowed by differences over a British trade deal to sell buses to Fidel Castro's Cuba. When Labour took office in October 1964, the new premier, Harold Wilson, had high hopes of emulating Churchill's close relations with the White House, yet Johnson never showed any sign of reciprocating. The President never looked forward to meetings with the new Prime Minister and his growing obsession with the Vietnam War meant that he judged Wilson largely on the refusal to commit even a token force of British troops to the conflict.[21] George Ball believed that 'Johnson took an almost instant dislike' to his British opposite number.[22] It should be noted, though, that the President, whose previous experience and future ambitions focused on domestic politics, had little relish for meeting any of his foreign counterparts.[23]

Bruce himself never seems to have had the personal warmth with Wilson that he found with Macmillan or Douglas-Home, yet he recognised the Labour leader's political acumen and the following diary entry, from just before Wilson's March 1966 election triumph, shows that, by then, the President may have come to appreciate the latter's public support on the Vietnam War (which is discussed more fully below):

> [Wilson] said he had been fearful of the last debate in the Commons on Vietnam, but had driven his opponents to the wall and did not expect any further trouble this month. There is perhaps a touch of paranoia in Wilson, but he is undoubtedly one of the most adroit politicians in the world. We receive almost daily copies of messages passing between the Prime Minister and the President. Their tone is cordial to the point of being on both sides effusive. The President is clearly grateful for the support given him by the PM on Vietnam.[24]

In any case, however one judges the Wilson-Johnson partnership, the important point is that relations between their officials does not seem to have suffered. Both sides worked to keep cooperation close. Philip Kaiser, Bruce's Deputy Chief of Mission in 1964–69, recalls that, whenever there was a summit meeting, the Embassy would get an account of it from the British before one arrived from Washington, 'reflecting the fact, we thought, that 10 Downing Street was…more sensitive to the obligations of the special relationship'. Kaiser adds that the relationship was close because of continuing cooperation in such areas as intelligence, nuclear weapons and US bases in the United Kingdom, all of which meant that both sides had a stake in friendship. He comments:

> In the intelligence field our two countries gave each other more information than either gave to any of its other allies. We exchanged information on both overt and covert sources for the preparation of joint estimates. The weekly report of the Joint Intelligence Committee ... was the product of a combined effort with the chief of our CIA station responsible for the American contribution.[25]

Diplomatic Challenges

A series of crises had an impact on Anglo-American relations during Bruce's eight-year ambassadorship. During 1961 Bruce had to deal with the effects of the Bay of Pigs fiasco (which he noted was 'undoubtedly in the minds of the British public, a blow to our prestige'[26]), Kennedy's poor performance at the Vienna superpower summit and the building of the Berlin Wall, none of which reflected well on America's position in the world. These were minor hiccups compared to the Cuban Missile Crisis the following year, which more than restored Kennedy's image. Less well-remembered is the long-running crisis between Greece and Turkey over the future of Cyprus, which dominated his diary entries during much of 1964. The London Embassy proved central to the diplomacy over that, partly because Britain was the former colonial power on the island and a guarantor of Cypriot independence.[27]

By then, three interlocking concerns loomed large in the Ambassador's mind, each with enormous, separate and combined, significance for Anglo-American relations. The first was Britain's economic decline relative to its industrial competitors, which forced the government into expenditure cuts. The second was an important aspect of these cuts, the country's military retreat from defence bases in the Far East and the Persian Gulf (the so-called 'east of Suez' position). This British retreat coincided with the third problem, America's growing involvement in the Vietnam War, which will be dealt with in greater detail below. The war stretched US resources and made it difficult for Washington to fill the power voids left by its ally's withdrawal from bases in Malaysia-Singapore.

Economic decline was of particular concern to Bruce, whose reaction to Britain's precarious position sometimes verged on panic. The country had never properly recovered from the financial strains of the Second World War and, with its 'great power' ambitions and expanded social expenditure, was already living beyond its means when Bruce arrived. The Conservative government of the early 1960s was unable to escape 'stop-go economics' whereby attempts to boost demand merely led to increased imports, which in turn damaged the balance-of-payments position and forced a return to deflation. By the time of the 1964 election defence took up about 7 per cent of the gross domestic product and there was a payments deficit of £400 million. Yet, despite its commitment to higher social spending, the incoming Wilson administration quickly ruled out devaluation of sterling and looked to the US to help prop up the currency in the money markets. The Americans were willing to help to an extent. After all, a British economic collapse could lead to a precipitate withdrawal from world affairs and, in any case, it was widely recognised that a devaluation of the pound was likely to be followed by currency speculation against the dollar. In late 1964, the Americans helped put together a $3 billion support package for sterling after a crisis triggered by Labour's first budget. The Americans also wanted to see Labour reduce its domestic spending plans, unwelcome news to a Prime Minister who had been elected with only a thin majority. Bruce was at the centre of several currency crises in 1964–66 before a seamen's strike in mid-1966 led to a large-scale 'run' on sterling and forced a major austerity package. Fortunately for Wilson, he had won a safe majority in parliament at a general election just a few months before. However, the Arab-Israeli war of June 1967 and subsequent closure of the Suez Canal helped bring a further, overwhelming crisis in November 1967 when the British pound was finally devalued from $2.80 to $2.40. Even then, speculation persisted for months afterwards, beyond the end of Bruce's post. The Ambassador himself was deeply troubled by these events and especially pessimistic in July 1966, to the point that even his own officials became critical of him.[28]

Bruce's pessimism was perhaps reinforced by the knowledge that economic decline had an inevitable impact on Britain's ability to maintain a world role. Even when Labour came into office in 1964 there was a desire, not least from the Prime Minister himself, to hold onto military bases in Singapore, Aden and the Persian Gulf, the so-called 'East of Suez' position. Bruce did not find an initial round of cuts, outlined by a British delegation to Washington, in January 1966, too troubling. The delegation 'allayed American fears that they would no longer, in view of diminished economic and financial resources, play a global political and military role'.[29] However, by the spring of 1967 the British had decided to withdraw from 'East of Suez' over the next decade and they rejected US pleas to defer the announcement. 'This action will be ill received in Washington', noted Bruce bluntly.[30] Then, in January 1968, following the devaluation of sterling, the pace of withdrawal was quickened, so that British forces would retire from the Indian Ocean by the end of 1971. Bruce was full of admiration for the 'wonderfully efficient' way his staff gathered information on the Cabinet discussions at this critical juncture, commenting in his diary on 16 January:

They have built up a sort of intelligence system, and it is quite remarkable how forthcoming, on the basis of personal trust and friendship, some of their British counterparts have been in keeping them advised of what is going on behind the scenes.

It is a comment that underscores the warmth of the Anglo-American relationship at the level of everyday, official work even at the moment when the British world role was coming to an end, calling into question their future value to the US. It is also interesting that, during a meeting with Wilson in Washington soon afterwards, Johnson chose not to dwell on the unwelcome British retreat. Indeed this, the last Wilson-Johnson summit, proved one of the warmest.[31] Then again, the President's reluctance to argue with the Prime Minister may have reflected the fact that he had much deeper problems to face at that point in Vietnam.

Vietnam

Conflict in South-East Asia was a consistent concern during the ambassadorship and may serve as a case study of the kind of problems Bruce faced. It illustrates the way he smoothed transatlantic tensions and also, notwithstanding his loyalty to the President, his readiness to question decisions taken in Washington. US involvement in Vietnam may only have escalated in 1965, yet even in 1961 there were serious problems over the neighbouring state of Laos, which had supposedly been neutralised by the 1954 Geneva agreements, but where communists threatened to overpower the royal government. Within days of arriving in London, Bruce had his first conversation with the Foreign Secretary, Lord Home, about Laos[32] and it remained a regular problem until July 1962, when a new agreement was reached to neutralise it. A year later, Bruce's attention shifted to Vietnam. In August 1963, he already felt the situation was 'deeply disturbing', especially because the South Vietnamese government were 'oppressing the Buddhists, who comprise 90% of the population'. Nor was he convinced by the arguments of the US military that the war could be wrapped up in 18 months. 'I heard the same sort of optimism expressed by the French for years about Indo-China.'[33]

Nonetheless, as a patriot and convinced anti-communist, Bruce believed it important 'that the Chinese, Ho Chi Minh and the rest realized they cannot gain full control of the area' and he expressed few doubts about the escalation of US involvement in 1964–65.[34] In November 1964 he agreed with the Defence Secretary, Robert McNamara, 'that we must either abandon our policy of protecting that part of the world against Communism, or else intervene more vigorously to assure its integrity'.[35] A year later, with US combat troops committed to the conflict and no signs of a communist willingness to talk, an air of despondency began to creep into Bruce's diary. He feared that 'American opinion, now in majority favoring our present policy will, as casualties mount, become more critical, demanding withdrawal or rash adventures through escalation.'[36] While defending American policy in public, Bruce was privately sceptical about the direction of the war. In May 1967 he sent a memorandum to McNamara advocating a policy of retrenchment, with a reduction in the bombing of North Vietnam, a cap on US ground forces and greater reliance on South Vietnamese troops, who must be properly trained in guerrilla warfare techniques.[37] Arguably, Bruce pointed the way forward for Washington, but such ideas would only be adopted after the setbacks of the 1968 Tet Offensive.

Aside from his own worries about the war, Bruce had to cope, of course, with doubts from the British. Wilson himself was sympathetic to US policy in Vietnam, as was the Conservative opposition, so that, when America's 'Rolling Thunder' bombing campaign began, Bruce correctly predicted a 'good deal of adverse newspaper comment…but support by Government'.[38] The opposition to US policy emanating from the left-wing of the Labour party was too strong for the Prime Minister to ignore, given his slim majority in parliament. Vietnam also divided the Commonwealth, with some members – Australia and New Zealand – sending troops to fight there and others – notably Tanzania and Ghana – condemning Johnson. Furthermore, Wilson hoped to become the mediator of a diplomatic settlement to the conflict. As a result Johnson became resentful of what he saw as a lack of cooperation from the Prime Minister. Bruce was therefore in a difficult position, as he tried to persuade the President that Wilson's moderate behaviour, including a refusal to send troops to Vietnam, was not unreasonable.[39] In this effort Bruce had strong supporters in Washington. George Ball told Johnson that British diplomatic support 'has been stronger than that of our other major allies', while McGeorge Bundy, the National Security Advisor, added that 'every experienced observer has been astonished by the overall strength and skill of Wilson's defence of our policy'.[40] Nonetheless, Vietnam did much to tarnish Anglo-American friendship, not least because of a rise in popular anti-Americanism.

By June 1965, British public opinion was so concerned about the war that Bruce asked Washington to send an eminent speaker to make its case during a debate at Oxford University. The former Ambassador to South Vietnam, Henry Cabot Lodge, was sent over, only to be barracked by the audience, to Bruce's dismay.[41] From now on there were regular anti-war demonstrations outside the Embassy building and handling the issue became a permanent headache for Bruce. Then again, Wilson's clear victory in the March 1966 general election eased his need to placate the Labour left. True, in June 1966, when US planes bombed targets near the major population centres of Hanoi and Haiphong, Wilson publicly dissociated Britain from the action. However, there was an element of stage management in this, in which Bruce was closely involved. Not only was the Prime Minister briefed about the bombings in advance, but also, American officials advised him on the precise wording of his 'dissociation'.[42] Wilson's readiness to be manipulated

had its reward: a few weeks later, at a summit meeting, Johnson even compared Wilson to Winston Churchill. It is an incident which confirms that,
even if the President soon regretted his action, Anglo-American relations
in the Wilson-Johnson years had their positive side. In February 1967 it
even seemed that London might be the scene of a diplomatic breakthrough,
bringing the conflict to an end. The Soviet Prime Minister, Alexei Kosygin,
visited Wilson and they tried to draw North Vietnam into peace talks with
the US.[43] The talks came to nothing and, for Bruce, the war continued to pro-
voke differences at both the elite and popular levels. In late October 1967
bricks were thrown through the Embassy windows and several policemen
outside were injured by one of the angriest anti-war demonstrations. The
following month Bruce found that the Secretary of State, Dean Rusk, 'was
caustic, even bitter, about the British...not sending troops to help us in
Vietnam'.[44]

The Embassy

Opinions differ on Bruce's management of the Embassy. 'He managed to
have you do things without asking you to do them', recalled one political
officer,[45] while another was thanked by Bruce for doing his job so unobtrusively. 'As you know, I don't like to get too involved', the Ambassador
remarked, 'and I am glad you didn't get me involved in too many things.'
To some staff it seemed that there were actually two embassies in London:
'There was David Bruce and then there was the rest of the Embassy and the
two didn't necessarily co-ordinate all the time.'[46] Such a 'detached' approach
could cause problems, for example if Bruce sent telegrams off to Washington
without showing them first to relevant staff. Willis Armstrong, the Embassy's
minister for economic affairs in 1964–67, considered the Ambassador 'not
very experienced in economic matters' and was particularly concerned by a
hysterical telegram he once sent to Washington about the state of Britain's
financial reserves.[47] Richard Ericson, who served in the political section in
1963–65, found that, beyond weekly meetings of the senior staff, Bruce was
'very difficult to see, very busy', that he focused on the 'top 3 or 4 percent'
of issues and that he 'never saw a damn thing that went out of that embassy
before it went out except the stuff that he wrote himself'.[48] Others, while
acknowledging that Bruce 'delegated responsibility for running the embassy,
both substantively and administratively, to the staff', believed that he kept
himself well informed of what was going on. 'He presided over the embassy
with the charm and ease of a Virginia patrician.'[49] It was not that the other
staff were helpless without him. London was still, arguably, the top posting
in the US Foreign Service and numerous officials who worked there under
Bruce went on to head embassies of their own. Just focusing on the political
section, these included William Eagleton (later Ambassador to Syria), Ron
Spiers (Pakistan and Turkey) and Monteagle Sterns (Greece). Spiers also went

on to be an Undersecretary of State, while Willis Armstrong, an Economics Minister under Bruce, became an Assistant Secretary of State. Another member of the economics section, Arthur Hartman, went on to head the Paris and Moscow embassies.[50] This was, therefore, a formidable staff.

The perceptions of British officials throw interesting light on the question of the Embassy's effectiveness under Bruce. Paul Gore-Booth, the Permanent Undersecretary of the Foreign Office, wrote to Patrick Dean in Washington, in 1965 about the 'widespread feeling, not confined by any means to the Foreign Office, that the US Embassy here at the moment is...deplorably weak'. There were clear reflections in Gore-Booth's analysis of the 'two embassies' idea. So, on the one hand, Bruce was 'a man of very considerable stature and, of course, has the advantage of at least part of one ear of the President. It is always worth talking to him and he is much respected in London...'.

However, other members of the Embassy failed to 'go around and gossip as an embassy ought to do' and in general 'one has great difficulty remembering the personalities at all'. Nor was this feeling confined to the British. Shortly afterwards, Dean talked to Johnson's National Security Advisor, McGeorge Bundy, who commented that the London Embassy 'was far too large and far too overpaid and really produced very little, apart from David Bruce himself'.[51] Such views seem to have persisted. In August 1969 (a little after Bruce left the post), Peter Hayman, Deputy Undersecretary of the Foreign Office, told an American colleague that 'members of the US Embassy were much less seen around, either in the Foreign Office or at diplomatic parties, than many other Embassies...'.[52]

Bruce undoubtedly had weaknesses as an ambassador. He had little liking for public speeches and ribbon-cutting, for example. Nor did he always enjoy the frequent visits from members of Congress, business leaders and other senior figures, who treated the Embassy like 'a bar room and restaurant for jet-borne countrymen'.[53] In February 1962, he complained that he had already 'received a total of 277 letters from Congressmen, all requiring an answer, and all asking favours of one kind or another'.[54] Furthermore, despite Bruce's diplomatic experience, his ambassadorship ran into public controversy at times. He was sometimes accused of interfering in British politics, as when he made a speech in favour of European integration – of which he was always a keen advocate – in Birmingham in 1962, during Macmillan's attempt to enter the European Economic Community,[55] and when he was falsely accused of favouring a Labour victory in the 1964 general election.[56] A more persistent problem, that Bruce could do little to counter, was that the Embassy in Grosvenor Square became the focus of media attention because of anti-American demonstrations. In Bruce's early years, these were against nuclear weapons and policy towards Cuba; in the later years, against the Vietnam War. By October 1967, the Ambassador was slipping out by the Embassy's back door to avoid the persistent demonstrations outside.[57] There was a particularly violent protest on 22 October 1967 when an angry mob managed to throw bricks through the Embassy windows. The following month, Bruce himself was the focus of another attack while speaking in Cambridge.[58] Perhaps the worst public controversy during Bruce's tenure, however, was of a very different order, the Profumo sex-and-spying scandal that broke early in 1963. Not only was the disgraced Minister for War a social intimate of Bruce, but also the Ambassador had had his portrait sketched by Stephen Ward, who was also central to the scandal. Before the dust settled, Bruce found himself the unwelcome focus of FBI attention.[59]

The air of the eighteenth-century aristocrat surrounded Bruce, who had a love of fine food, expensive wines and precious antiques. He was most at home with other wealthy, influential and cultured individuals. A lunch he attended in May 1961, to take just one example, included the eminent socialites Diana Copper and Nancy Lancaster, the photographer Cecil Beaton, the philosopher Isaiah Berlin, the head of Sotheby's auction house, Peter Wilson and choreographer Frederick Ashton.[60] In some ways, this suited the world of the early 1960s, when the Conservatives held sway and the premiership could still be held by a former Fourteenth Earl. However, the permissive society, an irreverent media and the triumph of the Labour Party threw traditional beliefs into doubt. It would be unjust to depict Bruce as backward-thinking. He had long been convinced, for example, that Britain's future ought to lie with Europe. In the long term, his criticisms of socialist spending plans can seem prescient. He was a political moderate, believed in racial equality and, like all successful diplomats, was always open to the views of others. In the context of the mid-1960s his liking for royal garden parties, the weekends at country mansions and visits to Ascot were increasingly ill at ease in the world of The Beatles, anti-Vietnam war demonstrations and a desire for social levelling. On seeing Bruce at a function towards the end of his ambassadorship, Barbara Castle, a Labour Cabinet minister, wrote 'Not for the first time I was able to see at first hand the secret of the British ruling class in action: they survive by just assimilating their enemies socially.'[61] It is a quote which suggests that, whatever his professionalism and patriotism, Bruce suffered from an element of 'localitis' in London.

For Castle and other left-wingers, the wealthy, patrician American Ambassador was little different to their own loathsome upper class. Another Cabinet minister, Richard Crossman, once dismissed Bruce as a 'very stiff, reactionary New England banker'.[62] It is noteworthy that, among Labour leaders, Bruce was closest to Roy Jenkins, a moderate figure and one who, like Bruce, enjoyed high society parties, fine food and witty conversation.[63] Like Bruce too, Jenkins believed that Britain's future lay in membership of the EEC and, as Chancellor of the Exchequer in 1967–70, he reined in government expenditure. This was not all good news for the Americans, since the spending cuts included the accelerated withdrawal from East of Suez. Nonetheless, for a time at least, it helped reverse the downward spiral of the British economy that so concerned the Ambassador. Significantly, when it came to dealing with the wider Labour movement, Bruce seems to have relied a lot on his Deputy Chief of Mission, Philip Kaiser who, at Oxford University in the 1930s, had known many future Labour ministers, including Roy Jenkins, Denis Healey and Richard Crossman, who all sat in Wilson's Cabinet.[64] As a former Assistant Secretary of Labour under President Truman, Kaiser also had good trade union connections, something which could not be said of Bruce.

Conclusion

A number of historians see a marked decline in the so-called 'special relationship', especially under the post-1964 Labour government. It would be pointless to deny that, in Washington eyes, Britain was becoming less important as an ally.[65] However, Alan Dobson has drawn an important distinction between a decline in the *importance* of the relationship and the continuing good *quality* of bilateral relations.[66] A look at the Bruce years in London confirms that, while personal relations between the President and Prime Minister may not always be warm, the tradition of cooperation can survive lower down. There can be no doubt that the Anglo-American relationship remained important to both governments. True, the British needed the US rather more than vice versa. A Foreign Office Planning Department paper of mid-1964 called the alliance 'the most important single factor in our foreign policy'.[67] The Americans also appreciated the value of Britain as an ally, as seen in a 1968 State Department memorandum which declared that, 'The special relationship has been pronounced dead as often as Martin Bormann has been reported alive. Indeed, perhaps the best evidence that it is still alive is the fact that its detractors feel obliged to re-announce its death every few months.'[68]

Given the sea-change in Britain's position in the 1960s, and its declining importance as an ally for Washington, Bruce's ambassadorship must be counted a success. The retreat from a world role, the constant economic problems and Lyndon Johnson's aversion to foreign leaders did not prevent Bruce and his Embassy acting very much as a 'bridge' between London and Washington. While there were constant direct exchanges between the White House and Downing Street, the Ambassador was able to clear up differences on a range of issues, from Cuba and Cyprus, to economic problems and Vietnam. Thanks to his remarkable social network and meetings with Cabinet ministers, Bruce was also able to keep Washington updated quite accurately about British thinking. Looking at the roles of an embassy as defined by Berridge,[69] Bruce's aversion to public speeches and 'ribbon-cutting' perhaps limited his value as a propagandist for the US and he does not seem to have become personally involved in arranging commercial deals (though he did meet many American business leaders in London). Nonetheless, he did enjoy the role of representing America at major state occasions, diplomatic receptions and at Buckingham Palace events. His political reporting and provision of policy advice seems to have been helped by the selective way in which he wrote to Washington. Above all, he worked hard to maintain friendly relations between the two countries, lobbying in London on behalf of his government but also, as seen over Vietnam, explaining British thinking to the White House and State Department.

There were problems in Anglo-American relations, of course. There always are. However, those who worked at the London Embassy in the 1960s were generally full of praise for Bruce, considering him 'one of the best ambassadors we've ever had',[70] 'a wonderful guy'[71] and even 'a god at the end of the hall'.[72] For Jonathan Stoddart, who served there in 1966–69, it was a 'superlative embassy' and Bruce was 'one of the finest men I have ever worked for . . .'. Stoddart felt that Bruce 'delegated very well, assuming he had competent people working for him'.[73] Hermann Eilts echoed such views, agreeing that, while Bruce 'delegated authority' he was also 'interested in everything that went on in the Embassy' and was 'one of the outstanding persons for whom I've worked'.[74] Philip Kaiser lauded Bruce as 'one of our outstanding ambassadors . . . an elegant host' and 'a superb interlocutor between President and Prime Minister'.[75] There clearly were problems with Bruce's management of the Embassy, but in an operation the size of London, these may have been inevitable. Bruce subsequently looked back on his time in the UK and complained that 'there were so many people in the embassy he didn't know who many of them were or what they were doing'.[76] On another occasion, he called his Embassy 'the little State Department'.[77] Of 1,163 staff in the UK in December 1962, many were engaged in consular work beyond London. Of the 688 based at Grosvenor Square, only 152 (including some locally employed personnel) were involved in the State Department; the others were working on defence, commerce, information and other vital matters. It was an immense and complex operation.[78]

The time had certainly passed when Americans could see Britain as an equal in terms of political, military or economic power, and Bruce was all too aware of the country's monetary problems. Yet he was ready to immerse himself in London society, admiring of the monarchy and determined to treat the British with respect as a close ally, however far they had fallen. At a time when personal ties between heads of government took a tumble, from the days of JFK and 'Supermac' to the uneasy relations of LBJ and Wilson, the Ambassador and the Embassy helped ensure that the Anglo-American partnership continued to work well. Clear inequalities in power did not necessarily rule out a partnership. In his memoirs, Douglas-Home wrote that, 'It is difficult to exaggerate the role which David Bruce played in maintaining trust and confidence at a juncture which was critical for both countries. His capacity to be totally professional whilst looking like an amateur was almost unfair.'[79] This professionalism included the need to cope with deep personal tragedy in the form of the death of Audrey, the only child of Bruce's first marriage, in a 1967 plane crash.

It may be true that the British Embassy in Washington, with its readier access to the State Department, Congress and other levers of power, was more important in transatlantic contacts. The value of the London outfit is confirmed by the event that dominated Bruce's last weeks in London, the visit by Johnson's successor, Richard Nixon to the United Kingdom. Planning for this confirmed that, while media attention during summit meetings may focus on the leaders, embassies are essential to support and prepare for them. Nixon distrusted the State Department, but his advance men had to liaise with Bruce for weeks before the President arrived. The Ambassador successfully resisted attempts by Nixon's aide, John Ehrlichmann, to dictate whom Wilson should invite for dinner, while the Embassy helped organise such events as a meeting between the President and leading figures in British media. The Ambassador also accompanied Nixon during his appointments in London and briefed him, on his arrival, about Harold Wilson, cheekily remarking that, 'Some people, Mr. President, think he's tricky.' Relating the story to an amused Kaiser afterwards, Bruce commented, 'I'm a great ambassador, Phil, I'm a great ambassador.'[80] It was a vain remark but, on the evidence of his London posting, not an inaccurate one.[81]

Acknowledgements

The author is grateful to the British Academy and the University of Nottingham for funding research into David Bruce's diaries and at archives in the United States.

Notes

1. Virginia Historical Society, Richmond, David Bruce Diary, undated remarks at the start of 1961. A selection of diary entries is now available in Raj Roy and John W. Young (eds.), *Ambassador to Sixties London: The Diaries of David Bruce, 1961–69* (Dordrecht: Republic of Letters Publishing, 2009).
2. See Nelson Lankford, *The Last American Aristocrat: The Biography of David K.E. Bruce* (Boston: Little, Brown, 1995), pp. 298–300; John F. Kennedy Library (JFKL), Oral History Program (OHP), Acheson interview, pp. 6–7 and see pp. 9–10. These suggest that Bruce was indeed able to choose his own post, partly because he had not been appointed Secretary of State.
3. Lankford, *The Last American Aristocrat*; Jonathan Colman, 'The London Ambassadorship of David K.E. Bruce during the Wilson-Johnson years, 1964–68', *Diplomacy and Statecraft*, Vol. 15, No. 4 (2004), pp. 327–52; and see the Introduction to Roy and Young (eds.), *Ambassador to Sixties London*.
4. George Ball, *The Past Has another Pattern* (New York: Norton, 1982), p. 452.
5. G. R. Berridge, 'The Resident Ambassador: A Death Postponed', Diplomatic Studies Programme, Discussion Paper 1 (University of Leicester: Centre for the Study of Diplomacy, 1994), pp. 3–20.

6. Bruce Diary, 28 March–12 April 1961.
7. Bruce Diary, 25 September–6 October 1961.
8. Bruce Diary, 20–22 December 1961.
9. Bruce Diary, 6 January 1962.
10. Bruce Diary, 17 August 1961.
11. Bruce Diary, 13 April 1962.
12. JFKL, OHP, Dean Acheson interview, p. 25, and Chester Cooper interview, p. 24.
13. JFKL, OHP, McGeorge Bundy interview, p. 25.
14. Association for Diplomatic Studies and Training, Arlington, Virginia, Foreign Affairs Oral History Collection (hereinafter FAOHC; available online at http://www.adst.org/Oral_History.htm), Sheldon Krys interview.
15. Lankford, *The Last American Aristocrat*, p. 312.
16. See Michael Hopkins, 'David Ormsby Gore', pp. 143–5, and Jonathan Colman, 'Patrick Dean', in Michael Hopkins, Saul Kelly and John Young,(eds.), *The Washington Embassy: British Ambassadors to the United States, 1939–77* (Basingstoke: Palgrave, 2009), pp. 163–4.
17. The National Archives (TNA), Kew, FCO 7/1445, Hayman to Greenhill, 27 August 1969.
18. London to State, 28 January 1964, copied in Bruce Diary.
19. Bruce Diary, 16 January 1963.
20. JFKL, OHP, David Bruce interview, pp. 1–2.
21. John W. Young, *The Labour Governments, 1964–70*, Vol. II, *International Policy* (Manchester: Manchester University Press, 2003), pp. 21–2; and in general see Jonathan Colman, *A Special Relationship? Harold Wilson, Lyndon Johnson and Anglo-American relations* (Manchester: Manchester University Press, 2004).
22. Ball, *The Past Has another Pattern*, p. 336.
23. See Elmer Plischke, 'Lyndon Johnson as Diplomat in Chief', in Bernard Firestone and Robert Vogt (eds.), *Lyndon Baines Johnson and the Uses of Power* (New York: Columbia University Press, 1988), pp. 265–9.
24. Bruce Diary, 3 March 1966.
25. Philip Kaiser, *Journeying Far and Wide* (New York: Scribner's, 1992), pp. 224–5.
26. Bruce Diary, 21 April 1961.
27. On the crises of 1961–63 see especially Nigel Ashton, *Kennedy, Macmillan and the Cold War: The Irony of Interdependence* (Basingstoke: Palgrave, 2002).
28. See Colman, 'London Ambassadorship', pp. 336–7.
29. Bruce Diary, 28 January 1966. The key text on these issues is Saki Dockrill, *Britain's Retreat from East of Suez* (Basingstoke: Macmillan, 2002).
30. Bruce Diary, 16 July 1967.
31. Bruce Diary, 8 February 1968.
32. Bruce Diary, 20 March 1961.
33. Bruce Diary, 23 August and 17 October 1963.
34. Bruce Diary, 22 May 1964.
35. Bruce Diary, 11 November 1964.
36. Bruce Diary, 22 December 1965.
37. Bruce Diary, Bruce to McNamara, 11 May 1967.
38. London to State Department, 7 February 1965, in diary.
39. For the general background see Sylvia Ellis, *Britain, America and the Vietnam War* (Westport, CT: Praeger, 2004); and John Young, 'Britain and LBJ's War', *Cold War History*, Vol. 2, No. 3 (2002), pp. 63–92.

40. Lyndon B. Johnson Library, Austin, Texas, National Security File, Memoranda to the President, Vol. 4, Ball to Rusk, 14 April, and Bundy to Johnson, 3 June 1965.
41. See especially: diary, 15 and 17 June 1965.
42. Bruce Diary, 11 and 23 May, 23 and 30 June; TNA, PREM 13/1083, Johnson to Wilson, 14 June.
43. See John Dumbrell and Sylvia Ellis, 'British Involvement in Vietnam Peace Initiatives, 1966–67', *Diplomatic History*, Vol. 27, No. 1 (January 2003), pp. 113–49.
44. Bruce Diary, 22 October and 8 November 1967.
45. FAOHC, Sheldon Krys interview.
46. FAOHC, Oscar Vance Armstrong interview.
47. Nonetheless, Armstrong admired Bruce's political judgment and lucid style: FAOHC, Willis Armstrong interview.
48. Yet Ericson too considered Bruce a 'great' ambassador, FAOHC, Richard Ericson interview.
49. FAOHC, William Galloway interview.
50. See Kaiser, *Journeying Far and Wide*, pp. 219–20.
51. TNA, FO 371/179615, Gore-Booth to Dean, 21 July, and reply, 26 July 1965.
52. TNA, FCO 7/1445, Hayman to Greenhill, 27 August 1969.
53. Bruce Diary, 1 February 1964; and see Lankford, *American Aristocrat*, pp. 302–5.
54. Bruce Diary, 6 February 1961.
55. Bruce Diary, 18 April and 27 July 1962.
56. Bruce Diary, 12 and 13 October 1964.
57. Bruce Diary, 17 October 1967.
58. Bruce Diary, 22, 23 October and 14 November 1967.
59. The FBI became involved after receiving a complaint from Thomas Corbally, an American friend of Ward: see Lankford, *The Last American Aristocrat*, pp. 320–5.
60. Bruce Diary, 7 May 1961.
61. Barbara Castle, *The Castle Diaries, 1964–70* (London: Weidenfeld & Nicolson, 1984), p. 559 – entry for 27 November 1968.
62. Richard Crossman, *The Diaries of a Cabinet Minister: Volume 3, 1968–70* (London: Hamish Hamilton and Jonathan Cape, 1977), p. 393.
63. Lankford, *The Last American Aristocrat*, pp. 327–8.
64. Kaiser, *Journeying Far and Wide*, pp. 59–71.
65. For example: C. J. Bartlett, *The Special Relationship* (Basingstoke: Macmillan, 1992), pp. 109–18; Dimbleby and Reynolds, *An Ocean Apart*, p. 256; John Dumbrell, *A Special Relationship* (Basingstoke: Macmillan, 2001), p. 72.
66. Dobson, *Anglo-American Relations in the Twentieth Century*, p. 138.
67. The National Archives (TNA), Kew, FO371/177830/7A, SC(64)30, 21 August.
68. Truman Library, Independence, Missouri, Philip Kaiser papers, box 8, research memorandum, 7 February 1968.
69. G. R. Berridge, *Diplomacy: Theory and Practice* (Basingstoke: Palgrave, 4th edn, 2010), ch. 7.
70. FAOHC, John Correll interview.
71. FAOHC, Charles Cross interview.
72. FAOHC, Mark Lissfelt interview.
73. FAOHC, Jonathan Stoddart interview.
74. FAOHC, Hermann Eilts interview.
75. Kaiser, *Journeying Far and Wide*, p. 222 and see pp. 218–19.
76. FAOHC, Herbert Horowitz interview.

77. FAOHC, Arnold Denys memoir, chapter on 'London in Springtime'.
78. Bruce Diary, 4 December 1962.
79. Lord Home, *The Way the Wind Blows* (London: Collins, 1976), p. 245.
80. Kaiser, *Journeying Far and Wide*, pp. 256–9; and on Nixon's visit see Roy and Young (eds.), *Ambassador to Sixties London*, pp. 427–36.
81. London was not Bruce's last post. He was recalled to take charge of the US team in the Vietnam peace talks in 1970–71, to head the 'liaison office' in Beijing in 1973–74 and to be Ambassador to NATO in 1974–76. He died in December 1977.

9
Walter H. Annenberg, 1969–74

James Cameron

Walter Hubert Annenberg – as one Foreign Office brief delicately put it – was 'an unusual diplomat'.[1] He had no expertise in foreign affairs and his impact on the Nixon administration's policy towards Britain was limited. Yet he remained US Ambassador to the United Kingdom for five years and returned to the United States with warm reviews on both sides of the Atlantic. Despite his marginalisation from the centre of power, Annenberg was eventually able to carve out a niche within the American diplomatic machinery with some success in a way that surprised his critics and says a great deal about both the Nixon administration and the state of the Anglo-American relationship during this period.

Appointment

Born in 1908 to successful media magnate, Moses L. Annenberg, Walter Annenberg expanded his father's holdings through a series of canny acquisitions and innovative publications, including the phenomenally profitable *T.V. Guide* and *Seventeen*, the first magazine to be marketed towards teenage girls. In addition to his wealth, Annenberg's influence primarily stemmed from his ownership of the *Philadelphia Inquirer* and the *Philadelphia Daily News*, as well as a host of television and radio stations across the country with a particular predominance in Pennsylvania. Dubbed 'Citizen Annenberg' by some of his detractors, he was not averse to using his media holdings to advance his political and business interests. As his critics were quick to point out, the Annenberg family fortune had been built on some shady foundations: his father had been convicted in 1939 for evading taxes totalling $3,259,000.[2] By the late 1960s, however, he had built a reputation as a generous philanthropist, endowing the Moses L. Annenberg School of Communications at the University of Pennsylvania.[3]

In sum, Annenberg's story was in many ways typical for mid-twentieth century American business leaders, but not one that necessarily suggested a natural progression into the realm of high diplomacy. Before his appointment as Ambassador, Annenberg's foreign policy record was slim. American journalists could find sparse evidence for any views on foreign affairs expressed by the would-be ambassador, save for a strong personal dislike of Charles de Gaulle and financial support of Israel's reconstruction after the 1967 war. His antipathy towards de Gaulle allegedly stemmed from his personal experience of what he perceived as French ingratitude during a visit to Paris immediately after the Second World War. He publicly condemned de Gaulle on the pages of the *Philadelphia Inquirer* and arranged for the editorials to be distributed in the European press. By contrast, his support for Israel was far more private. Although he never spoke about it publicly, Annenberg's biographer John Cooney has inferred that his post-war visit to the Dachau concentration camp had a deep and lasting impact on his support for the Jewish state.[4] Neither persuasion could be said to have chimed particularly well with – nor had much influence on – Nixon, who admired de Gaulle for his geopolitical skill if not his anti-Americanism, and viewed Israel as a pawn in the great power balance, rather than an intrinsically worthy cause. At Annenberg's confirmation hearing his sponsoring Senators, Hugh Scott and Richard Schweiker of Pennsylvania, had little to say to bolster their strong support for his confirmation, primarily citing his newspaper's coverage of global politics and his receipt of a few foreign honours.[5]

Given this lack of experience, Annenberg's nomination was controversial from the first. Attacks on him were sharpened to the point of vitriol by the highly charged domestic politics of late-1960s America. Annenberg was seized upon by liberal journalists as the confirmation of everything they suspected of Nixon: that he was corrupt and would do anything to advance his political interests – even appoint an ignorant media mogul who knew nothing of the art of diplomacy to the premier ambassadorial post in the Foreign Service. *The New York Times* intoned:

> Since 1961 the major American ambassadorships abroad have gone almost invariably to men of talent and experience in international affairs, many of them professional diplomats. Outstanding among these is the present ambassador to London, David Bruce, who had previously served as Under Secretary of State and as envoy to Paris and Bonn…It would be dismaying, after all Mr. Nixon's campaign criticisms of the Johnson administration for its poor conduct of foreign relations, to find the new president returning now to the unhappy practice of parcelling out key embassies to major campaign contributors.[6]

This theme was taken up by J. William Fulbright, Chairman of the Senate Foreign Relations Committee. Characteristically, Nixon responded by pushing forward with the appointment, opposition to which the President later ascribed to the same North-Eastern Brahmin snobbery that he felt had impeded his own rise to greatness.[7] Nixon's misgivings had some merit.

Annenberg had not given any money to Nixon personally, although his wife had contributed $2,500 to the campaign – a minuscule sum, given the family's vast wealth.[8] Annenberg's *Philadelphia Inquirer* had eventually come out in support of Nixon, but not before initially throwing its weight behind California Governor Ronald Reagan.[9] Although the number of political appointments to West European capitals would grow as the Nixon administration progressed, at the time of Annenberg's confirmation hearings evidence of widespread political cronyism was slight. Even *The New York Times* admitted in May 1969 that, 'career officers of the Foreign Service have an unusual preponderance both in the top diplomatic jobs abroad and in the State Department'.[10] Despite the media outcry, and apart from some tough questioning on his father's tax evasion and the extent of his interference in Pennsylvanian politics, Annenberg's confirmation hearing passed relatively smoothly.[11] On the Senate Foreign Relations Committee only Fulbright voted against his confirmation – a significant dissent from the chairman, but not fatal.[12]

Concerns about Annenberg's appointment were not merely confined to the editorial page of *The New York Times* and the committee rooms of the US Senate. When his name first appeared as the likely nominee for the post, British foreign secretary, Michael Stewart, questioned whether London could subtly influence the decision. Permanent Undersecretary Paul Gore-Booth cautioned against interfering in American domestic politics, particularly in the case of a new administration and advised that 'there was no good reason to raise objections'. In any case:

> If even the slightest question were raised about Mr. Annenberg, a friend of his would unquestionably get hold of the story and leak it to Mr. Annenberg who would then have it appear in the 'Philadelphia Enquirer' [*sic*], or whatever he owns. The fat would then be in the fire.[13]

The decision not to approach the Nixon administration was therefore taken in the spirit of resignation to rather than enthusiasm for Annenberg's appointment. Stewart concluded that 'if there was nothing you could do about a thing, it was better not to spend a lot of time on it'.[14] Publicly vilified at home, Walter Annenberg was dispatched by the Nixon administration to a host government that was unsure whether he was an appropriate choice.

A Foreign Policy Novice

Annenberg's acquaintance with Stewart and the rest of Harold Wilson's government was brief, Labour losing the June 1970 general election to Edward Heath's Conservatives. Yet Annenberg confirmed Stewart's early anxieties that he was a foreign-policy neophyte and upheld that reputation throughout his tenure as Ambassador. The record shows a plenipotentiary whose contributions to meetings were limited, both in the volume and the content of what he said. Minutes of discussions Annenberg had with British officials leave the reader with the impression of an ambassador who was highly dependent on the briefing papers submitted to him by his subordinates. When these had run their course, so had any hope of a productive dialogue between the Ambassador and his British interlocutor. This exchange between Annenberg and Heath's Foreign Secretary, Sir Alec Douglas-Home, on the American policy of bringing the People's Republic of China into the United Nations whilst retaining representation for Taiwan typifies the limited nature of the conversations he had with the British:

> *Sir Alec Douglas-Home* considered that Peking would not take her seat in the General Assembly unless she was also a member of the Security Council. She regarded herself as entitled to a permanent seat on that body. He frankly did not believe that the American proposals would work, and wondered whether President Nixon would still be able to go to Peking if the Americans continued to pursue a two Chinas policy. *Mr Annenberg* said that he was unable to speculate on what the president might have in his mind, and he was not competent to comment on the legalities of the matter.[15]

At times some members of Heath's government and their Foreign Office mandarins appear to have taken pleasure in engaging in what Kissinger described as 'ever-so-polite needling' of Annenberg, almost to the point of cruelty.[16] In December 1973 Julian Amery, then minister of state at the Foreign Office, asked Annenberg whether he could expand on what Kissinger meant when he talked of his ' "conceptual" approach to international affairs'. The Ambassador replied in a note a few days later that he was 'still struggling with "conceptual". Don't you think it might be a good thing if we were to table this for the holidays?' He appended some basic explications of the term from the *Encyclopaedia Britannica*, which he presumably believed might be helpful.Amery was unimpressed, scribbling on the bottom 'can we improve on his definitions?' His officials were clearly amused by the Ambassador's contribution, Hugh Overton of the North America Department commenting, 'I quite agree that Mr Annenberg's definitions do not help much!'[17] It appears that the Ambassador was never able to shake his reputation for ineptitude when it came to the intellectual heavy lifting that was so characteristic of the Kissinger style of diplomacy.

This was not merely due to his lack of diplomatic experience, but the deliberate product of the Nixon administration's centralisation of power over foreign affairs within the White House. In this context, it seems likely that Annenberg's inexperience was seen as an asset by the President – just as it was in the case of William Rogers, his beleaguered Secretary of State. Kissinger's conduct towards Annenberg was in agreement with the complete contempt expressed by one anonymous member of the Nixon White House staff: 'I don't feel sorry for him. I feel sorry for our country with a man like that representing us'.[18] The National Security Advisor frequently ignored and actively sought to exclude Annenberg during his time in London, with full cooperation from British officials. In preparation for a September 1972 visit, Kissinger manoeuvred to cut Annenberg out of substantive discussions with the Cabinet secretary, Sir Burke Trend. Kissinger desired to make a secret trip to Paris after the conclusion of these meetings, the Washington Embassy emphasising that, 'it is considered important that the United States embassy [in London] should not (repeat not) learn anything about Dr. Kissinger's clandestine departure'.[19] Many of these initiatives were seemingly petty and designed with the sole purpose of belittling Annenberg. Kissinger also proposed to remove the Ambassador from the guest list for dinner with the Prime Minister, an initiative that was successfully thwarted.[20] Donald Tebbit of the Washington Embassy took a dim view of these gambits, responding sardonically to a Kissinger request for some private time with the Foreign Secretary that he did 'not know whether Kissinger has something really private to say to the Secretary of State or whether it is simply that he enjoys this method of operation. I expect it is more of the latter.' However, the Foreign Office sought to facilitate Kissinger's intrigues in order to ingratiate themselves with him, a goal which was certainly considered worth any offence given to the US Ambassador.[21] Annenberg was offended and made his feelings clear in a telegram delivered to the new President, Gerald Ford and Kissinger, who had by then been appointed Secretary of State.

> The embassy could, if permitted to participate actively in the diplomatic process, make a more purposeful contribution to the imaginative and dynamic foreign policy of the Ford administration. To my chagrin, I have observed this mission become a bystander. Repeatedly we learn of significant statements for US policy in conversations with the British embassy, or British officials visiting Washington, but we are all too infrequently advised of such exchanges, especially those at a high level. Like our colleagues in Paris, we find that our host government is often better informed about US policy than we are. We lack the sense and reality of participation in the conduct of US policy toward the United Kingdom which is vital if we are to carry on the kind of dialogue and make the vigorous representations of US interests which are expected of us. Without adequate, timely information and reasonable insights into policy, our ability to engage in sustained advocacy of US objectives is materially weakened. British officials have expressed dismay at this situation. The authority and standing of this embassy have been downgraded in British eyes. I need not point out how demoralising this is for the professional members of my staff.[22]

Yet there were larger structural forces at work that served to further distance not only Annenberg, but London from the centre of American foreign policy. As Kissinger has admitted, the President was 'preoccupied with ending the Vietnam War and with openings to China and the Soviet Union. Nixon marked time on North Atlantic relations, promising himself that, as soon as the Vietnam War ended, he would return to his emotional priorities.'[23] With the administration's focus on *détente* and triangular diplomacy, Bonn had replaced London as the most important West European capital due to the growing economic and political might of the Federal Republic of Germany. This manifested itself in Willy Brandt's assertive policy of *Ostpolitik* – a course that Nixon and Kissinger feared would at once derail *détente* and steal some of its political lustre.[24] By contrast, Britain had become a bit-player on the international scene, its influence having shrunk dramatically in the wake of Harold Wilson's last-gasp attempts to maintain a global military presence and the consequent sterling crisis of 1967.[25] Kissinger was a frequent visitor to London, but increasingly used it as a venue for private meetings and a staging post for his trips to Paris. This approach cast Britain as a country of operational convenience rather than great-power importance.[26] The Heath government continually complained about a 'lack of consultation' on everything from the suspension of US dollar convertibility into gold in August 1971 to the worldwide alert of US nuclear forces during the Yom Kippur War of October 1973. Yet as British Ambassador to Washington Lord Cromer noted in a telegram to London in the wake of suspension of dollar convertibility, 'the Americans no longer consider it necessary to consult with the UK as an imperial or world power. They consult us when it is useful to them and not because they have to.'[27] This was the new reality, and Britain's role and that of the American Ambassador to London in US foreign policy-making suffered regardless of the Nixon-Kissinger *penchant* for secretive great-power diplomacy.

Compounding British decline, the state of the Anglo-American 'special relationship' was strained further by the bad feeling that existed between the Heath government and the Nixon administration. Given his bureaucratic marginalisation, Annenberg had little control over the course of Heath-Nixon relationship. The Prime Minister reflected that he 'knew that if [a message] came through the ambassador, it wasn't important'.[28] Even when Anglo-American affairs were in a state of benign neglect from 1969 to early 1973, Heath refused to use the term 'special relationship', referring instead to the 'natural relationship' that existed between the two countries. This was an attempt to calm French nerves over his government's foreign-policy priority: British entry into the European Economic Community (EEC).[29] When Kissinger's focus shifted to European affairs after British accession to the EEC on 1 January 1973, it merely served to exacerbate hitherto-latent tensions between the most Europhile British Prime Minister of the twentieth century and an administration that was seeking to reassert American leadership over the western half of the continent. If the Nixon administration's aim was for 'Britain ... to "deliver Europe" ', Kissinger's 1973 *Year of Europe* initiative was a disaster for American foreign policy. Heath's immediate reaction was to take a leading role in attempts to craft a unified European response to Kissinger's call for a 'new Atlantic Charter'. Kissinger responded to the British tilt towards Europe with heavy-handed threats, including the possible withdrawal of up to 95,000 US combat troops from the continent – a gambit that Douglas-Home denounced as 'a piece of quasi-blackmail' and 'an act of gross public indecency'.[30] When the Yom Kippur War erupted on 6 October 1973, relations sunk even lower, with British refusal to allow its bases to be used to support re-supply and reconnaissance flights. Kissinger responded by vowing to strike at another root of the special relationship – this time threatening to impair intelligence sharing between the two countries. Yet the Heath government again remained unmoved.[31] The dual issues of British intransigence over the Middle East and support for a new assertive foreign policy within Europe combined in the EEC's declaration of 6 November which called for peace talks between the Arab states and Israel within 'the framework of the United Nations', the withdrawal of Israeli forces to pre-1967 borders, and a recognition of the rights of the Palestinians. This prompted US Secretary of Defence James Schlesinger to accuse Britain of practising a form of 'decayed Gaullism'. Whilst the Heath government eventually joined in Kissinger's attempt to respond to the Arab oil embargo by presenting a united front of industrialised countries at the Washington Conference of February 1974, relations between the two allies had become severely strained.[32]

The US Embassy in London was as scathing as Schlesinger. In an analysis to the Secretary of State, signed off by Annenberg and copied to all West European and North Atlantic Treaty Organisation (NATO) capitals, the extent of both the Anglo-American rift and American perceptions of British decline was clear. It opened with the damning judgement that, 'the "special" quality of the Anglo-American relationship has been more apparent than real for some time ... By the late 1960's [*sic*] the United Kingdom no longer enjoyed the paramountcy it had once had in Washington and in London, US views no longer naturally assumed first place in British calculations'. The split had its roots in structural changes in the international system, but was exacerbated by Heath, who nurtured 'a strain of anti-American feeling. He is a kind of British Gaullist with a bias toward France and a receptivity to long-standing French arguments that in the end Europe must strive to depend on no one but itself'. This shift had resulted in tensions over Kissinger's Year of Europe, 'but the October War in the Middle East dramatically revealed the dimension of the change and surfaced divergences which had largely remained outside scrutiny'. Yet difficulties were not only the fault of the Heath government. As the telegram noted:

The US economic measures of August 1971 and the dramatic American opening of contact with the People's Republic of China, decisions taken without prior consultation in fields of first importance to Britain, brought the British government (and Heath personally) up sharply. That the United States had imperative reasons for secrecy and speed was of less significance to the Heath government than the fact that we had done so without apparent regard for British interests or sensibilities.[33]

The American Embassy had a clear view of the underlying reasons for Anglo-American difficulties. However, it judged that 'a community of interest in safeguarding Western values and promoting the welfare of the Atlantic community remains'. The British were resigned to a strong American role in Europe, if only because they 'realise that for the foreseeable future only the United States can ensure that the process of *détente* is safely managed and that the consolidation of Western Europe... develops in an orderly way without pressure or interference from the East'.[34] Whilst ruptures in the relationship were not chronic, it appears that the partnership between the two countries was increasingly viewed as a marriage of convenience from Grosvenor Square.

In contrast to Kissinger's occasional tendency to overestimate his ability to 'deliver Europe', Annenberg had a very clear view of his own diplomatic deficiencies. Apart from his passionate final telegram, he interfered little in Kissinger's machinations, whilst concentrating on providing a comfortable working environment for the employees on whom he relied for the smooth running of everything from his lavish Embassy functions to political assessments. Annenberg's biographers have been able to find numerous tributes to his managerial style. This combined a personable-ness towards Embassy staff with a laissez-faire approach to guiding operational issues that he considered the responsibility of middle management – a method he had lifted wholesale from his business career.[35] Isolated from the summit, Annenberg was also cautious not to interfere in the day-to-day operations of the career diplomats working below him. This was appreciated particularly by the more clandestine functionaries in the American Embassy, one Central Intelligence Agency (CIA) station chief commenting approvingly that the ambassador 'did not try to get into what didn't involve him'.[36] Those who suffered most from the Annenberg style of embassy management were his Deputy Chief of Missions, known as Ministers. As was reported at the time, Annenberg's second Minister, Joseph Greene, asked to be transferred from London because of an 'an unbridgeable personality conflict'. In this case, it was alleged that Annenberg had undermined Greene by liaising directly with heads of embassy sections rather than going through his second-in-command.[37] Word also appears to have spread throughout the State Department that Annenberg could be a difficult boss. According to Foreign Office records Ronald Spiers, the incoming Minister at the time of Annenberg's departure in 1974, 'made it clear to the State Department that he would not be prepared to serve under Annenberg'.[38]

Despite his bureaucratic marginalisation, Annenberg did enjoy some diplomatic triumphs. His business background helped in smoothing commercial ties, which were certainly strained during 1971 due to the crisis between Lockheed and Rolls Royce over the provision of the RB211 engine, the US suspension of dollar convertibility into gold and the imposition of a 10 per cent surcharge on imports. They were all primarily dealt with directly between 10 Downing Street and the White House, but Annenberg did act as a lobbyist in a small number of cases on behalf of specific British and American companies. In 1969, he reportedly helped British Petroleum fend off an anti-trust suit by the Department of Justice over its proposed merger with Standard Oil of Ohio. He successfully argued to the White House that such a move by the Department of Justice was purely motivated by resource xenophobia and was commercially illiterate, given the threat of retaliation by European governments – particularly the British when allocating contracts for the exploitation of North Sea oil. Companies as diverse as Chase Manhattan and McDonald's approached Annenberg for help in facilitating their entry into the British market. As his biographer Christopher Ogden has argued, Annenberg's keen business sense was particularly important during this period, given that American companies were making a new push to extend their operations outside the United States.[39]

Annenberg's business skills were useful in other areas too. One example was the successful negotiation of the April 1973 cost-sharing agreement for American military infrastructure based in Britain. The Foreign Office noted with frustration that 'the negotiations with the Americans proved difficult and inordinately protracted'.[40] A ten-year agreement had expired in 1963 and it took another decade to negotiate its replacement. The principal outstanding points by 1971 regarded the amount the US government should pay for work completed on facilities by the Department of the Environment. The US Embassy took the initiative and put forward a series of compromises, which were accepted by both parties.[41] The Foreign Office noted appreciatively, 'Mr Annenberg took a personal interest in the negotiations over the last few weeks and, we are told, exerted pressure on Washington to meet us over some of the outstanding points.' Moreover, the ambassador 'was particularly anxious that he personally should sign the US note to the Secretary of State covering the memorandum of understanding'.[42] Annenberg probably took well to this form of negotiation, given the numerous acquisitions and divestitures he had negotiated in the course of his business career. Having been excluded from so much by Kissinger, it is likely that Annenberg wanted to leave his mark on an agreement that strengthened relations between the two countries in a small, but significant way.

Indeed, whilst there were considerable ruptures between political leaders, working relations between mid-level functionaries remained good – even between Kissinger's National Security Council (NSC) staff and British civil servants. As Mary Sarotte has noted, on areas where Anglo-American interests coincided, the Nixon administration 'worked astonishingly closely' with the British. These included the June 1973 Agreement on the Prevention of Nuclear War, where the Foreign Office did much of the drafting.[43] Annenberg facilitated these strong operational ties by making the best of his position within the Nixon hierarchy: he played almost no role in the increasingly fraught relations between the White House and 10 Downing Street, but fostered contacts at the working level through a combination of laissez-faire approach over most operational matters both within the NSC and his own embassy, whilst occasionally intervening in disputes where he felt his commercial experience could make a real contribution and ensure he would receive a sympathetic hearing in the White House.

Public Diplomacy: A Quick Learner

Annenberg made his greatest impact as 'an ambassador of goodwill'. As Bobby Scalf, a political officer at the American Embassy argued 'it was the only thing that any ambassador could do after Bruce and with Nixon and Kissinger running everything'.[44] The role of public diplomat did not come easily to Annenberg and his initial entry into British public consciousness was as infamous as it was disastrous. On 29 April 1969, the Ambassador presented his credentials to the Queen. Overwhelmed by the ceremony and taking care to observe the minutiae of protocol, he stumbled over his words when Elizabeth II asked after his welfare: 'We're in the embassy residence, subject, of course, to some of the discomfiture as a result of a need for, uh, elements of refurbishment and rehabilitation.' This incident would have gone unremarked, were it not for the fact that a British Broadcasting Corporation (BBC) camera crew was filming the entire incident for the documentary *The Royal Family*. Instead, it became notorious, particularly after the film aired to an audience of over 25 million in Britain and 400 million globally. As Lord Carrington remarked, ' "elements of refurbishment" was considered an extremely good joke here'. The British Embassy in Washington unkindly showed the documentary at private screenings for two nights in a row, which must have hardly endeared them to the new Ambassador.[45] Annenberg compounded this error when he made his maiden speech at the Pilgrims Society in central London. The address focused on American domestic political turmoil rather than foreign relations. The main tropes of the speech were familiar to those who followed the Nixon administration's approach to the American university campus unrest of the period, with its exhortations for 'an end to giving in to students... and end to appeasement' and the way in which it laid the blame for riots at the feet of a 'permissive and apathetic older leadership, which, while providing innumerable advantages for youth has failed to inculcate in youth the understanding that there is a correspondent responsibility for each advantage enjoyed'. However, it struck the wrong note with an audience that was more at home listening to a series of platitudes on the strength and depth of the transatlantic relationship. The focus on Vietnam was also ill-judged, given its tangential relevance to Anglo-American relations and widespread opposition to the war in Britain. Moreover, it gave the press an additional reason to dislike the new envoy, one commentator observing that 'the British press corps, not without a slight touch of malice, is watching and waiting for the next brick to be dropped'.[46]

Annenberg recovered from these initial difficulties, and made a concerted and ultimately successful effort to present a positive image of American generosity to the British public, both in London and further afield. At the root of this approach lay a romantic identification with a traditional form of Britishness that, although increasingly at variance with reality, sustained the Ambassador throughout his five-year posting. As his verbal stumbling made clear, Annenberg was over-awed by the royal family and its imperial baubles and made a concerted effort to ingratiate himself with the Queen, the Queen Mother and Prince Charles.[47] He also shared the profound respect that many Americans had for Winston Churchill as the stand-out hero of the Second World War, often proudly recounting that, during an encounter in 1949, the wartime Prime Minister had advised him to 'look not for reward from others, but hope that you have done your best'.[48] This was a conservative, highly idealised and increasingly outdated vision of Britain, but one that held a continued and increasing attraction to a portion of the British population in the 1970s as the country's future came to look far less glorious than its past.

Annenberg combined his determination born of romanticism with a very practical approach to building his reputation in Britain, drawing on many of the techniques he had used in the past to break into the snobbish and anti-Semitic environment of Philadelphia's aristocratic and socially exclusive Main Line area.[49] As with many Jews of his generation, Annenberg had suffered from the deeply ingrained and pervasive anti-Semitism of American North-Eastern high society during the early and mid-twentieth century. At various points during the interwar years, Ivy League colleges such as Columbia, Harvard, Princeton and Yale restricted admission of Jewish students, whilst many other bastions of privilege such as dining and sports clubs did not allow non-Anglo Saxons to become members.[50] Amongst other indignities, Annenberg was excluded from joining the University of Pennsylvania's non-Jewish fraternities when a student there, as well as the Main Line's most exclusive country clubs. In a characteristic response, he built a golf course in his back yard.[51] As the first Jewish-American Ambassador to the Court of St James's, there is scant evidence that Annenberg suffered from any overt discrimination whilst in Britain.[52] However, in some respects he saw acceptance in his new home as a way to socially outflank the Anglophile boyars of his hometown, which he characterised to British Home Secretary James Callaghan as 'a bush-league London'.[53]

Just as he had in Philadelphia, Annenberg set out to 'collect paintings and support the Art Museum' in order to facilitate his integration into high society.[54] One of the first things Annenberg did in the wake of his uncertain start was to arrange to have a selection of his impressive art collection exhibited at the Tate Gallery. The exhibition included outstanding works of French Impressionist and Post-impressionist art, including paintings by Monet, Cezanne, Gauguin, Picasso, Renoir and Lautrec. In what was to become a pattern of 'chequebook diplomacy', the Ambassador paid for the logistical costs and insurance so that admission was free.[55] Annenberg donated approximately $1 million to various charities and good causes during his tenure, including contributions to the restoration of St Paul's Cathedral and the purchase of Henri Rousseau's *Storm with Tiger* by the National Gallery. He also sponsored production of a coffee-table book on Westminster Abbey, which included contributions by Sir John Betjeman, A. L. Rowse and Lord Clark. He gave 8,000 of the first print run to schools.[56] Annenberg also appreciated that, in the words of one of his subordinates, 'he was Ambassador to all Britain, not just the West End'. He also donated money to York Minster and a Roman dig near Nottingham during his tours of the country, which also included visits to Manchester, Sheffield, Liverpool and Edinburgh.[57] These visits gave him an insight to British life beyond the royal family and Winston Churchill – one that probably informed his charitable giving. Annenberg was acutely aware of how British economic difficulties had led to a national identity crisis. In his farewell telegram, he argued:

> Today, Britain is a divided nation. There is little sense of direction or national purpose. Regional interests are growing stronger and more strident, and in the case of Scotland could adversely affect the rational development of the North Sea oil boom on which so many hopes have been pinned. Militants in the trades unions, oblivious of the national good, pose a danger for the recovery of British industry. Nothing less than leadership by government to inspire an act of political will by the British people will overcome these divisions. I am not pessimistic of the chance of this happening, but the obstacles are formidable.[58]

In this context, Annenberg's philanthropy can be viewed not merely as an attempt to rehabilitate his own reputation, but to contribute to a regeneration of British national pride through professions of deep respect for what he saw as the best about the country, backed by infusions of much-needed cash. Recipients were certainly grateful for his generosity and responded with enthusiasm. Westminster Abbey's installation of a stained glass window was dedicated to him and Queen Elizabeth awarded an honorary knighthood in 1976 – both gestures deeply appreciated by this instinctive Anglophile. He is the only American Ambassador to have been so honoured by the Queen.[59] Annenberg's resolute determination to be liked by the British, combined with the application of a portion of his vast fortune to this cause, was one of the main reasons Douglas-Home could comment at his farewell that although 'there was a time when we thought your saddle had slipped ... you ran out a good, decisive winner in the end'.[60]

A Loyal Political Supporter in the Shadow of Watergate

Annenberg's success in public diplomacy was naturally overshadowed by the Watergate crisis that engulfed the presidency during Nixon's second term. Although Annenberg was never involved in any of these activities, Watergate reignited the row over political venality in Washington, specifically the claim that ambassadorships were awarded on the basis of campaign contributions rather than competence. There was more to accusations of political cronyism in Nixon's second term than there had been in 1969. Whilst the overall proportion of political as opposed to career ambassadors in the Foreign Service was approximately the same as or better than previous administrations, this was primarily due to the expansion of US overseas missions to newly independent countries in Africa. After a slow start at the beginning of Nixon's first term, the number of political appointees heading missions in 'Class 1' West European capitals returned to normal levels. Many of these ambassadors donated large amounts to Nixon's election campaigns.[61] Whilst Annenberg had not given significant amounts of money before his appointment, he did so afterwards. The Ambassador gave $254,000 to Republican campaign funds during Nixon's presidency, in some cases through an unconventional channel via an ex-White House aide that allowed the President to circumvent the Republican National Committee and hence have greater control over how the money was allocated. The Ambassador's wider family also contributed generously to the Nixon presidency, his sister donating hundreds of thousands of dollars to redecorate the Blue Room in the White House.[62] It is likely that the donations helped Annenberg retain his appointment to the Court of St James's in the face of challenges from other potential candidates, including another business magnate and philanthropist W. Clement Stone.[63]

Annenberg provided more than merely financial support. In early 1973, he wrote a letter on State Department stationery in support of Nixon's foreign policy that was then mailed out to voters. Enclosed were two supportive editorials, one from the *Sunday Express* and another from the *Daily Telegraph*.[64] The Ambassador denied any violation of political impartiality, telling the State Department that he had written the letter in a private capacity, before it was copied and distributed by the President's Special Counsel Charles Colson. Under Congressional pressure for further disclosure, Annenberg then said that Colson had asked him to write the letter before he distributed it.[65] As the Watergate crisis deepened during the course of 1974, the Ambassador's *T.V. Guide* began publishing a column called 'News Watch', the explicit aim of which was to combat bias in the news media. Pat Buchanan, a key Nixon media aide, was one of the main contributors. Annenberg claimed that he had no direct involvement in the establishment of the column, attesting that it was the decision of the *T.V. Guide's* editors alone. Sceptical commentators noted that it had been set up immediately after a meeting between Nixon and Annenberg in Palm Springs.[66] Yet any such support was motivated by a genuine gratitude towards Nixon. Annenberg continued to stand by the President long after others had considered it politic to distance themselves from the administration. He regularly provided his Palm Springs estate as a refuge for the embattled President, even after his resignation in August 1974.[67] Annenberg stated that he owed it to Nixon because the President 'gave me the greatest honour of my life'.[68] This uncomplicated and straightforward notion of loyalty in exchange for material reward must have been comforting to Nixon, who saw himself as constantly surrounded by deception and ingratitude.

Conclusion

Walter Annenberg was indeed an unusual diplomat, but the perfect one for a presidential administration as extraordinary as Richard Nixon's. An Ambassador who knew almost nothing about foreign policy was ideally suited to a President who sought to centralise decision-making in the West Wing. Kissinger ignored Annenberg, as he did most other American Ambassadors. Given his vast influence over the conduct of foreign policy, this effectively cut Annenberg out of any role he may have hoped for in shaping the high diplomacy during his tenure. It is telling that as many – if not more – column inches in the American press were devoted to the Ambassador's role in London high society as his influence on policy, whilst he was never recalled by either house of Congress to testify on foreign policy issues after his confirmation by the Senate.[69] At the same time, Annenberg displayed many strengths unanticipated by the host of newspaper commentators who rushed to condemn his appointment. He had the humility to accept his subordination, whilst concentrating on making sure working relations within the Embassy were good. He interfered little in day-to-day management, which allowed American diplomats the space to maintain contacts that were solid enough to endure the tempestuous relationship between Nixon, Kissinger and Heath. Occasionally he intervened to facilitate agreements between the two governments or remove barriers to British and American business transactions; important during a period when many firms were taking the first steps towards truly deserving the term 'multinational'.

Annenberg had so little impact partly because Britain did not occupy a central position in Nixon and Kissinger's grand design. Vietnam and triangular diplomacy dominated Nixon's first term. In these areas, Paris and Bonn were more important than London. Heath repaid the compliment by focusing on Europe at the expense of the Anglo-American partnership. Relations between the two countries reached a low ebb during this period; when they were not ignoring each other, tension and recrimination predominated over cooperation. Yet this mattered infinitely more to Britain than it did to the United States. Whilst British decline had been a constant anxiety and a growing reality during the 1960s, its full effects were felt during the 1970s. William F. Buckley, Jr was cruel, but correct, when he argued that the reaction to Annenberg's royal gaffe was so poisonous because, 'in England, form is almost everything, substance having been greatly liquidated, along with the empire, in the past 20 years: so that protocol becomes even more important than ever'.[70] Annenberg recovered well from this initial setback, his instinct leading him towards a public stance that gave many Britons what they desired from the senior American representative in their country: almost unbounded financial generosity for cash-strapped cultural institutions, smoothed by praise for their country's contributions to world history and culture. With this strategy, he took some of the edge off Nixon's high-handed approach to Britain. In doing so, he displayed far greater nous than many expected and deserved the laudatory editorials that accompanied his return to the United States.

Annenberg had been appointed to the United States' most prestigious diplomatic post with the expectation of support, and he was probably one of the few members of the Nixon administration who fully lived up to the President's domestic political requirements. The Ambassador gave money, and most probably stretched his political impartiality with his letter writing and media endorsements. Most importantly, however, Annenberg displayed the quality that Nixon – much to his chagrin – discovered that he could not guarantee through preferment: unqualified loyalty to his cause, right to the bitter end.

Notes

1. Briefs for President Nixon's visit (Folder 2) (1970), 'The Hon. Walter H. Annenberg United States Ambassador', p. 2. FCO 7/1813, National Archives, Kew, London. Accessed through Archives Direct, *The Nixon Years, 1969–1974*, available at: http://www.archivesdirect.amdigital.co.uk/Introduction/Nixon/default.aspx (accessed 19 December 2011).
2. D. Pearson and J. Anderson, 'The Washington Merry-Go Round: Annenberg Lifts Some British Brows', *Washington Post*, 24 February 2969, p. B7.
3. 'Nominations of Walter H. Annenberg, Jacob D. Beam, and John S.D. Eisenhower: Hearing before the Committee on Foreign Relations United States Senate', US GPO, 7 March 1969, p. 2.
4. J. Cooney, *The Annenbergs* (New York: Simon & Schuster, 1982), pp. 192–4.
5. 'Nominations of Annenberg, Beam and Eisenhower', pp. 1–4.
6. Editorial, 'Money and the Foreign Service', *The New York Times*, 11 January 1969, p. 32.

7. C. Ogden, *Legacy: A Biography of Moses and Walter Annenberg* (New York: Little, Brown & Co., 1999), pp. 406–7.
8. 'Nominations of Annenberg, Beam, and Eisenhower', p. 24.
9. FCO 7/1813 'The Hon. Walter H. Annenberg', p. 1.
10. P. Groose, 'Diplomatic Posts to Go to Careerists: Nixon Administration Finds Few Partisans to Appoint', *The New York Times*, 4 May 1969, p. 13.
11. 'Nominations for Annenberg, Beam, and Eisenhower', pp. 1–4, 6–29.
12. W. Unna, 'Fulbright Votes "No" on Annenberg', *Washington Post*, 13 March 1969, p. A23.
13. FCO 82/482 US diplomatic representation in UK (Folder 2) (1974) 'P.M. Gore-Booth Record for Confidential File Mr. Walter Annenberg', 29 January 1969, p. 1.
14. *Ibid.*, p. 1.
15. FCO/82/64 Political relations between UK and USA (Folder 1) (1971) Record of the Call of the American Ambassador on the Secretary of State at 12.15 on 2 August 1971, p. 1.
16. H. Kissinger, *Years of Renewal* (New York: Touchstone, 1999), pp. 608–9.
17. FCO/82/280 Kissinger press conferences and diplomacy (Folder 2) (1973), M. I. Goulding to H. T. A. Overton, 18 December 1973, p. 1; W. Annenberg to J. Amery, 13 December 1973, pp. 1–3; H. T. A. Overton to M. I. Goulding, 20 December 1973, p. 1.
18. D. McCardle, 'Not Everybody Likes the Joke', *Washington Post*, 21 September 1969, p. F13.
19. FCO/82/197 Visit by Dr Henry Kissinger of United States to UK, September (Folder 1) (1972), 'FCO Telegram No. 2608', pp. 1–2.
20. FCO/82/197, Call by Lord Cromer, 12 September 1972, p. 1.
21. FCO/82/197 D. C. Tebbit, 'Visit of Dr Kissinger', 8 September 1972, pp. 1–2; M. E. Sarotte, 'The Frailties of Grand Strategies: A Comparison of Detente and Ostpolitik', in A. Preston and F. Logevall (eds.), *Nixon in the World: American Foreign Relations, 1969–1977* (New York: Oxford University Press, 2008), p. 156.
22. W. Annenberg to President and Secretary of State, 'United States Relations with the United Kingdom – Ambassador's Retrospective', 23 October 1974, p. 4 from 1973–1976 Telegrams Transferred to NARA, Department of State FOIA Electronic Reading Room, available at: http://www.state.gov/m/a/ips/c22798.htm (accessed 24 May 2011).
23. Kissinger, *Years of Renewal*, p. 602.
24. Sarotte, 'The Frailties of Grand Strategies', pp. 157–8.
25. D. J. Reynolds, *Britannia Overruled: British Policy and World Power in the Twentieth Century* (Harlow: Longman, 1991), pp. 226–33.
26. Sarotte, 'The Frailties of Grand Strategies', p. 157.
27. A. Spelling, 'Lord Cromer, 1971–74' in Hopkins *et al.* (eds.), *The Washington Embassy*, p. 192.
28. Ogden, *Legacy*, p. 463.
29. Reynolds, *Britannia Overruled*, p. 241.
30. A. Noble, 'Kissinger's Year of Europe, Britain's Year of Choice', in M. Schulz and T. A. Schwartz (eds.), *The Strained Alliance: US-European Relations from Nixon to Carter* (New York: Cambridge University Press, 2010), p. 226.
31. Heath was willing to allow SR-71 reconnaissance planes to fly from RAF Mildenhall, but requested that the operations be deniable. Kissinger refused. G. Hughes, 'Britain, the Transatlantic Alliance, and the Arab-Israeli War of 1973', *Journal of Cold War Studies*, Vol. 10, No. 2 (Spring 2008), pp. 21–2.

32. Noble, 'Kissinger's Year of Europe', pp. 231, 233–4.
33. W. Annenberg to W. Rogers, 'The Changing Anglo-American Relationship', 28 November 1973, sections 1–5 in 1973–1976 Telegrams Transferred to NARA, Department of State FOIA Electronic Reading Room, available at: http://www.state.gov/m/a/ips/c22798.htm (accessed 24 May 2011).
34. *Ibid.*
35. Cooney, *The Annenbergs*, p. 347.
36. Ogden, *Legacy*, pp. 446–7.
37. R. Evans and R. Novak, 'Inside Report: Lobbyist Stumbles, Pollution Bill Gains', *Boston Globe*, 22 August 1971, p. 40.
38. FCO/82/485 US diplomatic representation in foreign countries (1974), C. J. Treadwell, 'US Ambassador to the Bahamas', p. 1.
39. Ogden, *Legacy*, pp. 435–6.
40. FCO/82/313 Agreements on cost sharing defence facilities (Folder 2) (1973) E. T. Davies to J. A. N. Graham, 'Cost Sharing Arrangements for United States Defence Facilities in the United Kingdom', 6 April 1973, p. 1.
41. FCO/82/313, 'Negotiations with the United States on Cost Sharing Arrangements for United States Defence Facilities in the United Kingdom', p. 3.
42. FCO/82/313, Davies to Graham, 'Cost Sharing Arrangements', p. 1.
43. Sarotte, 'Frailties of Grand Strategies', p. 151, 156–7.
44. Ogden, *Legacy*, p. 453.
45. *Ibid.*, pp. 428–9; McCardle, 'Not Everybody Likes the Joke', p. F13.
46. K. E. Meyer, 'Lost in the Words', *Washington Post*, 24 June 1969, p. B2.
47. Times Staff Writer, 'Desert Estate: Prince Visits Annenberg', *Los Angeles Times*, 17 March 1974, p. 22.
48. FCO/82/271 Internal political situation in the USA; changes in US Administration (1973), 'Remarks by United States Ambassador Walter H. Annenberg at Churchill College, Cambridge July 26 1973', p. 1.
49. L. H. Geller, 'Race Isn't only Barrier to Main Line Acceptance', *Philadelphia Tribune*, 15 December 1970, p. 14.
50. M. G. Synnott, 'The Admission and Assimilation of Minority Students at Harvard, Yale, and Princeton, 1900–1970', *History of Education Quarterly*, Vol. 19, No. 3 (Fall 1979), pp. 285–304.
51. Ogden, *Legacy*, pp. 126, 271–3.
52. Nor does he appear to have been on the receiving end of any anti-Semitic invective from the President. As a close advisor to Nixon, Kissinger was. Ogden, *Legacy*, p. 403; R. Dallek, *Nixon and Kissinger: Partners in Power* (London: Penguin Books, 2008), pp. 169–71.
53. A. Shutters, 'British Still Debate Merits of Annenberg as US Envoy', *The New York Times*, 17 November 1969, p. 16; Ogden, *Legacy*, p. 272.
54. Geller, 'Race Isn't only Barrier', p. 14.
55. J. Flannery, 'London's Dazzling Exhibitions: Annenberg Art Patron', *Los Angeles Times*, 17 September 1969, p. F10; A. Shuster, 'Annenberg Leaving London With Critics Mellowed', *The New York Times*, 15 October 1974, p. 4; Cooney, *The Annenbergs*, p. 360.
56. Times Diary, 'Annenberg's Debt to the Abbey', *The Times*, 22 November 1972, p. 16.
57. Ogden, *Legacy*, p. 453.
58. Annenberg, 'Ambassador's Retrospective', p. 3.
59. Ogden, *Legacy*, pp. 457–8, 496.

60. Shuster, 'Annenberg Leaving', p.4.
61. Staff Correspondent, 'Ambassadorship "Auctions" Toned Down – for Now', *The Christian Science Monitor*, 6 March 1974, pp. 1, 6.
62. M. Mintz, 'Large Contributors to GOP in '72 Listed', *The Washington Post*, 13 May 1973, p. M7; AP, 'Diplomats Aided G.O.P. Candidates: Funds Channelled through Ex-White House Aide', *The New York Times*, 27 December 1970, p. 22; L. Hutchinson, ' "It's No Secret": Pat Proclaims Visit to Russia', *Chicago Tribune*, 16 May 1972, p. A2.
63. D. McCardle, 'A Yacht of Money', *The Washington Post*, pp. B1, B3.
64. M. Berger, 'Eagleton Hits US's Paying for Letter Praising Nixon', *The Washington Post*, 26 February 1973, p. A2.
65. Washington Bureau of the Sun, 'US seeks explanation for Annenberg's silence', *The Sun (Baltimore)*, 4 May 1973, p. A6.
66. D. Adler, 'The White House vs. Television News: Part II: Administration Sees Bias, Seeks Balance', *Los Angeles Times*, 14 May 1974, pp. D1, 12.
67. Cooney, *The Annenbergs*, pp. 373–7.
68. Associated Press, 'Nixon to Enter Hospital Soon, Annenberg Says; Ailing Ex-President's Voice Firm during US-London Call', Ambassador Reports, *Los Angeles Times*, 19 September, p. A20.
69. Examples of Annenberg's prominence on the cocktail circuit include: J. Weinraub, 'Americans Dwindle on the London Scene', *The New York Times*, 10 September 1972, p. 80; J. Weinraub, 'Crowded "Little Season" Proves Hectic for Met Supporters on a Tour in London', 1 April 1972, p. 11; 'J-5 Gets Date with Royal Family', *Philadelphia Tribune*, 3 October 1972, p. 20.
70. W. F. Buckley, Jr, 'The Trials of Walter Annenberg', *Los Angeles Times*, 4 August 1969, p. B6.

10
Ambassadors Richardson, Armstrong and Brewster, 1975–81

Alex Spelling

The second half of the 1970s would not witness the same challenges to the US–UK relationship as experienced in the decade before and the period would largely see continuity and cordial relations at an official level. However, these years were a time of considerable flux for both countries in the domestic and international arenas. Britain's precarious economic position would dominate American perceptions and impact upon the defence commitments at the heart of their relationship. Inflation, low growth, unemployment and a weak currency bedevilled the Labour government as it tried to carry through tax increases and public expenditure cuts.[1] President Gerald Ford's assumption of power following Richard Nixon's resignation in August 1974 restored a degree of political stability in the US, but the new President faced a number of international challenges, particularly the fall of South Vietnam, unravelling of *détente* and the fallout from his controversial pardon of Nixon. And whilst not as severe as British problems, the US economy was also experiencing significant inflationary pressures and rising interest rates. The impact of the 1973 oil price rises would continue to have significant implications for all Western nations' economic and energy policies.

Elliot Richardson, 1975–76

Walter Annenberg's replacement in London, Elliot Richardson, had an impressive curriculum vitae and based on his recent appointments was a rising star. However, he was domestically oriented and a political appointment rather than a career diplomat, a fact which would influence his relatively short time in Grosvenor Square. In 1970 President Nixon made Richardson Secretary for Health, Welfare and Education, before transferring him to the Secretary of Defence post from January to May 1973, and then from May to October, Attorney General. In the latter post Richardson was elevated in the national consciousness as a result of the enveloping Watergate scandal; when asked by Nixon to fire Watergate special prosecutor, Archibald Cox, he refused and resigned. Born in Boston in 1920, Richardson graduated from Harvard with an AB (*cum laude*) in 1941 and in 1947 received his LLB. His studies were interrupted by service during the Second World War as a First Lieutenant with the US Army. He received a Bronze Star and a Purple Heart after landing with the 4th Infantry Division in Normandy on D-Day. After graduation, he served as a law clerk and, in 1949, was made an associate of a Boston law firm. During the 1950s he switched between private practice and a period as Legislative Assistant for a Boston Senator and from 1957 to 1959 he served as Assistant Secretary for Legislation for the Department of Health, Education and Welfare, thereafter being appointed as the US Attorney for Massachusetts. Two years later he became a partner at Ropes and Gray Law firm. He returned to public service as Lieutenant Governor of Massachusetts in 1965 and in 1967 was elected the State's Attorney General.[2]

As Ambassador, Richardson was given a special budgetary allowance from the State Department for entertaining, something perhaps needed given the extent of such activities under his billionaire predecessor (Annenberg reportedly spent $100,000 of his own funds per year on official entertaining, in addition to his $1 million restoration of Winfield House). Unconfirmed reports suggested Richardson said he could not take the job unless this was the case. The State Department thus increased the Embassy's representative allowance from $30,000 to $50,000 although this sum would be shared out amongst other Embassy staff requiring funds.[3] Richardson said he was prepared to use his official salary for additional entertaining (as he could live off his own means if necessary) but no more than that. In an introductory interview with Fred Emery of *The Times* on 20 February, Richardson deflected questions about his ambitions for a more prominent Cabinet role in Washington (although five days later the paper would carry a story in which he admitted he was ready to run as a presidential candidate or serve as Secretary of State) and said that it was the UK's historic role, and the 'leading centre of civilized relationships among people', that made this post appealing. More immediately, the UK was severely battered by the forces of interdependence, perhaps the central phenomenon of the Western world. During his time as Ambassador, he hoped these issues would be debated with 'great intensity and urgency'. His ambassadorial role would be 'a kind of channel, catalyst, an entrepreneur of ideas, rather than the traditional role of dealing simply in bilateral relationships'. The nature of the US–UK relationship necessitated much agreement on matters of international finance, energy, the European Economic Community (EEC), North Atlantic Treaty Organisation (NATO) and so forth. He also believed that Britain still had an important role in the world, not least as London's banking role ensured that financial problems converged there. Furthermore, world problems were now primarily economic which meant individual geo-political roles were no longer as valid as in the recent past. Countries must contribute transnationally and here the UK was very important. Beyond these sentiments, however, he had no long-range plans for his tenure.[4] This may have been because he saw the post as temporary.

E. J. Hughes of the Foreign and Commonwealth Office's (FCO) North American Department (NAD), thought it interesting that two of the unsuccessful candidates for the vice-presidential nomination in 1974 (the other being George H. W. Bush) had now been sent overseas. He wondered whether this was to cement Nelson Rockefeller's candidature. Moreover, Richardson's chances of getting the presidential nomination in 1976 ahead of Ford were small. The Head of the Department, Nicholas Gordon-Lennox, thought Richardson was so ambitious that he was unlikely to stay long. Nevertheless Richardson's abilities were readily apparent as were his social graces. Openly Anglophile, he was said to admire the British tradition of uncorrupt and loyal service. The Prime Minister decided to host a lunch for Richardson upon his arrival. The PM understood that protocol made it 'invidious' to single out one ambassador, but in these circumstances, it was a reflection of close US–UK ties.[5] Richardson's opposite number in Washington, Peter Ramsbotham, cabled London to say that he had seen lots of Richardson recently. He had had a big send off and was not just an ordinary envoy. Many high-ranking members of the administration had attended, demonstrating the weight of his standing in the country, although his appeal was mainly intellectual rather than in the public or press. 'There is little doubt that we could hardly have been offered a more impressive man as Ambassador.' He was eloquent and generous about Britain. Ramsbotham conversely thought they should not necessarily see him as short term; he might be there a long time and be a considerable asset.[6]

A Piece of the Action

Sir John Killick, the Deputy Undersecretary at the FCO, recalled a conversation he had had with Richardson at the Pilgrims Society Dinner. The American mentioned that he wanted to get involved in real business and whilst he understood Ramsbotham's function in acting as a bridge between the two countries, he wanted a 'piece of action' for himself. He did not like the idea of all business being conducted through Washington. Killick advised that Ramsbotham could not give direct information on the UK and the leading political figures; Richardson could. The Ambassador thought he could get an early 'jump' on Washington by reporting on the discussion of commodities at the forthcoming Commonwealth Conference. Killick thus thought they should do all possible to help Richardson to give him a sense of 'job satisfaction' by providing the material for significant reports to Washington. There would be the delicate issue of not prejudicing relations with Kissinger.

> There is no reason to suppose that he wants Mr Richardson to become a particularly significant Ambassador in London. But on the other hand it is clear to me that Mr Richardson will not be content to be as complacent

an Ambassador as Mr Annenberg. He would likely become disconcerted if no real business was pushed in his direction.[7]

Jack Binns who served in Grosvenor Square from 1974–79, first as a Political Officer and then in his final year as Political Counsellor, chief of the Political Section, believed that, because the British did not consider Annenberg a 'serious' representative, they conducted more business through Washington than London.

> I think that changed with the advent of Elliot Richardson, who was... at the peak of his peak of fame. He was regarded as a 'serious' person and politician and was extremely connected in the US... the Labour government was more comfortable dealing with us than with unknown persons in the State Department and other agencies in Washington... clearly the change of our ambassadors in London shifted the burden of dialogue from the British Embassy in Washington to the American Embassy in London.[8]

Killick, therefore, quickly understood the need to do more for Richardson than Annenberg without prejudicing the Washington operation. Richardson did not want to undercut Ramsbotham, but his active nature and judgement might lead him to seek a larger 'piece of action' than was correct, and thus there might be a need for restraining action.[9] Ramsbotham thought it 'lamentable' that the activities of the US Embassy had withered under Annenberg, but agreed closer cooperation should not prejudice the work done in Washington. To preserve the Kissinger relationship, relations with the UK Embassy would have to be pursued with discretion. They must not disclose what Kissinger revealed in the strictest confidence, especially if it was not to be communicated with other officials, whilst keeping the Washington Embassy abreast. But Richardson was full of bright ideas and 'we need them'. An element of this dilemma was apparent when Richardson informed Killick that he would not be at the lunch in Washington for the PM's meeting during his North American trip. He said, 'rather ruefully', that there could be no guarantee he would participate if he came. It seemed clear that he had been firmly 'dis-invited'. However, this was standard Kissinger practice and not serious.[10] Indeed, Kissinger told Ramsbotham in November that Richardson was the best deputy he had and would prefer him to be his successor at the State Department. Unfortunately, Richardson could not refrain from making 'stupid statements' about expectations for higher office. He had done it again recently and annoyed the President, diminishing, in Kissinger's opinion, his chances.[11]

Reflective of such experiences, in a retrospective interview about his role Richardson boldly (and unselfishly) claimed that, in practice, the Deputy Chief of Mission (DCM), Economic Counsellor and Information Officer were the important jobs in London, *not* the incumbent Ambassador. This was partly because the US–UK relationship functioned at a high level on the basis of President–Prime Minister and Secretary of State–Foreign Secretary contact. The correct people dealt ably with day-to-day issues. Richardson's role was to maintain cordial relations with a variety of individuals and groups.[12] Nevertheless, Richardson did try to temper the mood in Washington early on into the post when he responded to the growing frustration of Ford, Kissinger and Defence Secretary, James Schlesinger, over Britain's March 1975 Defence Review which cut some overseas commitments, including bases in the Mediterranean and Indian Ocean (thus focusing energies on Europe and the Atlantic). He felt Britain (and the North Atlantic Treaty Organisation – NATO) had come away better than might have been expected. Nothing 'vital has been lost'. A meaningful British contribution to Western defence was still available.[13]

Defensive Measures

Following a dressing down by Schlesinger, and pointing to the seriousness with which the US viewed the potential cuts, Secretary of Defence Roy Mason lunched with Richardson at the Embassy. Mason urged the Ambassador that 'anything we can do to strengthen his hand in stiffening Ministers' backbones on this issue would be greatly appreciated'. Richardson agreed.[14] He thus counselled Kissinger to raise the issue of defence cuts in his next meeting with the Foreign Secretary, James Callaghan. He believed the failure of Vice President Rockefeller to discuss this at his last meeting with Wilson would weaken the position of Mason in the Cabinet discussions about public spending cuts. 'Repeated and high-level expressions of US concerns are important in providing support for those who oppose cuts'. Cuts inevitably reduced Britain's 'heft' on the international scene, eroding the sense of its own role, with inevitable impacts on its value to its partners. That said there was a right way to go about this. From the 'grapevine' he had heard that Schlesinger had threatened to cut off intelligence sharing and assistance for Britain's Polaris missiles. 'We do not favour threats of this nature which have a "cut off your nose to spite your face quality"'. It was reasonable, however, to expect that such unique cooperative programmes would be vulnerable to criticism if Britain's role continued to shrink. In any event, clarification of the American position was needed.[15]

   As the source of British cutbacks was economic rather than political or ideological, the nature of the country's economic performance and the policies of the Labour government attracted criticism in Washington. Indeed, Richardson recalled that the abiding difficulties facing the relationship were economic.[16] The Embassy provided detailed reports on the nature of Cabinet discussions and prospects for recovery but it made for depressing reading. A June telegram declared there was little prospect for meaningful growth in 1975, slow growth in 1976 and perhaps an export-led recovery by 1977. The

UK was lagging in the cycle, with unemployment and inflation likely to rise in comparison to other countries. The major problems were inflation, driven by rising wages, sluggish growth and low business confidence, all of which discouraged investment and led to increased unemployment.[17] In public, on the other hand, the Ambassador tried to sound upbeat. Addressing the English Speaking Union on this issue in May 1975, and returning to his earlier exhortations, he told the audience that traditional values would pull Britain out of its present crisis.[18]

Unfortunately, matters reached a peak in December when following another round of reviews, it was decided that defence would have to lose somewhere in the region of £100–500 million per annum as part of total cuts of £3,750 million. Kissinger informed Callaghan that any further reductions would weaken the UK as a NATO ally with important implications for future European stability. 'I am sure you are aware that America's long-term relations with the UK will inevitably have to take into account Britain's standing as a partner in our common security enterprise'.[19] The effect of such warnings is uncertain, but in practical terms they had little effect. In fact, Wilson authorised cuts in the region of £225 million, a figure later reduced to £193 million as the Prime Minister sought to balance his Cabinet colleagues' views.[20] Even if unable to reverse Britain's economic realities, the Ambassador nonetheless played a useful mediating function during these debates and appeared sympathetic to the government's plight. Meanwhile, a sign of Richardson's growing involvement in the reporting side of the job was demonstrated in October when Political Officer, Alan James, was appointed to research UK domestic policy as the Ambassador wished to be better informed. And, despite the recent buffeting, the British briefing notes for Home Secretary, Roy Jenkins' meeting with the Ambassador, optimistically stated that there were no major problems in bilateral relations.[21] However, this growing involvement would be cut short when, at the end of the year, President Ford decided to make the Ambassador his new Commerce Secretary, ironically, in part to try to steer the US into an economic recovery of its own.

Back in the Cabinet

Richardson's ambassadorship was thus very brief and he returned to Washington in January 1976. Alan James believed Richardson would have been an outstanding ambassador if he had been given a longer run. The British regretted his departure after only ten months.[22] The briefing notes for Wilson's meeting with Richardson in January 1976 noted that the Ambassador had worked conscientiously and made a wide range of contacts in the UK. He had also been active socially despite his financial limitations, if less successful addressing large public audiences. On Northern Ireland, it was hoped he 'would not forget us' and the British were grateful for help; Richardson could make a huge difference in promoting a clearer understanding in the US of the realities of the situation. Primarily, they felt, this could be achieved by improving the visa stops against fundraisers; more barriers to hinder the transfer of arms and money; and persuading influential US politicians to speak out against the true purpose of fundraisers. In December Richardson had spoken to Senator Edward Kennedy on the matter; though Kennedy would not offer any assistance until there was a clearer indication of how Britain would proceed on power sharing.[23] Before departing London, Richardson told the press that he wanted to give the American people 'a better indication of what the situation really is' in Ulster. Some form of governmental intervention was necessary, but it should be 'precise, surgical and without side effects'.[24] This was more subtle than a strongly worded speech made by Wilson at the Association of American correspondents Christmas dinner in which he denounced American public financing of the Irish Republican Army (IRA).[25]

Whilst his diplomatic role had been limited, he had intervened wherever possible in ways calculated to be helpful. For instance, when negotiations over the US–UK Double Taxation agreement (ratified in 1976) had been in danger of breaking down, he had telephoned Treasury Secretary, William Simon, and persuaded him to change the decision to denounce the agreement. A new deal was later concluded. At his farewell call on the prime minister he spoke positively of his time in the UK; there was a tendency to describe the situation as the glass being 'half full' when in reality the country had many strengths.[26] This echoed comments to the press in which he claimed the US and Soviet role in the world had been diminished whilst Europe's (including Britain's) had increased. There was a 'wave of reasonableness' in the country, rooted in a clear understanding of its basic problems. The components of a viable economy were now being brought out, articulated and observed.[27] At a working level though, there was some dissension within the embassy following the departure announcement. Ronald Spiers, the DCM, said that if 'another Annenberg' was appointed he would not want to stay on. Morale in the Foreign Service was low as embassies seemed to be filled with political appointees and members of the Kissinger circle.[28]

Richardson's tenure had shown that on a day-to-day level US–UK relations were strong, but under the surface there were tensions due to the UK's economic malaise which directly affected the defence budget and its usefulness as an ally (although they remained the biggest net contributor to NATO after the US). Ford and Kissinger were seemingly genuine in talking up the quality of the relationship, yet in private could be disparaging about Britain's status and the capabilities of its government. Indeed, Mason wrote to Wilson after the spending decision to reiterate his worries over the depreciation of Britain's defence effort, his belief that a close relationship was simultaneously developing between West Germany and the US, and their growing belief that Britain's abilities were being dangerously downgraded and its reliability questioned.[29] In such matters, the US Embassy, save for the examples cited, could play little direct role in improving the situation. Britain's economic malaise and its relationship with the US would come to a head at the end of the year under the next occupant of Grosvenor Square. The new Ambassador would also, from April 1976, be working under a new Prime Minister, as Callaghan acceded to the top position following Wilson's decision to step down upon reaching his sixtieth birthday. Callaghan had displayed firm Atlanticist convictions as Foreign Secretary and developed a close partnership with Kissinger.[30]

Anne Armstrong, 1976–77

President Ford described Anne Armstrong as 'sugar and steel' in January 1976. Those who had worked in politics with her were, according to the accompanying *Time* article, 'equally extravagant in their notices. At once tough, gracious and articulate, Mrs. Armstrong is one of Ford's more distinguished appointments'.[31] The only criticism emanated from her dogged defence of Nixon almost until the end of the Watergate affair. Another political appointee, Armstrong was the first American woman to win a major ambassadorial role since the 1950s. Born in 1927, Armstrong was educated at Vassar College and worked briefly for the New Orleans *Times-Picayune*. As a result of her 1950 marriage to a Texan landowner, she became joint owner of a 50,000 acre ranch and the couple had five children. She was involved in local politics in the 1950s, progressing to a National Committeewoman, and from 1966–68 was chairman of the Texas Republican Party. She served as a member of the Executive Committee and co-chairman of the Republican National Committee from 1971–73, the first woman elected to this position, and delivered the keynote speech at the 1972 party convention. In 1973 she was appointed Counsellor to the President as well as serving on the Cost of Living and Federal Property Councils. There was some criticism at her decision to stay on during the Watergate scandal, not vacating the counsellor post until several months after Nixon's departure – for family reasons. Ramsbotham informed London that she was 'sympathetic and helpful', and similar positive sentiments were provided by Lord Cromer, Ramsbotham's predecessor.[32] At the swearing-in ceremony, President Ford described relations with the UK as 'good as they have ever been' and that he had enjoyed 'exceptionally fine' experiences with the Prime Minister.[33]

Following a luncheon with Kissinger, Ramsbotham reported that his attitude towards the British was most refreshing. There were no aspects of the relationship which seemed to worry him. In contrast to some of his earlier (and private) exhortations, he was sympathetic and only mildly concerned about defence cuts. However, he had earlier found 'very different attitudes' in the State Department (not elaborated upon) and it was his personal feelings which had made the difference (such self-promotion was a typical Kissinger ploy). He felt the new Ambassador, who had been briefed by top

American executives on their hopes and fears for the UK economy, would be different to Richardson, possessing neither his administrative experience nor intellectual capacity. Yet there were certainly no dissenting voices and Kissinger felt it would be easier to work with her than Richardson, whose political ambitions had made him uncomfortable. An additional note on US–UK relations stated that difficulties only tended to arise on economic and commercial issues, with current issues such as the US Transportation Department's resistance over granting landing rights to the new supersonic Anglo-French Concorde airliner (ostensibly over concerns of the sonic boom noise) and the dangers of trade restrictions. On 5 February, Concorde had been granted landing rights at Dulles and JFK airports. This allowed six monitored flights out of Dulles and four from JFK per day for 16 months. New York officials blocked the agreement, however; a decision later deemed unlawful by Judge Milton Pollack, of the Federal District Court of Southern New York.[34]

Learning the Ropes

Such issues were not immediately on Armstrong's agenda. The Court of St James's was an unexpected and totally surprising appointment in the year celebrating the US bicentennial. She was nevertheless 'thrilled' and in no doubt about taking up the offer. 'I think President Ford genuinely wanted to appoint more women and he had worked with me for a number of years. I think he thought I could do the job, and he really was reaching out to find women to give them top jobs.'[35] She recalled that there was good preparation by the State Department, but it would have been better to know what was expected of the Ambassador. The British press also gave her 'favourable' treatment, perhaps due to her gender and Texan background ('Texas was riding high then'). Britain's symbolic status, if reduced importance, is evident in Armstrong's comment that the UK was 'our closest ally, or certainly one of the top two or three'. London was a 'plum assignment', a place people yearned to go in their [diplomatic] careers. She was unsure of what her role was, but saw her task as cementing these relationships. Similar to Richardson, the most vivid impression she had on departure was the UK's economic woes – 'England was really in the depths then' – and the abiding political memory seems to have been economic issues. On such matters Armstrong would get to view 'the most important parts' of diplomatic cables and so forth.[36]

Ronald Spiers was a great complement to the new Ambassador, and essential, given her lack of experience. Although it was not the role he was looking for at that time, a point he communicated clearly, there was no better DCM, recalled Armstrong.[37] This standing was reflected on the British side. Ramsbotham, aware that Armstrong's stay may be short given the November 1976 presidential elections, passed onto London that it was important that Spiers remain as his knowledge of affairs and sympathy towards Britain was an asset.[38] The new Ambassador quickly found the administration indicative of 'a top flight embassy' and it confirmed the professionalism of the Foreign Service. With respect to issues like Northern Ireland, she was 'not sure' what a US envoy could do, but London was the hub of American activities in economics and military affairs and the Ambassador could be useful in such areas even if they were not confined to the capital. Thus, she believed that perhaps her strongest role was representing the US. Not that it was all smooth running, as common to other posts, the UK Treasury and US economic ministers did not often get along. Meanwhile, the 'Kissinger syndrome' of conducting diplomacy behind the Ambassador's back still played a complicating role:

> We had a big blow-up once. I picked him up at Claridge's, and I'd found out he was having some meetings with the foreign minister that I was not privy to, so I blew my top and told him, 'That better not happen again.' And Henry tells the story and claims I cried. Well, the last thing I was going to do was cry then. I might have bitten him, but I wasn't going to cry. So after that, that went better.[39]

She felt ambassadors, especially females, were supposed to be, 'easy on the head and hard on the feet'. However this socialising was less demanding than might have appeared, particularly in a post like London, given that, due to its 'sophistication', the need for formal calls was less than a smaller post. But the job did involve 'setting one of the best tables in London' on Spiers' recommendation. The budgetary allowance was acceptable for entertaining with supplements only necessary if a higher quality item was desired, 'at last they fixed it so you don't have to be rich'. In her representative capacity Armstrong carried out a number of ceremonial duties in the UK as part of the bicentennial celebrations. In the summer, this also involved accompanying the Queen on her state visit to the US.[40]

In general, Armstrong found the British people to be 'civil' and 'wonderful', who would only deign to bother the Ambassador in a nice way. Armstrong's gender contributed to being well known and a novelty:

> And so you certainly got your foot in the door as far as getting people's attention...Ambassadors can do good jobs in so many different ways, I've learned. One of my strengths was knowing how to deal with the public and enjoying it, and this was the kind of a post where that could be useful. In many countries, you wouldn't think of doing that – to be out and about often. I think it helped to be a woman.[41]

A month into her tenure, Armstrong became the first US envoy to visit Northern Ireland, announcing a US–UK initiative on gun-running, a significant issue for the British government who believed the IRA received significant quantities of automatic weapons from across the Atlantic. In November, Armstrong also met with a delegation from the Northern Ireland peace movement during a rally in London and passed on a personal message of support, consistent nonetheless with Washington's official position. Armstrong also reportedly formed a positive relationship with the British Foreign Secretary, Anthony Crosland.[42] And, like Richardson, Armstrong attempted to be upbeat about Britain's economic chances, citing signs of optimism.[43]

Profiled by *The Times*'s Brian Connell in September, the Ambassador noted some problems caused by reporters wanting her to discuss American politics and that, being a political appointee, she had to draw a difficult line. It was already clear to her that should the Democratic presidential nominee, Jimmy Carter, win the election, he would not keep her on. Nevertheless, she disagreed with his opposition to political appointees as she believed this was very much in keeping with the US outlook on government service in general, which required a 'salting' of citizens who did not come up through the ranks to cast a 'fresh look' on bureaucracy from time to time. Describing her character as 'assiduous and peripatetic', the report noted that she had travelled all over the UK, which had created a strong impression on the family. In her official reports home, she was 'guardedly optimistic' and opined that the special relationship should continue.[44]

One area in which the London Embassy was given some direct involvement concerned the renegotiation of the 1946 US–UK Civil Aviation agreement (the Bermuda agreement). Armstrong and Embassy officers discussed the situation with a number of officials and at a luncheon with the UK Trade Secretary, Edmund Dell. The Americans argued against a limitation of service as it would have effects on the tourist industry, offsetting any gain to UK airlines. Dell, however, said this was more of a US concern and that if tourists wanted to visit, they would, irrespective of flight frequency, and that higher numbers per flight would be better for US airlines. Armstrong felt that Dell's disavowal of the intent to push limitations too far was an acknowledgement of the validity of the American point. Measures were not being taken to diminish the impact on tourism, only to improve British carriers' share of the market and routes.[45] The most fractious issue in relations during Armstrong's tenure concerned Britain's protracted International Monetary Fund (IMF) loan in the winter.

The Sick Man of Europe

With pressure mounting on sterling, Dell again visited the Embassy to discuss Britain's balance of payments problems and remedial measures such as incomes policy and public expenditure cuts.[46] Spiers thought defence issues had now receded in importance and he tried to engage Kissinger's attention in Britain's overall economic predicament. Unfortunately:

> The Treasury Department was difficult to deal with because it considered itself independent and sovereign. Treasury officials would come to London without informing State and went about their business in

London without telling anyone what they were doing; they in fact were involving themselves with issues which were at the core of our relationships with the British. We found out what went on and then had to tell State and Kissinger what was going on. Kissinger would then have to talk to Treasury in Washington.[47]

International investors believed the pound was overvalued and devaluation might occur, triggering a large-scale sale of sterling. By the end of September the sterling–dollar rate had fallen from $1.77 to $1.63. Now convinced the pound was undervalued, the US Treasury agreed to partially fund a $5.3 billion loan to be repaid in December. The Exchequer thus applied to the IMF for $3–4 billion credit to finance the 1977 balance of payments deficit and loan.[48] President Ford undertook all that he could to be helpful and Callaghan writes that they worked well together because their interests transcended political differences. However, Ford's loss in the November presidential elections meant his 'influence quite naturally waned at the time when we most needed his help'. Moreover, William Simon, Ford's Treasury Secretary, and Arthur Burns, Governor of the US Federal Reserve, were not supportive. Callaghan's special advisor, Harold Lever, visited Washington to try and find a solution, but to little avail. Part of the problem stemmed from the impression of the IMF (over which the US had much influence) that the Labour government would not make the necessary public spending cuts.[49]

Callaghan struggled to find a consensus within the Cabinet and there were fears that the defence budget would once again come under scrutiny. Marshalling international support for the plans brought Spiers into the frame because US backing was crucial. He believed his personal friendships with Callaghan, Healey and Crosland 'helped considerably'.[50] Yet the available evidence points to a reduced role for the Embassy. Callaghan warned Ford that the scale of cuts the IMF required would see power shift to the left-wing group in the Cabinet. Yet the US remained firm and Callaghan acknowledged that Washington would not bring pressure to bear on the fund. Following heated Cabinet discussions, Callaghan ultimately cajoled his colleagues into agreeing to a reduction in public expenditure and monetary measures to tackle inflation in return for a $4 billion IMF loan. That Britain was negotiating from a disadvantaged position was a fact conversely acknowledged in Cabinet discussions: 'Our very weakness brings us strength . . . the IMF cannot afford not to give us the loan'.[51]

An Untimely Interruption

Armstrong would not get to see whether this weakness could be reversed and an economic recovery achieved as Ford's election loss to Jimmy Carter meant a second consecutive tenure in Grosvenor Square ended after less than a year. Hence it was 'an Ambassadorship in stages, because had Ford been re-elected, you know it's reasonably certain he would have asked me to stay on'. New Secretary of State, Cyrus Vance and Democratic Party Chairman, Bob Strauss, were known to the Ambassador and advised her to stay on and 'take your time'. However, she felt that it did not work either way. 'Since I was so political, it wasn't right. There'd be issues and people where it was slightly awkward for them and awkward for me ... whereas, for 90 percent of the Ambassadors, it would have worked. But I had been highly politicized.'[52] Upon leaving she declared that the posting had been the 'greatest year of my life', whilst reports noted that her already considerable reputation for skill, subtlety and charm had been enhanced.[53] Spiers recalled that the British 'loved her' and although brief, her tour was a 'real success'. Like Richardson, however, the relatively short stay meant that once both had gone through the protocol requirements, 'they weren't there long enough to grasp hold of the issues and get to know the people well'.[54]

Kingman Brewster, 1977–81

Kingman Brewster would complete the quintuplet of political appointees of the 1970s, but unlike his immediate predecessors, would have the opportunity to serve at least one full [presidential] term as the envoy in Grosvenor Square. Brewster was a close associate of Secretary of State Vance through the Yale Association and Vance had recommended him for the post. Since 1963, Brewster had been the President of Yale University and whilst highly political, like his recent predecessors in London, possessed no formal diplomatic experience. Born in Massachusetts in 1919, he graduated from Yale in 1941 with an AB and from Harvard in 1947 with an LLB. Despite being an ardent isolationist prior to US entry into the war, he volunteered for Navy service in 1942 and served as a naval aviator with active service in the Atlantic, before returning to his studies in 1946. After graduating, he spent a year in Paris as an Assistant General Counsel to Milton Katz, the US special representative for the Organisation for European Cooperation Administration (the body established to coordinate the Marshall Plan) before moving to the Massachusetts Institute as a researcher in the Economics Department. In 1950 he became an Assistant, then in 1954, full Professor of Law at Harvard with expertise in international commerce and relations before becoming Yale's provost in 1960. During his time as president he made a number of reforms including widening access to different social groups and admitting women. Politically, he had been a Republican before identifying himself as an 'independent' in the 1960s.[55] Such a background and contacts meant Brewster was firmly established as part of the liberal East Coast intellectual establishment.[56] Ramsbotham similarly endorsed Brewster in terms of his Ivy League credentials.[57]

Following his arrival in London, *The Times* picked up on these aspects, reporting that Brewster was a forceful education administrator. His relationship with Carter was unknown, but Carter had spent a week during

1975 at Yale as a Chubb Fellow and thus it was possible their paths had crossed then.[58] The paper's May profile carried the heading, 'The mission is the message for the ambassador from Yale'. He was described as being shy of the press, unwilling to give an interview before he took up the post for fear of creating a preceding aura. Nonetheless, he was loyal, thoughtful and importantly, an Anglophile.[59] Modestly, he called himself an 'amateur ambassador'. David Spanier wrote that, after the 'buttoned down' Richardson and 'electrifying' Armstrong, Brewster felt more in tune with the English style and had cited Harold Macmillan as a political hero. As a result, 'the special relationship looks like thriving from Grosvenor Square'. Despite Britain's attenuated international status Brewster believed that the idea that influence was dependent upon military and economic power was a defect in FCO thinking. 'In reality Britain stands a better chance than any other power to influence US policy.' The extraordinary information-sharing arrangements were cemented by a 'common scepticism of sweeping panaceas and dogmatic ideologies'. For his role, he understood much of the important bilateral business was handled by Carter and Vance, yet 'there are idiosyncrasies of our political process utterly mysterious to our English cousins and vice-versa'. Likewise, they were bound to differ on certain issues, even on Rhodesia, where despite agreement on the need for a peaceful settlement, wide latitude was needed for 'reasonable' differences.[60]

Reasonable Differences

Despite the travails of the IMF loan US–UK relations were viewed by Ramsbotham as close, constructive and workmanlike at all levels and the Cabinet had established good relationships with the new US administration. There were no differences in principle on international issues, just on emphasis and approach and this usually related to economic matters.[61] When Brewster made his first call on the Prime Minister at the end of July, he reported that although he had been a 'silent witness', the new Foreign Secretary, David Owen's recent visit to the US had been 'cheering' and that President Carter held Callaghan in high esteem. A detailed discussion on the most pressing international issues of the day followed and revealed some of the 'reasonable' differences that Brewster had spoken of. On Rhodesia, Callaghan acknowledged that the US could be more helpful in bringing South Africa forward due to the lack of hostility and less important economic ties between the two. He also thought it might be worth toning down the presentational aspect of the US presence in talks, as this created fears among the Patriotic Front of African nations of Western imperialism. Brewster acknowledged that the US position was only a starting point and it must be the UK that was in the driver's seat.[62]

The African issue was again evident when Brewster called on Callaghan in November. The Prime Minister made it clear that, whilst he accepted the United Nations Security Council (UNSC) decision to ban arms sales to South

Africa, Britain could not back economic sanctions due to its trade links with Johannesburg. Brewster told Washington that the British had been unhappy at the lack of consultation on the arms embargo paper which had apparently been shown to the African members before Britain. Vance thereafter contacted Owen to refute this and clear matters up. Relations were also better on the ongoing issue of Belize's independence; the Prime Minister was grateful for American help in attempting to persuade Guatemala to accept the present boundaries.[63] On nuclear weapons and the American position in the second round of Strategic Arms Limitation Talks (SALT II), the British felt the Ambassador could be helpful in relating to them what he had found out in Washington. Brewster duly told the Permanent Secretary of the FCO, Michael Palliser, and later Callaghan, that the US remained keen on Britain keeping its nuclear deterrent and that Carter had instructed Vance to tell Brewster to pass this message on. Brewster backed this decision as he believed that it gave the UK a legitimate, useful voice in American policy formulation.[64] As the months progressed, Carter and Callaghan established a close working relationship. Edward Kennedy volunteered to Ramsbotham that there was no other world leader of whom the President spoke in terms of such warmth and confidence. Carter attached 'exceptional' importance to this partnership.[65]

The Working Embassy

In London, a useful connection was established between Owen and Spiers who had known each other since the late 1960s.

> Much to the consternation of the British Foreign office bureaucracy, the first thing he did when he became Foreign Secretary was to call me to his office; I spent three hours talking to him about a whole host of foreign policy concerns. No one from the Foreign Office was in the meeting.[66]

Spiers also picked up on relationships with Denis Healey, now Chancellor of the Exchequer, and Callaghan. He was on a first name basis with most of the Cabinet. 'My friendships of the 60s stood me in very good stead.' With such good contacts on the British side and a close working partnership, one of the biggest challenges the Embassy actually faced was internal and concerned the level of representation. 'Everybody wanted to be represented in London. It was a constant problem for the Department of State', not least as State Department employees formed the minority of the Embassy staff. Carter was 'aghast' when he visited the UK in March 1977 and was told there was somewhere in the region of 741 employees. And this figure had actually fallen from that of a decade earlier. Some of this number accounted from the closure of consulates, but there were still only 46 Foreign Service officers, an even more surprising figure as this included all of the political, economic, consular and administrative staff. Cold War politics dictated a large CIA liaison detail, albeit 'declared' rather than covert agents. 'Everything was unnecessarily large. Almost every agency of government had representation.' One explanation was that London was an attractive post and thus an obvious place for federal agencies to establish posts. Reducing the presence was essentially an issue of cost control rather than a foreign policy problem. During his tenure, Brewster turned out to be more effective on this issue than his predecessors perhaps because Spiers had impressed on him the need for action. An additional, but less easily remedied, problem was the time and expense taken up with Congressional delegations, the majority of which were not for serious business, 'Most of them were shopping trips.'[67]

Another important role performed by the Embassy was that of political reporting. In May 1978, it was reported that Jack Binns had been promoted to the role of Political Counsellor; Brewster wanted him in charge during the run-up to the general election as Binns had a wide knowledge of British politics.[68] Even local politics proved interesting to policy-makers in Washington as the leftward drift of the Parliamentary Labour Party (PLP) had become a slight concern.

> If it had continued, it might have threatened the British commitment to the alliance, threatened their participation in European affairs and our collaboration in other areas of the world ... What concerned us most was what we called 'entryism' which because of the Labour Party's structure, permitted extreme left wing groups – usually Trotskyites – to enter a constituency party organization and with twenty or thirty people who were willing to dedicate time to the effort, could take over that organization.[69]

Whilst constituency parties were no threat to US interests, if such groups assumed control they could determine Parliamentary candidates. If this was to happen on a wide scale nationally, they could potentially dominate the Parliamentary party.[70] The Embassy's role in domestic British politics was also highlighted a year before when it organised the invitation and scheduling of appointments for leader of the opposition, Margaret Thatcher and Shadow Chancellor, Geoffrey Howe, in Washington.[71]

Emerald Politics

The place of Northern Ireland in the US–UK relationship was one of the issues that Brewster felt he could be most helpful in, building on the efforts of Richardson and Armstrong. Binns informed the FCO that it would be useful if Brewster could discuss the situation with Owen. Vance could then decide which line to take. A definitive US government statement could be an effective way of seeing off a fact-finding mission which had been proposed by a group of American Congressmen. Establishing good relations with the US Embassy on Northern Ireland could do nothing but good. The briefing notes for the Northern Ireland Secretary, Roy Mason's meeting with Brewster in September 1977, emphasised British gratitude towards US law enforcement agencies to counter fundraising efforts and gun smuggling. There had also been sympathetic press reports and editorials in the last two years. Altogether, these efforts had made serious inroads into the effectiveness of the US-based Irish Northern Aid Committee (NORAID). The UK government wanted to discourage proposals towards fact-finding or Congressional missions as this risked alienating Unionists and could make a settlement harder. Thanks were extended to Brewster at their next meeting for President Carter's 'helpful' statement which acknowledged the need for an internal solution; support for both sections of the community and the possibility of additional American investment.[72]

Such sentiments were echoed two years later, although a settlement was still nowhere near. Brewster was commended for having a good understanding of the problems facing the British government, particularly sympathy at the predicament London faced over the State Department's suspension of automatic weapons sales to the Royal Ulster Constabulary (RUC). It was hoped he may try to persuade State to end the ban. The Ambassador acknowledged the ignorance of some American politicians to the situation. Ireland played a different role in the primary campaigns and main presidential elections and due to it being a localised issue it was unlikely to feature in the 1980 campaign, even if Senator Kennedy was a candidate. Furthermore, the administration's position was unlikely to change now. However, a statement by Ian Paisley, the head of the Democratic Unionist Party (DUP), condemning loyalist terrorist actions would be useful for the US. Secondly, prior to the PM's next visit to the US, Brewster wanted to meet as he was sure Ireland would feature to some degree in the talks with the President. It would be helpful for him, and the US government, if the British could arrange more informal preparation at an official level between the Embassy, FCO and Northern Ireland Office.[73]

Mid-term Assessment

After 18 months in London, the British Chancery in Washington enquired as to Brewster's performance. The report described the Ambassador as having worked himself into the job, reading and mastering the briefs supplied, and that he was fully in control of the Embassy. He had engineered several changes in the political section which could be characterised as 'ruthless', but improved effectiveness. Over a range of issues, he was quietly putting the American case across. He had also made a number of first-class speeches, self-drafted, to various bodies. The only criticism was perhaps his keenness as he bothered busy Ministers and the Prime Minister without always having specific issues to discuss. Such '*tour d'horizon* takes up too much time and with little visible result'. The UK Embassy in Washington reported that the key point in the assessment was his relationship with Vance. When in

Washington, he usually stayed at the Vance residence.[74] Where there were disagreements, the Ambassador also had a conciliatory role. In May 1978, Vance conveyed a personal message to Callaghan and Owen via Brewster concerning the US UN Ambassador, Andrew Young's apology for any trouble his remarks about British policy in the Middle East and Africa may have caused them. Young was concerned to ensure this message reached them personally.[75]

At the beginning of 1979, British briefs emphasised that US–UK relations were in reasonable shape as there were closer contacts and to greater effect with the Americans than for some time. Ramsay Meluish, now Head of the North American Department, attributed this to a genuine wish of the Carter team to establish a close working relationship with the government, the British ability to respond swiftly and systematically, and the substantive nature of exchanges. From the FCO's point of view there was little difficulty ensuring the American dimension to all important foreign policy issues was considered. The 'bumpy moments' were a sign of strength and reflected a realistic perception of each other's interests. He nonetheless rejected the phrase, 'special relationship', which implied an offensive exclusivity and could not be taken for granted. The benefits of the connection were obvious to Britain, but also beneficial for the US, relieving the loneliness of being a superpower. Fundamentally, the price was not too high and a similar relationship with, for example, France or Germany, might require concessions. 'Britain's devotion... comes on the cheap.'[76] There was a balanced network of discussions, evidenced by the new US–UK plan on Rhodesia. Where there were differences, such as Belize and the Comprehensive Nuclear Test Ban Treaty (CTB), these were discussed frankly. The Civil Air negotiations demonstrated a 'no holds barred' attitude on both sides, likewise on shipping and anti-trust cases at different ends of the legal spectrum. Nevertheless, on Northern Ireland and Concorde, the administration was sympathetic and helpful.[77] Similar sentiments came from the UK Ambassador in Washington, Peter Jay. Whilst for the US government, Britain was only a 'bit of a bit of the world' and other countries commanded more attention, none were consulted more frequently for a second opinion on a wide range of problems.[78]

One potentially embarrassing development for the Embassy and the British government concerned the London visit in November 1978 of former President Richard Nixon who remained an extremely controversial figure. Any overt or official recognition of Nixon could potentially cause embarrassment in the press (in both countries) and criticism from opposition parties. The FCO advised that, as Nixon was coming as a private visitor, there was no need for any official recognition. The responsibility lay with the US Embassy and British officers to ensure that 'whatever their embarrassment they do not shirk their duties'. Only minimal courtesies should be established. Edward Streator, Spiers' replacement as DCM, was reported as sounding 'somewhat embarrassed throughout the conversation' and agreed to keep in touch. The UK Agriculture Minister, David Silkin, who had agreed to sponsor Nixon for his speech to the British-American Parliamentary Group (BAPG), was later persuaded to merely book the room for the reception and not to attend.[79]

The Iron Lady Cometh

In May 1979 the Conservative Party won the British general election, bringing in Margaret Thatcher, the country's first female Prime Minister. The election received widespread coverage in the US media. Recalling Thatcher, Binns was less enthusiastic. 'Personally, I never liked her. I found her very hard edged, opinionated, not open to reason and argument in my limited contacts with her at dinner parties and social events. But for the embassy it was "business as usual"'.[80] The arrival of a new government had a 'profound effect' in Meluish's opinion. There were now clear signs of divergence between the two allies in several fields. Greater British support for the SALT II verification would likely be sought and a meeting of minds was required on the CTB negotiations. Over the Arab-Israeli question the European position was quite distinct from the US and the European Community's decision to limit oil imports to 1978 levels up to 1985 had caused some consternation. On Southern Africa, despite the American maintenance of sanctions on Rhodesia and withholding of recognition, there might be division in the future and likewise on South Africa. Thus the department must draw attention to issues where there were likely to be disagreements, as a 'working partnership...is fundamental to British foreign policy'.[81]

However, Thatcher's visit to the US in December 1979 brought very positive responses. This had been helped by plenty of goodwill in advance from the press, public and politicians. British support over Iran was the leading topic. This should help Britain get its way with the US administration and reinforce Carter's belief that Britain was its soundest international partner.[82] Thatcher's 'Iron Lady' approach, however, was evident in the issue of US arms sales to the RUC (involving an order for 3,000 Magnum revolvers and 500 Ruger rifles), and she adopted a less diplomatic approach than her predecessor, albeit without any success. Feelings were running high in 1979 following the deaths of the Conservative MP, Airey Neave and Lord Mountbatten from terrorist bombs. The new Prime Minister declared that 'The Americans must be brought to face the consequences of their actions'. The issue was raised during her visit to Washington and Carter approached House Speaker, Tip O'Neill, in an attempt to moderate the stance. O'Neill refused on the grounds that it was inconsistent with American attacks on IRA fundraising and the propaganda would only benefit that organisation.[83]

Nevertheless, after a year in power, Brewster was impressed by the government and the 'new style of strength' displayed in international affairs, not least the 'marvellous zest' of the Foreign Secretary, Peter Carrington. Britain was a 'vital presence' in European, Atlantic and Third World affairs. Moreover, Thatcher's was the first British government, he felt, to confidently assert a positive role in the Third World since the Suez crisis, which had precipitated 'a great source of admiration as well as gratitude on the part of the American people and the US' (this was a reference to the 1979 Lancaster House initiative to deliver majority, representative black rule through the Popular Front to Rhodesia). In contrast to the criticisms of recent years, Brewster acknowledged that Britain's ability to do more than what might be expected from its Gross National Product (GNP) meant a 'great deal'. Furthermore, Britain was the only NATO member who dedicated its entire defence establishment to the alliance, an aspect that should be given special regard. On the question of substantive business being conducted in Washington (rather than through the Embassy), the Ambassador seemed satisfied, adding that he had not been made aware of any wires being crossed. If anything, there were more high level Atlantic meetings and consultations held in Europe than the US. Meanwhile, there were 'extraordinarily good relationships at all levels' in London and the permanent civil service meant a changeover of governments was much easier to accommodate than in the US. The visibility of the opposition parties meant that the new government were well known (the excellent political reporting of the Embassy was no doubt to thank for this also).[84] Hence they were dealing with 'friends not strangers' and this contributed to the strong relationship evidenced.[85]

Such was the changing political climate that this connection would however come to an end with Carter's defeat in the 1980 presidential elections to the Republican candidate, Ronald Reagan. The new President would choose his own representative. Brewster nonetheless was perhaps the most successful appointment of the 1970s. As Binns effusively recalled:

> He was an outstanding Ambassador. He was the best that I served, partly because he had a longer tenure, but also because of his relationship with Cy Vance...They were close personally and Brewster could reach Vance at any time and essentially get anything he wanted out of the State Department. Unless you have witnessed such a relationship, you don't realize how helpful it can be, whether you are talking about resources, policy issues or anything else. Brewster could make things happen.[86]

An illustration of this facility was described by Owen following an occasion when Brewster told him that the US could not supply the British Army with a specialised rifle due to Congressional pressure over Northern Ireland (lest the Army use them there). 'Normally our meetings were full of fun', but Owen refused to accept this decision, 'He was ashamed and I was angry'.

Owen requested a meeting with Vance, yet never heard anything about the subject again and the rifles were delivered. Similarly, this demonstrated the strength of the 'special relationship', which relied on 'actions often taken quickly, informally and in an atmosphere of trust'.[87] Meanwhile, the years in the UK clearly had an effect on Brewster who would return to London in 1984 as the resident partner abroad for a New York law firm before becoming Master of University College, Oxford in 1986.[88]

Conclusion

Bilateral relations and the US Embassy benefited from the stewardship of three highly capable American Ambassadors during 1975–81. Richardson and Armstrong made strong impressions and only the brevity of their tenures prevented them from building more substantial legacies. The post was a prestigious one for Armstrong and Brewster, less so for Richardson because of his political ambitions. Certainly, given the established nexuses of communication and the habit of direct consultation between the President–Prime Minister and Secretary of State–Foreign Secretary, the Ambassadors' function as a conduit of information was perhaps less important than in other foreign postings. The level of influence enjoyed by David Bruce did not return by the end of the decade. Indeed, one of the main aspects of the job appears to have been related to an active social presence and playing host to a wide range of groups and individuals. All three Ambassadors embraced British life during their respective stays and the positive experiences professionally, socially and culturally appeared to make them sympathetic to the nature of the challenges the UK faced in this period. Hence, with issues like Northern Ireland and the economy, they tried to bolster Britain's standing in the US and emphasise constructive solutions; and on certain issues it appears that both Richardson and Brewster were able to amend the outcome of decisions in Washington. Their contacts and friendships, particularly the Vance–Brewster link, could prove invaluable. Although more substantial matters such as the IMF loan, Africa and nuclear collaboration remained the preserve of the Cabinet.

Likewise, despite the conscious adjustments made to involve Richardson more directly than Annenberg, high-level communications carried on uninterrupted, a habit exacerbated until 1977 by Kissinger's method of conducting business directly through the FCO. The inverse importance of the relationship to the UK also meant that the UK Embassy in Washington performed a more substantial role than its London counterpart. However, the domestic strife experienced in Britain during these years and the potential impacts on its international position gave the London Embassy a valuable first-hand role in reporting on the state of affairs. Moreover, with the fluid changeover of parties and leaders on both sides of the Atlantic, the London Embassy contributed to a well-oiled machine which kept day-to-day matters running smoothly through continuity in information and communication.

Notes

1. Harold Wilson, *Final Term: The Labour Government 1974–76* (London: Weidenfeld & Nicholson, 1979), pp. 9–11.
2. UK National Archives (hereinafter TNA), Documents of the Foreign and Commonwealth Office (hereinafter FCO 82/627, US information Services, 'Elliot Richardson biography', 10 January 1975.
3. *The Times* (microfiche collection), 12 and 20 February 1975.
4. *The Times* (microfiche collection), 20 and 25 February 1975.
5. TNA FCO 82/627, Hughes (letter) to Lennox, 3 January 1975; Robin Butler (note), 10 February 1975.
6. TNA FCO 82/627, Ramsbotham (telegram) to Brimelow, 26 February 1975.
7. TNA FCO 82/627, Killick (note), 8 April 1975.
8. The Foreign Affairs Oral History Collection of the Association for Diplomatic Studies and Training (hereinafter FAOHC), Library of Congress, Jack Binns interview, 25 July 1990 (Charles Stewart Kennedy), available at: http://memory.loc. gov/cgi-bin/query/r?ammem/mfdip:@field(DOCID+mfdip2004bin03)   (accessed 29 June 2011).
9. TNA FCO 82 / 627, Killick to Ramsbotham, 22 April 1975.
10. TNA FCO 82 / 627, Ramsbotham (telegram) to Killick; Killick (note) to Lennox, 1 May 1975.
11. TNA FCO 82 / 540, Ramsbotham (telegram) to FCO, November 1975.
12. FAOHC, Elliot Richardson interview, 30 May 1996, (Alan James), available at: http://memory.loc.gov/cgi-bin/query/r?ammem/mfdip:@field(DOCID+mfdip 2004ric03) (accessed 20 August 2010).
13. Richardson (telegram) to Washington, 14 March 1975, available at: http:// aad.archives.gov/aad/createpdf?rid=47399&dt=2476&dl=1345 (accessed 27 June 2011).
14. Richardson (telegram) to Kissinger, 25 June 1975, available at: http://aad.archives. gov/aad/createpdf?rid=106620&dt=2476&dl=1345
15. Richardson (telegram) to Kissinger, 9 July 1975, available at: http://aad.archives. gov/aad/createpdf?rid=122713&dt=2476&dl=1345
16. FAOHC, Richardson interview.
17. US Embassy (telegram) to Kissinger, 'UK Treasury Views on International Monetary Questions and UK Balance of Payments Outlook', 19 May 1975, available at: http://aad.archives.gov/aad/createpdf?rid=92491&dt=2476&dl=1345; Richardson (telegram) to Kissinger, 14 June 1975.
18. *The Times*, 20 May 1975.
19. TNA FCO 82 / 577, Kissinger (telegram) to Callaghan, 9 December 1975.
20. TNA, UK Cabinet Papers, Cabinet Conclusions (hereinafter CAB) 128 / 58 / 1, 15 January 1976, available at: http://filestore.nationalarchives.gov.uk/pdfs/large/ cab-128-58.pdf (accessed 28 June 2011).
21. TNA FCO 82 / 627, P. J. Weston (note), 31 October 1975.
22. FAOHC, Alan James interview (Charles Stewart Kennedy, 20 November 1994), available at: http://memory.loc.gov/cgi-bin/query/r?ammem/mfdip:@field (DOCID+mfdip2004jam01) (accessed 20 August 2010).

23. TNA FCO 82 / 627, PM meeting with Richardson, briefing notes, 8 January 1976.
24. *The Times*, 3 January 1976.
25. Wilson, *Final Term*, pp. 205–7.
26. TNA FCO 82 / 682, Thomas (letter) to Cartledge; Account of Brewster's call on PM, 9 January 1976.
27. *The Times*, 8 January 1975.
28. TNA FCO 82 / 577, Moreton, record of conversation with Spiers, 24 November 1975.
29. TNA FCO 82 / 658, Mason (letter) to Wilson, 22 January 1976.
30. See Henry Kissinger, *The Years of Upheaval* (London: Weidenfeld & Nicholson, 1982), p. 933; *Years of Renewal* (London: Weidenfeld and Nicholson, 1999), pp. 608–9.
31. *Time*, 19 January 1976, available at: http://www.time.com/time/printout/0,8816, 913883,00.html (accessed 15 June 2011).
32. TNA FCO 82 / 682, US Information Service, Anne Armstrong biography, US Embassy, London, 6 January 1976; Cromer (letter) to Palliser, 7 January 1976; *Time*, 19 January 1976, available at: http://www.time.com/time/printout/0,8816, 913883,00.html (accessed 15 June 2011).
33. TNA FCO 82 / 682, Report of exchange of remarks, White House, 19 February 1976.
34. TNA FCO 82 / 683, Ramsbotham (telegram) to Callaghan, 3 March 1976; for Concorde dispute see *Time*, 21 March 1977, available at: http://www.time.com/ time/magazine/article/0,9171,946767,00.html (accessed 28 June 2011); Federal Judicial Centre, http://www.fjc.gov/public/home.nsf/hisj; *The Spokesman Review*, 11 May 1977, available at: http://news.google.com/newspapers?nid=1314&dat= 19770511&id=XvUjAAAAIBAJ&sjid=we0DAAAAIBAJ&pg=6851,5181775 (accessed 17 December 2011).
35. FAOHC, Anne Armstrong interview (Ann Miller Morin), 7 October 1987, available at: http://memory.loc.gov/cgi-bin/query/r?ammem/mfdip:@field(DOCID+mfdip 2004arm01) (accessed 20 August 2010).
36. *Ibid*.
37. *Ibid*.
38. TNA FCO 82 / 682, Thomas (letter) to Cartledge, 6 January 1976.
39. FAOHC, Armstrong interview.
40. *Ibid*.
41. *Ibid*.
42. *The Telegraph*, 31 May 2008, available at: http://www.telegraph.co.uk/news/ obituaries/2481470/Anne-Armstrong.html (accessed 25 June 2011); Armstrong (telegram) to Kissinger, Northern Ireland visit, 6 April 1976, available at: http:// aad.archives.gov/aad/createpdf?rid=50282&dt=2082&dl=1345; Armstrong (telegram) to Hartman, 22 November 1976, available at: http://aad.archives.gov/aad/ createpdf?rid=301489&dt=2082&dl=1345 (accessed 26 June 2011).
43. *The Times*, 20 May and 13 August 1976.
44. *The Times*, 27 September 1976.
45. Armstrong (telegram) to Kissinger, 28 October 1976, available at: http://aad. archives.gov/aad/createpdf?rid=269626&dt=2082&dl=1345 (accessed 28 June 2011).
46. Armstrong (telegram) to Kissinger, 28 October 1976, available at: http://aad. archives.gov/aad/createpdf?rid=269627&dt=2082&dl=1345 (accessed 28 June 2011).

47. FAOHC, Ronald Spiers interview, 11 November 1991 (Thomas Stern), available at: http://memory.loc.gov/cgi-bin/query/r?ammem/mfdip:@field(DOCID+mfdip 2004spi02) (accessed 29 June 2011).
48. James Callaghan, *Time and Chance* (Glasgow: Collins, 1987), pp. 428, 429–30, 431.
49. Callaghan, *Time and Chance*, p. 433.
50. FAOHC, Spiers interview.
51. http://news.bbc.co.uk/1/hi/uk_politics/6212557.stm (accessed 16 June 2011); Callaghan, *Time and Chance*, p. 433; TNA CAB papers, 29 November 1976, http://filestore.nationalarchives.gov.uk/pdfs/small/cab-129-193-cp-76-118-8.pdf; 1 December 1976, http://filestore.nationalarchives.gov.uk/pdfs/small/cab-128-60-cm-76-35.pdf (accessed 20 June 2011).
52. FAOHC, Armstrong interview.
53. *The Telegraph*, 31 July 2008, available at: http://www.telegraph.co.uk/news/obituaries/2481470/Anne-Armstrong.html (accessed 27 June 2011).
54. FAOHC, Spiers interview.
55. Kingman Brewster nomination, 7 April 1977, available at: http://www.presidency.ucsb.edu/ws/index.php?pid=7306#axzz1QcprUBdw; *The New York Times*, 9 November 1988, available at: http://www.nytimes.com/1988/11/09/obituaries/kingman-brewster-jr-69-ex-yale-president-and-us-envoy-dies.html?sec=&spon=&pagewanted=print (accessed 29 June 2011).
56. See Geoffrey Kabaservice, *The Guardians – Kingman Brewster, His Circle, and the Rise of the Liberal Establishment* (New York: Henry Holt & Co., 2004).
57. TNA FCO 82 / 810, Ramsbotham (telegram) to FCO, 7 January 1977.
58. *The Times*, 18 March 1977.
59. *The Times* (Michael Binyon), 22 May 1977.
60. *The Times* (David Spanier), 24 October 1977.
61. TNA FCO 82 / 10, Ramsbotham (telegram) to FCO, 7 January 1977.
62. TNA PREM 16 / 1908, Cartledge (letter) to Ferguson, 28 July 1977.
63. Ibid, note of Brewster's call on Prime Minister, 4 November 1977.
64. Ibid, Ferguson (letter) to Cartledge, 11 November 1977; note for Prime Minister, 17 November 1977; Cartledge (letter) to Ferguson, 18 November 1977.
65. TNA PREM 16 / 1910, Ramsbotham (telegram) to Callaghan, 7 October 1977; Callaghan, *Time and Chance*, pp. 481–3, 485–6, 488.
66. FAOHC, Spiers interview.
67. *Ibid.*
68. TNA FCO 82 / 941, Hughes (letter) to Jarrold, 5 May 1978.
69. FAOHC, Binns, http://memory.loc.gov/cgi-bin/query/r?ammem/mfdip:@field (DOCID+mfdip2004bin03).
70. *Ibid.*
71. TNA FCO 82 / 774, Russell (note), 25 May 1977; Meluish (note), 29 June 1977.
72. TNA, Northern Ireland Office (hereinafter CJ) 4 / 2663, J. A. Marshall (letter) to Mason, 11 July 1977; briefing notes for Secretary of State's meeting with US Ambassador, 14 September 1977; Secretary of State's dinner with US Ambassador, 5 October 1977.
73. *Ibid.*, meeting with US Ambassador, 31 May 1979; Notes for the Secretary's lunch with Brewster, 24 October 1979; Notes of meeting, 24 October 1979.
74. TNA FCP 82 / 941, Meluish, North American Department (note) on Brewster, 13 September 1978; FCO 82 / 569, UK Embassy, Washington (telegram) to Meluish, 4 October 1978.
75. TNA PREM 16 / 1908, Cartledge (letter) to Walden, 5 May 1978.

76. FCO 82 / 978, Meluish, 'Anglo-US Relations', 30 January 1979.
77. *Ibid.*
78. *Ibid.*, Jay (telegram) to Owen, 'How the Americans See Us', 13 February 1979.
79. TNA FCO 82 / 919, Meluish (letter) to Graham, 10 and 16 November 1978; Wall (letter) to Cartledge, 17 November 1978; Meluish (letter) to Cartledge, 20 November 1978.
80. FAOHC, Binns, *op. cit.*
81. TNA FCO 82 / 979, Meluish (letter) to Parsons, 26 June 1979.
82. TNA PREM 19 / 127, Henderson, UK Embassy, Washington, (telegram) to FCO, December 1979.
83. *Daily Mail*, 30 December 2009, available at: http://www.dailymail.co.uk/news/article-1239285/The-30-year-papers-How-Maggie-handbagged-world-just-8-months.html; *IrishCentral*, 3 January 2011, available at: http://www.irishcentral.com/news/President-Carter-wanted-to-lift-arms-sales-ban-to-RUC-112794369.html (accessed 30 June 1979).
84. See Giles Scott Smith, ' "Her Rather Ambitious Washington Program": Margaret Thatcher's International Visitor Program visit to the USA, 1967', *Contemporary British History*, Vol. 17, No. 4 (Winter 2003), pp. 65–86, at pp. 72–3.
85. *The Times* (Connell), 14 July 1980.
86. FAOHC, Binns, *op. cit.*
87. David Owen, *Time to Declare* (London: Michael Joseph, 1991), p. 797.
88. *The New York Times*, 9 November 1988, available at: http://www.nytimes.com/1988/11/09/obituaries/kingman-brewster-jr-69-ex-yale-president-and-us-envoy-dies.html?sec=&spon=&pagewanted=print (accessed 28 June 2011).

Part IV

The Cold War Closers, 1981–2001

Introduction

Alison R. Holmes

It was a 'new day in America' under Ronald Reagan. Jimmy Carter's moral high ground was abandoned for high flown rhetoric in terms of America's approach to both domestic and foreign policy. The new President's straightforward, some would say simplistic, worldview had resoundingly beat Carter's constant and public struggle with the complexities of the changing world. The social and political instability of recent years was being washed away by a heady combination of moral certainty and economic recovery.

In terms of transatlantic relations, the connection between Margaret Thatcher and Ronald Reagan became increasingly close, and arguably rose even beyond the level of that between Churchill and Roosevelt. Certainly, their link stands alone in terms of peace time interactions.[1] The trend noted elsewhere in the rise of face-to-face negotiation between leaders and technological advances, made near constant contact possible between every branch and leaf of governmental bureaucracy which created a mutual internalisation of process. These go a long way to explain what some authors have called the 'habits' of the special relationship.[2]

The three Ambassadors considered in this part again represent a range of options for diplomatic representation. Two were appointed by the same President and all three by the same political party. A key difference here is that at least two of the three did indeed have distinctly close links to the Presidents they served, regardless of their financial contributions – which were, in fact, generally not significant.

The influence of Annenberg alluded to earlier is felt in this grouping, as both Ambassadors Louis and Price (and their wives) were introduced to Ron and Nancy Reagan at an Annenberg New Year's Eve Party, albeit at very different times. Charlie and Carol Price met the Reagans through Walter Annenberg and his wife Leonore, or 'Lee' as she was known. Carol's mother knew the Annenbergs and suggested the two families get together when she knew they would all be in Sun Valley, Idaho at the same time in 1975. Some 6 years later, John Louis and his wife, Jo were introduced to the newly elected President and his wife the January he was to take office. The Catto–Annenberg link is more tangential, but still interesting by way of indication of how small the political world can be. From that same New Year, Annenberg's wife had gone on to be Reagan's White House Chief of Protocol from 1981–82, while Catto had held the position under Presidents Nixon and Ford from 1974–76. The relative weakness of Louis' connection to the President became a matter of concern almost from the outset, and he arguably suffered as a result of his lack of insider credibility. Conversely, Price, a longer-standing member of the Annenberg clique, came to have a very close relationship with the President. His reach was such that he came to frustrate the White House staff who wished to limit Price's influence, even if they were unable to curtail his access.

Louis, coming as he did at the end of a perceived weak projection of American power, suffered not only from his personal lack of charisma, but also from the consequent strength of the embassy machine which had grown into the space left by the lack of a strong ambassadorial presence. Media appearances and speechifying were never Louis' particular forte and he was dubbed 'the invisible man', an epithet that would be used again. In terms of patterns of ambassadorial track record, his experience does beg the question of whether it was possible, then or ever again, to be an effective ambassador without a 'telegenic' personality. Louis was not helped by the fact that his Deputy, Edward Streator, was already a long-term fixture in London, which might equally suggest that it would have taken quite a force of personality to overcome the 'incumbent'. Ronald Reagan's first appointment as Ambassador to London turned out to be one of the few to be listed by the London Embassy as having 'relinquished charge' rather than 'left post'.[3]

It fell to Price to provide that force and he offered it in spades. One of the longer-serving Ambassadors in the time covered here, Price stepped in after the rather mysterious departure of his long-time friend. Price had been appointed as Ambassador to Brussels at the time Louis came to London, thereby gaining invaluable experience, as well as useful contacts with both the NATO and European Union Embassy teams. When he left Brussels, he also, unusually, fought for and won the right to bring some of his senior staff, making his transition that much smoother while also providing a team of trusted advisors. This proved key in a situation that was potentially fraught with internal tension. Raymond Seitz, Price's Deputy Chief of Mission and later Ambassador himself, described Price as a

> big bear of a guy…a big laugh and a big presence…a wonderful guy…not the kind to take shit from anybody…the truth is Charlie could call the President and Charlie would call the President…you could put many a professional and many an officer in that situation and they wouldn't get through the switchboard.[4]

Price was also helped by his apparently instant rapport with Mrs Thatcher. He recalls his first meeting with the Prime Minister and being directed to an upstairs public room in Number Ten. Charles Powell, her advisor, was sitting on the couch, but no Prime Minister. Price was just about to ask, when the curtains of a set of tall windows suddenly parted. Mrs Thatcher popped her head out to explain that she was just 'wrestling with the window', but that he was in 'very friendly hands' and he should sit down, order a drink and make himself at home, which he promptly did – for several years.[5] The Thatchers and the Prices became firm friends beyond the call of public duty and extending well beyond his tenure in London.

The experience of Price also offers an important insight into the simultaneous operating levels of UK–US relations. Given that the relationship between the leaders could hardly have been stronger, it is intriguing to observe that the relationship on the ground was regularly fractious and heated. Protests and anti-American feeling still ran high with marchers in front of the Embassy and a constant vigil at Greenham Common. However, protest was not all that Price had to contend with. He arrived at the time of the Harrods bomb in 1983, was present in Brighton at the time of the bombing of the Conservative Party conference in 1984 when the IRA struck again, and left shortly after the Lockerbie bombing in 1988, thus witnessing the shift in the source of terror as well as in its means and methods. Terror tactics were also changing in other parts of the world that would later come to have a profound effect in London. The 1983 Beirut bombing was a wake-up call in terms of diplomatic security and the Inman Standards – named for Bobby Ray Inman, former Deputy Head of the CIA – would change Embassy protocol and specifications for ever. Inman's report, written in the aftermath of the Beirut incident, came into force under the 1985 Diplomatic Security Act – although Congress continued to refuse to fund much of these recommendations until years later.[6]

Another general theme of ambassadorial media coverage is illustrated in this period through the transition between Louis and Price. It can be generally observed, but particularly in course of this rather awkward shift, that the British media have a distinct tendency to compare Ambassadors, but only to each Ambassador's immediate predecessor. There is little or no attempt to compare similar circumstances, political parties or any other institutional/structural issues, but to jump instead to the most obvious contrasts of personality and presence. While this may have helped some Ambassadors, it is arguably unfair to the point of cruelty to others.

Henry Catto, the final Ambassador of this trio, was a relatively short-term Ambassador, arriving at the point of transition from Reagan to George H. W. Bush. Like Price, Catto could call on long experience of the President and previous diplomatic experience, but could also add to this skill set: experience in the White House, multilateral diplomacy and a long history in the business of information/communication. As such a trusted pair of hands with a broad range of both governmental and professional experience, it was Catto to whom the President turned when there was a mess to sort out back in Washington.

The end of the Cold War is understandably deemed to be a major turning point not only in transatlantic relations, but in international affairs. However, like so many purported turning points, each point of closure of a period or even epoch of time, also contains within it the trends and features of the future. These three Ambassadors are viewed very differently in terms of their success, but they offer a powerful demonstration of the importance of context and structure in relation to what they were able to achieve.

Notes

1. Alison Holmes, 'Ronald Reagan: Conviction Politics and Transatlantic Relations', *Transatlantic Studies Association Journal* (Winter 2010).
2. See David Reynolds, 'A "Special Relationship"? America, Britain and the International Order since the Second World War', *International Affairs*, Vol. 62, No. 1 (1985), pp. 1–10; David Reynolds, 'Re-thinking Anglo-American Relations', *International Affairs*, Vol. 65, No. 1 (1989), pp. 89–111; Alan Dobson, *Anglo-American Relations in the Twentieth Century: Of Friendship, Conflict and the Rise and Decline of Superpowers* (London: Routledge, 1995), p. 149.
3. The Embassy of the United States London UK website: http://london.usembassy.gov/rcambex.html (accessed 30 November 2011).
4. Alison Holmes, interview with Ambassador Charles Price, Beverly Hills, CA, 2008.
5. *Ibid.*
6. See John Mintz, 'Panel Cites US Failures on Security for Embassies', *The Washington Post*, 8 January 1999; Jordon Tama, *Terrorism and National Security Reform: How Commissions Can Drive Change during Crises* (Cambridge: Cambridge University Press, 2011).

11
John J. Louis, Jr, 1981–83

Paul Trickett

> I asked the Ambassador (Louis) if he recalled that when a writer
> for a British publication called *Diplomatist* had asked him what he
> considered the most important quality that a non-career diplomat
> brings to an ambassadorial post, he had replied, 'Ignorance. Fresh
> ignorance.'
>
> *The New Yorker*, 15 March 1982

John J. Louis, Jr formally served as American Ambassador to the United
Kingdom for 844 days, from 27 May 1981 to 19 September 1983. During
that time he was faced with a series of diplomatic incidents that threatened to weaken the relationship between America and Britain, from major
international events such as the Falkland Islands War to trade disputes such
as the collapse of Laker Airways. For many observers on both sides of the
Atlantic, within the British and American government and even inside the
US Embassy in London, Louis failed to present the case for the United States
vigorously and lacked the gravitas and the connections to be taken seriously
within London and Washington. At the same time, he was dismissed by the
British media as 'the invisible man'.[1] This, it is argued, ultimately led to
his unceremonious removal as Ambassador by President Ronald Reagan and
replacement by Charles H. Price II in 1983.[2]

The chapter will examine whether his 'fresh ignorance' was the cause for
his downfall. It will also argue that despite the shortcomings of the Ambassador, the Embassy functioned well in its role as a conduit of information
and an organising hub for the Anglo-American relationship. The chapter
pays particular attention to military, diplomatic, domestic political and economic events that shaped the special relationship from the perspective of
the London Embassy during the John Louis era. It will demonstrate that the
Embassy played an important role in the representation of the United States,
the promotion of friendly relations, lobbying, the clarification of intentions,
political reporting, policy advice and public diplomacy. However, it is first

important to understand Louis' background in order to understand why his appointment could have been considered problematic.

John Louis: Background and Appointment

John J. Louis, Jr was born on 10 June 1925, in Evanston, Illinois. He was a scion of the Johnson's Wax Company[3] as his father had married into the Johnson family.[4] From 1958 to 1961, he was director of international marketing of S.C. Johnson and Son. This made up his entire professional foreign experience before his ambassadorial appointment.[5] His personal wealth was estimated to be in the range of $300 million[6] and he had been a notable contributor to the Republican Party.[7] In 1972, Louis had given $300,000 to Richard Nixon's re-election campaign[8] and as a reward for his contribution, he was appointed Personal Representative of the President at the 12th anniversary of the independence of the Gabon Republic in 1972.[9]

Louis' résumé indicates the central problem for his suitability: his manifest lack of experience in foreign affairs. His colleagues at the Embassy noted this problem, with his Deputy Chief of Mission (DCM), Ed Streator, recognising that his Ambassador was someone with 'little experience with public speaking or international political affairs'.[10] Here was an example of the 'fresh ignorance' that Louis was alluding to in his 1982 *The New Yorker* interview. However, this failing would have been less of an issue if Louis had a strong connection with the President. However, Reagan and Louis were not close, as Secretary of State Alexander Haig observed, 'Reagan himself appointed John J. Louis, who had no diplomatic experience, as ambassador to the Court of St James's while at breakfast in Palm Springs, California, after being introduced to him at the dinner the night before'.[11]

Louis therefore lacked two of the main requisites to be a successful politically appointed Ambassador to the United Kingdom: status/experience and connections. He lacked the public prestige of his immediate predecessor, Kingman Brewster, the former President of Yale University or the influence and connections of Walter Annenberg, Richard Nixon's Ambassador to the United Kingdom, a billionaire philanthropist who advised two generations of Republican politicians and who spent nearly $1 million of his own money restoring Winfield House.[12] In fact, it was Annenberg who was the architect of Louis' appointment as he introduced Louis to Reagan as an ideal candidate to be Brewster's successor.[13] Louis' DCM, Edward Streator, later noted that 'I think that Annenberg met him one day and thought that this guy would make a great Ambassador to the UK. He was tall, distinguished looking and had great bearing and thought that he would be great at it. Walter, unfortunately, didn't take into account the fact that there's more to the job than simply standing there and being "red, white and blue." '[14]

Louis' nomination as Ambassador was formally submitted to the Senate on 3 April 1981 and was confirmed on 5 May 1981 with a vote of 96–0 in favour of the nomination.[15] Louis presented his credentials to Queen Elizabeth II on 28 May 1981, an event commemorated by *The Guardian* newspaper with a photograph entitled 'Polished Smile', a not very subtle reference to his background.[16] The public reaction to Louis in London was lukewarm with *The Times* noting that he was 'far and away the most obscure of the last five American Ambassadors to be sent to the Court of St James's'.[17] British officials were more positive that the appointment would be a success, in part due to hope that the dislike that Mrs Thatcher showed towards Kingman Brewster could be replaced by a better relationship.[18]

John Louis arrived in London at a time of worsening relations between East and West. The Soviet invasion of Afghanistan on Christmas Day 1979 signalled the effective end of détente and the return to a more aggressive anti-Soviet stance on the part of the United States.[19] Ronald Reagan was determined to vigorously oppose the USSR across the world. One of his key allies in this endeavour would be Thatcher but there were concerns in the United States about her chances of electoral survival.[20]

One of the first tasks that faced Louis on his arrival in London was to report on the condition of the Thatcher government and the United Kingdom as a whole. The report provides insight into the thinking in the Embassy towards the host country and the prognosis was not good. Louis' report of July 1981 remains classified, but the covering comments by National Security Advisor Richard V. Allen are indicative of the concerns that Louis and his staff had for the British government, stating that 'Thatcher had lost her grip on the political rudder'.[21] The report highlighted three areas of concern: Thatcher's political vulnerability, the potential for an 'increasingly fragmented' Labour Party to be harmful to the United States' security concerns, and the possibility that political turbulence would have 'an adverse effect on the country's reliability as a US ally'.[22] Louis went on to recommend that a visit by Reagan to the United Kingdom early in 1982 would help to strengthen the resolve of the United Kingdom and the Western Alliance. Allen replied on 17 August 1981, praising the 'very impressive' report and noting that this confirmed that they had the 'right man' in London.[23] The Ambassador's concerns were outlined further in a meeting between President Reagan and Louis in 9 November 1981 when the Ambassador focused on the problems that faced Thatcher domestically, the possible rise of anti-Americanism in the United Kingdom as well as the Middle East and Northern Ireland problems.[24]

The Deployment of Cruise Missiles

David Reynolds notes that traditionally there have been three *specialités* of the special relationship: intelligence, nuclear weapons and diplomatic consultations.[25] However, during the period of 1981–83 there were a number of events in these areas that caused difficulties for the two allies. These included the deployment of cruise missiles to bases within the United Kingdom and the shift in the nuclear strategy of the Atlantic alliance heralded by the Strategic Defence Initiative (SDI). In addition to these nuclear concerns, there were also problems in the UK–US relationship caused by the 1981 Defence White Paper[26] and difficulties within the intelligence community with doubts over security at Government Communications Headquarters (GCHQ) in Cheltenham.[27]

Away from nuclear and intelligence concerns, the Falkland Islands War of 1982 produced strain on the relationship (and had serious consequences for Ambassador Louis). The Grenada Crisis of 1983 introduced further complications for the two countries. However, the purchase of Trident II (D5) was emblematic of the cooperation that still existed between the two nations[28] although their purchase did offer a picture of Britain's strategic dependence on the United States.[29] The vast range of military relationships and events in this period are impossible to cover in detail in this short survey, so it is useful to highlight two cases that are illustrative of the role that the Embassy played in military relations between the two nations: the debate over cruise missiles and the Falkland Islands War.

In 1979 the Labour government had agreed to the deployment of intermediate-range cruise missiles as part of the NATO force modernisation programme.[30] The prospect of the arrival of the missiles at Greenham Common and Molesworth bases prompted fears of a 'limited' nuclear war in Europe and triggered the revival in the fortunes of the Campaign for Nuclear Disarmament.[31] Louis addressed the issue of the newly invigorated anti-nuclear movement in a speech to the European Atlantic Group in October 1981 where he condemned the 'wishful thinkers' of the nuclear disarmament movement who would force the alliance to 'lay down our arms and rely on the good will of the Soviets for our defence'.[32] However, Louis, during his visit to Washington in November, told officials that a greater sensitivity to British and European attitudes was needed and that the peace movement in Britain was rapidly gaining strength. He also urged that consultations with the British be improved and that more spokesmen for the Reagan administration visit Britain to state their case.[33]

Vice President Bush was sent to tour Europe in order to defend the deployment.[34] Edward Streator recalls the discussions that surrounding Bush's visit to London:

> I called my guys together and said 'we have to sell the missile deployment.' We've got a terrible problem with anti-nuclear protestors and we have a section of the country that is deeply unhappy with the deployment of Cruise ... After a great deal of discussion, we decided that the best thing we could do was to get the VP to make a speech at the Guildhall – a major address that would be covered by TV and radio.[35]

Bush's speech was judged a public relations success.[36] However, the deployment remained unpopular with many as a *Daily Telegraph* poll showed that

54 per cent of Britons were against the planned deployment of the missiles, although two out of three rejected unilateral disarmament, a problem that dogged the Labour Party in the 1983 general election.[37] The nature of the opposition to nuclear weapons in the UK caused serious concerns for security of the delivery of the missiles, so the Embassy acted as the coordinating centre for the various groups involved in the operation. Roger Harrison, the Deputy Political Counsellor, recalls that 'I suggested that we form a committee because we had all these different people involved. One of them was EUCOM (the European command) the military side who was in charge of that (the deployment). We had the FCO (Foreign Commonwealth Office) and the MOD (Ministry of Defence) and, of course, the embassy and the State Department'.[38] The Embassy therefore acted in a public and private capacity during the controversy; as facilitating agent in the deployment, advisor and organiser of public lobbying.

The Falkland Islands War

The Falkland Islands War between Britain and Argentina threatened to create a rift between London and Washington. Following the Argentine invasion of the Islands, the United States opted to remain diplomatically neutral, infuriating the British government.[39] This was due to the dilemma faced by the White House of having to choose between two allies: Britain, key member of NATO, or Argentina, a new partner in the war against communism in Central America.[40] As Lawrence Kaplan noted, 'here was a clear cut case of an old tradition confronting a new one'.[41] The administration's divided attitude towards the conflict was personified by Secretary of State Alexander Haig (who publically advocated US neutrality in the conflict) and Secretary of Defence Caspar Weinberger (who privately argued for the abandonment of neutrality and open support for the British).

On 30 March 1982, DCM Edward Streator was summoned to meet an irate Foreign Secretary, Lord Carrington, who had just received Alexander Haig's message regarding US neutrality.[42] Carrington told Streator that the UK government had supported American policy over Sinai and El Salvador without great enthusiasm, but out of a sense of solidarity to its ally. Now London expected support in return.[43] Streator felt that the attempts at equity on the part of the United States would be seen as hostility by the British.[44] It was Streator who faced Carrington because Louis was vacationing in Florida and did not return to London for a week and a half after the start of the crisis.[45]

Alexander Haig then embarked upon a bout of shuttle diplomacy designed to broker a peace deal.[46] Haig and his negotiating team arrived in London on 8 April[47] and were greeted by Ed Streator.[48] Before the first meeting with Mrs Thatcher, Streator advised Haig on the political situation in London, warning him that an agreement would be very difficult to reach.[49] As Haig later recalled, Streator told him that 'Britain was in a bellicose mood, more high-strung and unpredictable than we had ever known it'.[50] However,

Streator first had to ask Haig whether the Americans would ultimately support the British, to which Haig replied that they would.[51] As Streator later noted, the Embassy had no inkling that the official line was generally going to be favourable to the British.[52]

The shuttle diplomacy continued throughout April. The Embassy was heavily involved in these diplomatic efforts as Political Officer Edward Lanpher recalled that he was 'taken off the Africa beat and everybody in the embassy on the political side devoted just about full time to the Falklands War'.[53] The Embassy also played a role in intelligence dissemination during the conflict. At the start of the conflict, and as a response to a request from the Director of the Secret Intelligence Service (SIS) Sir Colin Figures, CIA Chief of Station at the Embassy Alan D. Wolfe presented a detailed briefing for the Joint Intelligence Committee about the current condition of Argentine armed forces.[54] Crucially for the British, Secretary for Defence Caspar Weinberger paid little attention to the official line regarding neutrality and was determined to support the British by supplying materiel.[55] Haig's efforts at maintaining neutrality and negotiating a peaceful resolution to the conflict were doomed and on 30 April, Reagan formally declared US support for the United Kingdom.[56]

The Falklands conflict reveals some of the strengths of the US Embassy in London. Streator became recognised as a reliable source of information for Fleet Street editors during the conflict, with early morning off-the-record briefings becoming a regular occurrence for the DCM in the first stages of the crisis. Streator dryly noted afterwards that 'after a few days I felt like I was writing the editorials for *The Times*'.[57] In sum, the events surrounding Cruise deployment, SDI and the Falklands conflict, demonstrate similar aspects of the London Embassy: an organising hub and a conduit for information and advice.

Economic Issues: The Siberian Pipeline Crisis

The most serious rift between the Thatcher and Reagan governments over economic issues was triggered by an international political crisis – the imposition of martial law in Poland.[58] At the heart of the problem was the question of what could be done about the Siberian gas pipeline, a vast project being constructed by a Western firm in the Soviet Union with the objective of supplying natural gas to Western Europe. The Americans wanted to halt the project altogether, or at least significantly scale it down, denying the Soviets foreign currency and reducing Europe's dependence on Soviet energy and trade.[59] On 29 December 1981, Reagan imposed a raft of sanctions against companies involved in the construction of the project while the European allies were given five hours' notification of the announcement.[60]

The British feared redundancies at the companies involved, most notably Rolls Royce, who had a contract to supply compressors for the project, and

John Brown Engineering, who would produce turbines for the pipeline.[61] The Embassy staff recognised that this was potentially the most serious rift in US–UK relations for many years and affected the US Embassy as it struggled to cope with the crisis.[62] Energy Attaché Tim Deal had the misfortune of having to inform the Chairman of John Brown about the sanctions[63] and was further entrusted by the Ambassador to run the press briefings designed to explain the rationale for the US policy to a hostile media.[64] Ultimately, the dispute was resolved by the new Secretary of State, George Shultz, who devised a compromise by which the existing pipeline contracts could be honoured.[65] Throughout the crisis, the Embassy played a role as a channel of communications, attempting to justify the American position and liaising with British industry.

The Collapse of Laker Airlines and the Issue of Extraterritoriality

The Embassy played a similar role in the other major economic dispute between the US and Britain during Louis' tenure: the fallout from the collapse of Laker Airways. The cut-price airline collapsed owing nearly $350 million.[66] However, there were allegations that there was a conspiracy of price-fixing by several other airline companies who colluded to undermine Laker Airways.[67] This caused consternation in the British government because one of the companies named was British Airways (BA).[68] As Michael Calingaert, the Minister for Economic Affairs at the Embassy, recalls, the British were unhappy for two reasons: first, the alleged action by BA was legal under British law, but the meeting took place in the US, and secondly, BA was about to be privatised and the threat of a damaging law suit in the United States would have lowered the share price.[69] The alleged conspiracy involved a meeting among airline officials who reached agreement to tell Boeing and Airbus, the principal aircraft suppliers, that if they continued to provide generous leasing arrangements to Laker, then the carriers would not buy aircraft from them any longer.[70]

The British government's complaints were rebuffed by the Embassy who apologised, but argued that it was a matter for the US courts and 'the Embassy could not tell them what to do'.[71] The Justice Department launched a criminal antitrust investigation into the accusations of price-fixing in March 1983.[72] The London Embassy needed to be informed about developments in the investigation which included hearings before a Grand Jury. Deal recalled the problems that arose: 'the judge in the case would not allow the transmission of information to the Embassy through normal State Department channels because too many people would have access to grand jury information so there was a special arrangement whereby a designated person in the European Bureau at State would pass on the information to me personally'.[73]

In both cases, the Siberian pipeline and the Laker antitrust lawsuit, the issue of extraterritoriality was the cause of friction between the two governments. John Louis touched upon this at a speech to the London Chamber of Commerce in July 1983, entitled 'US–UK Economic Relations: Conflict or Cooperation'. In the address, Louis recommended that talks with high level officials from both sides take place in order to find a framework to resolve the extraterritoriality disputes. Reporting to Washington after the speech, Louis noted that the FCO were in broad agreement with the sentiments of his address and were suggesting the possibility of an 'extraterritoriality hotline' that could be used to avoid future damaging trade conflicts.[74] A briefing document prepared by the Embassy at the time helps to illustrate the other economic concerns that they felt were important to the British government at that point: the inflationary impact of the US budget deficit, the common UK–US position on the reform of the Common Agricultural Policy and the issue of unitary taxation.[75] Thus it can be demonstrated in the economic sphere that the Embassy played a wide range of roles – clarifying intentions, representing the position of the US government, lobbying, policy advice and information gathering and reporting on developments between the two nations.

The London Embassy and British Domestic Politics: Northern Ireland

The vexed matter of Northern Ireland and the difficult relationship with the Labour Party were two of the major domestic UK issues that confronted the London Embassy during the Louis tenure at Grosvenor Square. The Ulster question was described by one senior US diplomat at the time as 'a pain in the butt' which presented considerable problems for the Anglo-American relationship.[76] The relationship between the London Embassy and the Labour Party was strained for much of the 1980s, especially after the arrival of Louis' successor, Charles Price in 1983.

The main American initiative towards Northern Ireland was designed to promote the cause of constitutional nationalism and lessen the flow of financial support for the Irish Republican Army (IRA).[77] This policy had been spearheaded since 1976 by a group of prominent Irish-American politicians who were dubbed 'the four horsemen': Senator Edward Kennedy, House of Representatives Speaker 'Tip' O'Neill, Senator Daniel Patrick Moynihan and Governor of New York, Hugh Carey.[78] The IRA hunger strikes of 1981 worsened the situation in Northern Ireland, causing an upsurge in sectarian violence and intensifying anti-British feeling in the United States amongst the Irish ex-patriot community. However, as Dumbrell notes, Reagan was reluctant to intercede in the matter for fear of offending an important ally by meddling in the internal affairs of another sovereign nation.[79] The view was echoed by the diplomats in London who viewed the Maze Prison hunger strikes as 'a domestic British matter' in which they did not intercede.[80] Louis recommended to Reagan that the best policy was to try to maintain this posture.[81] This is not to say that the Embassy were inactive on the Northern Ireland issue at the time – they acted as information gatherers, advisors, facilitators for potential economic incentives for the province and a neutral ground for the opposing factions in Ulster itself.

John Louis made few public statements on the situation in Northern Ireland, but he did visit Belfast in October 1981 on what the US Consulate described as a 'routine familiarisation visit'. There Louis met with leaders of the four main local political parties with little practical effect beyond demonstrating his willingness to support the efforts of 'the four horsemen'.[82] Ed Streator also visited the Province, meeting the Secretary of State for Northern Ireland, Humphrey Atkins at Stormont. As he recalls, 'I was there to find out what the two sides thought and to try to urge restraint...we had a series of officials at the consulate in Belfast whose job it was to keep us at the embassy and the Department appraised of the developments'.[83] Indeed, the US Consulate-General's house in Belfast acted as a 'neutral ground' for the various political factions where they could meet informally.[84] The London Embassy also acted as an organising point for the American attempts to find initiatives to provide economic incentives to aid the peace process.[85] Streator also acted as an advisor for members of the visiting 'four horsemen' group, such as Senator Moynihan, on the attitude in London regarding the Northern Ireland question.[86] However, the pace of the peacemaking initiatives was 'glacial'.[87]

The Labour Party

Two political officers maintained a close focus upon the Labour Party during the Louis era: Richard Melton and Robert Hopper. Their task was to develop contacts within a Labour Party riven by ideological civil war and deepening public unpopularity. A large portion of the Labour Party viewed the United States with great suspicion and, by extension, distrusted the Embassy. Melton's strategy was to develop relations with individual members of Parliament: 'I would see them privately; I would attend Labour Party conventions...[d]uring my tour, I think I had contact with almost every Labour MP and established personal relationships with many'.[88] Melton also attempted to introduce MPs to visiting Congressmen and other officials at the Embassy.

His successor, Robert Hopper, recognised that despite being at the zenith of her popularity (post Falklands War), Margaret Thatcher and the Conservatives would not be in Downing Street forever.[89] At some point the Labour Party would return to power: 'I concluded that my job should be to help identify moderate up-and-coming Labour people, put them in touch with the US political scene...it didn't have to be done right away; there was plenty of time and that this could be a long-term project'.[90] This quiet plan would develop throughout the rest of the 1980s despite some very public disagreements between the next Ambassador and the Labour Party. The Deputy Political Counsellor, Roger Harrison, also maintained an interest in the Labour Party. His focus was upon NATO matters, but he also wished to understand the nature of the opposition to the deployment of cruise missiles.[91]

Streator's formidable array of contacts also meant that the Embassy was kept in the loop regarding the developments at the higher level of the Labour Party. He invited Denis Healey, the deputy leader of the Labour Party, to lunch at which he asked Healey for his thoughts on the in-fighting within the Labour Party and the possible identity of the successor to Michael Foot as leader. Healey answered that it would be Neil Kinnock, a rising young Welsh politician, 'red haired with a radical wife', but himself relatively moderate in the terms of the Labour Party.[92]

Cultural and Education Programmes

The London Embassy also maintained a cultural diplomacy programme. The Public Affairs Officer (United States Information Service), Philip W. Arnold, headed a team that also featured Cultural Attaché, Christopher Snow.[93] The USIS team at the Embassy were responsible for administering the International Visitor Programme (IVP), which was an exchange programme designed 'to set up contacts, transfer ideas and establish long-running relations on an informal, but often fruitful basis' between US citizens and their counterparts in the rest of the world.[94] In 1981 this programme became increasingly politicised as it became part of the drive to make the USIS more assertive in opposing communist propaganda. It was also recognition of the fact that the United States was losing the battle for the sympathy of Europe's younger generation. Snow noted that part of the reason for this was the gradual dying out of the political generation on both sides of the Atlantic whose connections had been forged by war.[95] The funding of the programme was greatly increased and the number of IVP grants increased from 28 in 1981 to 68 in 1986 with the ultimate intention to identify future leaders and opinion formers in order to influence their attitude to the United States.[96]

The Public Diplomacy of John J. Louis, Jr

G. R. Berridge comments that 'representation, that often overlooked or naively minimised function of diplomacy, is chiefly concerned with prestige and is in certain instances impossible to distinguish from propaganda ... it embraces entertaining, giving public lectures, appearing on television and radio shows, and attendance at state ceremonial events'.[97] With regards to this definition of representation Louis was at a considerable disadvantage in one particular aspect in the public dimension of his job. He was not a comfortable public speaker, something that the staff at the Embassy soon realised. As Ed Streator notes, 'public diplomacy – by which I take to mean public speaking and appearances in the media – was anathema to John Louis. He could not operate without a script'.[98] The Embassy's Commercial Officer, Lange Schermerhorn, recalled Louis' public speaking performances: 'the moment came after dinner to get up and do the toasts and it was so painful; it became immediately clear that he [Louis] was not accustomed to public speaking and he found it extremely painful to do this…and at successive occasions afterwards it became more painful each time'.[99] This limited Louis' effectiveness on the public stage and meant that he made little impact on the national media as he was kept away from television appearances and made only fleeting appearances in the print media.[100]

An examination of *The Guardian* newspaper archives reveals that Louis is referred to on 17 occasions between 1 March 1981 (when the possibility of his appointment was first mentioned) to 16 September 1983 (when the news of his resignation appeared in the press). Taking out the stories relating to his arrival and departure, Louis makes eight appearances in the newspaper, in stories ranging from anti-nuclear protestors, the IRA, US–UK trade disputes, the royal wedding of 1981 and the Falklands. A crude sample, but it does illustrate the problems that the Embassy faced with Louis in the national media. His staff acknowledged that he was not a public figure – he did not do any television interviews of any substance during his time in London and while he did some speech-making around the country, these events were tightly controlled and the speeches were written for him.[101] The *Daily Mail* gossip columnist Nigel Dempster reported that Louis was so totally 'lacking in impact' that he was being called 'the invisible man' in London political circles.[102]

However, this does not tell the whole story of Ambassador Louis, public diplomacy and his role in promoting friendly relations between the UK and US. He undertook a wide range of public visits that included attending the Miner's Gala in Durham, visiting the Edinburgh Festival, Glasgow, the Shetlands and a North Sea oil platform. Louis' lack of confidence at public occasions can be demonstrated by his recollection of his appearance at the Miner's Gala in Durham where he was requested to sing. The Embassy found the Ambassador an appropriate song – written during a 1931 Strike in Kentucky and featuring a scathing attack on management. He recalled that 'I stood with great trepidation and I had a piano to help me, I got the miners to sing the chorus with me. I got a standing ovation. It went fine but I would not like to do it again.'[103]

Alongside his public engagements Louis diligently hosted a number of social events at the Embassy. Peter Osnos described a typical week for the Ambassador:

> In one typical week, they were busy every night including Sunday (dinner for visiting USIA director Charles Z. Wick), attending, among other

things, an American Airlines dinner, a Pilgrims Society dinner and a dinner for the American Banks Association in London. Recently, they had 50 people in for Prince Charles and Princess Diana, among them Julie Nixon and David Eisenhower, who flew over for the event. The queen came last month to meet a table full of top American businessmen.[104]

Louis' interview with John Bainbridge in *The New Yorker* reveals details of the scope of his contacts: over three luncheons at Winfield House, he hosted David Steel, the leader of the Liberal Party, the Home Secretary Willie Whitelaw and the editor of the *Financial Times*. He comments that these luncheons were very small, 'just myself, my guest, my DCM. The luncheons are very productive things, and the ambience here is much better than at the Embassy, I think'.[105]

The problem for Louis was that this was a form of diplomatic representation of an older age. It was certainly important to cultivate good relations in a social setting but of a greater importance, in a media-dominated world, was to be seen on television putting forward the American point of view. Assertive public diplomacy of this sort was a task that Louis found very difficult to perform and it became one of the main reasons for his recall as Ambassador in September 1983. In essence, Louis acted as a well-protected figurehead in the public diplomacy sphere, reliant on his DCM, Ed Streator. Roger Harrison recalled that Streator became known as the power 'not even behind the throne, kind of in front of the throne...because Louis was dependent entirely on Streator, Streator emerged as de facto ambassador for all substantive purposes'.[106]

Conclusion

The news of Louis' recall as Ambassador came as a surprise in London. The reasons for his removal can be broken down into four main areas: his failure to return at the start of the Falklands War; his lack of impact in public diplomacy; the desire of the Thatcher government to see a better connected Ambassador and, lastly, the presence of a readymade replacement in Charles H. Price II, the Ambassador to Belgium.

His absence at the start of the Falkland Islands War was seen by many as the chief contributing factor to his dismissal.[107] It was not the fact that he was on vacation when the conflict broke out that was seen as the problem – that was merely viewed as unfortunate timing. The reason for the controversy was that he took over a week to return from holiday in Florida. The Ambassador returned to take part in the second round of negotiations between Haig and Thatcher on 12 April. However, he was largely side-lined and was even a figure of derision within the Haig team. Haig team member, James Rentschler, recalled in his diary: 'Louis [was] hanging around this location with absolutely nothing to do, and looking rather pathetic doing it – a fate which some in Haig's party consider richly deserved since this Chief of Mission could not be bothered to interrupt his Florida vacation when the Falklands crisis first broke'.[108]

In his defence, Louis described himself as getting 'bad advice' about when he should return to London. 'I was told to get ready to come to Washington to join Secretary of State Haig when he goes to London. I was called the day he was to leave and told to get on the plane to Washington. I packed my bags, was about ready to get in a taxi to go out to the airport when I got a call saying, "Haig has left. If you come by commercial, you'll be chasing him all the way to Buenos Aires. Stay where you are" '.[109]

Compounding the problem of his absence was *The New Yorker* interview published in March 1982.[110] This article appeared concurrently with Louis' absence and painted a picture of an Ambassador who was more interested in social activities than the day-to-day grind of diplomatic activity. It was also an unfortunately prescient comment from Louis stating that the worst thing to do as an Ambassador was to take a holiday.[111] This article was seized upon by his critics and can be seen as indicative of the bad fortune that contributed to his fall.[112]

The initial Nigel Dempster article placed much of the blame for Louis' removal on the British government. They were partly influenced by Louis' performance during the Falklands, but also believed that they needed a more professional American Ambassador with better connections to the White House. The State Department was also viewed as partly responsible for Louis' downfall. They believed that the upcoming deployment of cruise missiles and the debate over nuclear disarmament and East–West relations needed a more vocal advocate on the American side. Louis' brand of laid-back diplomacy was not appropriate for waging a public relations war on behalf of the United States.[113]

The issue of his replacement also undermined Louis. The US Ambassador to Belgium, Charles Price, was perfectly positioned to take over from Louis. He was a long-time friend of Reagan, thus ensuring a more direct line to the White House for the British. His performance in Belgium had demonstrated that while he was another political appointment, he was much more aware of the key issues of international diplomacy and especially East–West relations. The personal dimension was also influential in that Price's wife, Carol, was a close personal friend of Nancy Reagan. This was seen by some in the Embassy as relevant to Price getting the post in London.

The result of all these factors was a perfect storm that undermined Louis and led to his removal. Ultimately, he paid the price for his low profile and lack of suitability for the task for which he had been appointed. *The Telegraph* commiserated with him that his removal was the inevitable outcome of the American practice of appointing non-professional diplomats as Ambassadors.[114] Louis himself indicated that he was not in agreement with the decision: 'Not surprisingly, my wife, my family and I are disappointed and saddened at the prospect of leaving Britain.'[115] Geoffrey Hodgson later observed that Louis was 'dignified and quiet, he was more of a traditional business conservative than an ideologue of the Reagan revolution'.[116]

It is easy to view Louis' tenure as a failure. His removal is indicative of the fact that the American government saw him as a weak link that needed to be removed. His connection to the levers of power was tenuous – he had little personal connection to Ronald Reagan to fall back upon. Streator notes that Louis did not have a 'standing' within the State Department – 'most people accepted that he was the ambassador to the UK, but few people at State actually knew him beyond those few he came through as visitors'.[117] He became enamoured of what some in the Embassy dismissed as 'the useless class', the aristocracy,[118] and he enjoyed socialising with them at weekends and going shooting.[119]

Despite these issues, much of note was achieved at the London Embassy during his residence, successfully fulfilling many of the roles traditionally expected of such a post. As has been demonstrated in the case studies of the extraterritoriality disputes over the Siberian pipeline and the Laker Airways anti-trust case, the Embassy acted as a lobbying entity that clarified and reported on the interests of the British government. With the deployment of cruise missiles, the Embassy contributed to the coordination of the planned roll-out of the weapons as well as playing an active role in the public diplomacy surrounding the anti-nuclear debate. In terms of political reporting and information gathering within the United Kingdom, the Embassy staff cultivated contacts in the media and the political class on issues such as the Labour Party and Northern Ireland. One positive consequence of Louis' enthusiasm for social events was that the Embassy 'provided an important meeting place, a chance for others in the embassy to meet with all kinds of people and talk... [a]s a result, the United States has the best plugged-in embassy in London'.[120] A benefit of Louis' reduced public profile was that he did not get involved in any public controversies while he was in London. He did not embarrass the United States, but he was fatally out of step with the tenor of the Reagan administration by the mid-1980s. In a quieter, less ideologically charged environment, Louis could have been a success as Ambassador, but he failed to represent 'the new activist right' in the Reagan administration.

There was one final indignity left for John Louis to suffer. On 24 October 1983, he was the guest at a farewell dinner given in his honour by Princess Alexandria where Mrs Thatcher was also in attendance.[121] The British had been informed several days earlier of the possibility of American intervention in the small Caribbean island of Grenada.[122] On the evening of Louis' farewell dinner the situation changed as the Americans launched Operation *Urgent Fury* without any consultation with the British. Thatcher was informed of the invasion at the dinner and she 'turned to Louis and said: "Do you know what is happening in Grenada? Something is going on." He knew nothing about it'.[123] Even at the end, he was undermined by his 'fresh ignorance'.[124]

Acknowledgements

The author would like to thank Edward Streator, Michael Calingaert, Penelope Dew, Roger Harrison, John Hervey and Andrew Riley for their help and offers of assistance in the writing of this chapter.

Notes

1. *The Associated Press,* 'US Ambassador to Britain Quitting Post', 14 September 1983.
2. P. Osnos, 'US Ambassador to Great Britain Is to Be Replaced', *The Washington Post*, 15 September 1983, p. A32.
3. Telephone interview with Edward Streator, 25 May 2011.
4. Ambassador Roger G. Harrison, interviewed by Charles Stuart Kennedy, 30 November 2001, The Association for Diplomatic Studies and Training Foreign Affairs Oral History Project, available at: http://memory.loc.gov/cgi-bin/query/r?ammem/mfdip:@field(DOCID+mfdip2010har01) (accessed 20 May 2011).
5. J. Bainbridge, 'New Man at Court', *The New Yorker*, 15 March 1982, p. 115.
6. Streator interview, 25 May 2011.
7. A. Brummer, 'Reagan Picks Executive as London Ambassador', *The Guardian*, 28 March 1981, p. 6.
8. D. Blum, 'After Years of Checkbook Politics, Choice for British Envoy Gets Wish', *The Wall Street Journal*, 21 April 1981.
9. Ronald Reagan, 'Nomination of John J. Louis, Jr., To Be United States Ambassador to the United Kingdom', 2 March 1981, available at: http://www.presidency.ucsb.edu/ws/?pid=43599 (accessed 18 May 2011). This was a relatively minor diplomatic function, so minor that Louis and Bainbridge did not mention it in the wide ranging *New Yorker* article of 15 March 1982 ('New Man at Court').
10. Streator interview, 25 May 2011.
11. A. Haig, *Caveat: Realism, Reagan and Foreign Policy* (New York: Macmillan, 1984), p. 68.
12. R. Davis and A. Bernstein, 'Hostess, Arts Patron Leonore Annenberg, 91, Aided Late Husband in Philanthropy', *The Washington Post*, 13 March 2009.
13. Telephone interview with Michael Calingaert, 12 June 2011.
14. Streator interview, 25 May 2011.
15. J. Adams, 'Logjam Breaks on Foreign Policy Nominees', *The Associated Press*, 5 May 1981.
16. 'Polished Smiles', *The Guardian*, 28 May 1981.
17. D. Cross, 'Shining Welcome for Reagan Man', *The London Times*, 15 May 1981.
18. Streator interview, 25 May 2011.
19. J. Dumbrell, *A Special Relationship: Anglo-American Relations in the Cold War and After* (Basingstoke: Palgrave Macmillan, 2001), p. 80.
20. R. Allen, 'Memo for President Reagan – Britain Drifts', 1981, Reagan Library (NSC Country File Box 91326), available at: http://www.margaretthatcher.org/document/56BE025F382E4911A99A24759251B3AC.pdf (accessed 3 May 2011).

21. *Ibid.*, p. 2.
22. *Ibid.*
23. *Ibid.*, p. 3.
24. J. Rentschler, 'Memorandum for Richard V Allen: President's meeting with John Louis', 1981, Reagan Library (NSC Country File Box 91326), available at: http://www.margaretthatcher.org/document/03DF378BD14C40BD9E1CD6E93652 C8EC.pdf (accessed 3 May 2011).
25. D. Reynolds, 'A "Special Relationship"? America, Britain and the International Order since the Second World War', *International Affairs*, Vol. 62, No. 1 (1985), p. 10.
26. Interview with Rear-Admiral John Hervey, London, 6 August 1997. Hervey was the British Naval Attaché in Washington in 1981.
27. J. Baylis, *Anglo-American Defence Relations, 1939–1984* (Basingstoke: Macmillan, 1984), p. 191.
28. J. Nott, *Here Today Gone Tomorrow: Recollections of an Errant Politician* (London: Politico's Publishing, 2002), pp. 216–17.
29. Baylis, *Anglo-American Defence Relations*, p. 187.
30. Dumbrell, *A Special Relationship*, p. 129.
31. *Ibid.*, p. 130.
32. P. Keatley, 'US Envoys Attacks Disarmers', *The Guardian*, 30 October 1981, p. 6.
33. R. W. Apple, 'US Nuclear Rift Disturbs London', *The New York Times*, 7 November 1981, p. 1.
34. D. Willis, 'The Women Who Worry Mrs Thatcher', *Christian Science Monitor*, 20 January 1983, p. 12.
35. Streator interview, 25 May 2011.
36. W. D. Nelson, 'Bush: "I think we did some good" ', *The Associated Press*, 10 February 1983.
37. J. Jones, *United Press International*, 10 February 1983.
38. Harrison interview, 30 November 2001.
39. M. Thatcher, *The Downing Street Years* (London: Harper Collins, 1993), p. 188.
40. N. Henderson, *Mandarin* (London: Weidenfeld & Nicolson, 1994), p. 448.
41. L. Kaplan, *NATO Divided, NATO United: The Evolution of the Alliance* (Westport, CT: Praeger, 2004), p. 90.
42. Lord Franks, *Falkland Islands Review* (London: HMSO, 1983), p. 63.
43. L. Freedman, *The Official History of the Falklands Campaign I: The Origins of the Falklands War* (London: Routledge, 2005), p. 191.
44. Ronald Reagan Oral History Project (2005) *Falklands Roundtable*, p. 17, available at: http://www.ccbh.ac.uk/downloads/falklands.pdf (accessed 27 April 2011).
45. P. Osnos, 'At Least our New Envoy to Britain Gives Good Parties', *The Washington Post*, 2 January 1983, p. B1.
46. Haig, *Caveat*, p. 272.
47. M. Hastings and S. Jenkins, *The Battle for the Falklands* (London: Michael Joseph, 1983), p. 385.
48. Haig, *Caveat*, p. 272.
49. Streator interview, 25 May 2011.
50. Haig, *Caveat*, p. 273.
51. Streator interview, 25 May 2011.
52. Ronald Reagan Oral History Project, *Falklands Roundtable*, p. 18.
53. Edward Lanpher, interviewed by Charles Stuart Kennedy, 25 June 2002, The Association for Diplomatic Studies and Training Foreign Affairs Oral History

Project, available at: http://memory.loc.gov/cgi-bin/query/r?ammem/mfdip:@field(DOCID+mfdip2004lan06) (accessed 18 May 2011).

54. N. West, *The Secret War for the Falklands* (London: Little, Brown, 1997), p. 48.
55. L. Freedman, *The Official History of the Falklands Campaign II: War and Diplomacy* (London: Routledge, 2005), p. 383.
56. Hastings and Jenkins, *The Battle for the Falklands*, p. 386.
57. Ronald Reagan Oral History Project, *Falklands Roundtable*, p. 18.
58. Dumbrell, *A Special Relationship*, p. 92.
59. Margaret Thatcher Foundation, 'The Polish Crisis of 1981–2', available at: http://www.margaretthatcher.org/archive/us-reagan%20(Poland).asp (accessed 19 May 2011).
60. Haig, *Caveat*, p. 254.
61. R. Allen, 'President's Notes for NSC Briefing on Siberian Pipeline', Reagan Library (NSC Meetings Box 91282), 9 July1981, available at: http://www.margaretthatcher.org/document/43FDB5BC3BC64DF6AFCF726C293A6300.pdf (accessed 29 May 2011).
62. Timothy Deal, interviewed by Raymond Ewing, 8 November 2004, The Association for Diplomatic Studies and Training Foreign Affairs Oral History Project, available at: http://memory.loc.gov/cgi-bin/query/r?ammem/mfdip:@field(DOCID+mfdip2007dea01) (accessed 25 July 2011).
63. Deal later recalled that the chairman 'exploded out of his chair in fury' at the news (Deal interview, 8 November 2004).
64. Deal interview, 8 November 2004.
65. Dumbrell, *A Special Relationship*, p. 97.
66. *The Associated Press*, 5 February 1982.
67. Deal interview, 8 November 2004.
68. *The Associated Press,* 'British Airways Agrees to Settle Laker Lawsuit', 12 July 1985.
69. Calingaert interview, 12 June 2011.
70. Deal interview, 8 November 2004.
71. Calingaert interview, 12 June 2011.
72. *The Associated Press*, 25 March 1983.
73. Deal interview, 8 November 2004.
74. 'US Ambassador (London) to Secretary of State (extraterritoriality)/ Declassified F97-013#61', Reagan Library: European and Soviet Affairs Directorate NSC (Thatcher Visit – Dec 84 [4] Box 90902), available at: http://www.margaretthatcher.org/document/109410 (accessed 24 May 2011).
75. 'US Ambassador (London) to Secretary of State (British Hopes for Thatcher US Visit)/ Declassified F97-013#59', Reagan Library: European & Soviet Directorate NSC (Thatcher Visit – Dec 84 [4] Box 90902), available at: http://www.margaretthatcher.org/document/109408 (accessed 24 May 2011).
76. Streator interview, 25 May 2011.
77. Dumbrell, *A Special Relationship*, p. 201.
78. J. Thompson, *American Policy and Northern Ireland: A Saga of Peacebuilding* (Westport, CT: Praeger, 2001), p. 93.
79. Dumbrell, *A Special Relationship*, p. 206.
80. Streator interview, 25 May 2011.
81. J. Rentschler, 'Memorandum for Richard V Allen: President's Meeting with John Louis', 1981, Reagan Library (NSC Country File Box 91326), available at: http://www.margaretthatcher.org/document/03DF378BD14C40BD9E1CD6E93652C8EC.pdf (accessed 24 May 2011).

82. *The Associated Press*, 'Britain Won't Negotiate with Maze Prisoners; U.S. Envoy Visits Ulster', 8 October 1981.
83. Streator interview, 25 May 2011.
84. Keith C. Smith, interviewed by Charles Stuart Kennedy, 5 February 2004, The Association for Diplomatic Studies and Training Foreign Affairs Oral History Project, available at: http://memory.loc.gov/cgi-bin/query/r?ammem/mfdip:@field(DOCID+mfdip2007smi01) (accessed 23 May 2011).
85. Richard H. Melton, interviewed by Charles Stuart Kennedy, 27 January 1997, The Association for Diplomatic Studies and Training Foreign Affairs Oral History Project, available at: http://memory.loc.gov/cgi-bin/query/r?ammem/mfdip:@field(DOCID+mfdip2004mel03) (accessed 24 May 2011).
86. Streator interview, 25 May 2011.
87. Melton interview, 25 January 1997.
88. *Ibid*.
89. Robert Hopper, interviewed by Raymond Ewing, 24 January 2002, The Association for Diplomatic Studies and Training Foreign Affairs Oral History Project, available at: http://memory.loc.gov/cgi-bin/query/r?ammem/mfdip:@field(DOCID+mfdip2010hop01) (accessed 23 May 2011).
90. *Ibid*.
91. Harrison interview, 30 November 2001.
92. *Ibid*.
93. Foreign Affairs Information Management Centre, *Key Officers of Foreign Service Posts*, 1983, p. 72, available at: http://www.columbia.edu/cu/lweb/digital/collections/cul/texts/ldpd_6260645_006/ldpd_6260645_006.pdf (accessed 16 May 2011).
94. G. Scott-Smith, 'Searching for the Successor Generation: Public Diplomacy, the US Embassy's International Visitor Program and the Labour Party in the 1980s', *The British Journal of Politics and International Relations*, Vol. 8, No. 2 (2006), p. 215.
95. *The Albany Herald*, 13 April 1983, p. 13A.
96. Scott-Smith, 'Searching for the Successor Generation', p. 218.
97. G. R. Berridge, *Diplomacy: Theory and Practice* (Basingstoke: Palgrave, 2002), p. 117.
98. Streator interview, 25 May 2011.
99. Lange Schermerhorn, interviewed by Charles Stuart Kennedy, 3 May 2002, The Association for Diplomatic Studies and Training Foreign Affairs Oral History Project, available at: http://memory.loc.gov/cgi-bin/query/r?ammem/mfdip:@field(DOCID+mfdip2010sch02) (accessed 24 May 2011).
100. Streator interview, 25 May 2011.
101. *Ibid*.
102. Osnos, 'US Ambassador to Britain to Be Replaced', p. A32.
103. Bainbridge, 'New Man at Court', p. 119.
104. Osnos, 'At Least our New Envoy', p. B1.
105. Bainbridge, 'New Man at Court', pp. 112–16.
106. Harrison interview, 30 November 2001.
107. *Ibid*.
108. J. Rentschler, 'James Rentschler's Falklands Diary', 1982, available at: http://www.margaretthatcher.org/archive/arcdocs/Rentschler.pdf (accessed 23 May 2011).

109. D. Radcliffe, 'Mrs Thatcher: In her Prime, at the Embassy', *The Washington Post*, 30 September 1983, p. E1.
110. Calingaert interview, 12 June 2011.
111. Bainbridge, 'New Man at Court', pp. 120–2.
112. Calingaert interview, 12 June 2011.
113. D. Mason, 'Today's Focus: The Unmaking of an Ambassador', *The Associated Press*, 23 September 1983.
114. *Ibid.*
115. Osnos, 'US Ambassador to Britain to Be Replaced', p. A32.
116. G. Hodgson, 'Obituaries: John J Louis, Jr', *The Independent*, 20 February 1995.
117. Streator interview, 25 May 2011.
118. Calingaert interview, 12 June 2011.
119. Harrison interview, 30 November 2001.
120. Osnos, 'At Least our New Envoy', p. B1.
121. Thatcher, *The Downing Street Years*, p. 331.
122. Dumbrell, *A Special Relationship*, pp. 99–100.
123. Thatcher, *The Downing Street Years*, p. 331.
124. Bainbridge, 'New Man at Court', p. 123.

12
Charles H. Price II, 1983–89

Paul Trickett

If the fate of John J. Louis, Jr was a warning of the potential dangers of political appointees with no depth of political connections as American Ambassador to the United Kingdom, then Charles H. Price II was a clear demonstration that the system of appointing Ambassadors by patronage could work successfully, provided that the appointee had the requisite connections to the levers of power. For over five years, Price combatively represented the foreign policy of Ronald Reagan, taking on anti-nuclear protesters, the Labour Party, the Irish Republican Army (IRA) and what he saw as anti-Americanism in Britain. In his time at Grosvenor Square he witnessed sweeping changes in the international and British political landscape – the Cold War, so bitter at the start of Price's tenure, was winding down as he left London. Price also observed the high water mark of Thatcherism and the friendly relationship between himself and the Prime Minister was one of the more notable aspects of his period as Ambassador.

Price was a very public ambassador and in this he contrasted greatly with the shy and retiring John Louis. Price was aware of the importance of public relations and of 'representation' and came to symbolise the United States in Great Britain from late 1983 to early 1989, a regular on television and radio news programmes and a frequent contributor of newspaper articles and letters to the broadsheet newspapers. While this period in Anglo-American relations is traditionally characterised by warmth and cooperation on a wide range of policies, it will be demonstrated that the special relationship suffered from tensions that could weaken the closeness between Thatcher and Reagan.

In fact, Charles Price arrived in the midst of one of the worst points in that relationship: the aftermath of the US invasion of Grenada. There would be other issues that would produce strains: the British reaction to the Strategic Defence Initiative (SDI), the nuclear debate in the United Kingdom and the Reykjavik Summit; American actions in the Middle East, in particular the 1986 bombing of Libya, and the many trade disputes that peppered the five years, most notably the wrangling over civil aviation. The role of Price and his Embassy in these events, as well as looking at Price's fractious relationship with the Labour Party and his actions in countering the actions of the IRA, will be addressed. The chapter will then consider Price's performance after the Lockerbie bombing before assessing the Ambassador's custodianship of the American Embassy. However, it is important to first look at Price's background to assess his suitability for the job and to place him within the wider international and domestic context.

Charles Price: Background and Appointment

Charles H. Price II was born 1 April 1931, in Kansas City, Missouri.[1] From 1955 until his appointment as Ambassador to Belgium in 1981, he was with the Price Candy Co. and served on the boards of a range of banking firms.[2] In short, Price was a successful businessman and banker with little experience of international politics before 1981. *The Guardian* noted that 'Price was born, brought up, and worked in Kansas City, Missouri, and until the last few years spent practically all his life there'.[3] However, the crucial difference between John Louis and Price was that Price had already served a diplomatic apprenticeship. In May 1981, he was appointed to be Ambassador to Belgium.[4] Price's appointment to Brussels follows a very similar pattern to that of Louis in London. Walter Annenberg, who recommended Louis for the London post, also introduced Charles Price to Ronald Reagan in 1975.[5] Reagan and Price became friends, meeting up for New Year at the Annenberg's home in California. Price became a fundraiser for Reagan and their wives became close friends.[6] In 1980, Price was contacted by President-Elect Reagan about the possibility of a job in Washington. Price turned to Annenberg for advice and the latter suggested that an ambassadorship would suit Price more because 'he was used to running his own business'.[7]

Price soon gained a reputation in Brussels for being a diligent worker and it was noted that 'he was a strong supporter of NATO's plans to deploy new nuclear missiles in Europe'.[8] He recognised his limitations (for example, he did not speak French) and utilised the experience of his Deputy Chiefs of Mission, Edward Killham and Charles Thomas.[9] The success of Price's tenure in Brussels was noted by feature writers profiling the new London appointee with Edna Robertson of the *Glasgow Herald* commenting on the difference between the outgoing ambassador and the incoming: 'Unlike his predecessor, he [Price] is a self-taught diplomat who took advantage of his previous post to not only acquire the ambassadorial arts, but also a thorough mastery of nuclear strategy ... a subject on which he sedulously defends Mr Reagan's record'.[10] *Washington Post* journalist Donnie Radcliffe noted that Price was part of Reagan's inner circle of friends and would have more 'clout' than John Louis.[11] That closeness, usually a great strength for a political appointee, could also be a weakness as it opened up Price to charges that they had used their influence (especially the connection between Carol

Price and Nancy Reagan) to undermine John Louis. Deputy Chief of Mission at the US Embassy in Brussels Edward Killham later observed that 'his wife commented several times that he, Charlie, knew Ron a lot better than this guy who was in London. She wanted London.'[12] However, Louis was also undermined by other factors connected to his failure to return to London after the start of the Falklands War, his lack of a personal link to the President, his general anonymity and failure to present American policy to the British public.

The Senate formally confirmed Price's nomination on 11 November 1983[13] and he presented his credentials to Queen Elizabeth II a month later on 20 December.[14] Many commentators observed that Price was assuming his role at a time of unusual tension within Anglo-American relations.[15] The invasion of Grenada in October had embarrassed the Prime Minister and Foreign Secretary as there was no prior consultation over the US military invasion of part of a Commonwealth member. The recent US decision to renew arms sales to Argentina had also provoked anger in London[16] and there was a stark reminder of the continued danger of Irish Republican violence with the bombing of the Harrods department store the day before Price's appointment at Buckingham Palace, which killed five and injured an American tourist, Mark McDonald.[17] Price was forthright in his condemnation of the attack stating that 'the American people and the president share the sense of outrage at what happened'.[18]

In the wider context, Price arrived in London as the deployment of cruise missiles to bases in the United Kingdom was beginning and the Cold War remained bitter with conflict between East and West through proxies in Afghanistan, Africa and Central America. The Middle East was also the cause of some instability with the American confrontation with Colonel Gaddafi and the aftermath of the massacre of US marines in Lebanon most notable areas of concern for America and its allies. Viewed superficially, the Reagan administration and its advisors did not seem to have learned the lessons of the failure of John Louis in London – here was another political appointee with only limited international experience. However, Price had demonstrated a clear facility for ambassadorial duties in Brussels and, crucially, he had a clear and long-standing relationship with the President. Charles Price was a readymade replacement for John Louis: a refinement of the political ambassador formula.

Military and Diplomatic Issues: Nuclear Matters and Public Interventions

It would be one of the ironies of Price's time in London that he would start by aggressively defending the deployment of cruise missiles to the United Kingdom while engaging vigorously with pro-unilateralist politicians, and end it by witnessing the removal of the very same missiles.[19] It was the nuclear issue that would produce one of the most public and contentious incidents of his ambassadorship – when he intervened during the 1986 Labour Party conference to attack the Party position on nuclear weapons and American bases.[20] It was an intervention that opened Price up to accusations of meddling in British politics.

Five months before the conference, Price addressed the theme of Labour's unilateral disarmament in an interview with *The Sunday Times* of 3 May 1986. In particular, he focused on their pledge to remove missiles from US Air Force bases in Britain. Price warned that 'if the Labour government took power and said, "All right, take out all of your cruise missiles and all your nuclear weapons," then we would have to think carefully about whether or not it was advantageous to continue to maintain bases in Great Britain'.[21]

Charles Price went to the Labour Party Conference in Blackpool at the request of his Deputy Chief of Mission Raymond Seitz, and James Kolker, the officer charged with Labour Party relations at the Embassy.[22] Before the start of the conference, Caspar Weinberger, Reagan's Secretary of Defence, had criticised the Labour Party's position on nuclear disarmament during an interview with the BBC, arguing that NATO would be 'severely weakened' by such a policy, and the 'special relationship' between the US and Britain even more so.[23] Labour Party leader, Neil Kinnock, reacted angrily and dismissed Weinberger's comments, claiming that they did not reflect official American policy.[24] In response, Price refuted Kinnock's interpretation of Weinberger's comments and stated that the White House fully supported the Secretary of Defence.[25]

Price was advised that this was the course to follow by his influential Public Affairs Officer,[26] Robert 'Bud' Korengold, who realised that 'they were invited observers; not participants, but I told the Ambassador we should not let Kinnock's comments get into the press cycle without our rebuttal'.[27] So Price went on the offensive, telling Robin Oakley of *The Times* and David Dimbleby on BBC television of the difficulties that the American government had with Labour policy.[28] Korengold and Price's rapid reaction meant that 'both sides of the matter hit the papers at the same time'.[29] Indeed, Kinnock's comments that, under Labour all US installations in the UK that contributed to NATO's defence would not be closed, were ignored as the agenda came to be dominated by the reaction of the United States to Labour policy.[30]

Certainly the Labour Party reaction to Price's intervention was hostile, with *The New York Times* reporting an altercation between Price and the Labour leader's wife, Glenys Kinnock: 'when [she] bumped into the American Ambassador at the party's annual conference here, she didn't try to hide her displeasure. Mrs Kinnock let him know, bystanders later said, that she thought his statement of an American position was an unwarranted interference in a British debate'.[31] The following day Price continued his attack, telling breakfast television about the potential hazards for NATO in

Labour's policy. The next day Oakley noted that 'Mr Price's latest comments underlined the Reagan Administration's determination to continue condemning Labour's proposals right up to the next election' while commenting that the Labour Party had been taken aback by the aggressiveness of the American reaction.[32]

The controversy eventually died down, but there were lasting effects, with Korengold recalling that Kinnock refused to talk to Price for some time after the Blackpool conference.[33] A coda to the incident was provided by Kinnock's visit to Washington in 1987, a disastrous event that culminated in a humiliation for Kinnock, who was granted a perfunctory meeting with the President who seemed to believe that Labour deputy leader, Denis Healey, was the British Ambassador.[34] Declassified cables would later reveal that the President's advisors wished to snub Kinnock altogether.[35] Labour would lose the 1987 election and many within the Party viewed the unilateralist approach as central to their failure.[36] However, other Labour figures looked to the intervention by Price as a factor in the defeat.[37] Price had taken a considerable risk. If Labour had won in June 1987, then he could have been seen as an impediment to good relations between London and Washington. However, in a cable a day after the election, Price was able to tell Washington with relief that 'the US–UK defence relationship is intact and Britain's alliance role assured...US bases here will remain, and we can expect a cooperative approach on the part of the British to future decisions to modernise US nuclear systems based in the UK'.[38]

Moving away from the public sphere of the nuclear debate, the Embassy participated in areas of Alliance nuclear cooperation. In 1983, at the start of Price's tenure, the Deputy Political Counsellor, Roger Harrison, hosted the committee overseeing the deployment of cruise missiles to the United States Air Force (USAF) bases in England.[39] However, according to Harrison, once the deployment began in earnest, in late 1983 to mid 1984, the Embassy began to find itself cut out of the loop as the British Ministry of Defence (MOD) and NATO's European Command (EUCOM) felt that the deployment should be carried out on a purely military level, coordinated by the MOD.[40]

The Strategic Defence Initiative (SDI) was also a cause of concern for the British. The initial announcement in March 1983 had been met with some hostility from officials who saw it as a radical departure from the traditional nuclear strategy.[41] Harrison consulted with his British colleagues who he viewed as 'scornful, they were trying to modernize their submarine base as a deterrent with a new missile. That was going to cost some money and now Reagan was saying that missiles were outmoded'.[42] UK reaction was articulated by the British Foreign Secretary at the time, Sir Geoffrey Howe, in a speech that expressed the government's concerns over SDI.[43] This was followed in quick succession by condemnation from the White House, a visit to the Foreign Office by Charles Price, and a statement by a

British spokesman saying that there were no differences between the two governments over SDI.[44]

A final area of nuclear disagreement was the reaction to the Reykjavík Summit of October 1986. As Political Officer Miles 'Kim' Pendleton recalled, 'Reagan's movement on arms control came like a thunderbolt to the Brits, and we had to do a lot of putting into perspective, which was hard to do, about our shifting position'.[45] For Margaret Thatcher, the Reykjavík Summit was an 'earthquake' that made her fear for Reagan's commitment to nuclear deterrence.[46] Such doubts were echoed by many in British political and intellectual elite, so Pendleton lobbied a group of academics to sell the change in policy. Pendleton noted that 'it was a hard sell because we had shifted so far…[it] did not result in much calming of British apprehensions'.[47] Thus the Embassy's role in nuclear issues was one of lobbying British public opinion, coordination and presenting the argument for NATO's nuclear strategy, even at points when the strategy changed rapidly.

The Bombing of Libya, 1986

The April 1986 bombing of Libya by the US raised considerable political problems for Margaret Thatcher. The key controversy for the British was the request to use UK-based planes which would require authorisation from the British government and would risk significant political fallout for the Prime Minister, who was already being accused of being too close to the White House.[48] In January 1986, the British had joined with the other European allies in rejecting President Reagan's call for sanctions against Colonel Muammar Gaddafi.[49] At his own request, Price met with Howe to explain the reasons for the call for sanctions. *The Times* reported that the Ambassador did not ask Britain to adopt similar measures, but that Britain not take steps that might undercut the American action.[50]

The 5 April bombing of the La Belle nightclub in Berlin that had killed two US soldiers and wounded 79 others had been blamed on Libya[51] and this pushed the US government to regard a punitive bombing strike as being the best option to halt Gaddafi's sponsorship of terrorism.[52] A decision was made to attack Libya on the night of 15 April and permission to use UK bases was justified by the British under America's right to self-defence under Article 51 of the UN Charter.[53]

The Embassy's role in the bombings was limited, despite much of the attack being coordinated from Grosvenor Square. Harrison was sent to the headquarters for United States Naval Forces Europe at 20 Grosvenor Square to observe the operation. As he dryly commented later, 'the admiral wouldn't have thought of asking me for any political advice, which was just as well because I didn't know anything about it, but I was sort of an embassy presence while he was conducting this operation'.[54] David Evans, the Political Advisor to the Commander-in-Chief, US Naval Forces Europe

(CINCNAVEUR) also witnessed the operation: 'one of the tricky diplomatic questions was getting flight permission for these Air Force planes to get down to Libya. The French refused them permission. So, the planes had to fly a longer way to get there, avoiding France'.[55] The eighteen F-111F strike aircraft from RAF Lakenheath were equipped with precision guidance equipment so the planes had to be used rather than the missiles from the US Navy taskforce.[56] Margaret Thatcher faced a welter of complaint after the attack from Members in the House of Commons who feared that she was exposing the United Kingdom to terrorist reprisals and aiding 'a kind of vigilantism'.[57] However, for many in the Embassy, she demonstrated 'considerable political courage' in allowing the use of British bases in the operation.[58]

For the Embassy, the main task came, following the bombing, as they dealt with the reaction.[59] The impact on American tourism to London was clear as Korengold recalls: 'many Americans, fearing some kind of retaliatory strike by the Libyans, decided not to come to Britain for a while at least. To get things going again, Margaret Thatcher agreed to host a reception for a band of American tourists in her Downing Street residence (that Ambassador Price and I also attended) to make the point that everything was all right for visitors to London'.[60] The Economic Counsellor, Lawrence Taylor, observed the impact of the bombings and felt that the reaction was largely predictable: 'The government of the day, which was supportive and a participant in the process, was quite strongly in favour ... it was not anything that brought the British public out in demonstrations in large numbers pro and con'.[61] Indeed, the reaction of many of the Embassy staffers to the British public response to the bombing was remarkably sanguine, feeling that the Libyan leader was too unsympathetic a character to engender much public sympathy.[62] This was despite a sit down protest with over 10,000 people opposing the bombings that took place outside the Embassy on 18 April.[63]

The major military and diplomatic incidents of the Price era were many and varied and this short analysis of two distinct areas, nuclear issues and the bombing of Libya, demonstrates the continuities between the Louis and Price Embassies. The Embassy acted as a channel of communication, as advisors and observers, clarifiers of intent and lobbyists. What had changed, however, was the tone of that lobbying. Price's campaign against Labour demonstrated an Ambassador that was not afraid to take risks in defending the policies of his country and was willing to confront those in the British public and political system with whom he disagreed.

Economic Matters: Civil Aviation

As with the Louis era, trade was a thorn in the side of the Anglo-American relationship. This partly manifested itself in matters of civil aviation such as in the dispute over the collapse of Laker Airlines and the subsequent anti-trust case or the negotiations over Airbus. The signing of the Single European

Act in 1986 provoked questions for the Anglo-American relationship on the issue of agricultural subsidies and the access for American firms into the new single market.

The matter of civil aviation deserves some attention – it was described by Assistant Secretary of State for European and Canadian Affairs Richard Burt in a now declassified briefing for George Shultz as 'the source of our most bitter differences'.[64] In 1984 President Reagan took the almost unprecedented step of halting a Grand Jury investigation into the Laker collapse conspiracy.[65] This was partly due to recommendations coming from the London Embassy. Energy Attaché, Tim Deal, had been charged with handling the negotiations surrounding the Laker case in London.[66] He and Deputy Chief of Mission Seitz agreed to ask the Ambassador to call Reagan to request that the case be dropped for the sake of bilateral relations and, as Michael Calingaert later recalled, 'then one fine day the court case just disappeared', the result, he suspected, of lobbying from Thatcher at a higher level as much as the Embassy efforts.[67]

The Americans were disappointed with the reaction from the British to the news. Burt noted that 'the highest levels of the Department and Ambassador Price have pressed British ministers to take some positive steps to liberalize the current civil aviation regime. The British have been singularly unhelpful'.[68] The topic was broached by Mrs Thatcher during the 22 December meeting with President Reagan at Camp David. Price was present at the meeting and played a significant role in the discussion. Thatcher argued that the civil aviation system was still unfair and that plans to introduce a treble damages clause would create more problems for the privatisation of British Airways.[69] She also highlighted the confusion in the pricing agreements which made lowering prices a long and drawn out process. Price commented that competition would help both countries and that the treble clause was not as much of an issue because first, there had not been a successful anti-trust suit in 15 years with the current system and secondly, a fund could be set up to pay for any potential future liabilities.[70] Thatcher responded by claiming that once it was known that there was money behind the fund then it would be an open invitation for a lawsuit. Ambassador Price added that British Airways chief executives had indicated to him that they could work within the framework of existing laws and regulations and he noted that the British government, in signing the Bermuda II agreement, knew it did not override or take the place of US anti-trust laws.[71]

The summary of the 1984 Camp David meeting demonstrates the problems faced by the negotiators dealing with the complexities of the civil aviation disputes. The Embassy played a key role in these negotiations, acting as 'a channel of communication, a facilitator between the Dept of Transport and the US Dept of Transportation'.[72] The summary also demonstrates Price's usefulness as an advisor and moderator between the President and Prime Minister. However, these arguments did not seriously impact on broader relations between the two countries. Indeed, Thatcher and Price's good personal relations can be demonstrated by the photographs published by *The Guardian* of the return flight to England from the Camp David meeting where they are seen pulling a Christmas cracker and by the simple fact that they travelled back to the United Kingdom together.[73]

The other significant civil aviation dispute of this period was related to Airbus.[74] This was a consortium of various European companies that had been formed in 1969 to challenge American dominance in aviation.[75] Airbus received heavy subsidies from the various European governments involved and the major American aircraft manufacturers such as Boeing argued that this would give Airbus an unfair advantage.[76] The negotiations over Airbus were complicated and the London Embassy bore the brunt of many of them.[77] A declassified memorandum from the Deputy Trade Representative, setting out potential talking points for Reagan in an upcoming meeting with Thatcher in 1988, referred to the three years' worth of negotiations over Airbus and commented that 'left unresolved, current trade tensions on this matter will grow between us and other Airbus governments and may get out of hand'.[78]

European Integration

On a wider multilateral level, the issue of European integration was confronted by the London Embassy. There was an initial fear in the Embassy that the planned creation of the single market in 1992 would mean that the Europeans were moving towards a 'Fortress Europe'.[79] Trade Policy Officer, Lynne Lambert, describes the worries over the single market: 'US business was very afraid that the single market shut it out. They thought it might produce something in industry and services akin to the Common Agriculture Policy'.[80] The Embassy responded to this by creating a high-level group to deal with European Community 1992 developments. The Ambassador, the DCM, the Economic Minister-Counsellor, Commercial Counsellor and the Treasury Counsellor were all involved and the group met frequently with the American business community to share opinions and discuss strategy.[81]

With regards to the special relationship and Europe, the Embassy team supported a strong British role in the European Community as they felt that the British would help to keep the European Union open and outward looking.[82] At the same time, they believed that the British would be one of the EU members most open to dealing with the United States. Meetings frequently revolved around how the British could help the United States gain support for their views within the European Union.[83] Lambert agrees with Ogden's interpretation noting that 'the British saw a benefit in being our intermediary for several reasons: telling other Europeans what the US position was one of their self-appointed roles ... also, the British tended to have the same positions as we did, and they used the US to bolster London's position'.[84]

Domestic Concerns: The Labour Party

The chapter has already dealt in part with Ambassador Price's fractious relationship with the Labour Party. However, it would be inaccurate to state that this was the only dimension of the relationship between the Embassy and the Opposition. While Price was clearly an advocate for the Prime Minister (one Embassy official noted that 'Charlie Price wanted us to support the Thatcher government. He made that message very clear to people in Britain')[85] others in the Embassy saw a longer game. The 1987 general election defeat created an opportunity for some in the Embassy to cultivate closer relations with more receptive members of the Party.[86] Charles Clarke,[87] Neil Kinnock's Chief of Staff often acted as a liaison with the Embassy.[88] The Embassy's political officers made a point of spreading their net as widely as possible to include people like security specialist George Robertson[89] and figures like Tony Blair, Gordon Brown and Peter Mandelson. John Reid[90] and Nick Brown[91] were also identified as potentially friendly to the United States[92] and when the Embassy had important visitors from the US, the political team endeavoured to get them invitations to Embassy receptions.[93]

Most were receptive to the Embassy's advances, although there was always a certain degree of ambivalence to the relationship. Most did not want to be seen as being too close to the United States or the Embassy as they wanted to be seen as someone who was carving out their own image within the Labour Party; thoughtful on policy issues and not reliant on the US Embassy to be told what to think.[94] Of all the people invited, only Harriet Harman[95] systematically refused the Embassy's invitations. Other sections of the Embassy were also involved; Lambert, for example, met with Blair and Brown to discuss the issue of Europe.[96] The architect of much of this outreach initiative was Raymond Seitz.[97] He maintained connections with the Labour Party through a team that featured Kim Pendleton, Lester Slezak and James Kolker.[98] However, the stridently pro-Thatcher rhetoric from the Ambassador still created distrust within Labour.[99] This policy of outreach and cultivating relations with the Labour Party continued the work started in the Louis era by officers like Richard Melton, Robert Hopper and Roger Harrison.

Northern Ireland

The Northern Ireland question was another issue that produced activity from the Embassy during the Price era. The Ambassador's first act when taking over at the Embassy in December 1983 was to visit the victims of the Harrods bombing and to condemn the IRA.[100] In 1984 Price publicly announced the start of a scheme to confiscate IRA funding within the United States.[101] The initiative was matched by a series of economic incentives to improve trade between Northern Ireland and the United States.[102]

On 14 October 1984, Price was in Brighton at the Metropole Hotel when the nearby Grand Hotel was bombed by the IRA.[103] The Prime Minister narrowly escaped death, but others were not so fortunate. Price appears in Thatcher's memoirs at this point in a bizarre little interlude that followed the evacuation of his hotel for safety reasons. The evacuation occurred so quickly, Price was left without a pair of shoes so he borrowed a pair from Denis Thatcher.[104] Four days later, Price highlighted and condemned the actions of NORAID in their fundraising efforts in the United States.[105]

Price later intervened in the debate surrounding the MacBride Principles in 1987, arguing that the proposals to put more Roman Catholics in jobs in Northern Ireland would create 'reverse discrimination'.[106] The attitude of the Embassy towards the Irish question can be found in an Embassy cable dating from August 1988 which summarises the prospects for the peace process. The report painted a bleak picture of the Troubles suggesting that 1989 (the 20th anniversary of the introduction of troops into Northern Ireland and the creation of the provisional IRA) meant it could be a 'bad year for commemorative terrorism'. The gloomy prognosis continued, judging there was no end in sight and the only real success was the establishment of Anglo-Irish security cooperation measures. This was balanced by failures by the Irish government to bring to justice prominent IRA activists. The report dismissed the possibility of the return of internment, but highlighted the British government's resigned policy of reducing the level of violence in the Province while recognising that the potential for finding an accommodation for both Protestant and Catholic factions was limited.[107]

Culture and Education

The scope of the International Visitor Programme (IVP) continued to expand. It was used by the United States Information Service (USIA) and the political section of the Embassy as a means of reinforcing and improving the contacts within the Labour Party: Tony Blair and Gordon Brown made visits to the United States in this period.[108] Korengold comments that 'with the IVP, we sent people we considered possible future leaders in our particular countries for a several months visit to the United States. No holds barred. We tried to let them see whatever they wanted and talk to anyone we could arrange for them in the hope that their future perception of the United States would be better based.'[109]

The USIA team's cultural diplomacy activities covered a wide range of duties that even included hosting a reception for the San Francisco 49ers American Football team when they came to play an exhibition game at Wembley in 1988.[110] The Ambassador also played a role in the cultural diplomacy function of the Embassy, hosting receptions designed to promote museum tours[111] and musical performers.[112]

The overview of the activities of the Embassy with regards to the special relationship during the Price era shows an institution working on several levels. At the highest level, the Ambassador was closely connected to the Prime Minister and the ruling Conservative Party. In this, he reflected the wishes of his political patron, Ronald Reagan, and the way he carried out his duties contrasted strongly with his predecessor: Price was a public ambassador. His performance at the 1986 Labour Party conference demonstrated the change in tone and the more assertive manner of his public diplomacy. However, on other levels, the Embassy remained consistent in action and intent with the Louis era. The Embassy remained a conduit for information and clarification of intentions between the US and UK on a range of issues, advising and reporting on key domestic, international and economic developments.

The Public Role of Charles Price: The Aftermath of the Lockerbie Bombing

The chapter now turns to the aspect of public diplomacy in Price's ambassadorship. However, there is another facet of public diplomacy – that of representation and symbolism.[113] Price's public diplomacy is demonstrated most clearly during the aftermath of the Lockerbie bombing. The bombing of Pan-Am Flight 103 over Lockerbie, Scotland on 21 December 1988 was one of the final events of Price's tenure. The terrorist attack left 270 dead, most of them American.[114] In the events that followed the bombing, Price acted as a focal point for the relatives desperate to get news of their loved ones.

Price and his team were amongst the first on site, as Korengold recalls, 'what we found was a scene of desolation that will never be erased from our memories – bits of the airplane and human bodies scattered on the ground all around'.[115] Price had been attending a black tie function in London when he was informed of the attack. Price's first instinct was to go to the scene of the crash, 'to demonstrate our concern on the ground and to lead our team on the ground'.[116] The Ambassador assembled his aides, amongst them Korengold and Press Officer, Aury Fernandez, quickly arranged a USAF plane to fly them directly to Lockerbie.[117] They arrived in the middle of night as the emergency services continued to search the wreckage for survivors.[118]

Price was able to report on developments to the media and provide an American voice for the concerned relatives watching the news.[119] Price's presence featured heavily in the following media coverage. As Pendleton recalls, 'all the pictures in the press the next morning showed Charlie and Carol Price standing near a very large fragment of the plane. That was indicative, I think, of the care the embassy and the consulate in Edinburgh gave to the process.'[120] Korengold later commented, 'the Ambassador and Carol Price were simply magnificent in their efforts to deal with the relatives' emotional concerns and demands, explaining the problems but simultaneously expressing their understanding and sympathy'.[121]

In the meantime, Fernandez and Korengold struggled to cope with the demands of the media as a sombre Price was interviewed by an array of networks, refusing to be drawn on reports of groups that claimed responsibility and offering sympathy for the victims from the plane and the town of Lockerbie.[122] After Christmas 1988, Price read the lesson at the memorial service for the victims of the bombing on 4 January 1989.[123] During the service he sat alongside Margaret Thatcher.[124] Price's time in London had started with a terrorist attack and it concluded with one. In both instances, Price demonstrated a keen awareness of the importance of being seen offering condolences and leading the mourners. Price was an ambassador who was aware of the symbolism of his role and was rightly praised for his leadership during the Lockerbie tragedy.

Nineteen days later, Price and Thatcher were again together, this time in happier circumstances in Grosvenor Square. There they unveiled a statue to General Eisenhower that had been paid for by contributions from Kansas dignitaries.[125] Three weeks later, during Prime Minister's Questions, Mrs Thatcher praised Mr and Mrs Price's time in London as 'marvellous'[126] and on 23 February 1989 Charles H. Price II formally relinquished his appointment as Ambassador to the United Kingdom.[127]

Conclusion

Charles Price's time in Grosvenor Square was marked by episodes of turbulence in the special relationship. However, he did not face the major incidents that threatened to undermine the special relationship as they did in the John Louis era when the Falklands War, the Grenada incident and the Siberian pipeline crisis all caused tension within Anglo-American relations. While the ongoing wrangling over Laker and civil aviation was a constant irritant, there was less scope for disagreement in Price's time. Price was selected because he would be an effective advocate for the United States in the United Kingdom. His friendship with Margaret Thatcher and her government mirrored the closeness in the relationship between Thatcher and Reagan. The regard that Price was held in by the British government was noteworthy in itself – one Embassy official later recalled sitting next to the Chancellor of the Exchequer, Nigel Lawson, at a meal and '[Lawson] without prompting or any real reason said to me, "Charlie Price is doing a very good job" '.[128]

Price was blessed with the good fortune that eluded his predecessor; he certainly did not commit an error of the scale that Louis managed to commit in the first couple of weeks of the Falklands War. Another short-term advantage for the special relationship was that Price's public interventions were not aimed at the Thatcher government, but at her opposition and enemies. Indeed, on occasions, such as the 1986 Labour conference dispute, government ministers openly approved of the American's intervention in British domestic political concerns. As has been noted, this was potentially a high risk strategy that could have rebounded on Price if Labour had won the 1987 election. He was also fortunate that he played a very peripheral role in the Iran-Contra scandal that undermined much of Reagan's second term.[129]

Price was particularly concerned by what he perceived to be the rise of anti-Americanism in Britain during the 1980s. The sale of a major portion of British Leyland to General Motors and the Westland helicopter scandal revealed uneasiness amongst the British public about the extent of American economic influence in the United Kingdom.[130] The American attacks on Libya had also created some anti-American feelings. Price commented that he viewed envy to be partly responsible for the attitude along with British insecurity at the loss of Empire and the popular view of Reagan as a Wild West gunslinger.[131]

It is also fair to say that Price worked hard. He was indebted to his DCM Raymond Seitz, who unobtrusively organised the running of the Embassy. Seitz moved to ameliorate some of the excesses of Price's public pronouncements, especially with regards to cultivating better relations with the Labour opposition. Seitz's influence was noted by some in the media, such as Alan Watkins of *The Observer*, but he deliberately remained more of a background figure.[132] This was in contrast to his predecessor as DCM, Ed Streator, who had been pushed into the limelight as a consequence of Louis' absence in April 1982.

As this chapter has attempted to demonstrate, Price succeeded because he was a public ambassador. He recognised the importance of television and radio news and he had an instinctive knack for grasping the important issues and presenting them in a clear manner. He was as comfortable on television as he was in the corridors of power and the higher echelons of British society. Price was very much of his time: he represented the more robust foreign policy and character of the Reagan administration during the Cold War. However, that time was ending and a new international consensus was being developed where the Cold War certainties were being replaced by the ambiguities of 'the new world order'. So, Charles Price, the 'very public ambassador', slipped quietly back into the private world of business and finance.

Acknowledgements

The author would like to thank Robert Korengold, James Kolker, Roger Harrison, Edward Streator, Raymond Seitz, Penelope Dew, Andrew Riley and Michael Caligaert for their help and offers of assistance in the writing of this chapter.

Notes

1. 'Nomination of Charles H. Price II to Be United States Ambassador to Belgium', 28 May 1981, available at: http://www.reagan.utexas.edu/archives/speeches/1981/52881c.htm (accessed 10 June 2011).
2. Public Papers of the Presidents, 'United States Ambassador to the United Kingdom', 19 Weekly Comp. Pres. Doc. 1276, 20 September 1983.
3. T. Coleman, 'Elements of Diplomacy', *The Guardian*, 2 February 1987, p. 23.
4. *The Associated Press*, 'President Announces Ambassadorial Appointments', 20 September 1983.
5. Coleman, 'Elements of Diplomacy' p. 23.
6. *United Press International*, 'US Ambassador to Britain Resigns', 15 September 1983.
7. Coleman, 'Elements of Diplomacy', p. 23.
8. M. E. Myers, *United Press International*, 20 September 1983.
9. Mildred A. Patterson, interviewed by Charles Stuart Kennedy, 6 May 2003, The Association for Diplomatic Studies and Training Foreign Affairs Oral History Project, available at: http://memory.loc.gov/cgi-bin/query/r?ammem/mfdip:@field(DOCID+mfdip2007pat01) (accessed 30 May 2011).
10. E. Robertson, *The Glasgow Herald*, 27 January 1983, p. 9.
11. D. Radcliffe, *The Washington Post*, 20 September 1983, p. C1.
12. Edward L. Killham, interviewed by Robert Martens, 18 December 1992, The Association for Diplomatic Studies and Training Foreign Affairs Oral History Project, available at: http://memory.loc.gov/cgi-bin/query/r?ammem/mfdip:@field(DOCID+mfdip2004kil03) (accessed 30 May 2011).
13. *The Associated Press*, 'Senate Confirms Ambassador to Great Britain', 11 November 1983.
14. E. H. West, 'Under the Eagle's Eye', *The Guardian*, 21 December 1983, p. 3.
15. M. Johnson, *The Associated Press*, 20 December 1983.
16. *The Associated Press*, 'Candy Heir Becomes America's New Ambassador to Britain', 21 December 1983.
17. *United Press International*, 'I Just Can't Comprehend the IRA', 20 December 1983.
18. *The Associated Press*, 21 December 1983.
19. D. Fairhill, 'Cheers as First US Missiles Leave Base', *The Guardian*, 9 September 1988, p. 1.
20. R. Oakley, 'Triumph and Trouble for Labour Leader: Kinnock Plays for High Stakes over Defence', *The London Times*, 1 October 1986, p. 1.
21. *United Press International*, 'US Ambassador Warns against US Nuclear Weapon Removal', 3 May 1986.
22. Telephone interview with James Kolker, 27 May 2011.
23. *Christian Science Monitor*, 'Trouble in Blackpool', 2 October 1986, p. 19.
24. J. Naughtie, 'Kinnock Makes Vow to Bind Up Nation's Wounds / Labour Leader's Blackpool Conference Speech', *The Guardian*, 1 October 1986.
25. Oakley, 'Triumph and Trouble for Labour Leader', p. 1.
26. Korengold's formal title was Minister-Counselor for Cultural Affairs and Information.
27. Correspondence with Robert Korengold, 2 May 2011.
28. Oakley, 'Triumph and Trouble for Labour Leader', p. 1.
29. Correspondence with Robert Korengold, 2 May 2011.
30. Naughtie, 'Kinnock Makes Vow'.

31. J. Lelyveld, 'US "Interference" Shaping Up as British Issue', *The New York Times*, 2 October 1986, p. A2.
32. R. Oakley, 'US Envoy Steps Up the Attack / Opposition to British Labour Party's Nuclear Defence Policy', *The London Times*, 2 October 1986.
33. Correspondence with Robert Korengold, 2 May 2011.
34. D. Jones, *America and the British Labour Party: The 'Special Relationship' at Work* (London: I. B. Taurus, 1997), p. 201.
35. Doc_NBR: 1987London09828 'British elections set for June 11', available at: http://politics.guardian.co.uk/foi/images/0,9069,1010587,00.html (accessed 2 June 2011).
36. Jones, *America and the British Labour Party*, p. 202.
37. I. Aitken, 'Labour at Blackpool: Standing Up to the Strain of Ovations – Points of Order', *The Guardian*, 5 October 1988.
38. R. Evans and D. Hencke, 'Revealed: Reagan's Secret Plans to Snub Kinnock if He Won the 1987 Election', *The Guardian*, 4 August 2003, available at: http://www.guardian.co.uk/politics/2003/aug/04/uk.freedomofinformation (accessed 2 June 2011).
39. Ambassador Roger G. Harrison, interviewed by Charles Stuart Kennedy, 30 November 2001, The Association for Diplomatic Studies and Training Foreign Affairs Oral History Project, available at: http://memory.loc.gov/cgi-bin/query/r?ammem/mfdip:@field(DOCID+mfdip2010har01) (accessed 20 May 2011).
40. *Ibid.*
41. T. Taylor, 'Britain's Response to the Strategic Defence Initiative', *International Affairs*, Vol. 62 (1986), p. 218.
42. Harrison interview, 30 November 2001.
43. BBC News Summary of World Broadcasts, 'Czechoslovak and Hungarian Comment on Sir Geoffrey Howe's "Star Wars" Doubts', 21 March 1985.
44. H. Pick, 'Howe Attack on Star Wars Defence Angers US', *The Guardian*, 21 March 1985, p. 8.
45. Miles S. Pendleton, interviewed by Charles Stuart Kennedy, 22 June 1998, The Association for Diplomatic Studies and Training Foreign Affairs Oral History Project, available at: http://memory.loc.gov/cgi-bin/query/r?ammem/mfdip:@field(DOCID+mfdip2004pen02) (accessed 25 July 2011).
46. N. Wheeler, 'Perceptions of the Soviet Threat', in S. Croft (ed.), *British Security Policy: The Thatcher Years and the End of the Cold War* (London: Harper Collins, 1991), p. 171.
47. Pendleton interview, 22 June 1998.
48. J. Dumbrell, *A Special Relationship: Anglo-American Relations in the Cold War and after* (Basingstoke: Palgrave Macmillan, 2001), pp. 102–4.
49. E. Pond, 'Sanctions against Libya: Relief and Dissent', *Christian Science Monitor*, 9 January 1986, p. 1.
50. N. Ashford, 'Washington Reassured by Britain / US Sanctions against Libya', *The London Times*, 9 January 1986, p. 1.
51. Dumbrell, *A Special Relationship*, p. 102.
52. David M. Evans, interviewed by Charles Stuart Kennedy, 22 November 1996, The Association for Diplomatic Studies and Training Foreign Affairs Oral History Project, available at: http://memory.loc.gov/cgi-bin/query/r?ammem/mfdip:@field(DOCID+mfdip2010eva01) (accessed 30 May 2011).
53. Dumbrell, *A Special Relationship*, p. 102.
54. Harrison interview, 30 November 2001.

55. Evans interview, 22 November 1996.
56. Dumbrell, *A Special Relationship*, p. 102.
57. *Ibid.*, p. 103.
58. Richard Ogden, interviewed by Charles Stuart Kennedy, 16 June 1999, The Association for Diplomatic Studies and Training Foreign Affairs Oral History Project, available at: http://memory.loc.gov/cgi-bin/query/r?ammem/mfdip:@ field(DOCID+mfdip2004ogd01) (accessed 25 July 2011).
59. Lawrence Taylor, interviewed by Charles Stuart Kennedy, 10 April 1998, The Association for Diplomatic Studies and Training Foreign Affairs Oral History Project, available at: http://memory.loc.gov/cgi-bin/query/r?ammem/mfdip:@ field(DOCID+mfdip2004tay02) , (accessed on 29 May 2011).
60. Correspondence with Robert Korengold, 2 May 2011; and *The Associated Press,*13 June 1986.
61. Taylor interview, 10 April 1998.
62. Harrison interview, 30 November 2001.
63. T. Marshall, 'Thousands in Europe Protest Raid : Anti-U.S. Groups Denounce Attack on Libyan Cities', *Los Angeles Times*, 20 April 1986, p. 1.
64. Declassified F97-013#18: Burt briefing for Shultz (Thatcher visit), Reagan Library: European & Soviet Directorate, NSC: Records (Thatcher Visit – Dec 84 [1] Box 90902), 19 December 1984, available at: http://www.margaretthatcher. org/document/109393 (accessed 2 June 2011).
65. *Ottowa Citizen*, 'Reagan Orders Halt to Air Travel Inquiry', 20 November 1984, p. 35.
66. Timothy Deal, interviewed by Raymond Ewing, 8 November 2004, The Association for Diplomatic Studies and Training Foreign Affairs Oral History Project, available at: http://memory.loc.gov/cgi-bin/query/r?ammem/mfdip:@ field(DOCID+mfdip2007dea01) (accessed 22 May 2011).
67. Telephone interview with Michael Calingaert, 12 June 2011.
68. Declassified F97-013#18: Burt briefing for Shultz (Thatcher visit), 19 December 1984.
69. Declassified NLS F97-013 #16, Thatcher-Reagan meeting at Camp David (record of conversation), Reagan Library: European and Soviet Affairs Directorate, NSC: Records (File Folder: Thatcher Visit – Dec 1984 [1] Box 90902), 28 December 1984, available at: http://www.margaretthatcher.org/document/ 109185 (accessed 24 May 2011).
70. *Ibid.*
71. *Ibid.*
72. Calingaert interview, 12 June 2011.
73. I. Aitken, 'Thatcher Back amid Camp David Euphoria', *The Guardian*, 24 December 1984, p. 1.
74. Calingaert interview, 12 June 2011.
75. R. Carback and J. Olienyk, 'Boeing-Airbus Trade Dispute: An Economic and Trade Perspective', *Global Economic Quarterly*, October–December2001.
76. R. Carback and J. Olienyk, 'Boeing-Airbus Subsidy Dispute: A Sequel', *Global Economy Journal*, Vol. 4 (2004), p. 2.
77. Ogden interview, 16 June 1999.
78. Deputy United States Trade Representative, 'Briefing for the President (MT visit to Washington)', Reagan Library, 1988 (WHORM Country File CO167 Box 606691), available at: http://www.margaretthatcher.org/document/ 9725F12D3D0447E4B81BD65B8CB55581.pdf (accessed 3 July 2011).

79. Ogden interview, 16 June 1999.
80. Lynne Lambert, interviewed by Charles Stuart Kennedy, 24 January 2002, The Association for Diplomatic Studies and Training Foreign Affairs Oral History Project, available at: http://memory.loc.gov/cgi-bin/query/r?ammem/mfdip:@field(DOCID+mfdip2007lam02) (accessed 28 May 2011).
81. Ogden interview, 16 June 1999.
82. Lambert interview, 24 January 2002.
83. Ogden interview, 16 June 1999.
84. Lambert interview, 24 January 2002.
85. Off the record comment.
86. Kolker interview, 27 May 2011.
87. Charles Clarke was Member of Parliament for Norwich South and Home Secretary (2004–2006).
88. G. Scott-Smith, 'Searching for the Successor Generation: Public Diplomacy, the US Embassy's International Visitor Program and the Labour Party in the 1980s', *The British Journal of Politics and International Relations*, Vol. 8, No. 2 (2006), p. 224.
89. George Robertson became Secretary of State for Defence (1997–99) and Secretary-General of the North Atlantic Treaty Organisation (1997–2004).
90. John Reid became Secretary of State for Defence (2005–2006) and Home Secretary (2006–2007).
91. Nick Brown became Minister of State for Agriculture, Fisheries and Food (1997–2001) and Chief Whip of the House of Commons (2008–10).
92. Scott-Smith, 'Searching for the Successor Generation', p. 228.
93. Kolker interview, 27 May 2011.
94. *Ibid.*
95. Harriet Harman is Member of Parliament for Camberwell and Peckham and became Secretary of State for Social Security (1997–98), Solicitor-General (2001–2005) and the Leader of the Opposition (May–September 2010).
96. Lambert interview, 24 January 2002.
97. Kolker interview, 27 May 2011.
98. Pendleton interview, 22 June 1998.
99. Scott-Smith, 'Searching for the Successor Generation', p. 224.
100. *United Press International*, 'I Just Can't Comprehend the IRA'.
101. *The Associated Press*, 'Ambassador Says US Confiscating Money Aimed at IRA Arms', 24 February 1984.
102. *The Associated Press*, 'U.S. Bid to Improve Trade With Northern Ireland', 2 March 1984.
103. *United Press International*, 14 October 1984.
104. M. Thatcher, *The Downing Street Years* (London: Harper Collins, 1993), p. 380.
105. *The Associated Press*, 'Ambassador Signals U.S. Clampdown on NORAID', 18 October 1984.
106. B. Rodwell, 'Envoy Condemns Ulster Jobs Code', *The Guardian*, 10 September 1987.
107. 88LONDON16998, 'Northern Ireland – Controlling the violence', 9 August 1988, available at: http://wikileaks.org/cable/1988/08/88LONDON16998.html# (accessed 4 June 2011).
108. Scott-Smith, 'Searching for the Successor Generation', p. 219.
109. Correspondence with Robert Korengold, 2 May 2011.
110. *Ibid.*

111. G. Heathcote, 'Washington To Show Chinese Treasure Found in Stately Home Attic', *The Associated Press*, 26 June 1985.

112. L. Goff, 'An International Rap', *The Washington Post*, 24 August 1987, p. 8.

113. G. R. Berridge, *Diplomacy: Theory and Practice* (Basingstoke: Palgrave, 2002), pp. 117–18.

114. M. Johnson, 'Jumbo Jet Crashes into Village; Hundreds Killed', *The Associated Press*, 22 December 1988.

115. Correspondence with Robert Korengold, 2 May 2011.

116. Pendleton interview, 22 June 1998.

117. M. Johnson, 'Outgoing U.S. Ambassador Reflects on Years in Britain', *The Associated Press*, 22 February 1989.

118. Correspondence with Robert Korengold, 2 May 2011.

119. J. Bilotta, *United Press International*, 22 December 1988.

120. Pendleton interview, 22 June 1998.

121. Correspondence with Robert Korengold, 2 May 2011.

122. E. Cody, 'Sabotage Questions Are Raised in Crash Probe; Search Teams Recover Jet's Black Boxes', *The Washington Post*, 23 December 1988, p. A1.

123. R. Barr, 'Pan Am Dead Remembered at Simple, Tearful Service', *The Associated Press*, 4 January 1989.

124. J. Randall, 'Service Mourns Flight 103 Victims; Scottish Churchman Exhorts Assembly, "Justice, Not Retaliation"', *The Washington Post*, 5 January 1989, p. A20.

125. *The Associated Press*, 'Eisenhower Statue Unveiled by Thatcher, U.S. Ambassador', 23 January 1989.

126. M. Parris, 'Little Green Men and a Blue Leader; Political Sketch', *The London Times*, 15 February 1989.

127. *The Independent*, 'Court Circular', 24 February 1989.

128. Off the record comment.

129. B. Schweid, 'Shultz Says Poindexter Assured Him U.S. Wasn't Trading Arms for Hostages', *The Associated Press*, 23 January 1987.

130. K. De Young, 'Thatcher Plan to Sell British Leyland Rouses Anti-American Sentiments; GM, Ford Bids for Parts of Ailing Firm Rekindle Political Row', *The Washington Post*, 22 March 1987, p. A23.

131. T. Coleman, 'Elements of Diplomacy / Interview with Charles Price II, US Ambassador to Britain', *The Guardian*, 2 February 1987, p. 23.

132. A. Watkins, 'The White House Candidate', *The Observer*, 25 May 1986, p. 9.

13
Henry E. Catto, Jr, 1989–91

Nicholas J. Cull

It is commonplace for citizens of other nations and even some members of the US Foreign Service to look askance at the time-honoured American practice that permits Presidents to use a certain proportion of ambassadorships as rewards for their friends and financial supporters. The system of political appointments has certainly thrown up its share of embarrassments and second-raters over the years, and by reducing the pool of appointments available to veteran diplomats it has frustrated careers that might otherwise have flowered to the benefit of US foreign policy. Yet the name of every lacklustre incumbent can be counter-balanced by the name of a political appointee who won the admiration of his staff and proved the value of a political pedigree. Henry Catto, Ambassador to the UK from 1989 to 1991, is a prime example of the second kind.

Henry E. Catto, Jr hailed from Dallas, Texas. He was born in 1930 without especial advantages. The family's lucky break came in 1936 when the Cattos moved to San Antonio and his father joined his uncle's insurance firm. Business success brought advantages to the young Henry. He was able to attend the best schools, studying at the Texas Military Institute and the prestigious Williams College in Massachusetts. Catto emerged as a dashing figure: elegant, charming and easy to get along with. In his own assessment, his personal lucky break came in 1958 when he married Jessica Hobby, an aspiring journalist who also happened to be Texas royalty: the daughter of the publisher of the *Houston Post* and former governor of Texas, William P. Hobby, Sr (eventual namesake of the Houston airport) and Oveta Culp Hobby, wartime head of the Women's Army Corps and Eisenhower's Secretary of Health, Education and Welfare. Catto developed an interest in politics, but his Republican convictions set him against the tide of Texas history which had effectively created a 'one party state for the Democratic Party. Catto ran twice for the State legislature and lost both times, but he fought a good fight and made good friends along the way, including George H. W. Bush.

Catto's party service paid off in 1969 when Richard Nixon made him deputy ambassador to the Organization of American States (OAS) working mostly on the education, science and culture committee, though he had a grandstand seat for the Soccer War. His fluency in Spanish helped. From 1971 to 1973 he served as Ambassador to El Salvador. In 1973 he became Chief of Protocol for the State Department, a post that required him to travel with Nixon to the Soviet Union and Middle East and oversee the state visits of foreign leaders to the US. Challenging tasks included his management of the visit of Emperor Hirohito of Japan. In the interval between the El Salvador Embassy and the protocol post, he completed a special assignment for the State Department on cultural relations with Latin America. In 1976, Gerald Ford posted him to Geneva as US Ambassador to the United Nations office there. This work gave Catto a deep working knowledge of the diplomatic process, a respect for the Foreign Service, and a particular appreciation of the importance of information work in international relations, all of which would become hallmarks of his later work including his London Embassy.

During the first Reagan administration, Catto was Assistant Secretary of Defence for Public Affairs from 1981–83, directing press relations for the Pentagon. In later years he joked that, at the Pentagon, he certainly learned the need to 'put one's mind in gear before allowing one's mouth to run'. Issues included the public flurry when the Navy decided to name a nuclear submarine the USS Corpus Christi, as some Catholics felt it was inappropriate to name a weapon after the body of Christ, even if the real namesake was the town in Texas. After leaving the Pentagon, Catto served as Vice Chairman and President of Broadcast Group at the Hobby family's H & C Communications. He ran a network of television stations in Houston and San Antonio, Texas and the Orlando-Daytona Beach area of Florida.[1]

Given Catto's extensive diplomatic experience and close relationship to George H. W. Bush it seemed inevitable that he would serve in his presidential administration in some foreign policy capacity. Within days of the election victory, pundits began to suggest possible roles for Catto. William Safire of *The New York Times* suggested that he might be a suitable director of the United States Information Agency which, since 1953, had overseen America's engagement with international opinion through channels such as information centres, press relations, exchange and cultural diplomacy and Voice of America broadcasting. Catto was already interested in the United States Information Agency (USIA) job, but the White House had other ideas.[2]

Catto's first inkling of his nomination to the London Embassy came at a Christmas party with the Bushes in the weeks following the 1988 election. He spotted the President-elect in animated conversation with his wife, Jessica. She explained the offer that was about to be made. Catto requested a day to think it over. While he was drawn to the post, which had a special meaning for him as the grandson of a British subject, it did not sit well with his family life. His wife had a career of her own. In addition to media work, she was designing and building eco-friendly homes in the western US. The Cattos agreed that he should take the post and that Jessica would join him when and as she was able. The arrangement reduced the level of formal entertainment at the Embassy, and the staff could see that it was hard on the couple. Some in the British media commented on the Ambassador's air of melancholy when his wife was away, and others speculated on marital disharmony, but Catto got into his stride regardless.[3]

Catto's transition into the life in London was much assisted by the outgoing Deputy Chief of Mission, Ray Seitz, who had a deep knowledge of British affairs thanks to two terms at Grosvenor Square. Catto was careful in his choice of Seitz's successor, selecting a veteran Foreign Service Officer named Ron Woods. Woods had led an impressive career, with service in Cairo, Rome, Paris and a spell as a senior staffer for Henry Kissinger. Woods became an essential element in Catto's administration of the Embassy and, for his part, he was impressed with Catto's approach: his efforts to get to know every element of his Embassy; his aversion to micromanaging; and his respect for the professionalism of his staff. It was a challenging transition nonetheless. Other senior staff joined the Embassy with Catto, including a new political counsellor, Bruce Burton, and a new economic minister counsellor, Anne Barry. It was an opportunity for Catto to remake the Embassy as he would wish, and so he did.[4]

Catto paid close attention to Embassy morale and was a master of calming troubled waters by treating a colleague to lunch. His relationship with Woods included regular tennis matches. Burton recalled Catto's mastery of the technique now known as 'MBWA' (management by walking around). He remembered many mornings glancing through his door to see the Ambassador gradually making his way down the length of the corridor from his office towards Burton's, stopping at rooms along the way, asking questions of his team. The Ambassador accumulated their answers and remarks on post-it notes, which he attached to his magnificent silk tie as he went. He adjusted his administration accordingly. He had a 'smile as big as Texas' and that worked wonders both outside the Embassy and within.[5] As events unfolded, Catto was soon called on to shepherd the Embassy staff through a difficult time: a colleague in the visa section named Marie Burke was brutally murdered in her home in circumstances which have still not been explained. His compassion and ability to listen displayed during the Burke case proved a scalable skill of value in the field. He was called on to visit families in Lockerbie, Scotland, who had lost family members in the bombing of PanAm Flight 103 a few months before he arrived and later survivors of a terrorist outrage in Northern Ireland.[6]

The other key appointment to Catto's staff was that of his minister counsellor for information – his senior public diplomacy officer. Here, Catto was fortunate that the White House staffing office was able to persuade one of the most experienced USIA officers – Charles 'Sam' Courtney – to defer his retirement to serve in the Embassy. Courtney's career had included a spell as Associate Director of USIA during the Reagan years and time as the minister for information at the Paris Embassy. He was a legend among his colleagues in public diplomacy, not least for having endured a kidnapping and punched a paparazzo who was harassing Duke Ellington when under Courtney's charge. He was well equipped to oversee Catto's relationship with the turbulent and potentially troublesome British news media without coming to blows. Specifically, Courtney understood that public diplomacy was not just about effective speaking, it also required effective listening. Courtney knew that his digests of British headlines and editorials which tracked the ebb and flow of British opinion found their way not only to his Ambassador's desk and his parent agency, but also reached the White House where – when necessary – the President himself paid attention.[7] Courtney's deputy – a rising star at USIA named Brian Carlson – remembered Catto's personal interest in the press. He regularly arrived in his office at the Embassy to find the Ambassador already ensconced in the day's newspapers, which Catto knew came to the public diplomacy staff first. Of course Catto could have asked for the papers to come to his own desk first, but Carlson felt he rather liked wandering the corridors of the Embassy, dropping in on his staff, and reading the papers *in situ*.[8]

Catto's investment in the Embassy extended to technology. To the chagrin of the guardians of the State Department's computer hardware, he insisted that the Embassy modernise its computer system, rejecting the clunky early 1980s Wang machines in favour of the latest Microsoft Local Area Network (LAN). The greater computing capacity obtained enabled the Embassy to do all sorts of things that were impossible on the old system, including – in the public diplomacy area – keeping closer track of movements of British opinion and staying on top of the kinds of questions British people were asking. Brian Carlson used the system to generate detailed analysis of the British political scene and found that Catto had a keen understanding of the value of knowing his audience before he spoke. The London Embassy would be way ahead of most other posts as the wave of digitisation washed forward. Some other European posts did not have even websites until the aftermath of the terrorist attacks of 11 September 2001.[9]

Lone Star over Winfield House

Running an embassy is only half of an ambassador's function. He, or she, has to reach out to multiple audiences in the nation to which they have been assigned. In the UK that meant managing relationships with such diverse realms as business, politics, media and that most idiosyncratic of British circles, the royal family. Catto knew how to play a part. He was aware that the British enjoyed having their expectations of a Texan fulfilled. This was doubtless why, when presenting his credentials, he greeted the Queen with an enthusiastic: 'How ya doin'?'[10] He soon added some Lone Star State touches to Winfield House. He flew the Texas state flag over the residence doorway and sometimes entertained in a Stetson. He installed a plywood cutout of a Hereford steer in the grounds (nicknamed Udder Pendragon) which gave him an excuse to raise the subject of European Community obstructions to US beef exports when any guest asked about it. At the receptions he threw at the residence, he served Tex-Mex food even though that meant training Winfield House's German chef to make nachos. His desk at Grosvenor Square included a small sign reading 'silencio, El jefe piensa' (silence, the boss is thinking).[11]

Catto saw his role – naturally enough – as keeping the Anglo-American special relationship on course. A prime concern was to facilitate the development of a sound working relationship between Prime Minister Margaret Thatcher and the new President. She had undoubted chemistry with Reagan, but that did not guarantee success with his successor by any measure. Catto was helped in this task by the early development of an excellent relationship with her private secretary and key foreign policy advisor, Charles Powell. Powell was a former diplomat and took readily to Catto's easy manner. The two men came to count on one another's guidance. Catto's discreet feedback following the first meeting between Mrs Thatcher and the President, that Bush preferred *both* parties to speak in an international meeting, was sufficient to produce far more balance in subsequent encounters of the two leaders.[12]

The most famous meeting between Bush and Thatcher was engineered by Catto early in his tenure, but took a long time to actually happen. He had long wanted Thatcher to speak at the Aspen Institute in Colorado with which he was associated and while preparing to take up his post in London managed to get the President to also commit to attend. They chose a day far in the future – 2 August 1990 – and planned around it. No one could have guessed that this would turn out to be the day Iraq, under Saddam Hussein, would invade Kuwait. The image of a united response so early in the crisis was a boon, but did not happen without cajoling. In a summit between the two leaders, hastily arranged at Catto's Colorado ranch, Woody Creek, the Prime Minister proclaimed this was 'no time to go wobbly'.[13]

It was an era of immense change in Europe. Reform gathered pace in Eastern Europe while leaders in Western Europe looked to take the European Economic Community to the next level. In 1990 Britain joined the European exchange rate mechanism, moving the British economy's connection to the continent into an unprecedented intimacy, but there were cross currents. Margaret Thatcher herself remained deeply sceptical of Europe and her hard line provoked significant splits with her cabinet colleagues at this time, including most famously her Chancellor of the Exchequer, Nigel Lawson, and Foreign Secretary, Geoffrey Howe. The United States generally welcomed European integration and felt that the reunification of West and East Germany was a positive step. Thatcher was not so sure and Catto had to become adept at managing the Prime Minister's concerns as the United

States worked to advance European integration and paid increased attention to Germany. In December 1989 President Bush publically and explicitly
endorsed the expansion of the European Community. The British press proclaimed the President's words to be a full-on snub to Thatcher. Alerted by
Powell, Catto called the White House and elicited both a call from President
Bush to Thatcher and a flying visit from Secretary of State Baker. Thatcher's
face was saved and the blip in the Anglo-American relationship passed. For
the political counsellor Burton, the speedy resolution of the problem was a
testament both to Catto's political instincts and his ability to get straight on
the phone to the White House, which a career appointee simply could not
have done.[14]

There were other hiccoughs. Catto's political work in London included
a timely brief to rebuild links to the opposition Labour Party, which was
then in the midst of rethinking its policies. A warming in party attitudes
towards the US was part of this process.[15] It was a barometer of the shift
in the Labour Party for the *Guardian* to note that Catto was taking their
leader – Neil Kinnock – 'seriously'.[16] Catto paid early visits to Kinnock and
his shadow foreign minister, Gerald Kaufman, and paved the way for a high
profile visit by shadow chancellor John Smith to visit Washington in April
1990.[17] His Embassy continued the established tradition of cultivating opposition politicians with International Visitor trips to the United States. Visitors
during Catto's tenure included Nick Brown (the future chief whip) and David
Clark (future chancellor of the Duchy of Lancaster). Catto paid a price for his
foresight. Sources close to Thatcher indicated that she was 'disappointed' by
his openness to the opposition, but the Ambassador's relationship with 'the
Iron Lady' was unaffected in the longer term.[18] Catto was correct in sens-
ing that the Thatcher years were coming to an end. In his final months in
London he was required to establish a working relationship with Margaret
Thatcher's successor, albeit from within her own party, John Major.[19]

Catto needed to reach not only the British establishment, but also the
wider British public. This required a concerted effort to engage the British
media. Catto was unafraid of the British media, despite its rather unkind
obsession with the absence of Jessica. With Courtney's encouragement, he
was a regular guest on BBC radio's flagship morning *Today* programme, typically speaking from the BBC's mobile studio built into a standard London
taxi, giving an American point of view on the great events of the moment.
His level temperament helped when the questioning slipped into absurd levels of partisanship. He also appeared on BBC television's premiere talk show:
Wogan in April 1990 and as a panellist on the current affairs discussion programme, *Question Time,* in January 1991.Catto did not take the British press
passively. He was prepared to rebuke journalists in private; gently upbraid-
ing columnist Simon Hoggart of the *Observer* for making merry over the
President's slips of the tongue.[20] He also took on the advertisers, persuading
Konica computers that using a picture of former President Ronald Reagan to

illustrate the billboard slogan 'anybody can learn to use a Konica' was rather insulting. The billboard disappeared forthwith.[21]

When really provoked, Catto was prepared to go public with his resistance to views expressed in the British press. In June 1990 he launched a stinging attack on the playwright Harold Pinter following an anti-American diatribe in the *Independent*. In a widely quoted letter to that paper, Catto quipped of Pinter: 'he would not be Vaclav Havel even if Britain were Czechoslovakia. He brings to mind Goethe's comment that when ideas fail, words come in very handy.'[22] When Pinter sniped back, Catto sought to bring the affair to a conclusion by inviting the writer for lunch at Le Gavroche, the Ambassador's favourite, just two blocks from Grosvenor Square. The writer accepted. Catto later recalled: 'I made no dent in his view of my country, but I enjoyed his company and he apparently enjoyed my wine.'[23]

As might be expected a considerable amount of Catto's time was occupied in the promotion of American trade interests. He lobbied in support of a bid for more landing rights in the UK for American Airlines and Pan Am, and against what Catto saw as 'the unseen but powerful hand of British Airways'.[24] Here Catto's perceived connection to the President paid dividends and added weight to his intervention, even though he did not need to call in any favours on that occasion. Courtney suspected that Catto's perceived relationship to the President brought the Embassy favours from the airlines as well. American Airlines was happy to provide two-dozen complementary first-class seats for Broadway performers to enable their participation in a gala theatre performance organised by the United States Information Service (USIS) post. It was the sort of help Courtney could not imagine coming to an Embassy headed by a foreign service officer.[25]

While all observers were aware of Catto's ability to call the President, Catto avoided actually making direct requests to the White House. One rare occasion when he felt justified in calling was to ensure that he was included in a meeting of Deputy Secretary of State Larry Eagleburger and CIA director Robert Gates with Margaret Thatcher, from which Eagleburger had wanted him excluded. Catto understood that to permit such a meeting without the sitting Ambassador being present would have sent a signal that he was irrelevant.[26] Courtney – though not Catto – remembered another call, made at the request of a senior executive at CBS News. On 21 January 1991, in the run-up to the outbreak of the first Gulf War, a CBS crew led by journalist Bob Simon and including the network's London bureau chief Peter Bluff, crossed from Saudi Arabia into Iraq. They were promptly captured by the Iraqi army and jailed. Conditions in custody were shockingly privative and roughly applied. CBS worked desperately to get their team back, but over a month went by without success. One problem was that there were few voices in the world to which the Iraqis would listen. One such voice was that of Soviet Premiere, Mikhail Gorbachev, but who could bring Gorbachev into play? Henry Kissinger wrote directly to the Kremlin. At the request of a CBS executive in London, Catto called the President and the President duly called Gorbachev, who asked Iraqi Foreign Minister, Tariq Ali, for mercy. It worked. Forty days into their ordeal, Iraq freed Bob Simon and his crew.[27]

Courtney recalled one further contribution of the London Embassy to the Gulf War. The news digests faxed daily to the White House tracked British attitudes to the war. In the final days of the campaign, these indicated a palpable revulsion against the bombing of the Iraqi army during its withdrawal along the so-called 'Road of Death' to Basra. Courtney believed that this material was instrumental in persuading the President that the war could not be prosecuted beyond the objective of liberating Kuwait.[28] The documentation to confirm or disprove this assertion has yet to be declassified.

Over Too Soon

Catto's time in London was unexpectedly cut short, and indeed was in question as early as a year in. In the spring of 1990, word reached London of an administrative problem back in Washington DC. The United States Information Agency was experiencing 'trouble at the top' owing to a clash between its director, Bruce Gelb, and the director of Voice of America (VOA), Richard Carlson, who disliked the VOA being a constituent part of USIA, especially when Gelb moved to clip his institution's wings. In March, Chase Untermeyer at the White House staffing office approached Catto to see if he might be willing to move, doubtless also understanding the difficulty of coordinating an Ambassador's schedule with that of his wife. However, the spat between Gelb and Carlson passed and Catto focused on other matters, including the mounting crisis between Kuwait and Iraq. He heard nothing more about a possible move until the following January, on the eve of the Gulf War, when Untermeyer raised the suggestion again. Catto agreed, and by the end of that month the press was reporting that the former Deputy Chief of Mission in London, career FSO Raymond Seitz, would be succeeding Catto. Seitz had played a valued role in Catto's transition to London, and Catto enthusiastically recommended him as an ideal successor, fully acquainted with the London scene.[29] It was unprecedented that a career diplomat should take the London job, but Seitz was the stuff of exceptions. He had excellent connections across the British establishment – having served twice in the Embassy before – and enjoyed a close relationship with Secretary of State Baker. He would do well in the post. The White House announced the change on 13 March 1991.[30]

London to USIA

While Catto had enjoyed his time as US Ambassador in London, he was excited by the prospect of directing a global agency like USIA and reporting directly to the President. He had quite fancied the job back in 1988.

Catto's varied experience in both communications and foreign policy certainly fitted him for the post, though his staff at the agency was equally glad of his excellent relationship with the President and his smooth and relaxed manner.[31] His priority on taking office at USIA was: 'to bring chaos to an end and try and create some order and *esprit de corps*'.[32] Catto's techniques included the same emphasis on personal relationships that had worked in London. On the day of his swearing in he hosted all the two-dozen top agency staff (both political and career) and their spouses for a cook-out at his home.[33]

USIA flourished under Catto's stewardship. He mended fences with Voice of America and it helped that its new director was his friend, Chase Untermeyer. He devised a new set of strategic goals for the agency and initiated a process to plan for the agency's future as the Cold War ended. In March 1992 he wrote to all agency personnel noting: 'If we [at USIA] were children of the Cold War, so the logic runs, are we now orphans?' He established a series of four study groups to evaluate key areas of the agency's operation.[34] Findings of these studies included a widespread feeling that USIA needed a mission statement that reflected global concerns including democracy building, the free market, and the environment. One subcommittee noted: 'the agency must make the point that public diplomacy is more cost-effective than military force ... and deserves to be funded accordingly'. But the reports would not be completed until the autumn, and their application would be hostage to the result of the presidential election.[35]

For Catto, the defeat of George Bush in the presidential election of November 1992 came as a bitter disappointment. He was just hitting his stride at USIA when the campaign began. Catto anticipated several more years of service, and even spoke to Untermeyer about the VOA director succeeding to the agency directorship in due course.[36] But it was not to be. The election was fought, not on the undoubted achievements of the Bush administration in the foreign policy field, but on matters closer to home.

In his letter of thanks to Henry Catto, written on the day before he left office, the President wrote:

> I thank you for your forward-looking efforts to define USIA's role in the post-Cold War era, and at a time when our efforts to educate other peoples about the principles of democracy and free enterprise are more important than ever, I salute you for reaffirming the agency's vital mission.[37]

Unfortunately, powerful figures in the Senate remained unconvinced about the post-Cold War value of USIA. The agency slipped back into vulnerability in the Clinton administration, and by the time that administration had woken up to the importance of public diplomacy, the agency had been cut to a shadow of its Catto-era self, offered as a sacrifice to please Senator Jesse Helms, and merged into the Department of State.[38]

Some of the investments made by Catto and his predecessors paid off in the 1990s. In May 1997 a New Labour government came to power in London led by Tony Blair. Over half of Blair's cabinet was made up of people who the London Embassy had cultivated through some form of international visitor (IV) exchange over the years. Visits typically lasted two or three weeks and included meetings arranged on behalf of the Embassy to fit the specific interests of the visitor. Former IVs included the Foreign Secretary, Robin Cook (1977), Board of Trade President Margaret Beckett (1976) and Anne Taylor, Leader of the Commons (1980). Tony Blair, his Chancellor Gordon Brown and Chief Whip Nick Brown were not only former IVs (1986, 1984 and 1990 respectively) but had also all returned at their own request in the Voluntary Visitor programme in 1992. George Robertson, the new Minister of Defence, and Ron Davis, Secretary of State for Wales, were alumni of USIA-funded NATO tours (1981 and 1985), while the Scottish Secretary Donald Dewar and Minister of Agriculture Jack Cunningham had been cultivated in their political infancy under the American Council of Youth Political Leaders Programme (1968 and 1973). Harriet Harman, the Social Security Secretary, had come as a Voluntary Visitor (1988). David Clark, the Chancellor of the Duchy of Lancaster had been an IV in 1982 and a Voluntary Visitor during Catto's time in 1990. There was no shortage of exchange alumni in subcabinet posts either. The Embassy had done well.[39] Future historians may debate the impact of this direct experience of the US in forming the distinctive openness to America that was such a feature of the 'New Labour' approach. Ironically, Blair's willingness to support the United States over Iraq would prove a major element in his political undoing a decade later.

Retirement

After leaving office Catto returned to Texas and the family business. He served on the board of National Public Radio. He retained an enthusiasm for diplomacy and public diplomacy especially, teaching courses on the subject for several happy semesters at the University of Texas in San Antonio while writing an informative and often entertaining volume of memoirs. He continued to press for proper investment in US public diplomacy and was appalled by the merger of USIA into the Department of State in 1999.[40] Catto was hardly less dedicated to extending his ambassadorial work in Anglo-American and transatlantic relations. He served as chairman of the Atlantic Council of the United States and a member of the British-North America committee. He supported many Atlantic themes in his capacity as vice chair of the Aspen Institute. He lost his wife in 2009. He died of complications from leukaemia in December 2011.

In the last analysis, Henry Catto did not have sufficient time in either the London Embassy or the USIA directorship to accomplish all that he might have done given his experience and political clout, but he was a first-class steward of the institutions under his charge and accomplished all that could have been expected in the time granted to him. Both were stronger as a result of his 'watch'. It is to Catto's credit that he was plainly admired by his career employees and was taken as a model of diplomacy by many. The career FSO Brian Carlson – the number two in the public diplomacy section at Catto's embassy – went on to become US Ambassador to Latvia (2001–2005) and paid a succinct tribute: 'I learnt a lot about being an ambassador from Henry.'[41]

His friend and interlocutor on Margaret Thatcher's staff Charles, now Lord Powell, had no doubt that despite his brief time in London Catto had made a difference. In the summer of 2011 he wrote:

> Henry Catto ranks justifiably high among America's Ambassadors to the United Kingdom. He was both highly professional, given his experience serving earlier Administrations in top-level posts, and political – in the sense that he knew President George H.W. Bush well personally and was able to convey his thoughts and priorities accurately as well as convey the British Government's concerns and preoccupations to the White House at the very top level. That is a rare and extremely valuable combination, and when added to his natural charm made him an ideal representative for the US, and notably more successful than Ambassadors from other countries at that time.[42]

One could hardly ask for more.

Notes

1. Interview with Henry Catto, 26 April 2004 and autobiography: Henry E. Catto, Jr, *Ambassadors at Sea: The High and Low Adventures of a Diplomat* (Austin, TX: University of Texas Press, 1998).
2. Catto interview, 24 April 2004. William Safire, 'Reading Bush's Mind', *The New York Times,* 24 October 1988, p. A17.
3. Jan Jarboe, 'The Lone Ambassador', *Texas Monthly,* November 1990, pp. 102–4, 164–8.
4. Interview with Ron Woods, 6 June 2011; and Bruce Burton, 2 March 2012.
5. Burton interview, 2 March 2012.
6. Woods interview, 6 June 2011; Catto, *Ambassadors at Sea,* p. 249. For a contemporary note see Stewart Tendler, 'Embassy Knife Death', *The Times,* 27 May 1989. Still unsolved, theories around the murder include Burke's having stumbled on a corrupt employee at the Embassy selling US visas to Jamaican gangs. This is advanced at: http://www.truecrimelibrary.com/crime_series_show.php?series_number=11&id=1346 (accessed 8 July 2011).
7. Interview with Sam Courtney, 28 April 2011. Catto, *Ambassadors at Sea,* p. 261. For memoirs of Courtney's career at USIA and response to the George W. Bush administration see Charles Sam Courtney, *Ignorant Armies: Tales and Morals of an Alien Empire* (Bloomington, IN: Trafford Publishing, 2007).

8. Brian Carlson to author, 8 July 2011.
9. Interview with Carlson, 19 September 2011.
10. T. Rees Shapiro, 'Henry Catto…', *Washington Post*, 19 December 2011.
11. Catto, *Ambassadors at Sea*, pp. 250, 265, 266, 367, n. 3; Jarboe, 'The Lone Ambassador'.
12. Catto interview, 24 April 2004.
13. Catto interview, 24 April 2004; Simon Tisdall, 'Colorado Summit to Examine Roles', *The Guardian*, 2 August 1990, p. 6.
14. Burton interview, 2 March 2012. Michael White and Martin Walker, 'Bush Bails Out PM on Europe', *The Guardian*, 6 December 1989, p. 22; Andrew Stephen, 'Baker Flies in to Calm Fears of Split with Thatcher', *Observer*, 10 December 1989, p. 14.
15. Alan Travis and Patrick Wintour, 'Labour Takes a Second Look at its Policies', *The Guardian*, 18 April 1990, p. 24.
16. Patrick Wintour and Michael White, 'Tactics of a Synthetic Crisis', *The Guardian*, 13 March 1990, p. 4.
17. Alex Brummer, 'Notebook', *The Guardian*, 20 April 1990, p. 12.
18. Andrew Stephen, 'Labour Registers under the Name of Mr. Smith', *Observer*, 22 April 1990, p. 15.
19. Catto, *Ambassadors at Sea*, pp. 290–1.
20. Simon Hoggart, 'Simon Hoggart', *Observer*, 1 December 1991, p. 24; Catto, *Ambassadors at Sea*, p. 261.
21. Catto, *Ambassadors at Sea*, p. 245.
22. Henry Catto, 'Why Harold Pinter Will Never Be Britain's Vaclav Havel', *Independent*, 10 June 1990, p. 30. Quotations of this include Polly Toynbee, 'Master of Strident Silences', *The Guardian*, 29 September 1990, p. 23.
23. Catto, *Ambassadors at Sea*, p. 262.
24. *Ibid.*, p. 272.
25. Courtney interview, 28 April 2011.
26. Catto, *Ambassadors at Sea*, p. 251.
27. Courtney interview, 28 April 2011. For press coverage see Mark Fineman, 'Iraq Frees CBS News Crew; Network Credits Soviet Intervention', *Los Angeles Times*, 3 March 1991. This report makes no mention of Catto or the President's role. Catto had no recollection of the call.
28. Courtney interview, 28 April 2011.
29. Catto interview, 24 April 2004; Martin Walker, 'Baker Aide Tipped as New US Envoy to Britain', *The Guardian*, 29 January 1991, p. 10.
30. Burton interview, 2 March 2012. Nomination papers are at George H. W. Bush Library (hereafter GBL) WHORM subject file FG 298, ID 218640 SS, Untermeyer to President, 24 February 1991, with an announcement on 13 March 1991.
31. Catto interview, 24 April 2004; Author's interview with McKinney Russell, 19 September 2011; Catto, *Ambassadors at Sea*, pp. 296-97.
32. Catto interview, 24 April 2004; Catto, *Ambassadors at Sea*, pp. 298, 313–14; GBL WHORM subject file, FG 298, 224301, Arthur E. Green (USIA) to Roger B. Porter (White House), 20 March 1991.
33. Interview with Robert Gosende (Associate Director, Africa, USIA), 29 February 2012.
34. National Archives II (College Park, MD) RG 306 A1 (1061) box 2, USIA historical collection, misc. files, 1940s–1990s, Catto to colleagues, 17 March 1992 and

29 May 1992 and Broadcasting Study file, esp. Penney to Schneider, 'interim report of the global issues and concerns subcommittee, n/d.

35. NA RG 306 A1 (1061) box 2, USIA historical collection, misc. files, 1940s–1990s, Broadcasting Study file, Penney to Schneider, 'interim report of the global issues and concerns sub-committee', n/d.

36. Author's telephone interview with Chase Untermeyer, Voice of America Director, 17 March 2005.

37. GBL WHORM subject file, FG 298, ID 361850, President to Untermeyer, 30 December 1992; President to Catto, 19 January 1993.

38. The author has written a book-length study of this story. See Nicholas J. Cull, *The Decline and Fall of the United States Information Agency: American Public Diplomacy, 1989–2001* (New York: Palgrave, 2012).

39. William J. Clinton Library (Little Rock, Arkansas) CPR ARMS (email) WHO 1997/01-1997/12 [Joseph Duffey] OA/ID 550,000, Duffey (director, USIA) to Erskine Bowles (Chief of Staff, White House), USIA Weekly Report, 7 April 1997.

40. Catto interview, 24 April 2004. Some years after the merger Catto met its co-author, Madeleine Albright at a dinner in Aspen. She approached and asked Catto sheepishly: 'Did we make a mistake folding USIA into the State Department? Catto confirmed that he believed they had indeed made a great mistake. He took her question as evidence that 'the mother of the thing had renounced the bastard child'.

41. Carlson to author.

42. Powell to author, 12 June 2011.

Part V

The Post-Cold War Ambassadors, 1991–2001

Introduction

Alison R. Holmes

The next three Ambassadors are relatively unusual for four, very different, reasons. First, this group includes both the only career Foreign Service officer as well as the most senior military figure to hold the post. These are important milestones in their own right, but it also means they made no financial contributions, nor did they gain their position by 'cronyism' (though they did have access to the presidents who appointed them), but by expertise in their chosen realms of government service. Second, they are all the appointees of a Democratic President. This is relatively unusual over the time frame of this volume, but it is also unusual that there are three under a single administration. This can be explained, of course, by the fact that Seitz was initially appointed by Bush 41, but held in post by President Clinton. Retention is certainly not a typical appointment profile and, in this case, explains the fact that Seitz had not even met Clinton until he went to Washington to help prepare for John Major's first, and rather frosty, trip. Third, they served in a period of relative peace and economic prosperity, colouring their mission and their workload as Ambassadors and which may have also had an influence on the fourth factor. Namely, they served at a time of a broad shift to the Left throughout most of the Western world and transatlantic/leader relations became heavily involved in what became known as the 'Third Way', a domestic political response to the process of globalisation.[1]

For these Ambassadors, the 'peace dividend' of the post-Cold War era was a statement of fact. Clinton had won on a slogan of 'It's the economy stupid' that he brandished as an attack on President Bush for his keen interest in foreign affairs which Clinton damned as both irrelevant to most Americans and something of an elite interest. This mantra was also his declaration that his focus was, and would remain, domestic issues. Ultimately, it was not possible to deliver on this policy goal as Clinton, like many Presidents, was forced to deal with the entire range of global issues that form the operational reality of UK–US relations. Foremost among these were the massive changes in South Africa, set against the bloody events in Mogadishu, Sierra Leone and Rwanda. The Balkans were a constant pressure, and one on which the Blair–Clinton axis would prove crucial, as was the ongoing issue, much closer to home, Northern Ireland.

Seitz and Crowe both represented departures from the 'norm' in that their ability to participate in the policy development process back in Washington was second to none. However, their capacity as 'civil servants' arguably meant they may not have been able, at crucial points, to argue their case as effectively as they might, had they been more traditional cronies. It is at this point that the parameters of what might be called the 'structure/agency' debate are particularly relevant to the conduct of transatlantic diplomacy as highlighted by the issue of Northern Ireland. As the presidency, as an institution, was being shifted from the 'bully pulpit' to the 'permanent campaign' made possible by the new world of 24/7 media, all three of Clinton's Ambassadors (especially those who felt a personal empathy for their governmental counterparts) were closed out of the political loop at various times and at a distinct cost to overall relations. Seitz and Crowe both recall their embarrassment and even shame at the way their government was handling various aspects of their dealings with the British government. Some might suggest this was due to the slightly cool relations between Major and Clinton at the time. However, even with the change to a more 'conducive' opposite number in Blair, there were signs that the diplomatic loop was not always being well tended. For the media era politicians, it would appear that the finer points of diplomatic exchange can be lost between the competing demands of domestic constituencies and the news cycle. Interestingly, Lader seems to have avoided these type of issues, but that may be explained one of three ways. First, it may be simply by virtue that the issue had moved on by this point. Second, Clinton's relationship to Blair was fundamentally different, which may have enabled them to resolve issues directly. Or finally, it may have been that Lader understood, on a more overtly political level, how to work in the wake of an 'activist chief executive'. As he points out:

> I had seen, and thought myself many times dealing with foreign government, I didn't go through ambassador. I haven't met many folks in the West Wing who did. If you had the relationship, you just called somebody – at Number 10 or in the Ministry of whatever. And so, do you spend all your time trying to – I'm being really honest with you – do you spend all your time trying to get yourself into the middle of conversations where other parties, who had the power, when they don't care whether you are there or not, or do you spend your time doing something where maybe Number 10 and the West Wing aren't spending as

much time . . . or that can genuinely advance the good relations between the two countries?[2]

A question for the future will be whether, as the office of the President continues to develop, and indeed as the office of the Prime Minister becomes more 'presidential', whether these sorts of issues will become more commonplace or be teased out of the system by a different tack in terms of the individuals appointed or in their training and experience.

The changing face of conflict from international to civil war at this time also produced unforeseen consequences for both Admiral Crowe as well as for the London Embassy and all Embassies around the world. In 1996, while Crowe was still in London, a truck armed with a bomb was driven into a US Air Force Dormitory in Saudi Arabia, killing 19 airmen. Two years later, a similar technique was used in both Kenya and Tanzania, killed over 200 people and injuring over 5,000. It is these events, rather than 9/11 as commonly assumed, that provided the impetus for major changes in Embassy security.[3] It is interesting to note that, despite his advancing age, Crowe was appointed by Secretary of State Madeleine Albright in October 1998 (and in accordance with the 1986 Diplomatic Security Act requiring reports on fatal incidents) to be the chair of a dual panel on the two events. Crowe used his military and recent ambassadorial experience (including his new understanding of terrorist organisations and tactics) to write a report that pulled no punches. He roundly criticised the administration for a lack of care and attention in terms of diplomatic safety, and took only some of the sting out of his attack by agreeing to be a lead campaigner on Capitol Hill for the funding required. Ironically, this process would eventually lead to the decision to leave Grosvenor Square and to what has been called a 'new era of fortress embassies . . . America's global image and the Architecture of Democracy had become the architecture of Fear.'[4] The saving grace may be, if Jane Loeffler is correct, that London has avoided the worst of these changes by embarking on a design for the new Embassy that she suggests could be seen as a 'positive statement' and potentially a 'new direction' for embassy architecture that may restore at last some of its ideals.[5]

Already, the post-Cold War Ambassadors can be looked on as a group apart. The hopes that the Clinton years might become a second 'Camelot' were left behind as scandal, impeachment proceedings and, more importantly, the reality of the world beyond the 'end of history' engulfed the administration and potentially its diplomatic representatives abroad. As Lader observes:

Government is a much more collaborative process and in diplomacy, patience and deliberateness, not deliberation, but deliberateness are essential ingredients . . . you can either be frustrated by that . . . or you can say 'This is part of my role' and you quietly go and have the conversations that are probably not seminal and are probably not even making a significant contribution to the end game, but as part of the whole, is shaping the clay...so that ultimately it can be sculpted. It's a footnote role to history.[6]

Notes

1. Alison Holmes, *The Third Way: Globalisation's Legacy* (Leicester: Troubadour, 2009).
2. Alison Holmes, interview with Ambassador Philip Lader, Charleston, SC, 2008.
3. Jane C. Loeffler, *The Architecture of Diplomacy: Building America's Embassies* (New York: Princeton Architectural Press, rev. 2nd edn, 2011), Preface.
4. Richard Arndt, *The First Resort of Kings: American Cultural Diplomacy in the Twentieth Century* (Dulles, VA: Potomac Books, 2005), p. 147.
5. Loeffler, *The Architecture of Diplomacy*, Preface.
6. Holmes, interview with Ambassador Philip Lader.

14
Raymond G. H. Seitz, 1991–94

Alison R. Holmes

Ambassador Seitz is remarkable in the story of US–UK diplomatic relations in at least three ways. Probably the most significant is the fact he was the first, and remains to date, the *only* career Foreign Service officer to be appointed Ambassador to the Court of St James's. The resistance of the London post to career officers in favour of political appointees also contributes to the second unusual aspect; Seitz served as Ambassador to the UK under two different Presidents. By itself, this is not without precedent.[1] Yet, the story by which he came to be nominated, which we shall return to, first by President H. W. Bush in 1991 and then held in post by President Clinton in 1993, is illuminating when examining the career of a foreign service officer in a world of political appointees. Finally, he is unusual within the Foreign Service – but not unique within London, again as we shall see – in that his tenure as Ambassador was his third tour of duty there. He served as a political officer from 1975–79, Deputy Chief of Mission (DCM) from 1984–89 and finally as Ambassador in the early 1990s. As he says himself, 'Nobody could have been better prepared for the job than I.'[2]

Raymond George Hardenbergh Seitz was born the youngest of three children to an army family in Hawaii on 8 December 1940. As he explained in his Churchill Lecture of 1999, five years after he had retired from the Foreign Service, his birth was auspicious to the extent that it occurred at 'almost at the same moment America became a world power'.[3] Indeed, on the day before his first birthday, he was already caught up in world events as he was scurried to safety, away from the 'Japanese aircraft that flew out of the morning sun over the Pacific Ocean and attacked Pearl Harbour'.[4] While he does not suggest these events were directly related, he went on to explain that this coincidence of birth meant that most, if not all, of his personal and professional life 'fitted snugly within a clearly bracketed, historical epoch that ran for exactly 50 years'. He went on, 'For this half-century the United States engaged in a titanic global struggle, first combating the threat of fascism in a hot war and then resisting the menace of communism in a cold war.'[5]

It is also true to say, that same sunny day he spent in his mother's care as his father struggled with the unfolding tragedy, also marked one of the formative moments of what eventually came to be known as the 'special relationship'. Taken with the early childhood years Seitz spent living in immediate post-war Germany, it would be understandable if Seitz had become a wholehearted subscriber to the 'special relationship' rhetoric. However, Seitz was no soft-hearted ideologue. He was a seasoned career officer who eschewed was he saw as the 'sentimentality' of a phrase that, in his view, allowed a dangerous lack of rigour to creep into the analysis of interests. Yet, whatever the wording, he clearly acted in the belief that there are two certainties of UK–US relations in this 'epoch': they are highly valued and run deep – on both sides of the Atlantic.

Seitz's mother died when he was 11 with the result was that he and his two older siblings[6] spent much of their childhood on the move. They lived for a time with his grandmother in Delaware, and then away at boarding schools and summers wherever his father's much-decorated career as an army general took them.[7] He studied history at Yale and graduated in 1963.[8] After graduation, he moved to Dallas to take up a teaching post and once again crossed paths with history by arriving not long before the assassination of President Kennedy, which had a 'tremendous effect' on him.[9] In a strange parallel, though a connection that would prove crucial later in his career, Seitz also arrived in Texas as the Republicans began to effectively take back the state. In Houston, the party was being led by George H. W. Bush, as Chairman of the Republican Party for Harris County, and assisted in this endeavour by a young Henry Catto[10] – later becoming President and Ambassador to the Court of St James's, respectively.[11] Slowly, Texas politics did begin to turn, evidenced by the fact that Bush went on to win a congressional seat in the House of Representatives and headed off to Washington in 1966 – the year Seitz was commissioned into the Foreign Service and also journeyed back east.[12] It would be many years before this particular loop was closed.

Upon meeting Ambassador Seitz, it is his east coast family roots and Ivy League education that are more apparent than a 'Lone Star state of mind'.[13] However, when one discovers that his past includes travelling across Europe by Vespa with a guitar slung over his back and singing hootenanny to help pay for the trip – one quickly realises there is clearly more to the man than meets the eye.

If his upbringing had an impact on his general approach, he also became steeped in State Department thinking. This struggle is a constant throughout his career, though arguably his training was usually to the fore as he consistently resisted what he saw as the 'sentimental' language of a 'special relationship'. He went so far as to express a distinct dislike for the 'typical anglophile' and declared himself to be instead an 'anglophilophobe'.[14] Seitz was known to his colleagues and the wider community in London for his muted approach, coloured by his understanding of power, national interest and the role of the diplomacy as a primarily government-to-government activity.[15] In short, he was an Anglophile in style if not in name and a man very much of the 'epoch' he identified as being his own.

The chapter will look not only at the experience of Seitz as Ambassador, but also at his two other postings to the UK. Each tour is significant because, separately *and* collectively, they bring light to different aspects of the workings of the London Embassy and impart lessons that can be applied across this study. In terms of his personal career, it was almost as if the State Department had a master plan, but for the man who wanted to live in exotic places and travel the world, he laughingly says of himself '...from 1972 onwards I was...Washington – London, Washington – London, Washington – London. So it didn't turn out the way I had expected – not because anybody had a plan or anything – it was accidental – but it wasn't the Foreign Service career I had expected.'[16] The result was a career that not only 'fit neatly' into an 'epoch' of history, but one that has been characterised by more than one commentator as being that of someone who should be considered near, if not at the top of the list for the title of 'most successful' American Ambassador to the UK. Ambassador Streator (one of the longest serving Deputy Chiefs of Mission in the London Embassy and Seitz's boss on the latter's first tour as well as his immediate predecessor in the post of Minister) sums up the views of many when he says of Seitz: 'He did a very good job in...all three positions. He was a political officer, minister and ambassador. I think he probably is the most successful ambassador in the post war period.'[17]

Political Officer, 1976–79: Getting Used to Being 'Over Here'

Seitz arrived in London in 1975 as a political officer to cover what was effectively the 'Africa desk' – an unusual feature of the London Embassy in that most US posts do not use a geographic designation system. This 'desk' arrangement is usually attributed to two factors unique to London; the sheer size of the Embassy and the fact the city is a regular gathering place for international and bilateral meetings that often – though not always – involve the United Kingdom. It was also helpful in that it reflected the organisation of the British Foreign Office:

> I thought that, if I returned...after two assignments there [Africa], I would be identified as an 'African-*ist*'...and while I was interested in Africa, I was not *that* interested in Africa. I wanted to see more...So a friend of mine...who had been assigned to London, called me and told me...there was this opening and the political counselor would be happy to have me come...to cover Africa. And – as I learned later – for many years, the embassy in London...had a political section that was organized

to have different officers following different regions around the world because so much went on in London…it is unusual in an embassy in Europe to have somebody whose responsibility is Africa or somebody whose responsibility is the Middle East. They don't have that in Tokyo or Beijing or Moscow, but I think there had always been [this job] in London and among African-ists it was a highly desirable job – because it wasn't in Africa![18]

At the time of Seitz's arrival, the UK was struggling to define itself, dealing with the remains of the Empire and developing a role for the changing Commonwealth. Rhodesia was a specific problem between the UK and the US and it fell to Seitz to follow, report on and, at times, even to negotiate on this increasingly fractious issue. He was later also charged with tracking the fortunes of the Conservatives – out of power at this point, but vocal on Rhodesia.

In Washington, President Nixon had stepped down in the aftermath of the Watergate scandal and Vice President Gerald Ford stepped in until he lost the presidential election of 1976 to Jimmy Carter. In terms of the London Embassy, the result was that the position of Ambassador passed relatively quickly from Nixon's second term appointee, Ambassador Elliot Richardson to Gerald Ford's replacement appointment, Ambassador Anne Armstrong before a return to a longer term under Ambassador Kingman Brewster. Somewhat ironically, this meant the Embassy was organised through this period in a more 'traditional' State Department fashion. The Deputy Chief of Mission, Ron Spiers, had arrived in 1975 at the beginning of this period of uncertainty, ran the day-to-day business more directly than might be the case if there were a 'hands-on' appointee in place. Spiers also had the advantage of having been a political officer in London from 1966–69 when he got to know a number of Labour politicians, many of whom were prominent members of the government by the time he returned as Minister. Thus, Spiers is the first of a number of key London 'two-' or even 'three-termers' whose careers crucially intersect and overlap, directly influencing the direction of Seitz's own career. It was also Spiers's tendency to a foreign-service-management style that meant younger officers, such as Seitz, had more direct input to the policy process. Again, as Seitz explains:

> And of course what happened – you talk about dumb luck, being in the right place at the right time – all these things come into play…it is a big Embassy – a big Embassy in a big European bureau…But what happened is – I was this secretary, second secretary with these two lowly responsibilities – the Conservative Party and Africa. Well, these two things began to converge and got more and more important until they got to a point that they were almost defining the relationship between the two countries and…because nobody else knew where Africa was…Suddenly I was

getting pulled into bigger and bigger situations...briefing Presidents – flying back to Washington with our then ambassador, Anne Armstrong, to brief Henry [Kissinger]...meeting with Zimbabwean Rhodesians at the Foreign Office – and the Foreign Secretary asking me to stay behind to talk...As the Ford Administration was coming to an end, the Carter Administration – Carter prior to his presidency – was identifying Africa as a central issue. In the meantime, the Conservative Party which was pretty 'right' in its orientation under Mrs Thatcher, certainly in Opposition, was stronger and stronger in defense of Ian Smith and Rhodesia...So Carter won and along comes Andy Young [Carter's Ambassador to the UN] and Carter himself, and gave a big push...I got to know all those people in the Conservative Party and the subject of conversation often was Africa and as part of the 'Carter initiative', if you will, an Anglo-American group was put together...and I was put on this too...I just got caught up in all of it.[19]

The Africa desk also meant that Seitz fortuitously met players on the British side who would later prove to be influential. Two in particular stand out: Robin Renwick and Charles Powell. At the time they were, like Seitz, both relatively young men just starting on their Foreign Office careers, serving together on the Rhodesia desk. They would later become Sir Robin, British Ambassador to the United States from 1991–95 (overlapping exactly with Seitz as Ambassador to the UK) and Charles Powell, famously Margaret Thatcher's closest advisor in Number 10. Powell's Downing Street career spanned eight years from 1983–91 of his nearly 30-year Foreign Office career (overlapping almost exactly with Seitz's time as DCM).[20]

Spiers, already noted as not wanting to serve 'another Annenberg', left London in 1977, shortly after the arrival of Kingman Brewster. Three years is generally considered a regular tour of duty.[21] However, in this case, Spiers's successor, Edward Streator, offers a different perspective on the former's tenure and departure, suggesting a deeper attitude towards political appointees:

Spiers...went off...he had been with Anne Armstrong. They didn't get along because Ron is a very bright man. Anne's a very bright lady, but Ron had the social graces of a porcupine and I think he found her too much of a lady, if you will...I mean she is of upper-level American society...and I think there was a basic clash because fundamentally Spiers was a socialist...He didn't know anybody, for example, in the Conservative Party...[22]

Things did return to a more 'usual' London pattern of approximately three–four year postings after the election and Jimmy Carter's appointment of Kingman Brewster who was, by all accounts, a close friend and ally of Cyrus

Vance, Carter's Secretary of State. Many in the Embassy, including Seitz, saw the practical value of such a relationship, though Seitz notes that the relationship 'was more with Cyrus Vance and less with Jimmy Carter. In fact, I didn't have much of a sense of Brewster-Carter relations at all – but the relationship with Vance was very close and they were friends for many, many years. And that was good because Brewster could talk to Vance any time he wanted.'[23] Seitz's boss at the time, Jack Binns, then Political Counsellor, concurs: 'they were close personally and Brewster could reach Vance at any time... unless you have witnessed such a relationship you don't realise how helpful it... can be... Brewster could make things happen'.[24] However, other views, notably again those of Streator, paint a slightly different picture as he felt that Brewster's 'other-worldly-ness' did not always help him. Certainly Thatcher, coming into Number 10 halfway through Brewster's term, seemed to view him with some scepticism. As Streator notes:

> Brewster hired me... and Kingman was one of the great people in my life that had extraordinary intelligence... not really very good at politics in many ways... he was interested, but his real interests were education and social policy, domestic social policy in the United States. And besides, he had the disadvantage of being there with Thatcher, who didn't like him very much because he was a Democrat and so he never really made much headway with her.[25]

The new government posed problems not only for the sitting Ambassador, but also for Seitz, the young Africanist in London because, while the Tories had been vocal in opposition, the situation was relatively containable. However, once they were in government and pressing a Democratic and activist White House, the issue was much more volatile. In London relations were also complicated by a mysterious lack of Conservative Party political intelligence on the part of the Embassy. Streator observed that 'the social secretary who had been with Kingman's predecessor, destroyed all of the records: the social records, the card files...'.[26] This unusual bureaucratic snafu evidently prompted Streator and Brewster to make a more concerted effort to recover ground with the Tories and so, according to Streator, it was under Brewster that Seitz officially added the Conservative Party to his portfolio.

> Kingman and I decided that we needed someone to cover the Tories because the guy who had been covering the Tories was just hopeless. And so we asked Ray if he'd, in effect, combine this Africa stuff with the Tories. He said 'sure of course'... So Ray got to know the Tories very well and he did a great job, as he did in everything... so that's how it worked out and then he was reassigned... Kingman got him a job... working for Vance who was Kingman's best friend.[27]

Brewster's laid-back style and Streator's longevity in post and clear ambition made for a functioning team especially in the early years of what was to become a long stint of Conservative rule. However, the combination was to prove not as effective or even sustainable for Brewster's replacement, John Louis.

Washington Hiatus

The time Seitz spent with Vance was relatively short-lived as events around the world reverberated back home, ultimately shifting the domestic political landscape. Political power struggles between Vance and Carter's National Security Advisor, Zbigniew Brzezinski, came to a head when Carter opted, against Vance's advice, to launch a rescue mission for the 53 American hostages taken in Iran (April 1980). Vance resigned even before the mission was completed, but the die was cast and Carter lost his bid for re-election. While the government, and arguably the country, grappled with a major shift in self-perception required by Ronald Reagan's promise of a 'new day in America', Seitz was working through a transformation of his own. He returned to Washington to work as Deputy Executive Secretary for Vance, but was shifted in relatively short order to Vance's successor, Edmund Muskie. With the change in government, he moved to the new Secretary of State Alexander Haig, albeit relatively briefly, only to land back in the team of Secretary of State George Shultz after a six-month stint as Deputy Assistant Secretary for Public Affairs. While his physical location had returned to the US, and despite the regular shift in his political bosses, it is interesting to note that Seitz was far from idle on British issues. At least two major events happened while he was in Washington that directly affected transatlantic relations.

The first was the Falklands War, which occurred during his brief stint as Deputy Assistant Secretary for Public Affairs. Seitz recounts going to see Larry Eagleburger – then Undersecretary of State of Political Affairs, because 'I was surprised that the US Government was having a hard time figuring out what to do, because to me, there was just no question of what we should do'. He goes on: 'But there really was a division of opinion in the US Government, which stunned the British and stunned me and stunned other Americans. And I went to see Larry and I just told him there can't be any question where we stand on this issue and there can't be any question about to whom we give material support . . . . I remember that very well . . .'.[28]

The second event was the invasion of Grenada and occurred after Seitz had moved back to work for Secretary of State Shultz. Seitz recalls this vividly as he was actually with the President and the Secretary of State at the crucial moment the US 'dropped the ball' in terms of keeping their ally informed.

I was working with Shultz at the time. And really, although it is true that there was this one person named John Howe who had assured the Foreign Office – and, therefore Geoffrey Howe had said in the House of Commons that nothing was going to happen. This is 48 hours before we invaded. Anybody else reading the signs would have known there was a very, very, very good chance. So anyway, that's not an excuse ... It was the same weekend I was down in Augusta with the President and Shultz. And this guy in a pickup truck drove through the front of this country club with guns in the back ... Then that night, we received word that a terrorist bomber had blown up the Marine camp in Beirut, 248 Americans killed, and – back in Washington ... that was the weekend that the decision was made to bomb Grenada. We dropped the ball. It wasn't professional.[29]

There is no evidence to suggest that Seitz's intervention prompted a change in policy on the Falklands or that he could have done more on the issue of Grenada and so these stories may be considered 'footnotes' to the main story of Seitz's career. However, they have relevance for three reasons. First, they highlight the fact that a career diplomat, not in the UK and whose brief had nothing to do with British issues, was nevertheless willing to use his access to lobby on what could only be described as 'British national interest'. Second, they demonstrate that career officers have the ability to be involved in issues over time in a way that is difficult, if not impossible, for a political appointee. Doubtless the fact he did engage, set him out among contenders for the post of Deputy Chief of Mission which followed in 1985 by Ambassador Charles H. Price II. Finally, a third point that would stand him in good stead for the future is best expressed by Seitz himself:

I started to learn things. You can't be in the Foreign Service and work effectively abroad if you don't know Washington and how Washington works – how policies are formed – how the State Department works ... in terms of the real foreign policy stuff – it's all the art of the possible and the only art possible is to find out what you can achieve politically in Washington ... that, in many respects, is the most important post that you can have in the foreign service, to be assigned home.[30]

The Return Flight to Heathrow

The Falklands also proved significant in terms of staffing in London. There are differing stories as to the appointment of John Louis. However, the change-over is relevant here due to the domino effect it had on personalities and positions effectively leading to Seitz's return, as well as distinctly colouring his tenure as DCM.

As indicated in Chapter 11 by Paul Trickett, John Louis was an unlikely Ambassador, a man not given to small talk, an uncomfortable public speaker and one who preferred an early night to almost any other activity. His story does, however, point to the influence of behind-the- scenes players in UK–US diplomacy. In this particular case, it is the continuing sway of Walter Annenberg, the Ambassador to the UK under Nixon who introduced Louis and his wife, Jo, to President Reagan at one of his infamous New Year's Eve parties. As both Seitz and Streator note, the Annenberg invitation list was considered an important indicator of 'clout'. As Seitz puts it: 'The big test for some things was who got invited to Walter Annenberg's New Year's Eve Parties...you had to draw a line somewhere – do you go to the Annenberg's or not?...Charlie was inside that line.'[31] This makes the case of Louis even more unusual in that it appears he was not a long-standing member of this group and was only introduced to the President the New Year's Eve immediately prior to the latter's inauguration. Elsewhere, Trickett quotes Alexander Haig's rather dismissive comment as to the specifics of this event – and while Louis' testimony at his Senate confirmation hearing suggests a slightly longer cogitation on the part of the President before contacting Louis about London, it remains a puzzle why Reagan should have been in such a hurry to go for a relatively unknown quantity.[32] Haig's comment is also ironic and rather sad given that Louis went out of his way to support Haig in a personal letter to the President at a time when Haig's own reputation was in trouble.[33]

Suffice to say, a shy, low-profile man by nature, serving in harness with a highly professional and ambitious DCM, was probably never going to be ideal. Streator even notes examples of this asymmetry while attending meetings with the Ambassador at which Streator's 'good friend', the Foreign Secretary, Peter Carrington, would wait for Louis to study his 'memorized brief and so when John would look away he'd wink at me – terrible...this whole Charlie McCarthy act was not working...It was very very tough.'[34] These tensions collided when Ambassador Louis was on vacation in Florida at the outbreak of the Falklands War (April 1982) and did not return to post immediately, though accounts differ as to exactly who at the Embassy told the Ambassador he should feel free to return on schedule. Ambassador Price, the member of the Annenberg klatch who had, in fact, introduced Louis to Annenberg, was godfather to Louis' first daughter (and the man who would take over the London post) contends that he spoke to Louis from Brussels, where Price was then Ambassador, the minute he saw the British press. 'When he [Louis] got back to London I called, in view of the Falklands, and said "Why the hell didn't you get on the god damn plane and get back to London?!" '.[35] Price says that Louis explained that he had been assured things were under control and there was little the Embassy could do – at least until Haig arrived for negotiations. Louis did not say who it was, but Price was certain – 'I know damn good and well the only possible person he could have talked to would have been Ed Streator'[36] – and the most logical choice by any standard of protocol. Streator himself says of his conversation with Louis that he 'pleaded with him to come back, but he didn't until Haig arrived to try and negotiate ... the tabloids were terrible about it'.[37] Timothy Deal, economics counsellor at the time, remembers Louis as generally 'ineffectual ... one of those cases where his alleged political clout didn't exist. He really was, I think, out of his depth.'[38] Whatever the timeline and whomever the source, the result was the same – and after a painful refusal on Louis' part to accept the writing on the wall, he offered President Reagan a letter of resignation the following September with an effective date in early November. In the letter, he outlined a 'great sense of accomplishment' and thanked the President for a job he declared to be 'the most demanding, most thrilling and the most satisfying of my life and I shall remain forever grateful to you for your trust'.[39] President Reagan, for his part, replied with 'special gratitude' for Louis' 'remarkable dedication and purpose' adding: 'The alliance today between the United States and Great Britain is adamantine and for that you are in no small part responsible.' He closed with the hope that he and Nancy could 'look forward to your continued friendship in the years to come'.[40] It is interesting to note that this exchange of letters was also issued, in full, by the White House press office on the same day.[41] Seitz, reluctant to dwell on the story, recalls simply that Louis had not come back from vacation, 'possibly on Ed's advice which was the worst part ... So that's how that happened.'[42]

Charles Price, Louis' replacement, recalls being telephoned while still in Brussels by Bill Clark, Reagan's National Security Advisor at the time, to ask when he would next be in Washington and requesting a meeting. At the subsequent meeting in July, Clark told Price Louis was going and asked if he would like the job. As an old friend of the apparently fatally undermined Ambassador, he felt torn. However, after assurances from Clark and repeating his concerns to the President later that day, he decided he would be foolish not to accept (though the official resignation did not happen for another two months). However, all parties acknowledge that the effect on Louis was profound, his long-standing friendship with Price and his family was never the same, and his public life was not what he had hoped due to rapidly declining health relatively shortly thereafter. Streator sums up the views of those who knew Louis with the stark conclusion that, 'his heart was broken'.[43]

Price arrived in London in December 1983 to find Streator well ensconced. This was hardly surprising given that, by this time, Streator had been in London for several years and the post of Ambassador had been under the shadow of Louis' limbo for six months or more. This meant Streator had free rein, as chargé d'affaires or acting Ambassador.[44] Streator and Price both quickly recognised that the situation was not tenable. Price recalls talking to Mike Deaver (Deputy Chief of Staff and long-time aide and advisor to both Reagans from California):

I didn't want him around. Ed thought he was ambassador. I mean I loved Ed and he was very knowledgeable. And Christ, he knew everybody in

London. He'd been there so long. And he was very good…but I called up Mike Deaver once and I said 'Look Mike, you have got to help me out because… there can only be one ambassador in this place and I am going to be it'…so that's the way he ended up getting that ambassadorship.[45]

Streator's recollection is not significantly different as he explains:

I knew everybody in London who mattered. You know Britain runs on 500 people. If you know the 500 people who run the country you know what's going on everywhere. You don't even have to leave your desk…so Charlie, quite sensibly had seen what happened to John Louis and was, in effect determined to be hands-on…I knew I was on my way out…he was the kind of guy and chief…who really wanted to be the whole show. There's nothing wrong with that. I think he's absolutely right.[46]

Though Streator does differ on the outcome in terms of his next post: 'Charlie had nothing to do with it…it was my friends in the White House…it was just a question of who would succeed me…[Price] wanted Ray to come because he had been an Executive Assistant to the Secretary.'[47]

Clearly there are some differences of opinion as to the tone and style of Streator's tenure in London, but one aspect of his management would remain a feature of the Embassy in London for some time. Deal (Economic Counsellor under Streator) explains that, while DCM, Streator had instituted a small, inner circle of the 5–6 most senior people that met weekly *in addition* to the regular country team meetings. These sessions were designed to discuss 'mutual reporting that was going to take place that week – what are we focusing on, what's of interest in Washington'.[48] They were chaired by Streator and, perhaps tellingly, did not include the Ambassador (Brewster or Louis). Seitz, during his first posting to London, and Deal both recall the significance of this approach in terms of Embassy/issue management as well as its impact on the perceived effectiveness of the post – so much so that they both adopted the approach during their respective tenures as DCM.[49]

Deputy Head of Mission, 1984–89

By the time Seitz returned as Deputy Chief of Mission in 1984, Ronald Reagan and Margaret Thatcher were in their second terms of office and had both the time and desire to get more involved in foreign affairs. The Falklands War and Grenada had undoubtedly been particular points of tension in the relationship. However, followed as they were by the tragedies of the IRA bomb in Brighton (1984) and later, the bringing down of PanAm Flight 103 over Lockerbie (1988) transatlantic attentions became focused and redoubled on common enemies.

Seitz returned to London with a great deal of useful intelligence gathered in his time in Washington. He had studied the Conservative Party in detail, now in power, and had watched a number of Ambassadors in action in London – as well as the means and methods of their coming and going. He also had local contacts both in and outside the Embassy right across the social and political spectrum. More importantly, as he explains, he felt he understood how the operation should work:

> the authority of a Minister is not the authority of an Ambassador over other agencies. So... your job is to run the Embassy, do whatever outside political work you can do – and basically alert the Ambassador to things that are coming down the road and things that you think he ought to do and how to plan his time and use his time. And then... make yourself available to do the dirty work in Washington, who he ought to see. And Charles was good at it... He had a good relationship with the President... you might not say he was connected in Washington in terms of the Congress, and the Senate or the State Department or the CIA or whatever, but if you're that much in the inner circle of the President, you don't have to be connected to these other people... at the end, those kinds of alignments in Washington make a lot of difference in terms of the Embassy's effectiveness and the ambassador's effectiveness.[50]

Price, sometimes to the chagrin of Reagan's White House staff, enjoyed a familiarity with the President that allowed him to suggest countless 'tokens of closeness' that were not in the 'usual' run of events. These communications were often relatively small, such as requests for letters of thanks and recognition of service by an Embassy staff member, to mark a particularly 'American' event, or just part of a regular stream of press clippings and speeches made by him and other prominent figures in British life. However, he also successfully made bids for larger symbolic gestures such as the idea of planning for the anniversary of the Marshall Plan, an official designation by Congress of a 'Winston Churchill Week' in the US and a request to break 'precedent' and have the President write a foreword for a book of speeches by Margaret Thatcher. Still not content with these exercises in 'relationship building', he extended his influence into areas such as the administration's presentation of major policy issues, the recommendation and facilitation of interviews for the President with major UK media outlets. He even made his views known through memos on the economic consequences of the Anglo-Irish Agreement, the strategy for upcoming summits and domestic lobbying efforts on the deficit debate back home. As he said to the President, 'Well here I go again! As you know, I have always told you precisely what I think; and you have kindly listened and never discouraged me from doing otherwise.'[51]

There is evidence to suggest that Reagan's staff spent some time attempting to circumvent Price's ability (and propensity) to maintain this close and consistent and personal line to the President – but remained frustrated as Charlie always seemed to find a way into the diary and onto the agenda – sometimes including going through Nancy. There are certainly not many presidents who, in thanking his ambassador for the gift of a shirt, would ask if he should 'send socks and undies' in return.[52] The President sums it up when he tells Price simply (and often), 'You make me very proud.'[53]

Deal also notes Price's capacity to focus on the crucial issues and his ability to raise it to the next level back in Washington if the need arose. Deal specifically names the Laker Airlines bankruptcy and the ensuing anti-trust investigation as a case in point (December 1984). Deal recalls that it had become a particularly contentious issue, especially with Thatcher, and that while they had worked hard to 'prepare the groundwork analytically for a change in policy', he goes on:

> I think it was his [Price's] personal relationship with Reagan that got to the point where Reagan ordered the Justice Department to kill the investigation. It was only the second time I think in American history that a president has ordered the Justice department to back off an anti-trust investigation. So, much to the relief of the British government, and much to the relief of the State Department as well, we got ourselves out of that.[54]

Price was also helped by his close relationship with both Margaret Thatcher and her husband Denis on both a professional and personal level. As puzzling as it might have been to Seitz and others, the link appears to have been genuine, if longevity is a reliable guide. Even after Price's return to the US, he remained in regular contact with the Prime Minister up to the present day. His closeness did, however, sometimes lead to conflict or accusations of preferential treatment for the Tories. As much as Price insists that he deliberately made an effort to spend time with the Labour Party and its leadership,[55] two very public rows over defence issues reinforced the view that Price was, at the very least, not comfortable with the Labour Party. One particular row occurred at the Labour Party Conference (October 1986), while the other surrounded Neil Kinnock's much publicised, and rather testy, meeting with the President (March 1987).

The Transition

Charlie Price was held in post by President Reagan for a second term and ended up staying in London six years – putting him in a category with David Bruce as one of the two longest serving Ambassadors in the post-war era and in the company of only a dozen others in the history of UK–US relations. If the Labour Party rows were considered part of his persona and a consequence of his partisan leanings, the more lasting impression of the Ambassador was probably created in the aftermath of the Lockerbie bombing. Price recalls hearing the possibility that an American plane was down while getting ready to attend a pre-holiday dinner. When the rumour was later confirmed, he went straight to the Embassy, walking in just in time to take a call from the Prime Minister who offered her condolences as well as transportation to the relatively remote Scottish town in the morning. The Ambassador, however, was firm in his determination to get there immediately. When informed by his staff that this may not be possible, he recalls telling them that it was not good enough.

> I said 'No wait a minute, you just call Mac' of the 3rd Air Force who I knew pretty well.[56] And I said, 'You just tell him that I want some damn plane to take me up to Lockerbie'... And I said 'Now I don't really want any kind of argument about this... I'll call the president and get him to authorise this'. Well that of course worked out just fine because he [Mac] had a C-130 that was presumably on some training mission... we got there about 1:30 in the morning and we went into the village of Lockerbie and it was just awful, the pilot still in the cockpit... the body parts... it was absolutely gruesome... the most wrenching part of the whole thing was that, of course, the families of those who had perished began to arrive and obviously I felt I should meet with them.[57]

Seitz also recalls this as the moment that Price's reputation, already relatively high, being confirmed in the public mind through a combination of instinct, connections and a very human touch.

> Lockerbie was really awful... and Charlie did a great job... I think he did just the right thing which is to go to the scene. And the public – he was just genuinely touched by it. It was an awful, awful thing. And in a way, I think the deep wound of Lockerbie healed other wounds in some respects and as I say Charlie did a wonderful job... there's something almost uncanny that you should end up with a tragedy that was Anglo-American, if you will, so that the two countries again, seemed to suffer a common unhappiness. Really. A bit like the twin towers...[58]

The year 1988 was also an election year back home and President Reagan was succeeded by his Vice President, George Herbert Walker Bush. No stranger to party politics or to diplomacy, President Bush was the first President in 130 years to have served as an Ambassador prior to holding the post of Commander-in-Chief.[59] His appointment therefore, of Henry Catto – his old friend from Texas campaigning days, and no stranger to Washington politics, public service or even to diplomacy – came as no great surprise.

While Price and Seitz formed a strong partnership with complementary skills, they were never particularly close as friends. Price explains:

> Ray was a very polished…well informed policy officer…I greatly admired Ray's intellect…I thought at the time when Ray and I got together…I am not an intellectual, but Ray is…I felt therefore we'd probably make a pretty good combination…Ray is not as much of a people person as I would say I am…And Ray is – he plays his cards very close to his vest.[60]

Seitz's experience as DCM, particularly under Price's tenure, was significant in three ways. First, Price's personal access to the President and the Prime Minister meant that Seitz's already extensive network, was pitched to the very top in terms of political personality, while still remaining well anchored in the governmental and diplomatic bureaucracy. Second, with a very publicly minded Ambassador, Seitz was able to concentrate on policy. Finally, in his effort to complement the Ambassador's strengths, he had the opportunity to build a political base with the Labour Party. Once again, and unbeknownst to him, this would be excellent preparation for his next and most unexpected return to London, and final Foreign Service posting.

As the Reagan dynasty gave way to the 'kinder gentler' conservatism of President Bush, so too the difference was felt in London. Bush's Ambassador, Henry Catto, and Seitz were more of a piece and hit it off almost immediately. Certainly Catto made it his business to 'turn around' ambassadorial relations with the Labour Party ('I courted the hell out of the Labour people'[61]) and quickly saw that the relationship between his President and the Prime Minister would need to be managed carefully ('I always had the feeling that the Prime Minister felt that George was sort of an imposter and really didn't – couldn't live up to Ronnie'[62]). Catto thus did what he could to ensure that the relationship worked as well as was possible, including the organisation of a meeting of the Aspen Institute at which both President Bush and the Prime Minister agreed to speak. Little did anyone know that the chosen date would become known not so much for the subject matter as for the fact it coincided with Iraq's invasion of Kuwait and the beginning of the next phase of Anglo-American cooperation in the Middle East.[63]

Catto was anxious to keep Seitz as long as possible, but it did not prove feasible and Seitz left London with another five years of service and two Presidential Awards for Meritorious Service (1985 and 1988)[64] under his belt. Upon his return to Washington, he became Assistant Secretary of State for European Affairs which provided another front row seat for history and the changes that were to mark the beginning of the end of the epoch Seitz later identified as the fifty years of American dominance. In this position, Seitz also became a trusted confidant and informed source for Secretary of State, James Baker, as well as the President who both watched the fall of the Berlin Wall and the events that followed in Germany and elsewhere very closely. Seitz, already familiar with the workings of the upper echelons of government, proved once again to be more than capable of handling complicated and delicate issues with care and foresight.

Thus, when President Bush sought to bring Ambassador Catto back from London to deal with a festering situation at the US Information Agency, Catto had no hesitation recommending that Seitz return, once again, to take on the post of Ambassador. The President, given his own diplomatic background, was pleased to accept the idea. Catto recalls:

> [I suggested Ray] because I thought he was terrific – we were friends – I was desperate to keep him on, but that was not possible... Ray didn't put me up to it... I just thought he was good and... how could you hope to be any better as far as understanding British-American relations?... it seemed perfect to me and I don't know how Ray feels about it. He may have resented a little bit that I weighed in... I just wanted to do it and I think it was a great thing – a great part of his career pattern and because of the uniqueness of it in history.[65]

The 'Last Bastion' Falls

Catto was not the only fan of the decision. As the Director-General of the Foreign Service and Director of Personnel of the State Department, Edward J. Perkins, indicates in his letter to Larry Eagleburger: 'The President's decision to send Raymond Seitz to London as our next ambassador has generated a great deal of favourable reaction among the Foreign Service officers... It seems to me that this is a manifestation of appreciation of the President's support for the Foreign Service.'[66] The memo was duly passed to the President who responded in kind: 'Ray will be an outstanding ambassador to the UK; and yes, this appointment does reflect my confidence *in* and respect *for* the Foreign Service'[67] (emphasis President's own). Such sentiments were also reflected in the departure from procedure in that, according to the Appointment Memorandum of 8 March 1991 by Robert Swanson, while the usual clearance questionnaire was completed, no personnel interview was deemed necessary.[68] Senator Biden's confidence at Seitz's confirmation hearing has already been alluded to, but it is worth pausing on Seitz's own testimony as it sets out the approach and mind-set of the first career officer ambassador in history as he is about to take up the post of Ambassador to the Court of St James's:

> The American ambassador to the United Kingdom is a position with an unusually distinguished lineage. As Minister at the American embassy in

London I served for the two most recent occupants of the job, Charles H. Price and Henry E. Catto, both of whom were representatives of great calibre and distinction. I am pleased the president has nominated me to join this diplomatic succession. Our relationship with Great Britain since the Second World War has been one of unique intimacy and collaboration It has often been tested...At each test the bonds have deepened...The relationship with Great Britain has become a fixed point in our foreign policy. It could not be re-created with any other nation.[69]

The President was no less effusive as indicated by the 'talking points' from Brent Scrowcroft for the photo opportunity/send-off for the now Ambassador Seitz. 'We are fortunate to have you there during this extraordinary period of change in Europe. I am well aware of the vital role you played in German unification, in eastern Europe and US-Soviet relations and in so many other areas...your appointment to...a post that had generally been viewed as off-limits to career diplomats shows the complete confidence Secretary Baker and I have in you'.[70] No higher compliment could be paid to a career officer, albeit one who was a familiar and a friend to many at the top table. Few career officers could claim such connections or demonstrate they knew how to use them to such good effect.

Third Time Lucky

Ambassador Seitz presented his credentials to the Queen on 25 June 1991,[71] which turned out to be one meeting among many as he had just seen her during her ten-day State visit to the United States. He had rushed from his own hearing and official White House send-off to London where he had six days before returning to greet the sovereign in his own country before being welcomed by his host in her own. It was only upon their respective returns to London he could be officially received and get down to the business of being Ambassador.

This time, the gap between Seitz's postings had been relatively short and his interim activities had everything to do with British attitudes and sensitivities given Mrs Thatcher's resistance to the reunification of Germany. However, just a few short months prior to his arrival, Thatcher had been unseated by her own ministers (November 1990) and John Major, a relative unknown except to those who had followed Tory fortunes closely, had become Prime Minister. Seitz arrived in the new environment with a clear strategy:

My advantages were numerous compared to anybody else who could have gone – including many people in the Foreign Service. But one thing I did know was that you did need to have a strategy. And you did need to, as much as possible, control your time and make priorities, but be sure to reserve at least 15% of your time for things that were not expected of you and to, I suppose in a traditional sense, to articulate American policy... on three tiers. One: the public. That is, speaking publicly. Two: background. That is with the press, which everybody reads of course, to help the press understand the context of issues in the United States and what is going on in the United States and then number three was to establish relationships within the government and, to a lesser extent, with the opposition so that you had easy access, if you will, when it came time to see somebody about some issue.[72]

Staffing was also a strategic enterprise and overlapping personalities came into play once again as Seitz chose Tim Deal, the same economic officer who had served with him under Streator, as his deputy. In the interim, Deal had returned to Washington as a member of the National Security Council staff, thus providing an economic complement to Seitz's political strength as well as an array of strong White House contacts. Deal offered himself to Seitz knowing that it would be his final posting in the Foreign Service – though, at that stage, neither appreciated it was to be Seitz's swansong as well. Deal sums up the organisation of the Embassy:

Ray Seitz was there and basically the Embassy functioned to serve him. He was the best political officer you could ever imagine, but he was also a very effective Ambassador... he knew everybody from his previous tours. He knew his way around and he wanted a DCM who could manage the day-to-day operations of the Embassy, who could divide up the representational responsibilities... he ran a very smooth operation... the whole operation was good... we had a very effective team... making sure that the other sections were reporting on things that mattered. That's why I reinstituted that idea of having that [Streator's senior team] meeting.[73]

Same Tune – Different Words

Seitz hardly had time for a full annual cycle of events before the US election was under way, and the work he had done on various issues such as the Middle East, Bosnia and Northern Ireland over the course of his first 12–18 months was to be significantly altered by the impending change in the White House. After President Bush, a new generation of political leadership was emerging in the United States. Politicians of a Second World War vintage were being replaced by baby boomers and the 'modern presidency' was being re-calibrated for the 'constant campaign'. The fifty-year epoch was in its final stages and the career officers who had built the post-war consensus and even the Cold War balance were waning in their power. The 'snug fit' that had characterised much of Seitz's career would become slightly less comfortable as it came to a close. President Clinton's retention of Seitz reflected a range of factors. There was some lobbying from the UK to retain Seitz – though he stresses he took no part in it. Indeed, he deliberately distanced himself from the process as he found himself in a diplomatic lacuna. Political etiquette requires appointees to offer their resignation at the end of the term of the President who appoints them, regardless of that person's potential political fate. Career officers, on the other hand, have a regular tour of duty and generally expect to be reassigned. As the first career officer Ambassador in London, there was no precedent and little effort from Washington to provide guidance given the lack of experience in the new team of such matters. Also significant is the fact that there was a changing tide in the regulations regarding political appointees, forcing nominees to increasingly disclose and divest themselves of any potential conflicts of interest; a tall order in terms of the UK given the depth and breadth of transatlantic business.

Rumours about the identity of a new ambassador are always rife in London and the post-Clinton election era was no different. The *Evening Standard,* a regular source for such gossip, reported that Pamela Harriman had turned down the post and Walter Mondale was under consideration.[74] Meanwhile, British publications and even British officials were said to be lobbying hard to retain Seitz. One name that did come up with some frequency was Admiral Crowe of Oklahoma who had served as Commander-in-Chief of both the Allied Forces in Europe and the Pacific Command, as well as Chairman of the Joint Chiefs of Staff for President Reagan. From retirement, he supported Clinton's presidential bid, and had become his Chairman of the Foreign Intelligence Advisory Board. Clinton had offered Crowe both Russia and China, but these were turned down at least initially for health reasons, but after a knee replacement, Crowe felt up to accepting a later offer of the UK. However, sources suggest that, as much as Admiral Crowe wanted to accept, he told the President that he could not comply with the divestiture as quickly as required. To bridge the difficulty, Crowe says he suggested leaving Seitz in place:

> I said two things: number one I'd like to go and number two you have a professional over there right now and I don't think you should order him out of that billet until he's had a full tour ... I said if he was a political appointee, sure pull him out of there right now. That's fair game, but you shouldn't pull Ray out ahead of time.[75]

The timing of these discussions and negotiations remain unclear, but in the meantime, the Clinton administration allowed its intention to keep Seitz in place – at least for the time being – to be known in March. "'We think it is an important gesture to the career Foreign Service" a State Department official said, speaking on the condition of anonymity.'[76] Interestingly, Deal's view from London was that:

> Both the British government and the American community in London very much wanted him to stay. I think there was enough of an expression of interest...that I think the Clinton administration decided to take its time in figuring out who they might send there...it was only as it got into the question of Northern Ireland...I don't think they would have kept him there indefinitely...it was only when he [Seitz] began to insist on some coherence in the policy toward Northern Ireland and the involvement of the Embassy that...motivated the Clinton administration to look for somebody to replace him...[77]

It bears pointing out, that despite precedent, his career history and credentials, Seitz had no direct connection to the President or his administration. Seitz was of the Bush generation, had been out of the country for years, took a much more traditional view of diplomacy and a rather dim view of the narrowing gap between the office of President and his politics. Their first ever meeting was only as part of the last-minute planning for John Major's visit to the US upon Clinton's arrival in the Oval Office. Given the leaking of Major's warm and supportive letter to President Bush before the election and the tensions during the campaign over governmental information-sharing as to Clinton's activities during his time as Rhodes Scholar at Oxford, the atmosphere was less than cordial. This simply highlighted the fact that this Ambassador had no personal 'oil' with the President that could be poured on the troubled waters. Again as Deal recalls, 'Because of the Washington connections that Ray Seitz and I both had, we felt more much engaged and involved in the foreign policy process during the Bush administration. The 1992 election changed that...Bill Crowe had personal lines to the White House, but it was still a much more difficult operating environment for the embassy in 1993–96.'[78]

The Irish Question

The issue at the centre of many of these difficulties was Northern Ireland. No ambassadorship can or should be categorised by a single incident, but as indicated by Seitz and others involved, it does seem to point to a whole series of significant issues and changes in the way US foreign policy operated at this time. It moved away from more 'traditional channels' and became increasingly focused on personality, summitry and ultimately the White House operation. The clearest moment of this shift was the issuing of a visa to the leader of Sinn Fein, Gerry Adams.

This story has been reviewed in-depth elsewhere, but essentially the Anglo-Irish Agreement signed under Thatcher had been followed up by John

Major who worked with President Bush personally, and the US generally, to great effect. Gerry Adams had applied for a visa in the past, but had always been refused for the sake of what Seitz calls 'the overall relationship'. However, Clinton had taken an early interest in Northern Ireland and literally brought it into the White House – putting it beyond the reach of the State Department and the Embassy. Deal recalls:

> The one that became a real firestorm for us in the Embassy was Northern Ireland. While Ray did actually stay on…it was during that time that the White House began dealing directly with Sinn Fein and Gerry Adams, outside of the State Department, outside of the Embassy. That became a problem that affected both Ray Seitz and Bill Crowe…it was the same problem that Tony Lake and Nancy Soderberg were really running policy toward Northern Ireland and doing so without any input from the State Department and not much from the Embassy either…we had some very difficult, difficult times. For one thing the British just couldn't believe that we were so out of the loop. They imagined that we were…disingenuous or something. No Ambassador in his right mind would allow these things to go on without his concurrence.[79]

This was echoed later by Crowe who adds:

> …it became obvious very quickly that State wasn't going to handle this problem. On Irish matters I did not deal with the State Department, I dealt with the National Security Council. State…wanted to, and they tried, but they discovered early on in the game that Lake wasn't going to let them…many times I sat there while people in Washington came to talk…including Lake. Lake would propose some outrageous scheme and I know they [the British] just detested what he was suggesting, but they would very calmly deal with it…and never get really upset. I was probably more upset than they were. I was sort of ashamed of my government at times…I didn't feel we were very ethical.[80]

In this light, one can begin to see how, despite intense UK lobbying, by the UK Embassy in Washington and of the US Embassy in London, it is possible that a visa could be granted to Adams without the prior knowledge of the UK Foreign Office – or the Ambassador in London. Worse still, there had been a sense that, at the very least, Adams would have to renounce violence to get the visa. Seitz recalls the agreement as, 'no visa without a renunciation of violence. And everyone was on board – the FBI, Warren Christopher, CIA, Tony Lake – everyone was on board and I recall – calling around – checking – so I went home thinking "got it" and then there was this meeting with the President. The President said, "No, there should be a visa".'[81]

When asked if he had rung, or tried to ring, the President directly Seitz replied, 'I was too late. By the time I found out, it was too late. He had already decided. I was stunned. I had no idea. I didn't know until the next morning and it was a done deal. And I thought it was a dreadful mistake and I still do.'[82]

Conclusion

Seitz observed at his ambassadorial hearing that 'history does not move at right angles' and certainly neither did his diplomatic career. In what might be more accurately described as an arc sweeping between Washington and London, Seitz became expert on the whole range of global issues that regularly appear on the transatlantic agenda. As the Foreign Service officer tasked to bridge the career/appointee gulf in terms of the London post, he negotiated at the highest levels using both political radar and institutional acumen. He was able to deliver his 'clout' through the one-two punch of diplomatic structures combined with deep connections. From each stage of his career we learn important aspects of the workings of the London Embassy as an institution in its own right, as well as what factors in the success or failure of any given ambassador, perhaps regardless of their initial starting point.

Through the eyes of the young almost-Africanist, we saw that connections are of paramount importance within the bureaucracy of the host country and at home. Fortuitous meetings with players who would go on to hold and wield power on the British side were invaluable as bright young stars rose within their respective organisations. It was also clear that links to political power, your own or through people close to you, could be used to create opportunities back home and the option and ability to seek positions rather than being merely posted. As Minister, Seitz was able to maximise his access through his Ambassador(s) as well as solidify and extend his own network on both sides of the Atlantic. His return to London as Ambassador was a case study in how to manage a large mission and the importance of having a clear strategy. However, on a slightly darker note, it may also offer evidence as to the inability of any ambassador, appointee or career, to totally escape changes in policy-making, the office and role of the President and the fundamental shifts in statecraft that have been in motion since the end of the Cold War.

Raymond George Hardenbergh Seitz had the intellectual power to recognise the 'epoch' in which he operated and the self-awareness and possession to know when it was time to step aside. He retired from both the Court of St James's and the Foreign Service in May 1994. Making London his permanent home, he offered the benefit of his experience to those who followed – but only when asked. He eschewed the language of the special relationship, but his skills and approach made him ideally suited to its special attributes.

Even he recognised that 'neither nation could replicate this relationship with any other country'.[83] His Senate testimony stands the test of time and reflects both a practical and theoretical understanding of an exceptional, if not unique, bilateral relationship:

> Our involvement with the United Kingdom extends well beyond the official structures of government. It is economic, cultural, individual. Over the decades, we have developed with the British a framework within which we share common aspirations and values, patterns of thought, ways of doing business, and how we look at things. This broad relationship is a good habit. Europe is moving into a new epoch in its long, rich history. The Soviet Union is withdrawing from Central Europe and our own military presence will be reduced. The Warsaw Pact is evaporating and NATO is adapting. Germany is united and there are new democracies in the East. The European Community and the CSCE are gathering momentum. The shape of the future is not clear, except to know that there will be new challenges from new quarters and to know also that our relationship with the United Kingdom will be a fundamental, essential ingredient in our own policy.[84]

Notes

1. David Bruce (1961–69) was 'held' in London by President Johnson on the death of President Kennedy – but served different political parties in other diplomatic posts: France under Truman (1949–52) and Germany under Eisenhower (1957–59).
2. Alison Holmes, interview with Ambassador R. G. H. Seitz, Orford, NH, 2008.
3. Raymond Seitz, Churchill Lecture, Guildhall, London, 18 November 1999.
4. *Ibid.*
5. *Ibid.*
6. His older brother would later follow his father, grandfather and uncle into the army and attend West Point.
7. Major General John F. R. Seitz and see: (No byline), 'Profile: Elegant Anglophile Stays Put – Raymond Seitz', *The Observer*, 4 April 1993.
8. The year before George W Bush arrived as a freshman at Yale.
9. Holmes, interview with Ambassador Ray Seitz.
10. Catto had been a Democrat, but turned to the Republican Party in his native San Antonio and came to Bush seeking advice as to whether or not to run for the Chairman's post in Bexar County. He decided against, but the two became firm friends and offered each other support and advice through their campaigning trials as Catto lost two bids for the state legislature in 1960 and 1961 and Bush lost his first bid for Senate in the election of 1964. Interview with author.
11. Henry E. Catto, Jr, *Ambassadors at Sea: The Highs and Low Adventures of a Diplomat* (Austin, TX: University of Texas Press, 1998), pp. 10–11.
12. Catto never ran again, but in 1971 he became US Representative with the rank of Ambassador to the Organization of American States in the Nixon administration. Ironically, he was interviewed by Elliot Richardson who was Deputy Secretary

of State at the time, but later became Ambassador to the UK (1975–76). After OAS Catto held other posts, both diplomatic and in the private sector, before being named Ambassador to the UK by Bush in 1989. Catto was also Seitz's boss and a key promoter to the post of Ambassador.

13. The only US Ambassador in the post-Cold War period to go to an Ivy League school – an alma mater and a fraternity affiliation (Delta Kappa Epsilon) he shared with both President Bush Sr and his son.
14. Raymond Seitz, *Over Here* (London: Weidenfeld & Nicolson, 1998), p. 13.
15. For example, then Senator Biden (DL) chaired Seitz's nomination hearing stating that 'Seitz brings to this position a sensitivity, quiet authority and a clear-headed approach that serves this country very well and have served it well . . . I truly mean it when I say you are one of the finest people I have dealt with in the government' (Ambassadorial Nominations Foreign Relations Committee, European Affairs Subcommittee, United States Senate [Washington DC: Federal News Service, 17 April 1991]).
16. Holmes, interview with Ambassador Ray Seitz.
17. Alison Holmes, interview with Ambassador Edward Streator, New York, 2009.
18. Holmes, interview with Ambassador Ray Seitz.
19. *Ibid.*
20. Charles Powell is also the older brother of Jonathan Powell, another Foreign Service officer who would play an important role in US–UK relations. The younger Powell, after 16 years in the Foreign Office (including a stint in Washington DC as political officer also at the time Seitz was Ambassador) left the civil service to become Tony Blair's Head of Office and longest serving advisor from 1997–2007.
21. Alex Spelling, TNA FCO 82/577 Moreton record of conversation with Spiers, 24 November 1975.
22. Holmes, interview with Ambassador Edward Streator.
23. Holmes, interview with Ambassador Ray Seitz.
24. Charles Stewart Kennedy, Interview with Jack Binns, 25 July 1990, The Foreign Affairs Oral History collection of the Association for Diplomatic Studies and training, Library of Congress, available at: http://memory.loc.gov/cgi-bin/quiery/r?ammem/mfdip:@field(DOCID+mfdip2004bin03
25. Holmes, interview with Ambassador Edward Streator.
26. *Ibid.*
27. *Ibid.*
28. Holmes, interview with Ambassador Ray Seitz.
29. *Ibid.*
30. *Ibid.*
31. *Ibid.*
32. Louis's testimony: 'I wish I could say that I have known President Reagan for years and years, but that is not the truth. But I did meet him for the first time, I think, on the 28th December of last year when he and his wife and I and my wife were the house guests of a mutual friend in California for a three or four day weekend. I did not seek this job and I did not know that the purpose of the three or four day weekend and our presence there was probably for the President to get to know me and my wife and to make a decision on something that he was thinking about, but I had no idea was happening [sic]. We had a social, friendly weekend. I found the President and his wife most approachable, wholesome people. The chemistry between us and our wives was very good and you can imagine my surprise when,

on the 2nd January, after the weekend was over a telephone rang in my home in Winnetka and the first voice I heard was one that said "This is Ronald Reagan".' John J. Louis, Jr, Testimony to the Committee on Foreign Relations, United States Senate, 10 April 1981.

33. Letter from Ambassador Louis to President Reagan dated 10 May 1982 to 'pay a personal compliment to Al Haig. I have had the pleasure of observing him firsthand and at close quarters, during the Falklands negotiations. I have been with him here in London with Margaret Thatcher and in Washington with Francis Pym. I am aware of the "battering" he has taken from the press over the past 15 months – punishment which I have to say is patently underserved'. The letter was passed from James Rentschler to William Clarke on the 27 May making it to the President on the 2 June, NSC#8203623 065298 TRO39-03 FE006-iv. Ronald Reagan Presidential Library (hereafter RRPL).
34. Holmes interview with Ambassador Edward Streator. Charlie McCarthy being the name of ventriloquist's, Edgar Bergen's, well-dressed dummy in a 1950s television programme.
35. Alison Holmes, interview with Ambassador Charles Price II, Hollywood, CA, 2008.
36. *Ibid.*
37. Holmes interview with Ambassador Edward Streator.
38. Alison Holmes, interview with Timothy Deal, Washington DC, 2009.
39. Letter from Ambassador John J. Louis, Jr to President Reagan, on London Embassy paper dated 14 September 1983, CF 162044 1150 FOOO2 CO169 PE009, RRPL.
40. Letter from President Reagan to Ambassador Louis dated 19 September 1983, CF 14719755 147197 1150 F0002 CO167 PE009 FE011, RRPL.
41. The White House Office of the Press Secretary 'For Immediate Release' 19 September 1983, RRPL.
42. Holmes interview with Ambassador Ray Seitz.
43. Holmes interview with Ambassador Edward Streator.
44. *Ibid.* Streator acknowledges his time in London was 'too long'. He would have left sooner, but he had a heart attack and was off work for some time and effectively kept on for a second tour.
45. Holmes interview with Ambassador Charles Price II.
46. Holmes interview with Ambassador Edward Streator.
47. *Ibid.*
48. Holmes interview with Timothy Deal.
49. Holmes interview with Ambassador Ray Seitz and interview with Timothy Deal.
50. Holmes interview with Ambassador Ray Seitz.
51. Letter from Ambassador Price to President Reagan dated 19 November 1984, RRPL.
52. Letter from President Reagan to Ambassador Price dated 8 October 1985, 3393 FO-005, RRPL.
53. Letter from President Reagan to Ambassador Price dated 23 March 1984, 218820 FO-002, RRPL.
54. Holmes interview with Timothy Deal.
55. Holmes interview with Ambassador Charles Price II.
56. Thomas G. McInerney: 1974–76 Air Attaché to US Embassy in London working for three Ambassadors; 1976–77 Vice Commander of the 20th Tactical Fighter Wing, Royal Air Force Station Upper Heyford, England; 1983–85, Commander of 3rd Air Force, Royal Air Force Station Mildenhall, England;1986 Vice Commander-in-Chief, Headquarters US Air Forces in Europe, Ramstein Air Base,

West Germany; 1988 Commander of Alaskan Air Command, Alaskan NORAD Region, and Joint Task Force Alaska.

57. Holmes interview with Ambassador Charles Price II.
58. Holmes interview with Ambassador Ray Seitz.
59. At President's Nixon's encouragement Bush stepped down from his Congressional seat to stand for Senate and lost (for the second time). Nixon then appointed him Ambassador to the UN where he served for two years (1971–73). He was also Chief of the US Liaison Office to the People's Republic of China (1974–75).
60. Holmes interview with Ambassador Charles Price II.
61. Alison Holmes, interview with Ambassador Catto, Woody Creek, CO, 2008.
62. *Ibid.*
63. While it is true that Mrs Thatcher took a firm line from the outset of the Kuwait conflict, it has been suggested that this Aspen meeting was the occasion for her now famous declaration that this was 'no time to go wobbly'. However, the Margaret Thatcher Foundation and George H. W. Bush Library sources all state this phrase was not used until a phone conversation between the two on 26 August in the context of UN Security Council Resolution 665. http://www.margaretthatcher.org/archive/us-bush.asp.
64. Consul's Office Appointment Files OA-ID 20150 20150-013, George H. W. Bush Presidential Library (hereafter GHWBPL).
65. *Ibid.*
66. Letter from Edward J. Perkins to Larry Eagleburger dated 12 February 1991, WHORM 221447 FO-002-01, GHWBPL.
67. *Ibid.*
68. Interestingly, Seitz presents a more sceptical edge in his responses to the same questionnaire for the European Affairs post. To the question: 'Have you ever had any association with any person, group or business venture that could be used, even unfairly to impugn or attack your character and qualifications for this position?' Seitz replied: 'I worked for two years as Executive Assistant to Secretary of State George Schulz. I have also been closely associated with Secretaries Haig, Muskie and Vance', Counsel's Office Appointment Files OA/ID 20150, 20150-013 and Counsel's Office White House Appointment Files OA/IF 20150, 20150-014, GHWBPL.
69. Ambassadorial Nominations, Foreign Relations Committee: European Affairs Subcommittee, chaired by Senator Biden (DL) (Washington DC: Federal News Service, 17 April 1991).
70. Talking Points from Brent Scowcroft to President Bush for photo opportunity, 1 May 1991, WHORM FO-002 Diplomatic affairs – Consular Relations 3092, 252555, GHWBPL.
71. No byline, 'Court Circular', *The Independent*, 26 June 1991.
72. Holmes interview with Ambassador Ray Seitz.
73. Holmes interview with Timothy Deal.
74. No byline, *The Evening Standard*, 13 January 1993.
75. C. S. Kennedy, Interview with Ambassador/Admiral William J. Crowe, 1998, Foreign Affairs Oral History Collection of the Association for Diplomatic Studies and Training.
76. Steven Holmes, 'Envoy's Appointment Seen as a Bid to Boost Foreign Service Morale', *The New York Times*, 27 March 1993.
77. Holmes interview with Timothy Deal.

78. Raymond Ewing, Interview with Timothy Deal, 2004, Foreign Affairs Oral History Collection of the Association for Diplomatic Studies and Training.
79. Holmes interview with Timothy Deal.
80. Kennedy interview with Ambassador/Admiral William J. Crowe.
81. Holmes interview with Ambassador Ray Seitz.
82. *Ibid.*
83. Seitz, *Over Here*, p. 338.
84. Ambassadorial Nominations, *op. cit.*

15
Ambassadors Crowe and Lader, 1994–2001

John Dumbrell

Admiral William Crowe's appointment as Ambassador to the United Kingdom coincided with widespread predictions that the heyday of the US–UK Special Relationship had passed. The ambassadorship of Raymond Seitz – itself a tough act to follow – had exposed the potential for Irish affairs to disrupt calm relations between London and Washington. More fundamentally, the global geopolitical shifts since 1989 seemed to have removed much of the rationale for close US–UK relations. Raymond Seitz himself was soon to record Bill Clinton's apparent willingness to treat the Special Relationship as an object of derision.[1] Shortly before Crowe's appointment, the British press was engaged in a conspicuous bout of 'end of the affair' editorialising. In January 1994, a leading article in *The Independent* argued that 'the arrival of a Democratic president' in Washington had exposed what 'was perhaps obscured by the warmth of Margaret Thatcher's friendship with Ronald Reagan: Britain seems not to figure large in American minds. Canada, Mexico and Germany probably matter more'. In March, Hugo Young wrote in *The Guardian* that any notion of London being 'at the head of Washington's transatlantic concerns' was pure fantasy. Such an idea 'would have been hard to credit even in the palmy days of Thatcher', much less in the post-Cold War era.[2] A widespread assumption existed that, bereft of its anti-Soviet underpinnings, the Special Relationship was running out of steam. It might be kept running for a time through the sticking power of sentiment and bureaucratic momentum. Yet such survival was likely to be little more than the smile on the face of the Cheshire Cat; minus Cold War mutual interests, the inner reality of 'special' relations was disappearing.[3]

The later 1990s saw some retreat in the view that London and Washington were pulling away from one another. President Clinton's relationship with Conservative Prime Minister John Major was far cooler than that developed with Major's successor, Labour Prime Minister Tony Blair, elected in 1997. The politics of the Irish peace process, which had pulled the US and the UK apart in the earlier period became, after 1997, an arena of conspicuous cooperation between Downing Street and the White House. Some tensions over policy in the Balkans remained, but diminished in comparison with rows over Bosnia that had characterised the Major years. Nevertheless, even after 1997, elite journalistic and policy-oriented opinion still tended to the view that the Special Relationship was something of a museum piece. The United States seemed to be looking to the Pacific rather than the Atlantic. A 1998 article in *Foreign Affairs* quoted Defence Secretary William Cohen as reflecting received wisdom in a speech to Asian business leaders: 'The Mediterranean is the ocean of the past. The Atlantic is the ocean of the present. And the Pacific is the ocean of the future'.[4] As America looked to the Pacific, so Britain appeared to be reorienting itself towards Europe. Alex Danchev offered a requiem for the Special Relationship: 'Unsinkable aircraft carriers... are fast becoming redundant'. Quoting predictions made in 1908 by Lord Curzon on the subject of post-imperial British decline, Danchev concluded: 'Britain is Belgium, though the British do not know it yet'. '*Requiescat in pace Anglo-America!*'.[5]

The prime concern of the two Ambassadors under discussion in this chapter was to keep the Anglo-American boat afloat in difficult circumstances, recognising and meeting problems rather than denying their existence. Both Ambassadors enjoyed good relations with President Clinton. Both Ambassadors – with varying degrees of emphasis – sought to align themselves with, and to promote, the Clinton doctrine of engagement, enlargement, 'democratic peace' and economic globalisation. The United States was moving beyond the New World Order – 'long on new and short on order' as Ambassador Crowe memorably put it – of President George H. W. Bush. In the post-Cold War world, the US would remain committed to cooperative internationalism and to a newly integrated era of global capitalism. As the 1990s developed, the US committed itself to enlarged membership of the North American Treaty Organisation (NATO), to military action in the Balkans, and to integration in global economic networks of post-communist Russia and still-communist China. The Crowe and Lader ambassadorships reflected these wider concerns, touching the survival and reorientation of American internationalism following the collapse of the Soviet Union. They also continued the traditional diplomatic function of trying to explain Britain to America, and Britain to America. Towards the end of the 1990s, two features of the new global order – the chronic leaking of information in the age of new technology, and the rise of international terrorism – came to have important implications for the popular reputation of the two Clinton appointees. Crowe is often now remembered as the author of leaked cables to Washington in the wake of the 1997 death of Princess Diana. Lader is remembered for his appearance on BBC television's *Question Time* in September 2001, following the 9/11 attacks. Speaking as a former Ambassador, Philip Lader, in obvious distress, was subjected to anti-American abuse from members of the studio audience.[6] The chapter will discuss each Ambassador in turn, paying particular attention to the circumstances of appointment; to the relationships of Crowe and Lader with President Clinton; and to the efforts of both men to negotiate the difficult currents of Anglo-American relations as both London and Washington sought to adjust to shifting priorities.

William Crowe, Chairman of the Joint Chiefs of Staff between 1985 and 1989, was the most distinguished military figure to appear as Ambassador at Grosvenor Square. The choice of Crowe to succeed Raymond Seitz was interpreted in contradictory ways. At one level, it could be seen as a sign that Washington was indeed committed to retaining close military relations with London, despite many predictions to the contrary, in the post-Cold War years. Conversely, perhaps Crowe was a senior military figure entrusted with the difficult job of selling US military disengagement to London? Crowe certainly saw the post as a very important and desirable one. He reportedly turned down the headship of the Central Intelligence Agency and the ambassadorship to Moscow before accepting the London posting. Crowe, whom many observers had previously presumed to be a Republican, had surprisingly endorsed Clinton in the 1992 presidential race, believing the Arkansas governor to 'be the candidate most capable of shaking off the inertia of Cold War habits'. Crowe resented what he called 'the conventional wisdom...that nobody in the American military was a Democrat'.[7] He also challenged those military officers who hinted that Clinton's avoidance of service in Vietnam called into question the Arkansas governor's ability to be an effective Commander-in-Chief: 'In the military I grew up in, it was our job to get along with the president, not the president's job to get along with us.' William Crowe was the most senior of some 21 retired military officers who together publicly endorsed Clinton. Crowe's support was widely seen as vital to the 1992 campaign, derailing the Vietnam service issue and at least stemming the military's resistance to Clinton.[8] Interestingly, Crowe's support for Clinton was given in the context of a clear understanding that the Democratic contender in 1992 was 'the candidate most capable of shaking off the inertia of Cold War habits'. According to Crowe, Clinton offered no radical departure from President George H. W. Bush in national security policy. However, Clinton was more prepared to re-balance Atlantic and Pacific relations, favouring 'a deeper cut in American troop strength in Europe', and being 'more inclined to emphasise the Far East'.[9] For the first year of Clinton's first term, Crowe chaired the President's Foreign Intelligence Board, where he offered conspicuous support to Clinton over the issue of gay rights in the US military.

Like Sir Joseph Porter in Gilbert and Sullivan's *HMS Pinafore*, Crowe was a senior sailor whose career had not involved large stretches of time at sea. Unlike Porter, Crowe was intellectually distinguished. His background was political (in the non-ideological sense) and academic. A Princeton PhD, Crowe spent six months of 1956 living in London, while researching a dissertation on the history of the Royal Navy. He served in Vietnam, assisting the South Vietnamese *riverine* force, and drawing lessons that melded rather easily into the Clinton administration worldview. Crowe shared the almost universal military view that the fighting services had been unfairly blamed 'for disastrous political judgements'. However, he also saw the war as teaching the limits of American power: 'We could not bring about a government in Saigon capable of motivating its own people or sustaining the support of the American people.' As Chairman of the Joint Chiefs, Crowe played an important role in the US–Soviet diplomacy of the second Reagan term. Crowe's 1993 memoir recorded his closeness to Soviet military chief, Sergei Akhromeyev, who – unable to adapt to shifting political circumstances – had committed suicide in 1990. Crowe's pre-1994 experience had given him an appreciation of the value of Anglo-American relations, not least in terms of London's willingness to allow US bombers to attack Libya in 1986. Crowe had not only to manage inter-service rivalry – the traditional preoccupation of Chairmen of the Joint Chiefs of Staff (JCS) – but also to help mitigate the hostility between Defence Secretary Caspar Weinberger and Secretary of State George Shultz in the later Reagan years. Crowe brought to the London posting significant political and diplomatic skills, a credibly close relationship with the White House, and a keen awareness of the need constantly to adapt and redefine America's global role.[10]

Crowe's success in ambassadorial public diplomacy was greatly aided by his amiability, lack of pomposity and lightness of touch. He was probably best known to British people for his appearance, as himself, in a 1989 episode of the TV comedy, *Cheers*. As Ambassador, he was once attacked at a meeting of UK business leaders for being less than committed to the retention of Northern Ireland within the United Kingdom. He was asked: 'How would you feel if Mexico took back Texas?' Crowe responded: 'I'm from Oklahoma. We've been trying to give Texas back to Mexico for a hundred years.'[11] He gave frequent off-the-cuff illustrations about the problems of Anglo-American understanding, stating that it was impossible to 'explain' Madonna or O. J. Simpson: 'As (fellow Oklahoman) Will Rogers put it, it's like explaining the difference between a conservative Democrat and a moderate Republican.'[12]

Ambassador Crowe found himself particularly preoccupied with developing Anglo-American policy towards Bosnia, and with Northern Ireland. By 1994, transatlantic disagreements over Bosnia were putting intense pressure, both on US–European and US–UK relations. Richard Holbrooke later recorded the strains in the Special Relationship as they appeared in September 1994, at the time of his appointment as Assistant Secretary of State with special responsibility for Bosnia: 'the strains in the Anglo-American alliance had been at a level that was nearly intolerable, and rebuilding the relationship, which I still believed was "special" – a once-standard phrase that had been banned by the Major government – had been a high priority'.[13] By the time Crowe was confirmed as Ambassador in May 1994, significant rifts had developed between London and Washington over policy for the Balkans. By this time, the US supported air strikes against Serb positions, together with a lifting of the arms embargo on the Bosnian Muslims. London opposed such action on the grounds that it would endanger the 2,000 British forces involved in UN operations in the region. From the European perspective, Washington was unwilling to risk direct engagement, but could not (in the words of Christopher Meyer, UK Ambassador in Washington, 1997–2003) 'desist from back-seat driving'.[14] From Washington's standpoint, the Europeans were simply demonstrating their chronic inability to provide a coherent response to the Serbian aggression. Clinton privately saw the Europeans as cynical and referred to 'the hypocrisy of the British and French, who used their troops on the ground as a shield to preside over the slow dismemberment of Bosnia'.[15] Crowe was plunged immediately into the diplomatic rows over Bosnia, described by John Major as a 'running sore' between London and Washington. Holbrooke recruited the new Ambassador to 'make the case to his senior British counterparts for bombing', coordinating this pressure with lobbying by Robert Hunter, US Ambassador to NATO.[16] The London Embassy offered diplomatic assistance at the time of the July 1995 London conference – held after the massacre at Srebrenica – where the Europeans successfully resisted the US policy of generalised bombing.[17] By October 1996, Ambassador Crowe was able to point to important successes, both in terms of Holbrooke's achievement of the Dayton Peace Accords and in the context of post-Cold War roles for NATO. Crowe argued that no-one would have *chosen* Bosnia 'as a test case for NATO reform and adaptation'; however, as events had unfolded, 'the future character of NATO, Russian reform, the EU, the UN, bilateral alliances – all have a heavy stake in the Bosnian outcome'. In a major address at Chatham House, Crowe linked progress in Bosnia to the emerging Clinton agenda of NATO expansion and Russian integration. Characteristically, Crowe set the challenges of Bosnia and expanded NATO membership in the context of an underpinning commitment to post-Cold War adaptation.[18]

The granting of a visa to Sinn Fein leader Gerry Adams in 1993 had opened up divisions between the Clinton White House and Grosvenor Square, which vigorously opposed the strategy of bringing in terrorists from the cold.[19] The administration's 1993 Irish initiatives had caused new rifts between the White House and the Major government, for whose point of view on Northern Ireland many senior London Embassy staff had sympathy. According to Irish journalists Trevor Birney and Julian O'Neill, Anthony Lake (Clinton's first National Security Advisor) was especially unpopular at Grosvenor Square.[20] Ambassador Crowe's role became one of running with Clinton's Irish play as he received it, attempting to smooth relations with

Downing Street as he proceeded. The Embassy – along with the US consulate in Belfast – was closely involved in the diplomacy surrounding Clinton's post-1993 Irish initiatives, including the President's 1995 visit to Northern Ireland. Blair Hall, political counsellor at Grosvenor Square, played a central role in planning the choreography of Clinton's Belfast trip. Crowe's style was to combine general support for American diplomatic interventionism with blunt talking towards the Republican side. Prior to the presidential visit, Crowe appeared on the *Today* programme on BBC radio to insist that the various London-Dublin-Washington peace initiatives must be answered by positive action on arms decommissioning on the part of Sinn Fein and the Provisional Irish Republican Army. Crowe insisted in March 1995: 'The ball is now in Sinn Fein's court and the United States is going to be monitoring this commitment that we feel we got out of Sinn Fein'.[21] John Major recalled Crowe's contribution in mid-1995 in the following terms: 'the straight-talking US Ambassador in London, Admiral William Crowe, met Adams to protest about the Provisionals' refusal to move on decommissioning and their threats to return to violence, saying that President Clinton had taken risks, and "you ain't given a goddam thing to him" '.[22] The breaking of the IRA ceasefire with the Canary Wharf bombing of February 1996 exposed the fragility of the hopes expressed in the Clinton peace initiative, and in Crowe's efforts to cajole Sinn Fein.

Despite his concern for policy adaptation, Crowe was a strong believer in a fairly traditional version of the Special Relationship. Echoing President John Kennedy's words, Crowe continued in retirement to affirm the uniqueness of the US–UK partnership, and its ability to transcend high-level differences of opinion and conflicting leader personalities. In 2001, he compared the Special Relationship to an iceberg: 'there is a small tip of it sticking out, but beneath the water there is quite a bit of everyday business that goes on between our governments in a fashion that's unprecedented in the world'.[23] Especially revealing of Crowe's understanding of US–UK relations were his cables – released to *The Guardian* newspaper under Freedom of Information legislation – to Secretary of State Madeleine Albright, sent in the wake of Princess Diana's death in September 1997. The cables revealed Crowe's admiration for Prime Minister Blair, who he saw as a Clinton-esque adapter and moderniser. Crowe had played a significant role in bringing Blair and Clinton together in London in November 1995. By 1997, Crowe had clearly come to the view that Blair was good for the UK and for US–UK relations. In the cables to Albright, Crowe referred to Blair's 'uncanny ability to correctly read the nation's mood': 'If the public are disillusioned with the tawdry excesses and rigidities of the Windsors, they still revere royalty and the British tradition. Tony Blair has once again taken the public pulse and steered a conservative course that nonetheless brings the nation a small step closer to his modernist ideal'. For Crowe, the Conservative Opposition under William Hague was at best an irrelevance: 'Hague has now called for Heathrow to be renamed Diana, Princess of Wales airport, a gesture that will likely be seen as too obvious and too late'.[24]

Crowe's 'Diana cables' were despatched to Washington as Philip Lader, the third Ambassador to serve at Grosvenor Square under Clinton (following Seitz and Crowe) was settling into his new job. Unlike Crowe, who came into the Clinton political orbit with the 1992 endorsement, Lader was a fully paid-up 'Friend of Bill'. Introducing Lader at his 1993 Senate confirmation hearing (for the post of deputy at Office of Management and Budget (OMB)), Senator Ernest Hollings referred to his fellow South Carolinian as 'the Renaissance Man, a man who has distinguished himself as a lawyer, a politician, a businessman, an academic, and a man of ideas'. Lader – whose father had migrated to America from Ukraine and his mother from North Africa – also, according to Hollings, 'embodies the American dream'. Before taking up the OMB post, Lader had been a business manager, primarily connected to land recreational development projects and 'later managed the real estate of Sir James Goldsmith's far-flung corporate empire'.[25] Between 1967 and 1968, Lader studied law at Oxford University, just overlapping with Bill Clinton. Philip Lader ran unsuccessfully for the governorship of South Carolina in 1986. Most famously, Lader was founder – with his wife, Linda LeSourd – of the 'Renaissance Weekend', a New Year's Eve event in Hilton Head (South Carolina) attended by Bill and Hillary Clinton every year between 1984 and 1999. The Weekends became a key focus of networking for the Clintons, with several key presidential appointments deriving from contacts made at Hilton Head. Though the Weekends were not primarily religious events, Linda LeSourd Lader developed a career as an organiser of women's prayer groups in Washington, and of the National Prayer Breakfast, an interfaith event on Capitol Hill. Bill Clinton described Linda as 'a whirlwind of theological sophistication mixed with Evangelical roots she traced through several generations'.[26]

At OMB, Lader was a central part of the Clinton–Gore effort to 'reinvent government' – cutting waste and promoting efficiency in the federal government. In November 1993, Lader moved to become Deputy Chief of Staff at the White House under Mack McLarty. In October 1994, he moved to become head of the Small Business Administration, serving on the National Economic Council (the body set up by Clinton to coordinate economic policy, especially to factor considerations of economic competitiveness into US foreign policy). By the time he reached Grosvenor Square, Lader had become a White House insider, with a special commitment to what had become the defining purpose of the Clinton presidency: the management and encouragement of economic globalisation.

The foreign policy priorities of the Clinton administration shifted significantly over the two terms. The early years were preoccupied with post-Cold War adjustment, including military retrenchment. The administration attempted to develop standards by which to calibrate (especially) military engagement, in accord with pragmatic limits on the use of American power, but also in line with emerging doctrines of liberal internationalism and 'assertive humanitarianism'. After 1995, the administration gained in confidence regarding the possibilities of effective power projection. The computer revolution and the consumer boom had reversed perceptions of American international decline. Clinton remained very cautious about ground troop commitments but (notably in Kosovo in 1999) was certainly willing to take controversial military action outside the remit of the United Nations. Partly in response to the Republican domination of the US Congress after 1994, Clinton increasingly accepted the logic both of unilateral action and of increasing military spending. By the end of the presidency, international terrorism stood clearly at the head of priorities. Throughout these changes, however, the commitment to free trade and to managing globalisation remained constant. During his presidency, Clinton agreed around 500 bilateral and regional free trade deals, ranging from wide-ranging agreements (such as the North American Free Trade Agreement) to *ad hoc* understandings regarding tariff relief on particular US exports. Bill Clinton and Vice President Al Gore made innumerable speeches extolling the virtues of free trade, linking globalisation to notions of 'democratic peace': the Kantian idea that nations who trade with each other tend not to fight one another. As Sandy Berger, Clinton's second National Security Advisor, put it in 2000: 'Globalization does have qualities that we can harness to advance our enduring objectives of democracy, shared prosperity and peace'.[27]

Far more than Crowe, Lader emerged as a publicist for this economics-oriented foreign policy. Lader reflected Al Gore's enthusiasm for the Internet and the generally positive administration orientation towards globalisation and technological innovation. Far from drowning out American power in a sea of economic competition, economic globalisation was seen in this narrative as underpinning America's position as 'indispensable nation' in a world of growing market-oriented democratisation. Lader developed these ideas in a June 1998 speech at Chatham House and in a May 2000 address to the London Business School. Speaking to the Royal Institute of International Affairs in 1998, Lader stressed the close economic ties between the US and the UK: 'Today, more than one million Americans went to work at British-owned businesses.' The Special Relationship, however, needed to broaden its focus to take account of newly global interrelationships. This broadening of focus, argued Lader, must occur within the context of a deepening British commitment to Europe: 'the transatlantic partnership must embrace our entire societies. Its reach must be global. Its scope must increasingly include Europe.' The 'pragmatic and intangible' qualities of the US–UK alliance must be applied to 'a broader European-American relationship'. Britain should foster both its European and its American connections, just as the US would achieve a new balance between Pacific and Atlantic interests in the context of globalisation.[28]

In the May 2000 address, Lader took as his main theme the 'twin revolutions' developing in technology and enterprise. He emphasised the interconnectedness of Britain and the UK within the wider inter-linkages of the globalising world economy: 'Not since tea was dumped at Boston Harbor has any one or several revolutions affected our two nations so much.' One-third of foreign businesses in the UK were already off-shoots of American companies; looking to the future, the upheavals in technology and the globalisation of free trade would 'make our prosperity even more intertwined'. Echoing President Clinton's familiar phrase about the 'inexorable logic' of globalisation, Lader portrayed the twin revolutions as irresistible. Yet history could be given a shove, and individual countries had to appreciate the dangers of missing the revolutionary boat. Thus Ambassador Lader urged greater commitment by the UK to technological research and development.[29]

Willliam Crowe had been nearing 70 years of age when he took the Grosvenor Square job in 1994. Lader, who took the post at the age of 51, brought huge energy to the job. He famously walked the entire length of England and Scotland during 1997 and 1998. His rather extraordinary walking tour gave Lader an unusually sympathetic understanding of the diversity of the UK landscape and population.[30] Ambassador Lader put great emphasis on personal engagement and encouragement of US-related activities in the UK.[31] He strove to smooth ruffled Anglo-American feathers at every opportunity. In 2000, he criticised the film, *The Patriot* (a story of the War of Independence, starring Mel Gibson) as 'damaging Anglo-American relations by falsely portraying British soldiers as evil and vicious'.[32] Lader consistently emphasised the need for cultural sensitivity between allies; his Great Walk was a physical embodiment of such a commitment. Yet, no less than Crowe, Lader saw adaptation as the key to alliance success. For Lader, as we have seen, such adaptation tended to be conceived in economic rather than military terms. In 1998 he listed recent Anglo-American quarrels – 'the Suez crisis, Skybolt, the Vietnam War, Grenada, the Strategic Defence Initiative, Bosnia'. Transatlantic amity would be restored not only by building on the history of Anglo-American cooperation, but also by embracing a globalised (and, for the UK, an unequivocally Europeanised) future.[33]

As the Lewinsky scandal developed into Clinton's impeachment trial, Lader rather conspicuously declined to offer a vigorous defence of the President. Lader's stance on the impeachment to some degree reflected his own religious position, while also partaking of the strong disapproval of the presidential conduct exhibited by Lader's boss, Secretary of State Madeleine Albright. It is an indication of the intensity of partisan American politics in this period that, in February 1999, the conservative journal *The Weekly Standard* actually attacked Lader for failing to criticise Clinton over the scandal. Much less seriously, Lader was also caused some embarrassment by remarks made by his teenage daughter Catherine (and reported in *The Tatler*) that British boys were 'scrawny, pale and unhealthy looking', compared to their 'tanned and athletic' American cousins.[34]

Ambassador Lader and his staff were involved in the principal Anglo-American military and diplomatic events of the later Clinton years. Following the Canary Wharf bombing of 1996, highly active diplomatic cooperation between Washington and Prime Minister Blair resulted in the landmark Belfast Agreement of 1998. Britain and the US undertook joint air strikes on Iraq in 1998 and on Serbia during the Kosovo campaign of spring 1999. Lader made public statements on the Belfast negotiations, and also defended Anglo-American action in Iraq and Kosovo. However, his substantive role in these events does not seem to have been huge, and has left little mark in the memoirs of key participants. Ambassador Lader does not, for example, make an appearance in Tony Blair's 2010 memoir, *A Journey*. Lader's absence is perhaps surprising in view of the apparent convergence between Blair and Lader in terms of clear adherence to Christian belief as a guide to political action. Like Crowe, Lader certainly saw Blair as a highly skilled political leader. He later commended Blair's 'instinctive intellectual understanding of the mutual security relationships between the UK and the US'.[35]

More than Admiral Crowe, Lader seems to have conceived his ambassadorial role in terms of public diplomatic engagement. It may also have been the case that the close personal relationship between Bill Clinton and Tony Blair tended to lessen the role of diplomatic intermediaries. By the end of the century, Lader was explaining to British audiences how America intended to combat international terrorism. In October 2000, David Frost questioned Lader about US reactions to the bombing off Yemen of the *USS Cole*. According to Frost, the press view was that 'it's got the name of Bin Laden written all over it'. Lader responded by referring to the 'implosion' of the Israel-Palestinian peace process at Camp David and in the Middle East itself. He pointed to Clinton's continuing efforts to keep the process in train, to 'maintain the kind of balance that allows him to play an honest brokerage role'. Lader also rather poignantly mentioned the worries of the US electorate about the degree of international backwash against the United States. There was 'a heightened sensitivity' prior to the 2000 presidential elections 'about how perilous is the role of being a global peacekeeper'.[36] Less than a year later, Lader would be sitting in another BBC studio as he faced the extraordinary expression of (albeit minority) anti-American feeling, even as the US was still reeling from the 9/11 attacks.

The trajectory of American foreign policy during the Clinton years can be traced through the ambassadorships of Crowe and Lader. Admiral Crowe's tenure at Grosvenor Square was dominated by issues of American post-Cold War international reorientation. As we have seen, Crowe saw Clinton as a leader unafraid to tackle such questions. Crowe's own experience – from

Vietnam to Soviet diplomacy in the late 1980s – had confirmed a strong awareness of the need to adapt. During the years of the George H. W. Bush presidency, Washington had shown signs of regarding Germany, rather than the UK, as its principal European interlocutor. The military and intelligence pillars of the Anglo-American Special Relationship remained in place, but seemed under threat in the face of reduced American commitment and of possible European defence integration. During the mid-1990s, Washington proffered public support for a European defence identity, while still identifying NATO as the 'primary institution'. The decision by Washington to recommit to NATO was made in the form of deciding to back adaptation through expansion. This commitment was made by the Clinton White House around the time of Crowe's appointment to Grosvenor Square. Crowe's role involved an effort to refashion the Special Relationship in this new environment: rescuing the alliance from the depths to which it had sunk in 1994, but not trying to pretend that it could escape change. Crowe emphasised that there was no question of 'a retreat from global engagement' by Washington, but that the US 'would like to see Europe do more in solving European problems and to rely less on US involvement'.[37]

Crowe certainly was not put in post in order to help dismantle US–UK military cooperation. However, 'adaptation' to Crowe did seem to mean a degree of pulling apart from Cold War alliance patterns: probably some weakening of 'special' US–UK defence and intelligence ties; the move by London towards a degree of European cooperation which would help obviate the need for the US constantly to become involved in regional disputes which did not affect core interests; and also a considerable degree of rebalancing by the US between Europe and Asia. In retrospect, and in the context of Anglo-American relations, we can see his ambassadorship as contributing to these trends. In the long term, the partial erosion of 'special relations' was reversed by the onset of the War on Terror in 2001 – and especially by Prime Minister Blair's support for the foreign policy of President George W. Bush. Even before 9/11, however, the closeness between the Blair and Clinton governments – over Ireland, Kosovo and Iraq, but also in terms of world outlook – had put a brake on the cooling of relations under John Major. Ambassador Lader embodied the spirit of the reviving Special Relationship in the latter 1990s with the emphasis on economics and globalisation. Partners in military terms in the later 1990s, London and Washington were also partners in spreading the gospel of 'third way' modernisation and marketised democratisation. Lader also supported the Blair doctrine of strengthening US–UK relations within the context of a deepening British commitment to (especially economic) European integration.[38]

In the absence of detailed archive releases, it is difficult to be confident about any judgement about the relative success of the two Ambassadors. They were very different figures, whose distinction was apparent in their post-Grosvenor Square careers. Crowe, who died in 2007, taught classes at the US Naval Academy and retained his connections with the University of Oklahoma. He chaired boards of enquiry which investigated the terrorist bombing of US Embassies in Africa, and made a series of recommendations for enhancing the safety of diplomats serving in dangerous regions. Crowe also signed a declaration in 2004 to the effect that President George W. Bush was unfit to lead American foreign policy 'in either style or substance'.[39]

In line with his business background and his commitment to the 'twin revolutions', Philip Lader in 2001 became chairman of WPP group, a major global player in advertising and communications. In broad terms, Crowe contributed directly to the easing of transatlantic tensions over Bosnia and played a significant role in Irish diplomacy. Lader, focusing more on public diplomacy, was less directly connected to the major diplomatic and foreign policy questions of the era. A reasonable case can be made, however, that both Ambassadors made important contributions to the survival and adaptation of the Special Relationship in the years between the collapse of the Soviet Union and 9/11: years when Anglo-American ties were weakening.

Notes

1. Seitz, *Over Here*, p. 322.
2. *The Independent*, 22 January 1993; Hugo Young, 'Sleeping with America when We Should Be Courting Europe', *The Guardian*, 1 March 1994.
3. See John Dumbrell, 'The US-UK "Special Relationship" in a World Twice Transformed', *Cambridge Review of International Affairs*, Vol. 17, No. 3 (2004), pp. 437–50.
4. See S. A. Cheney, 'The General's Folly', *Foreign Affairs*, Vol. 77, No. 1 (1998), pp. 155–7.
5. Alex Danchev, 'On Friendship: Anglo-America at Fin de Siecle', *International Affairs*, Vol. 73, No. 4 (1997), pp. 747–59, at pp. 757, 759.
6. See 'BBC Chief Apologises for Terror Debate', 15 September 2001, available at: http://news.bbc.co.uk/1/hi/entertainment/1544897.stm (accessed 30 July 2010).
7. William J. Crowe, *The Line of Fire* (New York: Simon & Schuster, 1993), pp. 340, 344.
8. See Godfrey Hodgson, 'Admiral William Crowe: Obituary', *The Guardian*, 24 October 2007.
9. Crowe, *The Line of Fire*, p. 344.
10. Crowe, *The Line of Fire*, pp. 297, 127; Bruce Anderson, 'An Admiral at the Court of St James's', *Stanford Magazine*, September/October 1997, pp. 23–30.
11. Anderson, 'An Admiral at the Court of St James's', p. 24.
12. Dennis Hevesi, 'Adm. William Crowe Dies at 82', *The New York Times*, 19 October 2007.
13. Richard Holbrooke, *To End a War* (New York: Random House, 1998), p. 333.
14. Christopher Meyer, *DC Confidential* (London: Weidenfeld & Nicolson, 2005), p. 98.

15. Taylor Branch, *The Clinton Tapes* (London: Simon & Schuster, 2009), p. 217.
16. Holbrooke, *To End a War*, p. 99.
17. John Major, *The Autobiography* (London: HarperCollins, 1999), pp. 497, 545.
18. William J. Crowe, 'Transatlantic Relations and the Future of European Security', *State Department Dispatch*, Vol. 7, No. 45 (4 November 1996).
19. See Michael Cox, ' "Bringing in the International": The IRA Ceasefire and the End of the Cold War', *International Affairs*, Vol. 73, No. 4 (1997), pp. 671–94; Timothy J. Lynch, *Turf War: The Clinton Administration and Northern Ireland* (Aldershot: Ashgate, 2004); John Dumbrell, 'The United States and the Northern Irish Conflict: From Indifference to Intervention', *Irish Studies in International Affairs*, Vol. 6 (1995), pp. 107–25.
20. Trevor Birney and Julian O'Neill, *When the President Calls* (Derry: Guildhall Press, 1997), pp. 35–6.
21. Stephen Castle, 'Cracks Show in Ulster Peace', *The Independent on Sunday*, 12 March 1995.
22. Major, *The Autobiography*, p. 477.
23. 'US and the UK: Special Relationship?', 23 February 2001, available at: http://news.bbc.co.uk/1/hi/world/americas/1185177.stm (accessed 20 January 2011).
24. David Hencke and Rob Evans, 'The Royals: Aloof, Rigid, No Empathy', *The Guardian*, 3 December 1999; see also 'Diana's Landmine Campaign "Panicked" Major', 3 January 2000, available at: http://news.bbc.co.uk/1/hi/uk/589313.stm (accessed 10 May 2011).
25. United States Congress: Senate: Committee on Governmental Affairs, *Nomination of Philip Lader: Hearing before the Committee on Governmental Affairs, US Senate, 103rd Congress, 1st Session* (Memphis, TN: General Books, 1994), p. 4.
26. Hillary Clinton, *Living History* (London: Headline, 2003), p. 167; Bill Clinton, *My Life* (London: Arrow, 2005), p. 314; Branch, *The Clinton Tapes*, p. 426.
27. John Dumbrell, *Clinton's Foreign Policy: Between the Bushes* (London: Routledge, 2009), p. 46.
28. Philip Lader, 'Lessons from Walking: Anglo-American Relations for a New Century', 12 June 1998, available at: http://www.mailarchive.com/ctrl@listerv.aol.com/msg00893.html (accessed 23 May 2011).
29. Philip Lader, 'The Enterprise Spirit', 2 May 2000, available tat: http://web.ebscohost.com/ehost/detail?sid=803ee0ea-6b01-4e5a-b8a4-a727912b5356 (accessed 17 May 2011).
30. Lader, 'Lessons from Walking'.
31. 'American Centre Opens with President's Approval' (opening of Liverpool American Studies Centre), *American Studies Today*, 7 July 1998.
32. Larry Pratt, 'The Patriot: A Great Movie', available at: http://www.spectacle.org/0800/patriot.html (accessed 10 May 2011).
33. Lader, 'Lessons from Walking'.
34. 'The Lader Chronicles', *The Weekly Standard*, 1 February 1999, p. 23; 'Are British Lads so Bad', 21 August 2000, available at: http://news.bbc.co.uk/1/hi/talking_point/874201.stm (accessed 10 May 2011).
35. David Rennie, 'The Special Bond that Has Soured into an Awkward and Unrequited Force', *The Telegraph*, 13 November 2004; Tony Blair, *A Journey* (London: Hutchinson, 2010).
36. 'BBC Breakfast with Frost Interview with Philip Lader', 15 October 2000, available at: http://news.bbc.co.uk/1/hi/programmes/breakfast_with_frost/973346.stm (accessed 17 May 2011).

37. Crowe, 'Transatlantic Relations and the Future of European Security', p. 2.
38. See John Dumbrell, *A Special Relationship: Anglo-American Relations from the Cold War to Iraq* (Basingstoke: Palgrave, 2006), pp. 235–41.
39. 'Ex-Officials Lash Bush Policies', 16 June 2006, available at: http://newsvote. bbc.co.uk/mpapps/pagetools/print/news.bbc.co.uk/1/hi/world/america (accessed 20 January 2011).

Part VI

The Post-9/11 Ambassadors, 2001–2008

Introduction

Alison R. Holmes

George W. Bush came into office in 2000 to find a relatively long-standing opposite number in Tony Blair and, once the media speculation over their 'chemistry' died down, it proved to be a strong and resilient bond. Consistency was also a feature at the ambassadorial level with two appointments to the Court of St James's for the Americans and three to Massachusetts Avenue for the British.[1] What neither leader could know was that they would become wartime premiers and step down from their respective posts at nearly the same time, arguably forming a distinct period of transatlantic relations; beginning with the events of 9/11, through Iraq writ large and ending in 2007/2008 with the handover of power from Blair to Gordon Brown, his patient Chancellor in London and, after two terms, the Republican loss of the White House. Unlike the experience of their predecessors at the beginning of the Second World War, there was no slow motion slide from peace to conflict, but a single strike that created both the foundation of a 'friendship through fire' between the leaders and a wake of diplomatic challenges for their Ambassadors.

Thus, in some ways, the final two Ambassadors bring us back to the very beginning of the period under review, especially if we think of the two considered here as representing different pressure on diplomacy in times of war. However, such a suggestion of 'comparability' rests on a presumption that the Second World War and what became the Global War on Terror (a contested phrase, but intended here to encompass Afghanistan, Iraq and foreign/domestic cooperation on terrorism) can be placed in the same category, and may therefore benefit from some explanation as to our choice of 'break point'. By using the events of 11 September 2001, there are (at least) two considerations. First, while this division has become commonplace in academic analyses, it is not without difficulties. Observers such as John Dumbrell note that:

foreign policy of the first George W. Bush administration divides naturally into pre- and post-9/11 phases. The first nine months of 2001 were already distinguished by transatlantic bad temper. Bush's 'Americanist' foreign policy, though portrayed as a departure from Clinton, in some respects actually grew rather naturally from the late 1990s.[2]

Peter Riddell argues that 'In retrospect, the international solidarity after 9/11 was deceptive, despite continuing cooperation between intelligence and police forces in fighting al-Qaeda and other terrorist groups... Europe, (or rather most of Europe) and America had increasingly distinct strategic outlooks and security concerns. These differences were highlighted rather than blurred by 9/11.'[3] Thus, events of 9/11 are perhaps not as clear a break as often portrayed and, to compound the difficulty from our perspective, the presentation of it as a distinct shift in terms of diplomacy may also perpetuate or even reinforce the often overly rigid war versus peace narrative of UK–US relations. That said, the decision to use 9/11 as a division was based primarily on the fact that, for those in power, the change of course required by the events of that day was perceived as being as stark as it was sharp with inevitable consequences for diplomacy.

The second issue is our proximity to these events and our lack of 'formal' or historical records. As these chapters have progressed chronologically, our authors have gradually lost both source material and mental distance from the topics at hand. Writing 'in real time' about the period in which one is currently living – especially one of emotional events and controversial policies – has many hazards. It is a bit like trying to make a bed while lying in it. It is not *im*possible, but hospital corners are out of the question. The whole thing will probably look at least rumpled to the attentive observer and unforgivably untidy to the perfectionist's eye. If the use of corroborated primary sources is the sole test of scholarly pursuits, such writing is doomed because there is precious little in the way of 'objective' material; the files remain firmly closed, or it is perceived as 'tainted' by personal prejudice or media bias. Perhaps counter-intuitively, the rush to memoir now commonplace in modern politics compounds this problem by creating a cacophony of 'me-centric' versions in which the views of others are not generally deemed worthy of note let alone explored and compared. On the positive side, memories are fresh and there is at least the possibility an author can exert some test of credibility, something that does not exist for the chroniclers of ages long gone. Similarly, the 'culture' of the subject is also that of the observer, potentially making 'interpretation' less of an issue.[4] However, none of these benefits should divert attention from the pitfalls, making it perhaps safer to think of this as an altogether different project. The ideal of reconstruction may not be feasible, but it remains possible and even enlightening to examine the different individuals' views of the events as they lived them, and thereby gain a more 'real' sense of the uncertainty that surrounded their decision-making process.

As individuals in our daily lives, we operate largely in the dark as to the ebb and flow of events in the lives of our colleagues, let alone their motives and hidden agendas. To compensate, we continuously and often unwittingly weave new information and 'received wisdom' into our own story and version of events, adding speculation based on our experience and personality as we go. One result may be that while later versions are more 'correct' in terms of 'what happened', they can also be less 'accurate' as to the sense of what was 'going on'. Given that much of the later debate over Iraq turns on whether or not leaders and governments 'lied', what anyone believed at any given moment becomes all the more crucial to the overall story. It may be understandable then, on a personal level, that Bush would turn to a Clausewitzian phrase to describe his frustration and powerlessness to penetrate the 'fog of war' aboard Air Force One on 9/11as he strove to sift facts, haunting enough, from even more terrifying rumour.[5] He also applies this observation more broadly to 'the nature of the presidency' and concludes that 'Perceptions are shaped by the clarity of hindsight. In the moment of decision you don't have that advantage'.[6] Similarly, Blair regularly refers to the constraints of knowledge at any given moment, a phenomenon he calls the 'conditions of understanding'.[7] Both men clearly seek to not only explain their actions, but also to remind their readers of the context in a very specific, and uncertain time.

The goal here is not an accounting of the foreign policy of the United States post 9/11 or the motivation for the United Kingdom to join the Global War on Terror; nor is it an exploration of the relationship between President and Prime Minister which dominated the period; and it is certainly not an analysis of the intricate political and social issues surrounding the Iraq war. It is, instead, a collection of 'raw data' available at this point in the hope it will (a) provide a stimulus for future scholars; and (b) provide a glimpse into the impact on the transatlantic diplomatic space of three factors: a particular *style* of leader relations; a war that was not a war against an enemy as we had known it (and certainly not imagined when the special relationship was born); and the interplay between layers and levels of government.

Dubya's Men

As appointments of the same President, it is perhaps not surprising that William Stamps Farish III and Robert Holmes Tuttle have features in common. Fundraising may be one, but the most relevant may, ironically, be the fact that neither man was a long-term personal friend of the President. That said, their respective pedigrees in terms of family connections can more than explain the decision to appoint them. Ambassador Farish was born in Texas and returned to Houston to begin a career in business, primarily oil, after boarding school and college 'back east'. Although there had been some previous business dealings between their families, Farish came to know George Herbert Walker Bush shortly after the latter arrived in Houston from Midland and became the Chairman of the Republican Party in Harris County. Their business paths also crossed when Bush sold his interest in Zapata Oil and Farish came to have the controlling interest in the company. An indication of their growing closeness is the fact that Farish acted as Bush's driver in the Senate race of 1964, travelling the state at his side in what was, ultimately, a losing campaign. They remained close, hunting together and their young families effectively growing up together through shared vacations and holidays. As Bush Senior became more active in politics, Farish acted on his behalf in various business matters, including becoming the holder of his blind trusts. Interestingly, Bush talked to his friend about becoming the Ambassador to the United Kingdom when the latter became President. Farish refused for personal and business reasons, but clearly the President's invitation was not forgotten when his son came to make the same decision.

Similarly, Ambassador Tuttle also had more dealings with the father than the son. Tuttle was born in California, the son of Holmes Tuttle, an original Okie who rode the rails to California to become a successful businessman and a member of the original Reagan 'kitchen cabinet'. The young Tuttle also attended boarding school back east, but returned to the West Coast for college and his MBA. He gradually got more involved in California politics including fund-raising, but it was as President Reagan's second-term Head of Personnel that his path crossed more significantly with the then Vice President Bush. Personnel was a key post for Reagan's strategy of 'people are policy', laying some of the groundwork for his approach to his later posting to London. If there is such a thing as a unifying 'Bush style' between father and son, loyalty and dependence on old friends would be on the list. Of George W., Fred Barnes makes the point: 'As First Lady Laura Bush once said, she and the president didn't come to Washington to make new friends. And they haven't. They chiefly socialize with old friends, many of them Texans.'[8] Clearly his father's old friends were also on the list.

Once in post, another thing the two Ambassadors shared, or had to similarly bear, was the effect of terrorism on their mission and an unprecedented level of anti-Americanism. If Ambassador Price marked a shift, these two lived with the consequences of that change on a daily basis. Post 9/11, the need for heightened security altered every aspect of their respective tenure. From representation on policy issues and consular functions to the management of the Embassy, safety of their staff and their own personal safety, the new millennium was substantively different. The State Department had struggled for some time with the issue of Embassy security around the world, but it was Ambassador Farish who took the decision that the Embassy was no longer 'fit for purpose'. Farish began the process of the Embassy's final departure from Grosvenor Square that Tuttle would finalise before his own departure. The reason for their caution was all too clear as the consequences of terrorist attacks were almost the first order of business for both men. Ambassador Farish was still in boxes from his move to the United Kingdom when the planes hit the Towers, while Ambassador Tuttle was in Washington to be confirmed at the time of the 7/7 attack in London and not due in London until the 1 August. He immediately changed his plans to ensure an American presence and at least try and reciprocate the care and attention received from the British four years earlier. In terms of anti-American feeling, both men indicate that while they did not personally suffer any direct/overtly anti-American attacks, verbal or physical, such views undoubtedly created constant 'background noise' in terms of the political mood, perpetuated by its prevalence in the British media. It is interesting to note that it resulted in not entirely dissimilar strategies for dealing with the British press, though from very different starting points.

Whatever the common 'heritage' of the two Ambassadors, there were two clear points of change in the Bush administration that affected them both. The first is obviously 9/11. 'The focus of my presidency, which I had expected to be domestic policy, was now war…September 11 redefined sacrifice. It redefined duty. And it redefined my job. The story of that week is the key to understanding my presidency' wrote Bush.[9] This perception in Washington is also key to understanding the role and mission of the Embassy in London, if not Embassies all over the world at the time. As Glyn Davies, Deputy Chief of Mission under Ambassadors Lader and Farish (now Ambassador and Permanent Representative of the United States to the International Atomic Energy Agency and the United Nations Office) puts it:

> 9/11…created a new agenda…policy just kind of collapsed back into Washington in a very, almost palpable sense…it became about how to react to this existential threat and the story of what we were doing in London was completely derivative of the directives and pronouncements and policies coming out of Washington, which began rapid fire to wash over us – and all offices. Everything from homeland security to military movements to sanctioning and…terrorist-related organizations…that was one of these periods where it didn't matter where you were, there was a megaphone and it was turned up all the way out of Washington and it was telling you what to do and you just did it. You just. Did it.[10]

By the second term, some sense of normalcy had returned, and a new Secretary of State and former National Security Advisor, Condoleezza Rice, came in with a desire to work in a more multilateral fashion with allies, particularly in Europe. Her ideas of transformational and public diplomacy were made manifest through an approach that resembled the Reagan idea of 'people are policy' and a plan to fill appointee slots with people the administration could trust to 'get the message out'. It was also strategically linked to 'transformational' and 'active' diplomacy strategies being developed in both the US and the UK as a new approach to public diplomacy generally.[11] Barnes, quoting a 'senior White House official' suggests there was anger in the White House with 'Ambassadors who were instructed to get out there in their capitals and actively support the policy, publicly ... and refused on the grounds they didn't agree'.[12] Such sentiments made the mission of new political appointees very clear with a consequent effect on the ground. No one understood that better than the man who had implemented a similar policy from the Reagan White House, Robert Tuttle. The urgency from Washington was not gone, but there was new room for Embassy initiative. David Johnson, Deputy Chief of Mission to Ambassadors Farish and Tuttle (retired, Ambassador and Assistant Secretary of State for International Narcotics and Law Enforcement Affairs) also argues that it is important to put London in the context of what was going on elsewhere. Having come to London from Afghanistan, he attributes the changes simply to 'Different time, different opportunities and I think not just even, but especially in the public sphere. If you look at what was being attempted abroad by diplomatic representatives during the ... '01–'03 period, I think you will find that it is different in scope and size than it is in the second [term] ... you've got to adjust for when it took place.'[13] The story of the post 9/11 period is clearly one of the 'art of the possible'.

Notes

1. British Ambassadors to the United States in this period were: Sir Christopher Meyer, Sir David Manning and Sir Nigel Sheinwald. They consolidated what had become a pattern of moving to Washington directly from positions in Number Ten, indicating the perceived importance of continuity and closeness to the Prime Minister. Meyer, a slight exception, had worked in Number Ten, but was posted to Germany as Ambassador and served less than a year before being moved on to the US.
2. John Dumbrell, *A Special Relationship: Anglo-American Relations from the Cold War to Iraq* (Basingstoke: Palgrave Macmillan, 2006), p. 148.
3. Peter Riddell, *Hug them Close: Blair, Clinton, Bush and the 'Special Relationship'* (London: Politicos, 2003), p. 226.
4. Specifically, I worked with Ambassador Farish in a professional capacity while head of a transatlantic business membership organization (2001–2005) and directly to Ambassador Tuttle as speech-writer and communications adviser (2005–2008).
5. George W. Bush, *Decision Points* (New York: Crown Publishers, 2010), p. 131.
6. *Ibid.*, p. 180.
7. Tony Blair, *A Journey: My Political Life* (New York: Alfred Knopf, 2010), p. 349.
8. Fred Barnes, *Rebel-in-Chief: Inside the Bold and Controversial Presidency of George W. Bush* (New York: Three Rivers Press, 2006), p. 15.
9. Bush, *Decision Points*, pp. 139 and 151.

10. Alison Holmes, interview with Ambassador Glyn Davies, Washington DC, 2008.
11. Alison Holmes, 'Transatlantic Diplomacy', in Alan Dobson and Steve Marsh (eds.), *Anglo-American Relations from the Cold war to the Present* (London: Routledge, 2012).
12. Barnes, *Rebel-in-Chief*, p. 172.
13. Alison Holmes, interview with Ambassador David Johnson, Washington DC, 2008.

16
Ambassadors Farish and Tuttle, 2001–2009

Alison R. Holmes

William Stamps Farish III, 2001–2004

It is standard practice for political appointee ambassadors to prepare to leave post shortly after the inauguration of a new President. It is also standard practice for the British media to begin to speculate on a replacement even before the chair is empty. The year 2001 was no different in that Ambassador Lader did not officially leave post until the 28 February, but the British media had already named his successor as William Farish by Valentine's Day. The consensus, and rather tired observation, was that London was a 'plum' job handed out to cronies. Clearly the case could be made of Farish that the stereotype applied, especially given his long-standing links to the Queen. Farish, a horse breeder and polo player had met the Queen when he replaced an injured player in the Queen's Cup many years previously. She had subsequently made private visits to his Kentucky stud farm, Lane's End, and has bred horses there over the years.[1] *The Guardian* in particular concluded that 'With the special relationship in robust shape and British and US heads of state increasingly bypassing their diplomatic placemen in favour of personal chats on the hotline, London does not provide the more rigorous examination of diplomatic skills'. Further, 'Given the socializing and schmoozing', Mr Farish's 'constitution' was more likely to be 'tested than his tact'.[2]

His name may have been in the public domain, but his arrival was not destined to follow as planned. Senator Jeffords (VT), a Republican, chose this moment to become an independent, altering the balance of committee positions and holding up various confirmations. While Farish used the time productively in terms of briefings and so on, the matter was forced by the President's impending visit to the UK, scheduled for July. Farish was ultimately among the first to get confirmed. As it happened, the Ambassador and his wife, Sarah, arrived on the rather inauspicious day of Friday 13 July and the President, Condoleezza Rice and Andrew Card arrived five days later. As he puts it: 'We were still unpacking over the weekend. I had meetings on Monday and Tuesday and the President arrived on Wednesday.

That afternoon we had gone to the Queen's annual garden party...came home and went to the airport to meet the President...the day before I had had a meeting with Jack Straw who had just become Secretary of State... [for] foreign affairs'.[3] Farish's perceived late arrival would later be added to the media's accusations of being low key or even 'invisible', but as we shall see, that charge is not as straightforward as it might appear, and certainly the rest of the Ambassador's stay was not destined to get any less hectic.

The press typically sought to make light of the Ambassador's role, and while he did not have extensive foreign or public service experience, he did have a long-standing interest in foreign affairs. He lists issues such as the Middle East, the changing relationship with Russia and China as well as the developing European Union as areas he was concerned with long before heading to the United Kingdom, as well as areas of the globe where he had business interests.[4] In terms of topics more directly related to US–UK relations, Farish felt that economic issues were a primary concern, and one that, as a businessman, he could bring his own expertise to bear both in terms of the operations of the Embassy and in its projection of American interests. As he says, 'economic issues...are very important for an ambassador, particularly a political ambassador because the State Department employees really haven't been directly or personally involved in the economic world to the same degree, and in countries like the UK...the economy plays a major role'.[5]

Internally, and like other Ambassadors before him, he wanted to streamline what he saw as the overly large Country Team meetings and bring it down to a more manageable or business-like process. In terms of external initiatives, he decided that the 'jealousies' between Canada, Mexico and the US had gone on long enough and that there should be more of a 'united front'. To that end, he invited his counterparts to jointly host a series of events at the annual conferences of the political parties for the first time.[6] As things turned out, the initial event went forward as planned, but future events were put on hold as the aftermath of 9/11 took precedence. He did, however, continue to take an active interest in globalisation and spoke to numerous business groups along the theme of the challenges and opportunities it presents to transatlantic business. David Johnson, Deputy Chief of Mission to Ambassadors Farish and Tuttle (retired, Ambassador and Assistant Secretary of State for International Narcotics and Law Enforcement Affairs) characterises this in his direct fashion, saying that the Ambassador tended to 'get involved when there is a need or an issue or a problem... not during the entire time, but when we were going hot and heavy on aviation negotiation, there was water for the ambassador to carry ...on defense issues... [on] big ticket trade advocacy issues'.[7]

One specific issue that had long caught the Ambassador's attention was the developing drama of Northern Ireland. The Clinton administration had become heavily involved, as Glyn Davies, Deputy Chief of Mission under

Ambassadors Lader and Farish (now Ambassador and Permanent Representative of the United States to the International Atomic Energy Agency and the United Nations Office) recalls from his time under Ambassador Lader. Davies argues that Clinton had effectively become 'the desk officer for Northern Ireland. He called Blair constantly, he called Trimble, he called George Mitchell, he worked the issue personally. He worked that issue the way George Bush's father worked the first Gulf War. He did it himself.'[8] Ultimately, this had caused some delicate moments with the British government with Ambassador Meyer, UK Ambassador to the US at the time, even suggesting that Clinton never 'gave the bite on Sinn Fein/ IRA at crucial moments'.[9] At the end of the day, this was one area in which there was little change in policy despite the change of party at the helm. Dumbrell suggests that while on most foreign policy issues Bush's intention was to be 'ABC – anything but Clinton', Northern Ireland was to be the exception that proved the rule. Farish was therefore alert to problems on this front from the outset and made a special effort to be on top of the issues, be present in Northern Ireland when it was helpful and, when necessary, willing to make pointed comments to colleagues back home. On one such occasion, Farish recalls speaking to Representative King-R of New York who had been having a series of fundraising lunches for Gerry Adams and 'took him to task', arguing that 'George Mitchell's been over here working his tail off and you're raising money for Gerry Adams and Sein Fein. It just makes no sense.'[10]

Yet, whatever the original strategy, preparations made or delays in arrival and quick succession visits of the leaders, all the best laid plans were to be shifted heavily to one side less than two months later. As Farish says, 'the changes that occurred...were not the kind of things that you could ever expect, are never trained for...I could have spent a lot of time, I could have spent my life in the State Department – and it wouldn't have prepared me anymore than I was – as it turned out.'[11]

When the Planes Hit

President George Bush – Emma E. Booker Elementary School, Sarasota FL: Andy Card pressed his head next to mine and whispered in my ear. 'A second plane hit the second tower' he said, pronouncing each word deliberately...'America is under attack'.[12]

Prime Minister, Tony Blair – Trades Union Congress, Grand Hotel, Brighton UK: Alistair [Campbell] came back in, turned on the television and said 'You'd better see this'. He knew I hated being interrupted just before a speech so I realized I better look. The TV was showing picture of the Trade Center like someone had punched a large hole in it...Just over fifteen minutes later, a second plane hit...This was not an accident. It was an attack.[13]

UK Ambassador Christopher Meyer – Massachusetts Avenue, Washington DC: We had John Major...staying with us...I joined [him] for coffee...when...our social secretary burst onto the terrace...'An aircraft has crashed into the World Trade Center'...my first reaction was to assume that this had been some small private plane that had wandered off course...Catherine [his wife]...suddenly called out and urged us to come in and watch her television: 'Something terrible has happened'...This was the second aircraft...hitting the South Tower just after 9 a.m...I went straight to my office...One crash could have been an accident; two had to be something else.[14]

US Ambassador Will Farish – Winfield House, London, UK: I was having a lunch with...a couple of press people actually and Sarah [his wife] came in and said 'Something very odd had happened'. She said 'a plane's gone into the World Trade Center...it's on the television'. So we came out because that kind of thing happens...planes get off course...it's not common but it does happen. And so we are watching the television and all of a sudden...I saw this other plane and bam it went in...within minutes the Embassy called and one of the Special Branch guys came in and said this just happened. I said 'I know. I am on my way'. I rushed straight back to the Embassy...and so that's how it all started...I went to the office and met with Glyn and our intelligence people and we got started.[15]

That is how it all started. The same story repeats itself over and over, regardless of location or position, and, because the news spread in a wave across the globe, there was enough time for thousands if not millions to watch it in real time. To those in power, the message was clear: the United States was under attack. To those on the ground, the driving force was the relentless stream of crises coming from every imaginable direction. Emergency plans, standard operating procedures, and risk assessment training all kicked into action on both sides of the Atlantic. It is interesting that, at such moments, the wheels of government and party political activity become compressed. The practical and the symbolic, the official and the intensely personal are merged as everyone was swept before the unfolding tragedy. The period immediately after the attacks can be broadly divided into three 'phases' – the necessary instant/public reaction, the aftershocks that played out across the first week or ten days and finally, the adaptation of embassy operations to a new mode of 'business as usual'.

What Do We Say

Perhaps ironically, Tony Blair was able to watch, in real time from his suite in Brighton, the pictures it would take some time for the President to see for himself. Having spoken only briefly to the assembled conference, Blair made his way back to London to ensure the various emergency and communications networks were being put into place. The President was similarly occupied, but as a likely target, his efforts were circumscribed by the concern for his own safety, whereas Blair was able to begin, even that first afternoon, to take soundings and gather information from other world leaders. However, the two leaders were anxious to speak to one another as soon as time allowed – a gesture that was repeated in different locations and levels throughout the two governments. Meyer recalls:

> After my council of war on the morning of 9/11 I called Condi Rice. I offered my condolences for the thousands of Americans who must have died. We feared that British casualties could run into the hundreds. We were ready to help in any way we could with the search for the victims at the World Trade Center...Condi sounded very cool and collected....I said that the Prime Minister would like to speak to the President as soon as possible. She immediately agreed to set this up. Bush would welcome an early contact with Blair.[16]

In the UK, the Prime Minister's statement from the TUC shortly after the second plane hit was one of the first public responses, and certainly the first by a world leader. His tone and message were consistent from the first and reminiscent of his famous shift in British foreign policy in his 'Chicago Speech'[17]: 'terrorism is the new evil in the world today' and 'democracies of this world are going to have to come together to fight it together'.[18]

The President's first statements from the school in Florida were very brief, stating only that the country had suffered a 'national tragedy' from an 'apparent terrorist attack' and, before asking for a moment of silence for the victims, ended by saying 'terrorism against our nation would not stand'.[19] Meanwhile, for the London Embassy, as for the President, the first requirement was to cope with the immediate issues and to make a public statement of their own. A later concern would be the creation of an *ad hoc* infrastructure to deal with the global stream of demands. The Ambassador recalls

> We were getting information from the State Department right away...within minutes we have a core Country team together, particularly intelligence, telling us what to do plus preparing what to say publicly...it sounds like it's all a great big sort of a mess but it really isn't because everybody is talking to their counterparts and we're all getting the same information and there are automatic plans in place for crises like these...the duties are allocated. It worked very smoothly...and you've got a lot of professionals who know their job...it doesn't mean they're not aching inside, but they know what they have to do to handle a given situation.[20]

As part of that immediate reaction, Farish spoke directly to the Prime Minister that afternoon and thanked him for his 'words of sympathy and strength' from the TUC and, through his own statement, said of the conversation with Blair: 'His comments remind us all that the United States and Great Britain stand together in every circumstance, as allies, partners and friends.'[21] Farish and his wife then spent much of the day in Grosvenor Square offering what support they could. In much the same way Ambassador Price went immediately to Lockerbie, they could only offer the symbolic presence of the United States at a time of uncertainty and fear.

> As the day went by, and particularly that evening, Sarah and I were down in Grosvenor Square meeting with people who were afraid they'd lost their relatives personally – and not be able to – not telling what had happening because nobody knew at that point...By the next day...the magnitude was apparent...and the people started...coming in droves to Grosvenor Square and I was...I guess I was talking to the media more in those two days than I'd ever in my life...it was that sort of situation.[22]

It is a reality of the transatlantic relationship that, unless events happen in the middle of the night European time (such as the death of Diana, Princess of Wales), British reactions to world events readily carry into American news cycles. In the case of 9/11, Blair's slight alteration of this TUC statement in time for his Downing Street comment that evening that, Britain would 'stand shoulder to shoulder with our American Friends'[23] came to epitomise the new character of UK–US relations. Bush's own official statement that night reflected the same themes:

> Today, our fellow citizens, our way of life, our very freedom came under attack in a series of deliberate and deadly terrorist acts...Thousands of lives were suddenly ended by evil, despicable acts of terror...Terrorist attacks can shake the foundations of our biggest buildings, but they cannot touch the foundation of America. These acts shatter steel, but they cannot dent the steel of American resolve...Our first priority is to get help to those who have been injured and to take every precaution to protect our citizens at home and around the world from further attacks. The search is underway for those who are behind these evil acts...We will make no distinction between the terrorists who committed these acts and those who harbor them.[24]

The next day the President returned the Prime Minister's call as the first business of the day. Bush recalls Blair saying that he was 'in a state of shock' but that they would support the US 100 per cent with 'no equivocation in his voice'. Bush comments that it was a moment that 'cemented' their relationship.[25] For his part, Blair remembers 'I spoke in turn to Putin, Schroeder, Chirac and Berlusconi and the next day to President Bush. The collective sense of solidarity was absolute...It is hard now to realise just how fearful people were at that time. For all we knew, there were other attacks about to happen. At any moment, we expected to hear of some new atrocity.'[26]

What Do We Do

After the initial statements and emergency actions were set in train, there was an obvious need to adjust the operational systems in London. As both the Ambassador and his staff point out, old diplomatic practices were no longer appropriate or even possible. The Ambassador notes: 'there were things like the condolence books, closing Grosvenor Square, shutting things down that the Embassy had to do on its own, to react to . . . the police were terrific. You know they all had their own parameters for a crisis.'[27] Davies, on the other hand, could comment on the process from the perspective of other postings as a career diplomat.

> The initial period was dealing with the immediate aftermath, that was fascinating – those two weeks because that was dealing with all these Americans stranded in London because of US airspace for 72 hours, dealing with the just outpouring of affections that began with people leaving New York Yankee baseball caps and ticket stubs from Broadway plays and postcards from new York and whatnot on that little traffic island in Grosvenor Square . . . we had to move it over to the Square . . . and had I don't know many many . . . well over 100,000 visitors. So the first ten days we were doing all that stuff and we . . . our counselor people spun out because we were getting calls . . . I mean you can imagine . . . 'where's Sally, where's Jimmy' . . . Followed quickly by cables 'the names of the following five banks, we want you to go into HMG and tell them they've got six hours' and you just shut these things . . . it became a 14 hour a day deal and that went on for months and months and the ambassador – daily meetings, filling him in, he had to learn it real fast . . . meeting cabinet officials and these sub-cabinet officials, hosting them, having events, going to things – and he did a good job – you know it just began to [pause] there was a fire hose coming out of Washington . . . traditional diplomacy had a role but it was a diminished role, it just was . . . we were out of that business, we were into the business of triage.[28]

Part of that immediate aftermath also included a series of tributes and memorial events. The condolence book, moved from the traffic island in front of the Embassy to Grosvenor Square itself, was set up almost immediately and next in line to British throne Prince Charles was the first to sign it. Two days after the strikes, Ambassador Farish received a call from Buckingham Palace to request his attendance. He understandably hesitated as there were so many other issues that required urgent attention – not least the service in St Paul's scheduled for the following day, but only momentarily. Davies again recalls, 'the phone would ring and it would be . . . St Paul's tomorrow. 5:00. The Queen. The Prime Minister. Be there. Boom. Stuff was – stuff was just happening...it was crisis time.'[29] If symbolism typified the moment, Buckingham Palace became the first in a series of three events that are now looked back upon as representing the range of what they meant to different people. The Ambassador says:

> We didn't know what was going to occur, except that they felt it was very important...I got there about 15 minutes or so before and I was told what was going to happen and Prince Andrew and I walked out and...they played the Star Spangled Banner and there were all these people. I don't know the number that had come and it was – it was tough. I mean it was the closest – in fact I get teary thinking about it...but I knew that I had to not blink...it was her relationship with our country.[30]

The day that started with cheers and tribute ended with a second iconic event at the other end of the emotional spectrum in the form of the behaviour of the audience during the BBC programme, *Question Time*. Ambassador Lader, the former Ambassador, made it his practice, in accordance with protocol, to not make public statements, but he became increasingly frustrated by what he perceived to be the lack of Embassy presence in the media. He contacted the Embassy to be told the State Department had 'not authorized any public statement, so I understood', but after a call to his wife, he decided to accept a variety of media invitations culminating with the *Question Time* programme the next day. The invited audience was restive and asked accusatory questions, others began to heckle the Ambassador, the main charge being that America had brought the events of 9/11 on itself through its foreign policy. From the outset, Lader felt 'It was clear it was a total set up...and every time I would try to say something I would get shouted down'.[31] In the last few moments of the programme he did manage to make a short statement, but was visibly upset. Some reports the next day going as far as to say he was 'in tears'. Lader received calls the next day from the Prime Minister, the Chancellor and members of the royal family to apologise while the BBC, unusually, formally apologised two days later for apparent bias.

Whatever the agenda of the *Question Time* programme, it did not diminish the impact of the memorial at St Paul's the next day. Farish remembers:

> I got a call when she [the Queen] and Prince Philip came down...to go through the planning of the St Paul's service...and we went over and met with them...late that afternoon for tea...there were so many things that happened that were amazing...the services, the meeting with so many of the families of the victims...it was just one event after another. That month or the next six weeks were – there wasn't a day or an hour that wasn't involved in that, along with all of the things that went on at the embassy.[32]

There is a public relations term known as 'slip-streaming' by which events or statements are grouped so as to create a more coherent public narrative and one of the positive effects of the control imposed from Washington was the ability to control and initiate events that would have resonance on both sides of the Atlantic at the same time. A good example of such ordering of the messaging is the almost immediate outreach to the Muslim community. On 18 September President Bush visited the Islamic Center in Washington while, at the same time, Ambassador Farish invited a delegation of Muslims to the Embassy in London. The intention was to demonstrate quickly and publicly that the US government did not blame a religion or a culture for the recent events, but the extremists. A message spectacularly lost in the months that followed.

A second, but more ambitious example of such coordinated activity is the visit made by the Prime Minister to the US two days later. Blair went first to New York for an emotional service near ground zero, attended by most of the significant actors on the American side. By this time, it was also clear that 9/11 had also been among the largest attacks on British civilians giving particular focus to Blair's participation. Blair and his entourage continued on to Washington to be present at the President's address to Congress that evening and even had dinner with the President before his speech. The timing and portrayal of the events was designed to signal the gratitude of the Americans and a reciprocation of the 'shoulder-to-shoulder' sentiment Blair had already espoused. However, they also provide an interesting glimpse into the inner workings of diplomatic and political intrigue that are constants of operations at this level.

'Wheels within Wheels'

The UK Embassy in Washington is one of the largest and busiest posts for the British Foreign Office. Though historically considered a 'hardship' posting due to the conditions and the weather, it has always been considered a senior posting.[33] In more recent years, senior roles in Washington have gone to someone with, at the very least, Cabinet-level experience if not direct experience in Number Ten and the Prime Minister's own team. This has meant, for some Ambassadors, that their link to the Foreign Office has become less important over time than their connections with Downing Street. Davies offers an explanation as to how it operates in a large chancery and the balance between the two Embassies:

> If you curl up in a ball and die if you don't know exactly everything that going on...[or a] type triple A who just absolutely had to...be involved in everything...I would have been lost. I would have lost my mind...I had an office in the West Wing of the White House. There are no secrets left in how the government operates as far as I'm concerned and there is just some stuff that happens...if you have an activist Chief

Executive of the United States he's going to 'do'...he's not going to call you first...there were wheels within wheels.[34]

As to the particular importance of the UK Embassy in Washington, Davies argues it is based on

> a variety of reasons...[that] they're in the same time zone as Washington DC, the capital of the free world, doesn't hurt, and because they entertain the powers of the capital of the free world and because they are – they have been spectacularly successful, maybe even the best in the world, though the French are close to them – system of educating, cultivating...spectacular diplomats and then sending them over to Washington.[35]

The sentiments of this career diplomat are echoed almost identically by Ambassador Meyer, particularly in relation to the events surrounding 9/11. On the morning of the 9/11 Meyer had also been dealing with similar issues in terms of consular affairs, security issues and the constant exchange of information between governments. His counterpart, Consul-General Tom Harris in New York had been coping with the non-stop consular issues surrounding the growing list of missing people and the arrangements for their families. As Meyer says of himself, his access was second to none:

> There were wheels within wheels. Blair and Bush spoke quite often on the phone. I would receive the records of these conversations...American records of these conversations would emerge slowly, if at all. But the records that I received from London were of conservations only a few hours old...I thus found myself in the curious position of telling him [his senior contact in government] what was going on in his own government as well as in mine. In return, I received invaluable information for London.[36]

However, such access can easily be jeopardised and even professional diplomats cut out of the political inner circle as Meyer found during the September trip. The Ambassador was to escort the Prime Minister and his team throughout their trip and met them in New York for the service. It was on the way to the White House that difficulties became apparent in that one of Blair's own Downing Street team had told the White House that the Ambassador would not be joining the party for dinner. Meyer recalls being told this information by Jonathan Powell on the plane on the way to Washington. He replied, as he says, with words that were

> ...furious and expletive laden, 'If this happens you will cut me off at the fucking knees for the rest of my fucking time in Washington. Is

that what you want?'…if I had been absent from these wider meetings, and the President's supper was one such – then I would have lost credibility in the eyes of the President and senior members of the administration. They would have concluded that I did not enjoy the Prime Minister's confidence. If, on 20 September 2001 they had made that judgment, then the effectiveness of the embassy would have been damaged at just the moment when the British Government had rarely needed it more.[37]

As it turns out, according to Meyer, it was not the British side that spared him such ignominy, but Rice who came to his rescue.[38]

Squandered Goodwill and the Media Sea Change

As early as the end of 2001, British opinion was beginning to shift significantly against the country's involvement in the Global War on Terror. Bush's State of the Union in 2002 and his statement on the 'axis of evil' marked a turning point in terms of relations with world leaders, particularly the traditional allies of Europe. The French were becoming more vocal in their opposition and the domestic German campaign had used distance from the US as part of their own, increasingly rancorous, debate. Meanwhile, violence between Israel and the Palestinians continued to be a major concern on both sides of the Atlantic. From the beginning, Blair put himself in the position of go-between for the US in Europe. However, his efforts began to have less and less effect and receive more and more flak from the British public and his own party. The portrayal of Blair as Bush's 'poodle' became ubiquitous in the press. As Dumbrell records, 'Tony Blair's predicament in 2001–2003 rapidly reached the proportions appropriate to the Jacobean tragedy',[39] while Riddell comments baldly 'Tony Blair's transatlantic bridge collapses in early 2003'.[40] Interestingly, it is also at this point there is a gap in representation on the British side in the US. Meyer was set to retire, but was convinced by the Prime Minister that he should remain in post for an undetermined length of time. For personal and health reasons, Meyer was anxious to get back to the UK and finally did leave in February 2003. Despite being aware of Meyer's issues and position, the Prime Minister did not release David Manning from his role in Downing Street until August of that year. Ultimately, Massachusetts Avenue was vacant for half a year. Whether this was the result of a real absence of need on the ground in the face of such intense leader-to-leader diplomacy or a consequence of Blair's desire to keep the team tight and small remains unclear.[41]

Back in London, Ambassador Farish's work throughout this period continued unabated. Issues from 'doggie passports' (finally successful in 2002 after a five-year campaign)[42] to the treatment of prisoners in Guantanamo Bay crossed his desk, while the usual business of Embassy life was constantly punctuated by memorials and anniversaries to mark each passing

9/11 milestone. However, in terms of press coverage and reaction to his work, there was a significant shift:

> I got nothing but really good press for the first year and a half which was amazing, everybody commented on it. Then things changed. It was one thing...after September 11 everybody was positive, the country was fabulous the press were ... very sympathetic to the situation...As we then went into Afghanistan and then we went into Iraq and all the build up to that, things changed and the press's attitude toward US changed and therefore toward the embassy changes because we were obviously moving forward with our foreign policy...and telling it as the President wanted it told – or as it was. And we were in lock step with the Prime Minister so we were all getting blasted by the press...the one thing that stuck, which was unfortunate, was the 'America's invisible envoy' comment in the *Evening Standard*.[43]

As the British national press became less willing to report anything other than the war, they left more traditional transatlantic issues to one side to make their own agenda. The Ambassador and his team decided on a change of tack in terms of the media strategy. Rather than following in the vein of his most recent predecessor with regular national media appearances, Farish began to favour press engagements outside London, going to major cities around the UK and particularly in Northern Ireland. He also used personal by-line pieces on particular issues, again using both papers outside London as well as national titles.[44] It was a natural strategy for a cautious spokesperson and a press team conscious that there was no way to win 'hearts and minds' of significant sections of the London media at that point in time. As the Ambassador says: 'I really enjoyed going to those other places where we really did tell our story and get it reported back...they would report what you said accurately and usually not with a positive or a negative twist, just a story...whereas you know you couldn't get that in London'.[45] Such strategic planning did not, however, mean the Ambassador was not engaging with key London opinion-formers at a variety of levels.

'Invisibility' as a Good Thing

As with the accusation of Blair being 'Bush's poodle', the Ambassador recognises the charge of invisibility was one that stuck. It is, however, relevant to the question of his success or failure as an ambassador to consider the question of whether or not such 'invisibility' can be made to work and what kinds of attributes must accompany that determination. While various journalists accused the Ambassador of 'shunning the spotlight',some journalists representing publications on both sides of the Atlantic, were willing to argue that the Ambassador was not absent, but merely taking a different approach.[46] For example, Don Melvin of the *Austin-American Statesman* in 2002 and Alice Thomson of the *Daily Telegraph* in 2003, both make the case that the Ambassador had always been a 'quiet man' who preferred to work behind the scenes, but that he was no less effective for that choice.[47] Further, given the circumstances of the time, including the strictures placed on all Embassies by Washington, such a strategy was not only sensible but necessary.

If it is tempting to think that such a theory is the defence of a weak ambassador, his own DCMs corroborate this reasoning both in relation to the space 'granted' by Washington for Embassy initiative alluded to above, and the context of Farish's relationship to the President. As Johnson indicates:

> It was a very personal relationship...it was not something that he, in my experience ever...used as a cudgel to anyone, it wasn't that kind of...that would not be the way he used a personal relationship. At the same time, I think there wasn't anyone who had any sort of encounter with him or really understood who he was, that did not believe that if there was a need for him to get in touch with the president that was something easily done by him.[48]

The Ambassador himself is slightly more guarded, but does acknowledge that various individuals and groups came to him clearly on the understanding that he could get messages to the President – meetings that included some whose own group would not be pleased to know they had tapped the Ambassador or had sent messages of support to the United States. By way of example, and without naming names, the Ambassador relates the story of some prominent Labour Party politicians who came to see him the week before the important parliamentary vote on the Iraq war. They came, he explains, because they wanted him:

> ...to convey to the President that if they were successful that this was not a vote against America, but that they just honestly didn't believe in this war and they thought that the Prime Minister was out of line. It was a very friendly conversation, but they came to tell me something that they wanted Washington to, or that they wanted the President of the United States to understand...people that wanted the President to know something and they knew that I was close to him and hoped that I would convey their thoughts.[49]

He did not relate whether or not he passed on all such messages, but he clearly viewed it as a position of trust, and one he took seriously both towards his President and his hosts.

Conclusion

It is ironic that Ambassador Farish was almost ridiculed for being closer to the royals than to the politicians at the time of his appointment, especially in light of the fact that later it would be the symbolic links between the two countries that would mean so much. Moments of tribute and memorial stand out as a dominant theme of his tenure and the royal family was a presence throughout, as allies of the United States, but also as personal friends to the Ambassador. Their desire to reach out on both of these levels affected transatlantic relations in a deeply emotional way. As Condoleezza Rice recalls, it was the moment the Coldstream Guards played the Star Spangled Banner that she, for the first time, began to cry.[50]

There is no escaping the fact that Farish was also accused of being absent. Given his wife was not well and was being treated in the US at various points during their stay it is true he did travel back to the US. However, it also seems clear that he was quietly working on the softer edges of power at a time when American power was perceived as being too 'hard'. Doing so, he provided advice and encouragement wherever he could, and on both sides of the Atlantic. Both of his deputies talk of their time as one of managing the Washington flood of instructions and cables as well as the 'concierge function' involving a 'revolving door' that was 'spinning fast',[51] delivering officials, politicians and all manner of experts to deal with the detailed military and policy concerns of war. Not unlike ambassadors during the Second World War, Ambassador Farish had to work with, and around, others sent by various agencies and departments to deal with their own area of expertise. 'Traditional diplomacy' by most standards was not the business of the day. As he puts it, 'I did what I was asked to do [by the State Department]...there are always some things in anything you do that you might do differently...the restraint with the press was one of them.'[52] Whatever the Ambassador's regrets, they clearly didn't affect the President's esteem given he asked Farish if he would like to continue in the post after he was re-elected, an invitation the Ambassador was honoured to receive, but nonetheless declined.

Ambassador's Farish's first major public speech, by tradition delivered to The Pilgrims, offers perhaps the best summary of his tenure in Grosvenor Square. The speech was given exactly five short, very long, weeks after 9/11:

> From the day back in March when President Bush honored me with the nomination for this post, through my arrival in July and right up through September 10th, I saw my role quite clearly: to articulate America's foreign policy; to explain to the British what America was thinking, and what the President was trying to achieve; to report back to the President on the mood here in Britain, and to oversee the work of the embassy's 700

employees. Years building up my own companies had prepared me to represent the interest of American businesses... Years of keeping in close touch with international affairs and foreign policy had left me prepared to face delicate and complex issues like Northern Ireland, the Balkans and Missile Defense. But like everyone else, nothing had prepared me for what happened on September 11th. Suddenly there were hundreds of people looking to me for comfort, for leadership, for answers. And all I had to draw on was my own heart – the heart of a fellow human being.[53]

Robert Holmes Tuttle, 2005–2009

Ambassador Farish left during the summer of 2004 as the election back home heated up and Embassy business slowed down. There was some comment in terms of the date of his departure, but he had completed three full years, the length of any Foreign Service posting. However, the position was not filled again for nearly a year, despite the fact President Bush was returned to the White House. Ambassador Tuttle recalls the invitation vividly. He and his wife, Maria, had been to Washington to various inaugural events in January 2005 and returned home via a weekend in Santa Barbara. Tuttle was not feeling well and had become increasingly ill over the course of the weekend and was not sleeping well. Much to his chagrin, the phone rang at 6:30 a.m. and a voice coolly responded to his angry 'hello' to say that the President was on the line. The President came on 'almost immediately' and proceeded to ask if he would like to be Ambassador to the Court of St James's. The President's explicit exhortation was that he wanted a 'public diplomat' in London and thought Tuttle was the man for the job. It was a message Tuttle immediately took to heart and came to think of not only as a strategy, but more of a vocation during his tenure in London.

Humble Beginnings

Barnes suggests that a distinctive feature of George W. Bush is the fact that he is 'neither an elitist nor a champion of elite opinion. He reflects the political view and cultural tastes of the vast majority of Americans who don't live along the East or West Coast.'[54] On the surface, Tuttle may not obviously fit into such a category, but his California roots are not deep. His father, Holmes Tuttle, was born in Oklahoma Indian Territory to a Chickasaw mother and raised in Tuttle, Oklahoma, named for his father, and literally rode the rails (at least until he and his friend were kicked off the train) to make their fortune in California. Holmes Tuttle eventually became part of what was famously known as Ronald Reagan's Kitchen Cabinet, but it was around their own dining room table that his son, Robert, came to shape his views about politics. Tuttle recalls watching the McCarthy hearings on television as a boy and discussing politics and history, not only with his own family, but with the rising circle of California Republicans, including the Reagans, who came to dinner. Tuttle attributes the trust placed in this small klatch of business-men by Reagan to the fact they were all in it for 'better government'. He recalls, '[Ronald Reagan] came from a very humble background [and] they were all strong men. They all spoke their piece...nobody was ever saying "Ron, I want this. Ron I want that"...they were all concerned about the size of government and high taxes, which we had after the war.'[55]

People Are Policy

That sense of rootedness was a strength of the father and an asset to the son as the young Robert got more involved in politics. After his return to California from school back east, Tuttle, slowly became attracted to national issues and the rise of Ronald Reagan, a man he so admired. Many political appointee ambassadors bring business acumen or political clout to the table, but few have worked so closely with a President whose personnel strategy is so widely considered to have been a success. Even before Reagan took the oath of office, he was working on his appointments and ensuring that not only were the people he appointed capable, they also knew they were there to convey the message of the President. It became the President's policy to ring senior appointees personally, ensuring they understood that not only did they have his support, but that he expected theirs in return. Tuttle refers to this as 'the two C's: commitment and competency' and qualities that he looked for in every appointment. This combination of professionalism and ideology, particularly under Tuttle's tenure for the entire second term, meant that nearly every available slot was filled with a 'Reagan supporter'. This gave the White House more control, albeit indirectly, over more of the system. Most importantly, the experience gave the later ambassador the opportunity to see the process from the inside and the various ways in which both career officers and political appointees could make a success or a failure of their posting.

It was in Washington that Tuttle met George W. Bush. He already knew the Vice President in relation to his work and recalls that:

> at the beginning of the Reagan Administration there was a feeling you were a Bush person or a Reagan person, it dissipated, but George Bush was a great Vice President, and so loyal. He didn't call me often on per-sonnel, but when he called me I paid attention to it. And he'd send good people. That's something. I paid attention to people who gave me good recommendation.[56]

Tuttle explains he 'hadn't been in Washington long' when 'Vice President Bush invited me up to a dinner...And there was his young, younger than me, son George W. We were not...close, but we got to be friendly and saw each other socially Washington.'[57]

As the Reagan era gave way to Bush senior, Tuttle returned to California and to his family business. He remained involved in various political campaigns and in fund-raising, but during the Clinton years devoted a good deal of his time and energy to his lifetime love of contemporary American art. Political paths continued to cross and, as the name of someone he knew and had stayed broadly in touch with became the favourite for the next presidential race, he decided to rejoin the effort to rally Republicans in California.

Bush's Second Term

After the turmoil and initial shocks of 9/11, the US government machinery had begun to stabilise and return to some kind of normalcy, and even the rising unpopularity of the war was not enough to prevent Bush from gaining a second term. He may have been helped by the fact that terrorism was never far from the headlines. For example, three days before the Spanish general election in March 2004, explosions on the commuter train system killed 191 and wounded nearly 2,000 people – the worst European attack of its kind and shocking even in a country familiar with the terrorism of the separatist group, ETA. The wisdom at the time was that the Spanish government's support for the war in Iraq had made Spain a target, which was seen as a significant factor in the defeat of José Aznar and the Partido Popular (PP).

The returned Bush administration was anxious to try to close some of the distance that had emerged between the US and its European allies, which underpins the motivation for the President's trip to Brussels in February 2005. His European effort was designed to try and bridge the differences and to mark a new beginning for cooperation not only on Iraq, but on a range of security issues. As part of the same effort, a month later, Bush appointed Karen Hughes to be the Undersecretary of State for public diplomacy with the rank of ambassador – a nomination the Senate confirmed in July. Unfortunately, this was the same month four bombers in London attacked the Underground and a bus killing 52 and injuring 700. It was at this junction that Tuttle rushed to London and began to put his own public diplomacy strategy into action.

Transformational

Hughes was a controversial appointment from the start, and her kick-off 'listening tour' through the Middle East was viewed with scepticism at home and ridiculed abroad. However, it was not an isolated initiative, but part of a much wider shift in approach from the administration. The appointment of Condoleezza Rice as Secretary of State was the beginning of a re-engineering of the State Department with public diplomacy at its core. Rice announced what she called 'transformational diplomacy' in January 2006 and emphasised the importance of communication, right-sizing and better cooperation through the creation of 'media hubs' around the world.

In practical terms, this involved the immediate dissemination of 'rapid response' talking points to spokespeople, especially ambassadors, and even incentivising staff through their promotion goals to talk to the media. This new approach placed Tuttle directly in line with the strategy from Washington. Interestingly, these efforts by Rice were also echoed in the UK by the Foreign Secretary, Jack Straw, who launched what he called 'Active diplomacy' almost at the same time. As part of this transatlantic information-sharing, Ambassador Tuttle was invited by Nigel Sheinwald, at this point still working in Number Ten prior to becoming Ambassador in Washington, to a briefing on the British government's public diplomacy efforts with the top Public Affairs staff.

Tuttle's efforts immediately after the July bombings were well received and gave him an excellent start with many of the key players in London. Unfortunately, the lines of communication were not always clear and the effort to 'get the message' out could be dangerous as he found very early on. Issues such as the extradition treaty that was progressing at the time of his arrival was controversial, particularly in light of the opposition in the UK to the treatment of prisoners at Guantanamo Bay, giving rise to some pointed question in the House of Lords,[58] as well as other military issues that were heavily covered in the British press. The extradition treaty was successfully completed with Baroness Scotland and the Ambassador exchanging instruments in 2007, but two specific incidents suggest that the lines from Washington were not as clear as they might be.[59] The first involved a question in the media as to whether white phosphorous was being used by troops as a weapon against civilians. The issue revolved around whether the substance was used as a weapon against civilians and it was admitted that it was indeed used to 'move insurgents'.[60] The new Ambassador intervened in the debate via a letter to the *Independent*, only to have his statement contradicted by the Pentagon a day later. A month later there was a second issue which arose in the course of a radio interview in which the Ambassador denied US rendition of suspected terrorists to Syria, with a known record of torture. The Embassy later felt the need to 'clarify' his statements.[61]

On a more operational level, there was also some territory to be delineated in terms of the new 'media hubs'. London is a major media centre for the world's press, making it both an easy and potentially dangerous place if lines crossed as they get quickly amplified. The Ambassador had been involved with discussions with Karen Hughes, but recalls at least one moment that the London press team and the 'hub' team ran into difficulties that he had to step in to sort out: 'we had very clear discussions and said hey we'll be the media here; don't get into our territory. Your job is to run the hub here ... and that was the last time it ever happened.'[62]

Undeterred, the Ambassador continued to build a network and act on his commitment to get out of London and travel the country. It was a strategy that, by his own admission, was not entirely thought out on arrival, but one that 'evolved'. It involved using Winfield House as a 'public diplomacy tool' as well as a showcase for contemporary American art. The Ambassador had brought some significant pieces from his own collection as well as making good use of the 'Art in Embassy' programme to obtain other important pieces for the public spaces of the house. He also decided to do at least two trips per month to places around the country, especially mosques, and moreover, to incentivise his staff to get out and speak publically as well. Such activity was not required by the State Department, but their own push in this area meant it was easier to get more staff on board.

> I made it clear from the beginning that public diplomacy was a high priority for me…and there was a push too from the State Department to get everyone involved in public diplomacy…we really wanted to reach out and we wanted all the Foreign Service officers out speaking as much as possible…this was something relatively new, but it was something the State department was pushing…and within a year we had quadrupled what the Embassy had been doing…it was my being in the right place at the right time and pushing something that was being pushed by Washington.[63]

Leader Relations

The main message Tuttle took from that first phone call from the President was public diplomacy, but there was a second, equally important message that the Ambassador and President discussed again during the course of the latter's visit to the UK; the closeness of the relationship between the President and the Prime Minister. It speaks volumes that the president was so sensitive to the impact this might have on the ambassador. Once in the job, the Ambassador was indeed impressed by their connection and respected the way in which the two leaders had taken one another into confidence. He was also aware that such a link made for certain nuances in terms of the way their personal teams and diplomats operated.

> I had thought about the closeness between the leaders of the two countries, mainly Churchill and Roosevelt, Reagan and Thatcher, which of course I knew first hand and I'd talked a lot to Charlie Price. I knew about the relationship between Bush and Blair, but I don't think I realized how close it was. But once I got there, it was obvious they were talking once a week and sometimes more frequently. And Blair was often in Washington…remember '05 and '06 were not great years…they were talking a lot. I don't think I realised the depth of the relationship at all levels. I also don't think I knew then that the Embassy gets between 15,000 and 18,000 official visitors every year. And that was not just the military, or intelligence, which of course is a lot of it, but visitors from throughout

government, judicial, agricultural, financial, you name it. The relation-ship is very, very deep.... sometimes briefing the Ambassador was not the first thing on anybody's mind...but I developed very good relation-ships because one thing I learned previously in Washington it's not just the people at top, it's everybody...[so] we were getting good readouts both from the White House and the State Department, but in those early days we sometimes got readouts only from the British side...[64]

Conclusion

Ambassador Tuttle arrived in London at a moment of change in the Bush administration; after the initial shock of 9/11 and the difficult engagements in Iraq and Afghanistan as well as the ongoing global war on terror, Bush's advisors concluded that a different approach towards US allies was required. Not 'softer' per se, but a step-change resulting in inevitably different tac-tics in terms of the nation's diplomacy. Tuttle, like Farish, was part of an older conception of Republican ideas and ideals. They are clearly not in the same generation as each other, but neither of them were part of the younger Bush's cohort either. It is also interesting to note that they were not part of the Republican 'right' that became a defining feature of the growing divisions in the party's leadership. Tuttle's experience in the Reagan White House clearly played a huge role in the way he dealt not only with his Embassy team, but also the way in which he networked in Washington, dealt with any gaps in the communications and understood the ways in which political leaders thought and operated. All of which stood him in good stead. Equally, as he says himself, he was in the right place at the right time. His personal mission of public diplomacy had moved to the top of the agenda on both sides of the Atlantic enabling him to innovate, initiate and experiment in ways that were simply not possible in the first aftershocks of 2001.

These two Ambassadors do indeed bring us full circle in that they repre-sent the ways in which crises limit and constrain diplomatic action as policy 'collapses back to Washington'. They demonstrate, once again, the way in which war requires specific competencies that necessitate the Ambassador stand aside on some major issues of the day. Ambassador Farish, as close as he was to two Presidents and whatever the ease with which he could pick up the phone, could only hope to perfect the 'listening ear' and 'car-ing shoulder' role of diplomacy. In contrast, Ambassador Tuttle, coming as he did in a period in which the State Department was on the offensive in terms of America's image, needed all his White House-honed skills to stay in the loop and move his Embassy forward along the desired track. As he says:

> To go back to the beginning the President called me and said 'I want you to do this job and this is what I want you to be'...we tried to reach

out to all segments of British society; students religious groups especially Muslims groups, cultural, political, business. We tried to balance our approach. I think that's important and easy sometimes to forget ... you've got to know how to work the system, and you've got to reach out. I suppose it goes back to my White House days. You've got to try to remember what you're trying to do.[65]

Both men sought to do as they were asked, to fulfil their mission and to serve their President as best they could. The circumstances in which they found themselves simply required very different strategies. As Glyn Davies points out: 'The Embassy serves the Ambassador's needs because Embassies are very hierarchical organisations ... Ambassadors are ... strongly symbolic figures ... [they] *are* the Embassy and if they don't succeed the Embassy doesn't succeed.'[66]

Notes

1. Alison Holmes, interview with Ambassador William Stamps Farish III, Gasparilla FL, 2008; and Royal Family website, http://www.royal.gov.uk/HMTheQueen/Interests/Overview.aspx (accessed 30 March 2012).
2. Among others. Paul Kelso, 'Soft Touch for Uncle Sam's Envoy: London Post Calls for Tact and Strong Constitution', *The Guardian,* 15 February 2001.
3. Holmes interview with Ambassador William Stamps Farish III.
4. *Ibid.*
5. *Ibid.*
6. *Ibid.*
7. Holmes interview with Ambassador David Johnson.
8. Holmes interview with Ambassador Glyn Davies.
9. Riddell, *Hug them Close*, p. 83.
10. Holmes interview with Ambassador William Stamps Farish III.
11. *Ibid.*
12. Bush, *Decision Points*, p. 127.
13. Tony Blair, *A Journey: My Political Life* (New York: Alfred Knopf, 2010), p. 345.
14. Christopher Meyer, *DC Confidential* (London: Phoenix, 2005), pp. 186–7.
15. Holmes interview with Ambassador William Stamps Farish III.
16. Meyer, *DC Confidential*, p. 190.
17. Tony Blair, 'Doctrine of the International Community', speech delivered at the Economic Club of Chicago, 22 April 1999.
18. Tony Blair, Trades Union Congress (TUC) statement, 11 September 2001, available at: http://keeptonyblairforpm.wordpress.com/911-tony-blairs-response-at-tuc-conference/
19. George W. Bush, ABC News, 11 September 2001, http://www.youtube.com/watch?v=F-qHSeMKjZU.
20. Holmes interview with Ambassador William Stamps Farish III.
21. William Farish, Press Statement, 11 September 2001, US Embassy, London, available at: http://www.usembassy.org.uk/ukamb/farish4.html
22. Holmes interview with Ambassador William Stamps Farish III.
23. Blair, *A Journey*, p. 352.

24. George W. Bush, CNN, 11 September 2001, http://articles.cnn.com/2001-09-11/us/bush.speech.text_1_attacks-deadly-terrorist-acts-despicable-acts?_s= PM:US

25. Bush, *Decision Points*, p. 140.

26. Blair, *A Journey*, p. 351.

27. Holmes interview with Ambassador William Stamps Farish III.

28. Holmes interview with Ambassador Glyn Davies.

29. *Ibid.*

30. Holmes interview with Ambassador William Stamps Farish III.

31. Holmes interview with Ambassador Philip Lader.

32. Holmes interview with Ambassador William Stamps Farish III.

33. Michael Hopkins, Saul Kelly and John Young (eds.), *The British Embassy in Washington between 1939 and 1977* (New York and Basingstoke: Palgrave, 2009).

34. Holmes interview with Ambassador Glyn Davies.

35. *Ibid.*

36. Meyer, *DC Confidential*, p. 241.

37. *Ibid.*, pp. 202–3.

38. *Ibid.* p. 204.

39. Dumbrell, *A Special Relationship*, p. 154.

40. Riddell, *Hug them Close*, p. 224.

41. Meyer, *DC Confidential*, pp. 272–3.

42. British quarantine laws for pets are particularly onerous, requiring animals to stay in kennels for a minimum of six months. New technology involving embedding a chip in the animal meant this could be avoided, but the British government was deemed to be slow in taking up the option. Various ambassadors (not only from the US) became involved in the issue beginning in 1997. They were finally successful in 2002.

43. Holmes interview with Ambassador William Stamps Farish III.

44. For example, a byline piece 'One Hundred Days of Re-building Iraq', *Western Mail*, 13 August 2003 or 'One Year of Freedom in Iraq Should Not Be Lightly Dismissed', *Daily Telegraph*, 19 March 2004.

45. Holmes interview with Ambassador William Stamps Farish III.

46. Elisabeth Bumiller, 'In Hour to Shine an Envoy Instead Shuns the Spotlight', *The New York Times*, 24 November 2003.

47. Don Melvin, 'Ambassador to Britain Works out of the Spotlight Works behind the Scenes', *Austin American-Statesman*, 1 July 2002; and Alice Thomson, 'The Quiet American at the Heart of Power', *The Daily Telegraph*, 12 April 2003.

48. Holmes interview with Ambassador David Johnson.

49. Holmes interview with Ambassador William Stamps Farish III.

50. Condoleezza Rice, *No Higher Honor: A Memoir of my Years in Washington* (New York: Crown Publishers, 2011), p. 82.

51. Holmes interview with Ambassador Glyn Davies.

52. Holmes interview with Ambassador William Stamps Farish III.

53. William Stamps Farish, Speech to the Pilgrim's Society, US Embassy, 16 October 2001, available at: http://usembassy.org.uk/ukamb/farish8.html

54. Barnes, *Rebel-in-Chief*, p. 15.

55. Alison Holmes, interview with Ambassador Robert Holmes Tuttle, Beverly Hills, CA, 2008.

56. *Ibid.*

57. *Ibid.*

58. Baroness Scotland of Asthal, *Hansard HL 11 July 2005 Col 647.*

59. 'UK/U.S. Treaty Ratified', Press release, US Embassy, 26 April 2007, available at: http://london.usembassy.gov/ukpapress48.html
60. David Charter, 'Chemical Rounds Used against Rebel Fighters', *The Times*, 16 November 2005.
61. Ewen MacAskill, 'US Embassy Close to Admitting Syria Rendition Flight: Statement Contradicts Ambassador's Interview: Correction Could Leave British Open to Challenge', *The Guardian*, 27 December 2005.
62. Holmes interview with Ambassador Robert Holmes Tuttle.
63. *Ibid.*
64. *Ibid.*
65. *Ibid.*
66. Holmes interview with Ambassador Glyn Davies.

Appendix: Table of Ambassadors, Presidents and Prime Ministers

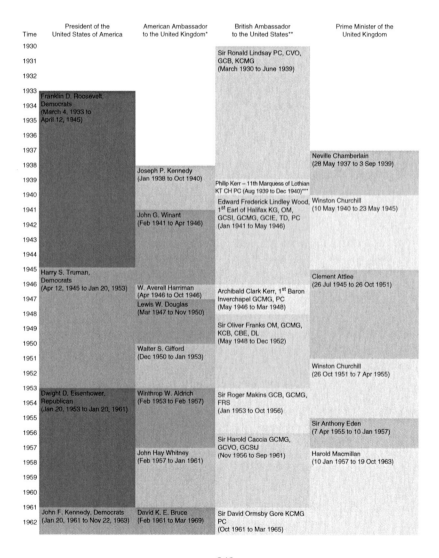

Time	President of the United States of America	American Ambassador to the United Kingdom*	British Ambassador to the United States**	Prime Minister of the United Kingdom
1930			Sir Ronald Lindsay PC, CVO, GCB, KCMG (March 1930 to June 1939)	
1931				
1932				
1933	Franklin D. Roosevelt, Democrats (March 4, 1933 to April 12, 1945)			
1934				
1935				
1936				
1937				Neville Chamberlain (28 May 1937 to 3 Sep 1939)
1938		Joseph P. Kennedy (Jan 1938 to Oct 1940)		
1939			Philip Kerr – 11th Marquess of Lothian KT CH PC (Aug 1939 to Dec 1940)***	
1940			Edward Frederick Lindley Wood, 1st Earl of Halifax KG, OM, GCSI, GCMG, GCIE, TD, PC (Jan 1941 to May 1946)	Winston Churchill (10 May 1940 to 23 May 1945)
1941		John G. Winant (Feb 1941 to Apr 1946)		
1942				
1943				
1944				
1945	Harry S. Truman, Democrats (Apr 12, 1945 to Jan 20, 1953)			Clement Attlee (26 Jul 1945 to 26 Oct 1951)
1946		W. Averell Harriman (Apr 1946 to Oct 1946)	Archibald Clark Kerr, 1st Baron Inverchapel GCMG, PC (May 1946 to Mar 1948)	
1947		Lewis W. Douglas (Mar 1947 to Nov 1950)		
1948				
1949			Sir Oliver Franks OM, GCMG, KCB, CBE, DL (May 1948 to Dec 1952)	
1950		Walter S. Gifford (Dec 1950 to Jan 1953)		
1951				Winston Churchill (26 Oct 1951 to 7 Apr 1955)
1952				
1953	Dwight D. Eisenhower, Republican (Jan 20, 1953 to Jan 20, 1961)	Winthrop W. Aldrich (Feb 1953 to Feb 1957)	Sir Roger Makins GCB, GCMG, FRS (Jan 1953 to Oct 1956)	
1954				
1955				Sir Anthony Eden (7 Apr 1955 to 10 Jan 1957)
1956			Sir Harold Caccia GCMG, GCVO, GCStJ (Nov 1956 to Sep 1961)	
1957		John Hay Whitney (Feb 1957 to Jan 1961)		Harold Macmillan (10 Jan 1957 to 19 Oct 1963)
1958				
1959				
1960				
1961	John F. Kennedy, Democrats (Jan 20, 1961 to Nov 22, 1963)	David K. E. Bruce (Feb 1961 to Mar 1969)	Sir David Ormsby Gore KCMG PC (Oct 1961 to Mar 1965)	
1962				

348

Time	President of the United States of America	American Ambassador to the United Kingdom*	British Ambassador to the United States**	Prime Minister of the United Kingdom
1963	Lyndon B. Johnson, Democrats (Nov 22, 1963 to Jan 20, 1969)			Sir Alec Douglas-Home (19 Oct 1963 to 16 Oct 1964)
1964				Harold Wilson (16 Oct 1964 to 19 Jun 1970)
1965			Sir Patrick Dean GCMG (Apr 1965 to Feb 1969)	
1966				
1967				
1968				
1969	Richard Nixon, Republican (Jan 20, 1969 to Aug 9, 1974)	Walter H. Annenberg (Mar 1969 to Oct 1974)	John Freeman MBE (Mar 1969 to Jan 1971)	
1970				
1971			Rowland Baring, 3rd Earl of Cromer KG, GCMG, MBE, PC (Feb 1971 to Jan 1974)	Edward Heath (19 Jun 1970 to 4 Mar 1974)
1972				
1973				
1974	Gerald Ford, Republican (Aug 9, 1974 to Jan 20, 1977)		Peter Ramsbotham, 3rd Vicsount Soulbury, GCMG, GCVO, KStJ, DL (Mar 1974 to May 1977)	Harold Wilson (4 Mar 1974 to 5 Apr 1976)
1975		Elliot L. Richardson (Feb 1975 to Jan 1976)		
1976		Anne Legendre Armstrong (Jan 1976 to Mar 1977)		James Callaghan (5 Apr 1976 to 4 May 1979)
1977	Jimmy Carter, Democrats (Jan 20, 1977 to Jan 20, 1981)	Kingman Brewster, Jr. (Apr 1977 to Feb 1981)	Sir Peter Jay (July 1977 to July 1979)	
1978				
1979			Sir Nicholas Henderson, GCMG, KCVO (recalled from retirement) (July 1979 to July 1982)	Margaret Thatcher (4 May 1979 to 28 Nov 1990)
1980				
1981	Ronald Reagan, Republican (Jan 20, 1981 to Jan 20, 1989)	John J. Louis, Jr. (May 1981 to Nov 1983)		
1982			Sir Oliver Wright, GCMG, GCVO, DSC (recalled from retirement) (Sep 1982 to July 1986)	
1983		Charles H. Price, II (Nov 1983 to Feb 1989)		
1984				
1985				
1986			Sir Antony Acland KG, GCMG, GCVO (Aug 1986 to May 1991)	
1987				
1988				
1989	George H. W. Bush, Republican (Jan 20, 1989 to Jan 20, 1993)	Henry E. Catto, Jr. (Apr 1989 to Mar 1991)		
1990				John Major (28 Nov 1990 to 2 May 1997)
1991		Raymond G. H. Seitz (Apr 1991 to May 1994)	Robin Renwick, Baron Renwick of Clifton, KCMG (Nov 1991 to July 1995)	
1992				
1993	Bill Clinton, Democrats (Jan 20, 1993 to Jan 20, 2001)			
1994		William J. Crowe, Jr. (May 1994 to Sep 1997)		
1995			Sir John Kerr, Baron Kerr of Kinlochard, GCMG (Sep 1995 to Sep 1997)	
1996				
1997		Philip Lader (Aug 1997 to Feb 2001)	Sir Christopher Meyer KCMG (Oct 1997 to Feb 2003)	Tony Blair (2 May 1997 to 27 Jun 2007)
1998				
1999				
2000				
2001	George W. Bush, Republican (Jan 20, 2001 to Jan 20, 2009)	William S. Farish III (July 2001 to July 2004)		
2002				
2003				

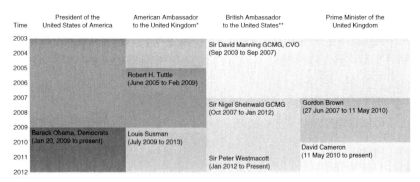

Time	President of the United States of America	American Ambassador to the United Kingdom*	British Ambassador to the United States**	Prime Minister of the United Kingdom
2003			Sir David Manning GCMG, CVO (Sep 2003 to Sep 2007)	
2004				
2005		Robert H. Tuttle (June 2005 to Feb 2009)		
2006				
2007			Sir Nigel Sheinwald GCMG (Oct 2007 to Jan 2012)	Gordon Brown (27 Jun 2007 to 11 May 2010)
2008				
2009	Barack Obama, Democrats (Jan 20, 2009 to present)	Louis Susman (July 2009 to 2013)		
2010				David Cameron (11 May 2010 to present)
2011			Sir Peter Westmacott (Jan 2012 to Present)	
2012				

*US London Embassy website http://london.usembassy.gov/rcambex.html at 16 September 2012, for further details see the following table.

**The British Embassy in Washington (and the Foreign and Commonwealth Office) websites refer readers to Wikipedia which lists only years of arrival/departure – but not the month. We decided to pursue further information so as to provide comparable information. The FCO historians kindly provided a partial list while the US State Department website http://www.state.gov/s/cpr/94544.htm also has a partial list of British ambassadors with commencement month (and year) but not departures. This list has, therefore, been compiled from a variety and, unfortunately, some conflicting sources with different definitions of 'arrival' e.g. appointed, in country, first day on the job, officially received etc. We understand this may result in some confusion, although the individual chapters provide substantive detail in achieving our ultimate goal of identifying longer gaps in representation and a general 'matching' of personalities between the US and UK posts.

***Philip Kerr – died in post 12th Dec 2012

American Ambassadors to the United Kingdom

Appointment	Presentation of credentials		Termination of Mission	Note
Joseph P. Kennedy Non-career appointee *Ambassador Extraordinary and Plenipotentiary* New York	Jan 17, 1938	Mar 8, 1938	Left post, Oct 22, 1940	
John G. Winant Non-career appointee *Ambassador Extraordinary and Plenipotentiary* New Hampshire	Feb 11, 1941	Mar 1, 1941	Appointment terminated, Apr 10, 1946	
W. Averell Harriman Non-career appointee *Ambassador Extraordinary and Plenipotentiary* New York	Apr 2, 1946	Apr 30, 1946	Left post, Oct 1, 1946	
O. Max Gardner Non-career appointee *Ambassador Extraordinary and Plenipotentiary* North Carolina	Dec 6, 1946			Took oath of office, but died in the United States before proceeding to post. A commission signed by the President during a recess of the Senate, which had not yet been dated and attested, was returned to the President by the Acting Secretary on Dec 6, 1946, Gardner having declined a recess appointment. Recommissioned Jan 13, 1947.
Lewis W. Douglas Non-career appointee *Ambassador Extraordinary and Plenipotentiary* Arizona	Mar 6, 1947	Mar 25, 1947	Left post, Nov 16, 1950	
Walter S. Gifford Non-career appointee *Ambassador Extraordinary and Plenipotentiary* New York	Sep 29, 1950			Commissioned during a recess of the Senate. Did not serve under this appointment.
Walter S. Gifford Non-career appointee *Ambassador Extraordinary and Plenipotentiary* New York	Dec 12, 1950	Dec 21, 1950	Left post, Jan 23, 1953	

Appointment	Presentation of credentials	Termination of Mission	Note
Winthrop W. Aldrich Non-career appointee *Ambassador Extraordinary and Plenipotentiary* New York	Feb 2, 1953	Feb 20, 1953	Left England, Feb 1, 1957	
John Hay Whitney Non-career appointee *Ambassador Extraordinary and Plenipotentiary* New York	Feb 11, 1957	Feb 28, 1957	Left post, Jan 14, 1961	
David K.E. Bruce Non-career appointee *Ambassador Extraordinary and Plenipotentiary* Maryland	Feb 22, 1961	Mar 17, 1961	Left post, Mar 20, 1969	
Walter H. Annenberg Non-career appointee *Ambassador Extraordinary and Plenipotentiary* Pennsylvania	Mar 14, 1969	Apr 29, 1969	Left post, Oct 30, 1974	
Elliot L. Richardson Non-career appointee *Ambassador Extraordinary and Plenipotentiary* Massachusetts	Feb 20, 1975	Mar 21, 1975	Left post, Jan 16, 1976	
Anne Legendre Armstrong Non-career appointee *Ambassador Extraordinary and Plenipotentiary* Texas	Jan 29, 1976	Mar 17, 1976	Left post, Mar 3, 1977	
Kingman Brewster, Jr. Non-career appointee *Ambassador Extraordinary and Plenipotentiary* Connecticut	Apr 29, 1977	Jun 3, 1977	Left post, Feb 23, 1981	
John J. Louis, Jr. Non-career appointee *Ambassador Extraordinary and Plenipotentiary* Illinois	May 7, 1981	May 27, 1981	Relinquished charge, Nov 7, 1983	
Charles H. Price, II Non-career appointee *Ambassador Extraordinary and Plenipotentiary* Missouri	Nov 11, 1983	Dec 20, 1983	Left post, Feb 28, 1989	
Henry E. Catto, Jr. Non-career appointee *Ambassador Extraordinary and Plenipotentiary* Texas	Apr 14, 1989	May 17, 1989	Left post, Mar 13, 1991	

Appointment	Presentation of credentials	Termination of Mission	Note
Raymond George Hardenbergh Seitz Foreign Service officer *Ambassador Extraordinary and Plenipotentiary* Texas	Apr 25, 1991	Jun 25, 1991	Left post, May 10, 1994	
William J. Crowe, Jr. Non-career appointee *Ambassador Extraordinary and Plenipotentiary* Virginia	May 13, 1994	Jun 2, 1994	Left post, Sep 20, 1997	
Philip Lader Non-career appointee *Ambassador Extraordinary and Plenipotentiary* South Carolina	Aug 1, 1997	Sep 22, 1997	Left post, Feb 28, 2001	
William S. Farish Non-career appointee *Ambassador Extraordinary and Plenipotentiary* Texas	July 11, 2001	August 2001	Left post, July 10, 2004	
Robert Holmes Tuttle Non-career appointee *Ambassador Extraordinary and Plenipotentiary* California	June 30, 2005	Oct 19, 2005	Left post, Feb 06, 2009	
Louis B. Susman Non-career appointee *Ambassador Extraordinary and Plenipotentiary* California	July 29, 2009	August 17, 2009		

US London Embassy website http://london.usembassy.gov/rcambex.html at 16 September 2012

Index

Note: 'n' after a page reference indicates a note number on that page.